The Fourth Estate

The Fourth Estate

*A history of women
in the
Middle Ages*

SHULAMITH SHAHAR
Translated by Chaya Galai

METHUEN
LONDON AND NEW YORK

First published in 1983 by
Methuen & Co. Ltd
11 New Fetter Lane, London EC4P 4EE
Reprinted 1984 and 1985

Published in the USA by
Methuen & Co.
in association with Methuen, Inc.
733 Third Avenue, New York, NY 10017

Printed in Great Britain at the
University Press, Cambridge

British Library Cataloguing in Publication Data

Shahar, Shulamith
The fourth estate.
1 Women – Europe – History – Middle Ages,
500–1500
I. Title   II. Die Frau in Mittelalter *English*
305.4'09'02   HQ1147.E85
ISBN 0–416–35410–6
ISBN 0–416–36810–7 Pbk

Library of Congress Cataloging in Publication Data

Shahar, Shulamith.
The fourth estate.
Translation of: Die Frau im Mittelalter.
Bibliography: p.
Includes index.
1. Women – Europe – History – Middle Ages,
500–1500.
I. Title.
HQ1147.E85S5213   1983   305.4'09'02   83–13224
ISBN 0–416–35410–6
ISBN 0–416–36810–7 Pbk

To the memory of my father

Contents

List of Illustrations

Foreword

The chronological framework of this study encompasses the High and Late Middle Ages, that is, from the early twelfth century until about the second quarter of the fifteenth. It has sometimes been necessary to refer to an earlier period in order to trace the origins of a particular idea, law or custom, or the beginning of a process, and in the section dealing with witches it was necessary to follow the subject into the second half of the fifteenth century, which was when the great witch-hunting era began in Western Europe, although the ideas and beliefs comprising the doctrine of the witch as Satan's accomplice had arisen in the Late Middle Ages. Here the chronological boundaries had to be exceeded, while illustrating the culmination of a process whose origins lie well within the period under discussion.

Geographically, the study covers Western Europe, not including the Scandinavian countries, Scotland and Ireland. England, the Low Countries, Germany, France, Italy and the Iberian peninsula all had feudal social systems. The twelfth and thirteenth centuries are commonly described as the second feudal age in Western Europe, whereas the fourteenth saw the decline of feudalism, especially in the military and political spheres. The above-named countries had much the same kind of economic system, material culture and class structure; they were also united in the Roman faith and Church organization. In all these countries Latin was the language of higher culture, and the same literary genres prevailed, even when written in the local languages.

Given this uniform background, it is possible to discuss the history of women in the High and Late Middle Ages in these countries within the compass of a single study. Yet on the other hand laws and customs differed not only from country to country in the area under discussion, but also from district to district within each country. The very nature of feudalism varied from land to land. In Spain, for example, it bore the imprint of Muslim rule and of the reconquest. Regions were characterized by distinct economic developments – as, for example, the early advent of urban economy in northern Italy and in Flanders. Then again, the heretical movements were especially widespread in certain regions, notably northern Italy and southern France. In England, charges of witchcraft were different from other countries. I have endeavoured to keep these differences in view, by referring to existing studies about the particular features of these issues in the respective regions. Nevertheless, a certain blurring of distinctions was unavoidable in writing a general history of women in medieval society. Inevitably, too, the number of examples used to illustrate problems and developments had to be restricted for reasons of space. Research into this subject has only begun.[1] Undoubtedly, specific studies will not only serve to broaden our knowledge and understanding, but will also reveal errors in the present work.

The idea of studying the history of women in the Middle Ages came to me while I was researching the heretical movements in the High and Late Middle Ages. Noting that women enjoyed higher status and better rights in these movements than they did in the Catholic communities, I attempted to explore the relationship between the status of women in the theology and in the actual society, on both the Catholic and heretical sides.[2] My conclusions led me to take up the comparison between the general image of women both in medieval theology, in the texts dealing with the structure of society, and in literature, and her actual position in medieval society. I dealt with the subject in three seminars which I conducted in the years 1974–6, under the auspices of the School of History at the University of Tel Aviv.

The problem of sources for this study is especially acute. There are very few sources that deal specifically with women, e.g. books of instruction for women, or sections dealing with so-called feminine sins in confessors' manuals. The Catholic theologians' view about woman's place in creation, her role in the Original Sin and in the redemption of mankind were incorporated in their general writings on these subjects, and in canon law. Similarly, women's rights of inheritance were included in the various compilations of feudal and urban laws, and in the manorial customs books. To pinpoint women who had inherited estates and ruled over them, it was necessary to examine a considerable number of feudal records. A long chronicle may contain a few paragraphs about one particular noblewoman. Similarly, to study the role of women in the urban economy, it was necessary to search through all the general sources that deal with the guilds, and with all other spheres of urban life. In effect, all the sources that serve the study of the Middle Ages may yield information about the position of women in that period. Research into additional sources, or into those that have previously been studied with another aim in mind, will no doubt help to produce a fuller and more accurate picture than that offered by the present volume.[3]

I am grateful to my students, who took part in the seminars dealing with aspects of the history of women in the Middle Ages. Their questions, comments and contributions were of great help to me. I have to thank my friend and former student Mrs Yehudit Naphtali, who helped gather the material for one of the sections dealing with women in urban society. Finally, I owe special thanks to my friend Dr Zvi Razi, who read the manuscript several times, commented on it, and placed at my disposal his doctoral dissertation on the peasants of Halesowen, England, 1270–1460,[4] and brought to my attention every reference in the sources and in the literature which might be of importance and interest in the study of the history of women in the High and Late Middle Ages.

SHULAMITH SHAHAR

Beyond that place there was a land where women had the minds of men, while the men lacked reason and resembled large and hairy dogs.

Medieval travel book on the East

They neither kill nor wound, nor lop off limbs,
They do not plot, or plunder or persecute.
They set no fires nor disinherit others
They poison no one, steal no gold nor silver
Nor deceive in order to gain an inheritance.
Nor falsify contracts, nor cause the slightest harm
To the kingdom, the duchy or the empire.
No evil follows the deeds of even the worst of them.
And if there is one such – judgment cannot be given or
rules laid down from this exception.

Christine de Pisan, 'L'Épistre au Dieu d'Amour'

I

Introduction

There has never been a book about the 'History of men in the Middle Ages', nor is it likely that there ever will be one. But apart from the fact that far too many books about the Middle Ages make no mention of the part played by the women, leaving a lacuna in the description of medieval society, is there any justification for a special study to be made of the history of women in the High and Late Middle Ages? In the extremely hierarchical medieval society the social classes differed greatly from each other in their legal rights, economic circumstances and modes of living. Was there any condition that was shared by all women in medieval society? Nowadays, despite the remaining diversity in the status and way of life of women in the different social classes, some sociologists have defined them collectively as a 'minority group', although not necessarily a numerical one; others, rather more reasonably, use the term 'marginal social group'.[1] But let us discard the terminology of modern sociologists and examine the contemporary definitions that were applied in the Middle Ages.

From the beginning of the eleventh century onward, contemporary writers repeatedly describe society as made up of three classes (*ordines*) – Worshippers, Warriors and Workers (*oratores, bellatores, laboratores*). This triune society is depicted as horizontal, purposeful and harmonious. Each class fulfils a certain function which the other two need, as it needs theirs. Together they comprise the single, harmonious, Christian society which expresses the divine will. This description does not include a specific reference to women. But from the twelfth century on, with the great social and economic transformations that marked the age, the triple society, though not entirely discarded, was partially replaced by a new popular description. It continued to express mainly an ideal and finally also a political conception that was realized in the representative assemblies, while the new description was based on a division into 'socio-professional' classes, to use the phrase coined by J. Le Goff.[2] To designate these classes contemporary writers used the terms *conditio* and *status*, in place of *ordo* as in the triple society.

The 'literature of estates', as historians sometimes call the writings about the 'socio-professional' classes, does not present a uniform description of society, but there are two features that occur throughout. The old, horizontally-balanced division has been replaced by a vertical one, reflecting a human rather than a divine order. Secondly, the old *ordines* were subdivided on a 'socio-professional' basis. The Worshippers are divided into the Regular and the Secular clergy, the latter being graded hierarchically from the pope down through the cardinals and all the lower ranks, to the parochial priests at the bottom of the ladder. Warriors are divided into dukes, counts, knights and sergeants. The class of Workers is made up of free peasants, serfs, merchants, notaries, physicians, various artisans, beggars and thieves. (As Max Weber put it, in the city every activity becomes a profession, including beggary, crime and prostitution.) Each of the above-listed trades or titles have particular faults and sins peculiar to them.

In these descriptions of society, and in other writings from the twelfth century onwards, women are almost always categorized separately. They are described as a distinct class, subdivided according to their social-economic, rather than 'socio-professional' position. Otherwise, they are subdivided according to their personal, i.e. marital, status, a division never applied to men. This may be illustrated in several ways. The thirteenth-century manual for preachers, *De Eruditione Praedicatorum*, by the Dominican Humbert de Romans, has a separate section on preaching to women. The first chapters of this section are devoted to nuns, having different sermons for each order. These are followed by a chapter for lay women (*ad omnes mulieres*), followed by separate chapters for noble ladies, wealthy bourgeoises, poor country women, maidservants and whores.[3] An example of women being described as a distinct category, subdivided according to their marital status, is to be found in Etienne Fougères' *Livre de Manières*, written in the second half of the twelfth century. The author deals separately with maidens, married women and widows and the proper way for them to conduct themselves.[4]

Sometimes the division is based on both the 'socio-professional' or social-economic and the marital status. This was done in the fifteenth-century Dance of Death, which is documented in wall-paintings and in poetry. Here women, as a distinct category, were added to the Dance, which had previously comprised only male figures. Among the female figures dragged along by the corpse are a queen, an abbess, a nun, a pedlar and a sister of mercy, showing a subdivision based on occupation or title. In addition, there are also women in various familial, biological and psychological phases – the virgin, the beloved, the bride, the newly-married and the pregnant woman.[5]

Being thus ranged together as a class, women, like the other classes, have special faults and sins attributed to them. These are sometimes subdivided to match the internal division of the class, and sometimes given as applying to the feminine class as a whole. Among the faults and sins attributed to women as such are: vanity, pride, greed, promiscuity, gluttony, drunkenness, bad temper, fickleness, and more. The authors also declare that women must be kept out of public office, must not serve as judges nor wield any kind of authority, may not take part in councils or public assemblies, and must devote themselves to their domestic functions. A good woman is one who loves and serves her husband and brings up her children.[6] In the manuals for confessors, too, a special section was usually devoted to the characteristic sins to be expected in women.

In contrast to the inequality between the condition of men and women in the temporal Church, as well as in society and the state, Christianity viewed the sexes as equal with regard to grace and salvation: 'There is neither Jew nor Greek, there is neither bond nor free, there is neither male nor female: for ye are all one in Christ Jesus (Epistle to the Galatians 3:28). Nevertheless, a twelfth-century ecclesiastical author, Abbot Hugh of the Flavigny monastery, in describing the metaphysical hierarchy, placed women separately at the bottom of his list. His celestial hierarchy went as follows: Peter and Paul, the other Apostles, the saintly hermits, the perfect monks living in communities, good bishops, good laymen, women.[7]

Like the homiletics and the works dealing with the hierarchy of grace, the 'estate literature' was written by men. In his *Canterbury Tales* Chaucer has the Wife of Bath speak the following words:

> By god, if wommen hadde writen stories,
> As clerkes han with-inne hir oratories,
> They wolde han writen of men more wikkednesse
> Than all the mark of Adam may redresse.[8]

A reasonable asumption. But in reality, when a woman in the Middle Ages did write on social and moral questions, she too defined women as a class unto themselves. Christine de Pisan, who, in the late fourteenth and early fifteenth century wrote many books of poetry, history and morality, and who was aware of the fact that the image of women had been created by men, was also the author of 'The Body Politic' (*Corps de Policie*). In this treatise on political morality she discusses the classes that comprise the political body and their respective duties, making no mention of women. To them, she devoted a special volume entitled 'The Book of the Three Virtues' (*Le Livre des Trois Vertus*), or 'The Treasure of the Ladies' City' (*Le Trésor de la Cité des Dames*), as it is called in certain manuscripts. It is a parallel work to 'The Body Politic', dealing with the duties of women in the different classes, and also includes precepts for maidens, married women and widows.[9]

It would seem, therefore, that most medieval writers treated women as a distinct class, thereby providing the justification for the actual separate study of the history of women in the Middle Ages. This, however, is only the theoretical background. The social scheme wherein women are a distinct class is part of the theory about woman in the Middle Ages and of her described image. It remains to be seen to what extent theory matched reality, and whether the generality of women did in fact bear the distinguishing marks of a medieval order with its own law (*jus*). We have seen that contemporary writers were aware of the special situation of women in the different classes, and expressed it in the subcategories into which they divided them. Needless to say, if we wish to discover the functions performed by women, the rights they enjoyed and the discrimination to which they were subjected, we shall have to study each class separately. If we wish to visualize their lives, we shall have to deal with the way of life of women in each and every social class. We shall have to study the mode of living, privileges and deprivations of a noblewoman, and compare them with those of a nobleman, and then do the same with the townswoman and the peasant.

Moreover, women were denied access to one of the routes by which men of the lower classes could rise, namely, education at a church school, admission into the service of the Church and an ecclesiastical career. In the words of Philippe de Novare: 'The Church often made it possible for poor men to become great churchmen and rise to wealth and honour.'[10] To say that it happened often is an exaggeration, but it did happen. Women, on the other hand, had no such option: the secular Church was closed to them, and only the upper class took the veil.

While some writers stressed the economic differences between women in their respective classes, others laid emphasis on their marital status. It was also for this reason that in registers and censuses the marital status of women was invariably noted: if a woman was single nothing was appended; if married, her husband's name; or it was noted that she was a widow. This was never done where men were concerned. (Had the registers shown the widowed state in men, too, it would have helped modern demographers to determine the relative life-expectancy of men and women in the Middle Ages!) Modern European languages have retained special titles for women of different marital status – Miss, Mrs; Mlle, Mme; etc., while no such distinction exists for men, suggesting that to this day the public view of women is more affected by their marital status than the view of men.[11] During the Middle Ages this was not merely a matter of opinion: the legal status and real rights of the married woman differed from those of the unmarried and widowed. This held for all classes of society, as we shall see. One illustration may suffice here: according to the ordinances of the lepers' house at Amiens, a patient who called a married serving woman a prostitute was sentenced to twenty days' penance, while one calling an unmarried serving woman by the same name was sentenced to only ten ...[12]

There is no doubt that all the subdivisions, social and marital, existed in reality to a great extent. But no general model or image fits reality perfectly, nor do they in this case. Moreover, in the Middle Ages the law did not fully reflect the real status of some women. The question whether women were in fact a distinct class will be dealt with throughout this volume. Here we shall propose only one example to illustrate the disparity between the situation as described in the 'estate literature' and in reality. It will serve to point out the difference between reality, on the one hand, and literary images, theoretical models and even the law, on the other. We have seen that in his categorization of all lay women Humbert de Romans lists noble ladies, wealthy bourgeoises, maid-servants in the towns, poor women in the villages and prostitutes. In the

fifteenth-century Dance of Death the feminine category is represented by a queen, an abbess, a nun, a pedlar and a sister of mercy –
as against some forty trades and noble ranks among the men. Setting
aside the wealthy bourgeoises, who did not engage in any trade,
townswomen would thus seem to have worked only as servants,
pedlars, sisters of mercy or prostitutes. But the thirteenth-century
'Book of Trades' (*Livre des Métiers*) by Etienne Boileau, which
contains the rules of all the guilds of Paris at the time, shows that
out of a hundred occupations women engaged in eighty-six! A
similar picture of a broad spectrum of occupations engaged in by
women emerges also from the rules and registers of guilds in other
Western European cities at that time, and the part played by women
in medieval industry may be the most fascinating aspect of the
history of women in medieval cities.

Similar if not greater discrepancies are found between the image
of women in literary works and their position in actuality. As F. L.
Lucas, in his book on the Greek tragedy, points out:

> It remains a strange and almost inexplicable fact that in Athena's
> city, where women were kept in almost Oriental suppression as
> odalisques or drudges, the stage should have produced figures
> like Clytemnestra and Cassandra, Atossa and Antigone, Phaedra
> and Medea, and all the other heroines who dominate play after
> play of the 'misogynist' Euripides ... the paradox of this world,
> where in real life a respectable woman could hardly show her face
> alone in the street, and yet on the stage woman equals or
> surpasses man, has never yet been satisfactorily explained.'[13]

Greek drama deals with the human soul and its eternal verities by
means of psychological and social archetypes; it does not reflect
contemporary realities, political, social or domestic, with regard to
women. The medieval courtly romance does not plumb the depths
of the human soul as does classical Greek drama, but it does not
hold up a mirror to contemporary life either. The only aspect it
reflects realistically is the lifestyle of the nobility. Above all, it
expresses an ideal, as A. Auerbach puts it in his *Mimesis*:

> The courtly romance is not reality shaped and set forth by art, but
> an escape into fable and fairy tale. From the very beginning, at the
> height of its cultural florescence, this ruling class adopted an
> ethos and an ideal which concealed its real function. And it
> proceeded to describe its own life in extra-historical terms, as an
> absolute aesthetic configuration without practical purpose.[14]

Courtly lyrical poetry, which exalted the woman, had even less to do with the realities of life. We must therefore beware of deriving unequivocal assumptions about the position of women in the aristocracy from their image in the courtly romance; we shall return to this subject further on.

Urban literature, which was primarily moralistic and satirical, showed greater realism and faithfulness in its depiction of the relative positions of men and women in urban society. Neither tragic nor sublime, it actually portrayed townsmen's conscious attitude towards women. Whether a tale with a moral, a broad jest, a conventional piece depicting the 'class type', or a more original work portraying an individual character, whose author's views and tastes do not necessarily match those of his public, it does serve to fill gaps in our picture of woman's place in that society. As we shall see, this literature abounds in expressions of hatred for women. However, it must be kept in mind that such manifestations, either in comic or serious-realistic writings, do not necessarily indicate an inferior status. In the second half of the twentieth century, when women in the western world have won, if not full equality, at least a more nearly equal legal status than in any known historical society, misogynistic literature has been written as vituperative as anything in the urban literature of the Middle Ages.[15]

We have not referred to all the literary works of the age that dealt with women from one viewpoint or another. In the mid-twelfth century, for example, Bernard Silvestris wrote a cosmogonical poem entitled 'About the Universe' (De Universitate Mundi), described by E. R. Curtius as a combination of speculative cosmogony and a hymn to sexuality. In this poem, which is dominated by the cult of fertility, the Noys, a female emanation of divinity, plays an essential role. She is entreated by Natura, i.e., the mother of all creation and the inexhaustible womb (mater generationis, uterus indefessus). Natura governs reproduction and the cycle of life. She gives form to matter, places the stars in their orbits and the seed in the earth. She is bound to God through the Noys and her handmaidens.[16] While there is much interest in the 'Great Mother' archetype as depicted in this exceptional poem, it remains a literary creation which neither reflected reality nor affected it. The 'Great Mother' fertility cult had been all but obliterated in the Christian civilization of the Middle Ages, with the possible exception of the 'Open Virgin', a statue of the Holy Mother which opened to reveal the images of God the Father and God the Son – whom the dogma had as the Lords of Heaven graciously raising the Virgin to their presence – nestling within her body. Needless to say, the statue was abominated by the orthodox.[17] No attempt has been made to encompass conventional literature as a whole either, but only to introduce examples from the various literary genres to complete the picture of woman's place in the Church, the state, society, and the family, in medieval civilization.

Since women were a 'marginal social group' in the Middle Ages, it is legitimate to ask the questions generally asked about such groups. Were they aware that they had fewer rights than members of the central, ruling group? Or did they unthinkingly accept this state of affairs as part of the natural order of the world? If they were conscious of being oppressed, did this give rise to resentment and anger, or did they acquiesce in it by a process of psychological adjustment? If they felt resentment and anger, how did they react – by escaping into unreality, or by rebelling within the existing system? We know of women who tried to rebel within the system and of others who escaped from reality, but it is futile to attempt to define which reaction was an escape and which a rebellion: these are value judgments which change from age to age, and even vary from one person to another in the same age. Nor can we determine how significant was the role of these women in their time. As a rule, the women themselves wrote little, and most of the evidence is indirect.

Certainly there never was anything more extensive than attempts to seek a personal solution. None of the medieval movements of political or social revolt sought to improve the status of women, nor was there ever a feminine movement to improve the condition and extend the rights of women. A singular case is reported tersely in the annals of the Dominicans of Colmar: 'A maiden came from England who was comely and well-spoken. She said that she was the Holy Spirit who had become incarnate for the salvation of womankind. She baptized the women in the name of the Father, the Son and Herself.' The writer concludes: 'After she died she was burnt at the stake.'[18] Was this an escape into unreality, or an attempt to revolt against the existing system?

We know that some women took the veil not because they felt a vocation for the religious life, but because the convent afforded them relative freedom from male domination, a better schooling than they could obtain in the world, and, if they became abbesses or held other convent functions, they might wield broad authority and exercise their talents as leaders and organizers. We know of women who, being unhappy in their marriage, chose to enter a convent.

Others, when widowed, preferred to remain in that state rather than remarry. Christine de Pisan, who was widowed in her youth and did not remarry, wrote that it is better for a woman to remain in her widowhood, because the lot of the married woman is sometimes no sweeter than that of one who has been taken captive by the Saracens. Many women joined the heretical movements, in which they enjoyed higher status and wider rights than in the Roman Church, and were also somewhat freer of male domination, although the improvement of the status of women was not a particular object of any of these movements. Likewise the popularity of the courtly literature (most of which was written by men, but women cultivated its authors), which idealized extramarital love and portrayed the lover as the vassal of his mistress, may be explained if not as a protest against existing reality, at least as a longing for a different one. We shall return to this subject again.

The structure of the present work and the sequence of its chapters were largely dictated by the authors of the 'class literature' of the Middle Ages. Chapter 2 deals briefly with the public and legal rights of women. Chapter 3 with women in the order of *oratores*, namely, the nuns. Chapter 4 is devoted to married women, for, as we have seen, marital status was one of the criteria for the categorization of women. Subsequent chapters deal with noble women, women in urban society and in the peasantry. The chapters devoted to women in the different classes deal with their respective problems as defined in the chapter about their legal and public rights, and in the chapter on the marriage laws in their respective classes. The final chapter is devoted to women in the heretical movements, and to those who were accused of witchcraft.

We make no reference to queens, because in the High and Late Middle Ages no woman succeeded to the throne (not even Matilda, the daughter of Henry I of England, and Constance, daughter of Roger I of Sicily). Nor have we attempted to deal with the figure of Joan of Arc, both because she is an entirely exceptional phenomenon, and because there is no shortage of written material about her. Nor is it within the scope of this work to discuss the many women who, as the sisters, mothers, wives and mistresses of kings and great feudal lords, and having a strong character, were able to manipulate developments from behind the scenes. These women have been popular subjects for far too long in historical literature. Thus Agnès Sorel, for example, although she sat in the council of Charles VII of France, will not be discussed in this book, whose purpose is to elucidate the general situation of women in medieval society, in life and in law. There may have been many other, less famous women who helped their sons, brothers, husbands or lovers, manipulated and perhaps even dominated them in private, but who did not attract the attention of chroniclers.

2

Public and Legal Rights

Distinctions were made in the rights of women on the basis of both marital status and class. However, there were also restrictions imposed by law on all women *qua* women, which is one of the justifications offered for treating them as a distinct class in the literature of the estates. By law, a woman had no share whatsoever in the government of the kingdom and of the society. A woman could not hold political office, or serve as a military commander, judge or lawyer. The law barred her from filling any public office and from participating in any institutions of government, from manorial courts to municipal institutions, royal councils and representative assemblies in the various countries. The literature of the estates declares explicitly: 'Women must be kept out of all public office. They must devote themselves to their feminine and domestic occupations.'[1] Or, as the English jurist Glanville put it: 'They are not able, have no need to, and are not accustomed to serving their lord the king, either in the army or in any other royal service.'[2]

It goes without saying that legislation always reflects the psychological, sociological and moral assumptions of the legislator, these assumptions being sometimes implied in the law and sometimes offered explicitly in defence of it. The attitude evinced by medieval civilization towards women was not determined by an unconscious ideology (although, as in every society, there were also unconscious factors which influenced the relations between the sexes),[3] and so the denial of rights to women by both state and Church was supported by plain and direct justifications. Ecclesiastical law usually based the curtailment of the rights of woman on her secondary place in creation and on her part in Original Sin. We shall discuss this subject in detail in the chapter dealing with nuns. Secular law justified the restrictions of the legal and civil rights of woman on the basis of her limited intelligence, her light-mindedness (*imbecilitas sexus*), her wiliness and avarice[4] – reasons which had already been given in similar terms in the Roman period. These were also sometimes adduced by the canonists in addition to their other reasons (secondary place in creation and part in Original Sin).

Reality generally matched the law. It matched it with regard to all offices not held as fiefs, and to most assemblies in which the participation was not based on the possession of a fief. Thus, women did not fill posts or perform functions on the manor, or in the institutions of municipal authority, or in the systems of government of the feudal lords and kings who, beginning in the twelfth century, increasingly resorted to the services of professional, wage-earning functionaries. Women took no part in the town councils and assemblies, or in the representative assemblies which were making a gradual appearance in Western European countries. They were not called upon by their kings to attend the representative assemblies, nor were they elected to represent their estates or regions, nor did they inherit the right to participate in assemblies. In England peeresses had the right to transmit the title and the prerogative of sitting in the House of Lords to their husbands and sons, but not to sit there themselves.[5] Even on the manors, where single women and widows participated in the manorial court assemblies, they did not hold office or perform any function.

But women did inherit fiefs, and in consequence there were some women who ruled over territories, participated in the feudal assemblies of their lords alongside the other vassals, and headed the feudal assemblies of their own vassals, whether to sit in judgment, to legislate or to discuss political or economic issues. When a woman inherited a fief that carried with it a certain office, it was sometimes given to another person to perform, but sometimes she herself performed it.[6] Abbesses exercised wide prerogatives in the fiefs that belonged to their convents. In this way, there were noble women (and abbesses, too, were almost without exception members of the nobility) in the Middle Ages who, in utter contradiction of the law, wielded powers of government such as they never had in Roman or Germanic society, nor in modern Western Europe before the twentieth century. We shall be dealing with this extensively in the chapter devoted to women of the nobility. The special status of these women, who inherited fiefs involving powers of government, was an obvious exception which does not match the description of the position of women in the estates literature, nor the generalized statements of the jurists.

We know that in medieval society civil rights and duties did not correspond. The very duties from which women on the manor were exempted, constituted for the men a heavy burden often enforced by humiliating punishments. In most of Western Europe, the nobles of both sexes were exempt from taxation (except in England and in the Italian cities). Yet townswomen and countrywomen alike, though they were denied civil rights, were subject to the civic duty of paying taxes. Single women and widows were subject to the same taxes as were laid upon men of the same class and income. The duty of paying a married woman's taxes fell upon her husband (and it was thus that they appeared in the records, e.g., *Johannes Smyth et uxor ejus*). Only if the married woman had an independent occupation of her own, in commerce or as an artisan, did she have to pay her own taxes.[7] Information about taxpaying women may be gathered from the tax returns and the town regulations. The tallage returns of the city of Paris for the years 1296, 1297 and 1313 list single women, widows and married women of independent occupations.[8] In London in 1319, 4 per cent of the taxpayers were women, including widows with income-bearing property, and women who worked at their occupations.[9] The records of the poll tax in England in 1377 also list single, widowed and married women.[10] The charter given to the town of Oppy in Artois, which includes an undertaking not to apply pressure in tax-collection, extends the undertaking also to the taxpaying widows of the town.[11] In London, women's personal possessions were seized in default of taxes, and if these were not redeemed by the appointed date, they were sold by the town authorities.[12]

LEGAL RIGHTS

A legal system is to a large extent a function of the social and political structure. In the High and Late Middle Ages not only were women barred from serving as judges or lawyers (a woman could serve as an agreed voluntary mediator, whose decision was not binding upon the parties),[13] they could not even appear as representatives of other persons in court (*procurator*). The only case in which a woman could appear as another person's representative in court was when she appeared on behalf of her own husband. In

England the peeresses, whose right to be tried only by their peers in the House of Lords was recognized in 1442, were barred from sitting in judgment in that institution.[14] Nor could a woman testify in court or serve as an oath-helper. The French jurist Beaumanoir stated: 'A woman's testimony is not acceptable, except where another witness supports her evidence, and no man may be put to death or mutilated upon the testimony of a woman alone.'[15] And the English jurist Bracton puts it as follows: 'In the trial involving a woman, also, the oath helpers (*compurgatores*) must be men.'[16]

Women had property rights, but their right to bring suit was restricted. The law allowed an unmarried woman to bring suit in civil law, to draw up a contract or a will or to borrow money. In most regions she was allowed to appear in court, but in some places, such as Sicily and Brabant, it was the custom, though not a legal requirement, for a woman to be represented in court by a male member of her family, or by a jurist engaged to appear on her behalf for a fee.[17] A married woman could not press a civil suit without her husband's permission, only independent merchant women being allowed to file suit in civil law even if they were married. This subject will be dealt with more extensively in the chapters devoted to married women and women in the towns.

In criminal law married and unmarried women had the same rights. Any woman could press charges for bodily harm, for rape and for insult. A married woman could press charges for the murder of her husband, as specified *inter alia* in Article 54 of Magna Carta.[18] No woman, whether married, single or widowed, could press criminal charges in any other matter. This restriction of the right of women to press criminal charges was of greater significance prior to the thirteenth century than thereafter. Before that time, criminal charges in most countries were preferred by the individual; from then onwards, it gradually though not entirely became the function of the public authority to do so.

So much for the letter of the law. Departure from it was expressed in the fact that, despite the rulings of the jurists concerning the inadmissibility of women's testimony, and despite the barrier against their serving as oath-helpers, in certain cases courts did have recourse to female witnesses, and women did occasionally serve as oath-helpers. This occurred both in secular and ecclesiastical courts. Women testified which of a pair of twins was born first, or to the existence of an heir who had died immediately after its birth as claimed by one of the litigants (two questions which sometimes arose in inheritance suits). When a wife applied to the ecclesiastical court for separation from her husband on the grounds of his impotence, women were sent to investigate the allegation. In secular court, in cases of rape, women gave evidence after examining the plaintiff; in cases of infanticide women were appointed to examine the breasts of all the women in the vicinity to find out if any of them had secretly given birth. In none of the cases could a man give evidence, and the court in effect recognized the testimony of women.

In Paris, in Normandy, and in certain other places there was actually a special office held by a woman whose business it was to collect evidence in cases such as these. According to the records of the court of Paris, a certain 'Emmeline La Duchesse, a sworn matron of the King and of ours' (i.e., of the court) appeared seven times as a witness in suits brought by women who claimed that they had been beaten when pregnant, or had been beaten and as a result miscarried, or that they had been raped. In Normandy women who fulfilled this function were titled 'good-wives and legal matrons'.[19] In France the evidence given by women in criminal cases was sometimes accepted, but only when, as the law demanded, it was not a single testimony.[20] In England women sometimes brought charges of murder not only when the husband was the victim, but also when it was a son, brother or nephew.[21]

Despite the ruling of the jurists that even a woman's oath-helpers had to be men, in several English towns women appeared as oath-helpers of a woman. In one case where a woman was sued for failing to repay a loan which she denied owing; in the case of a woman who was charged with the brewing and sale of ale in contravention of the royal assize; and in cases such as one that appears in the records of the city of London, where six women served as oath-helpers for a woman who was charged with failing to return possessions that had been left in her keeping – 'this was done' says the record 'in accordance with the custom of the city.'[22] Women served as oath-helpers in the ecclesiastical court when a woman was charged with fornication or adultery. Even a nun who was charged with fornication was ordered to produce oath-helpers from among her sister nuns.[23] Exceptionally, we find in the records a case where a woman appeared as representative (*attornata*) of another woman before the town court.[24] Some women appeared as signatories on charters. The charter of a donation made by a widow to the convent of Rievaulx bears the signatures of five men and six women.[25]

It is probable that there were other such exceptional cases here and there. Women were occasionally appointed guardians together with men, not only for their own children, but sometimes for the orphaned children of men who were not their husbands, and were appointed executors of their wills.[26] A striking exception made in the thirteenth and fourteenth centuries to the rule barring the testimony of women in ecclesiastical court was the important role of women witnesses who testified concerning the lives, and especially the miracles, wrought by candidates of both sexes for canonization. In some cases more than half the witnesses were women.[27] Also noteworthy was the evidence given by women in the inquest ordered by Charles VII in 1456 on the trial of Joan of Arc. The witnesses were women from her native village, her godmothers, in their seventies and eighties, and her early girl-friends who described her childhood and youth.

Before we pass on to the subject of women as defendants in court, we might briefly pause on that special claim pressed by women, namely rape. Rape was not treated with equal severity throughout Western Europe. In England and France it was a criminal act and by law a rapist might be blinded, castrated or even put to death.[28] The legislation of Frederick II for Sicily stipulated the death sentence for rape, even if the victim was a prostitute, and a man could be fined for failing to respond to a woman's cry for help.[29] In Germany, on the other hand, the penalty for rape was flogging, the victim sometimes being allowed to help carry it out.[30] By the laws of Cuenca and Sepúlveda, a rapist was fined and expelled from the city.[31] In England and France, despite the laws of the land and the rulings of the jurists, which imposed very severe penalties for rape where members of the peasant class were concerned, the actual punishment was usually a monetary fine. Marriage sometimes followed rape, and the court encouraged these unions by pardoning the rapist if he married the victim.[32]

Neither legislator nor judge favoured the plaintiff in cases of rape. Most codes allowed for the possibility that a woman would falsely charge a man with raping her, either to force him to marry her, or in order to revenge herself on him and cause him to be put to death or mutilated. In the legislation of Frederick II it is said that such false accusations by women often led to socially unsuitable unions.[33] There can be no doubt that women did sometimes falsely accuse men of raping them, as the court records show.[34] But the court not only took pains to verify, as the law required, whether rape had in fact been committed but even where there was no doubt as to the fact, there was a suspicion that the woman had enjoyed the act. In southern France in the thirteen century a woman testified before the court of the Inquisition that she had been raped by one of the guests at the castle while her husband was visiting the stables. She said she had not told him about it, because she feared that he would accuse her, as men were wont to do, of enjoying the act.[35] The woman was voicing her fear of what her husband might think of her, not merely as his own anticipated reaction, but as the common one, which suggests that the idea would not have seemed novel to the judges.

In England in the thirteenth century, judges would dismiss a charge of rape brought by a woman if she conceived as a result.[36] This was because, according to the medieval concept of woman's sexual and physiological nature, she needed to secrete a certain seed to enable her to conceive, and this did not happen unless she was sexually satisfied. Pregnancy meant that she had enjoyed the rape and had no right to press charges. This interpretation, based on a misguided biological concept, was no more absurd than the inter-pretations based on psychological concepts, which also maintain that women enjoy rape.[37] If men in the Middle Ages were quite clear in their minds about the pleasure felt by a rape victim, they laid down a definite yardstick which, at least by law, narrowed the assumption of pleasure to a particular case.

We can now consider the situation of women as defendants in court. Although their own legal rights were limited, women, regardless of marital status, could be sued in the same way as men. Court records show that women were sued in civil law in such matters as non-repayment of debts, violation of contract, and the illicit brewing of ale. Weavers were charged with pawning or selling their customers' good raw silk and weaving the cloth from inferior materials. In the cities women were charged with excessive opulence of dress, forbidden by the town's sumptuary laws. In villages and towns alike, women were accused of abusive and blasphemous conduct, trespassing, and fist-fights with both men and women. They were charged with theft, heresy, witchcraft, arson, infanticide and murder. We shall discuss these criminal charges against women in greater detail in the chapters devoted to the cities and to the peasantry.

It may be noted here that in the Middle Ages the number of women charged with murder was considerably smaller than that of men, just as it is today. According to the rolls of the sessions of the eyres in the counties of Norfolk, Oxford, London, Bedford, Bristol and Kent in the thirteenth century, only 8.6 per cent of the persons accused of murder were women. (77.6 per cent of the women

convicted had killed men). The number of men found guilty and
executed for the murder of women was larger than the number of
men condemmed and executed for murdering men. Some 50 per
cent of the men charged with murdering women were put to death,
as against 15 per cent of those charged with murdering men.[38] This
means that there were fewer false accusations of murder of women
by men, than of men by men. In fourteenth-century court rolls of
Norfolk, Yorkshire and Northamptonshire, where most of the
defendants were villagers, women also accounted for only 7.3 per
cent of all those convicted of murder. Of the murders committed
within families, the highest percentage was that of husbands
murdering their wives, and vice versa.[39]

Did men and women pay the same penalties for the same crimes?
There were crimes for which the penalty was identical for both
sexes, such as heresy and – from the late Middle Ages – witchcraft,
for which men and women alike were burned at the stake. However, it must be remembered that the number of women charged with
witchcraft was greater than that of men, not only in the sixteenth
and seventeenth centuries, but also in the Middle Ages. We shall
come back to this in the chapter on witches. On the other hand,
men were sometimes burnt at the stake for sodomy, whereas it
would appear that women were never prosecuted for lesbian
relations, and even the manuals for confessors describe homosexual
relations between women as a lesser sin than between men.[40] For the
murder of a master by his man, which was considered tantamount
to treason, as when a vassal murdered his lord or a servant his
master, the penalty was burning at the stake. The murder of a
husband by the wife was seen as belonging to the same category.[41]
Thus, if we accept the definition that for a woman to murder her
husband is tantamount to the murder of a man by his subordinate,
then this may count as another instance where the penalty was
applied equally to both sexes.

When a case of adultery was brought before the ecclesiastical or
the secular court, the same penalty was usually imposed on the man
and the woman. However, as we shall see in the chapter devoted to
married women, a man's extramarital relations were not everywhere
invariably considered adulterous, whereas such behaviour in a
woman was invariably considered adulterous. Moreover, the ecclesiastical court recognized judicial separation more frequently on
the grounds of the wife's adultery than of the husband's. In the
legislation of Frederick II of Sicily, a particularly cruel penalty was
imposed upon the adulterous wife, that of having her nose cut off; it

was not imposed on the adulterous husband.[42] In most countries, however, the penalties for this crime were the same for men and women. For other crimes, the penalties imposed upon women were sometimes milder than those paid by men for the same crimes. On the other hand, as we shall see, in some European countries the methods by which women were executed were the most cruel.

In Germany women were sometimes kept under house arrest instead of in gaol. Women were not broken on the wheel. For committing perjury for the second time a woman had her ear cut off – a man was put to death.[43] In Brabant it was easier for a woman to have a physical punishment commuted to a monetary fine than for a man. Pregnant or nursing women were not tortured in France or in what is today Holland.[44] In most countries the execution of a pregnant woman was postponed so as to spare her baby's life. When a woman who was condemned to death declared that she was pregnant, she was examined by the 'matrons', and if her claim was true the execution was put off. Court records show that a certain woman of Brandeston in Northamptonshire, who was pregnant at the time of her trial, had her execution postponed. Her husband was put to death immediately after the trial. She managed to become pregnant twice more while being kept in a prison where men and women were confined together, and her execution was repeatedly postponed. The records do not show whether she was finally killed or not.[45]

In some places prison conditions for women were rather more humane than for men.[46] In France women were not held in chains. King Jean II decreed that male and female prisoners be kept separately, and that 'respectable women' should guard the female prisoners.[47] The purpose of the decree was to maintain morality in the prisons, but it also provided a measure of protection for the women. In Paris in the fourteenth century a special prison was established for women. Also in fourteenth-century England, in some prisons separate wings were assigned for male and female prisoners.[48] In France women convicted of blasphemous and abusive conduct, and shrews, were sentenced to be tied with a rope under their arms and ducked in the river three times. A man who passed by and jeered at them while in this state was fined and ducked as well![49]

Where women were plainly discriminated against in legal penalties was in the method of their execution in France, Germany, Italy and Brabant – there women were either burnt at the stake or buried alive, whereas men were usually hanged. Although not all the legal codes of France stipulated that a woman must be executed by burning at the stake or burial alive,[50] throughout the Middle Ages this was the manner by which women were put to death for murder, infanticide, vicious pandering leading to rape, and even for theft.[51] This was in addition to the crimes of arson, heresy and witchcraft, for which men and women alike were burnt at the stake. The chronicler Jean Chartier reports that two gypsies, a man and a woman, were hanged at the gates of Paris in 1449 for the crimes of theft and robbery. According to him, this was the first time that a woman was hanged in Paris. At about this time a woman was also hanged for the first time in Montpellier in southern France.[52] In Italy, Germany and Brabant also, throughout the Middle Ages women were executed by burning at the stake or burial alive.[53] Men were burnt at the stake, as we have noted, for heresy, witchcraft, sodomy, the murder of a master by his man, and arson.[54] Burning at the stake was thus reserved for what were held to be the very worst crimes. In general, men were put to death by hanging; nobles were decapitated with an axe.

Historians have repeatedly suggested that the manner chosen for the execution of women, in preference to hanging, was due to ideas of modesty: the bodies of the condemned were left hanging naked for many days to warn all malefactors, and in the opinion of the age it would not do to display the bodies of women in the same way. When in the fifteenth century execution by hanging began to be applied for women, they were hanged clothed in long garments which were tied around their ankles. The German historian Wilda extolled the modesty of the Germans, which led them to execute women by fire or by burial alive. The French legal historian Viollet thought that the custom of burning or burial alive reflected the influence of Christianity. The French legal historian Brissaud also repeated that the cause was modesty (though he does not find it praiseworthy).[55] It is remarkable that these historians accepted uncritically the explanations of the authors of didactic literature concerning the supreme value of feminine modesty, and overlooked the monstrous agonies entailed in these forms of execution. That there was awareness of these agonies is evidenced by the fact that men were subjected to them only for those crimes which their contemporaries held to be the most outrageous, and which they feared might rouse the ire of God against the whole community in which they were perpetrated.

Although the authors of didactic literature often described feminine modesty as a supreme value, by and large medieval attitudes to sex were far from unequivocal, as we shall see further on. The sensual aspect of medieval civilization is well known. In the same city of Paris, where 'for reasons of modesty', women were put to death by burial alive or by burning, there were twenty-six public baths for the use of both sexes (in separate wings, but the proprieties were not observed in practice), and prostitution was recognized. Women who committed suicide usually did so by hanging themselves. Out of thirteen known cases of suicide, eight were by hanging,[56] because this was a quicker and less painful way to die.

Women belonged to the civilization of the Middle Ages, in which acts of cruelty were carried out in public, providing sadistic and emotional relief for the multitudes which gathered to watch them.[57] The chronicler who described the hanging of the gypsy woman in Paris reported that large crowds came to watch the execution because of its novelty, and that women and girls in particular flocked to see it.[58] Though there were far fewer violent criminals among women than among men, nevertheless, medieval women hardly personified the qualities of gentleness and mercy. But the laws were enacted by men, and the judges who administered them were also men, and it was they who determined that women should die by the cruellest methods of execution known to the cruel society of the Middle Ages. Did they see the condemned woman as a better scapegoat than the man condemned for the same crime, a scapegoat that would bear all the guilt and sinfulness, and which should therefore be totally consumed by the flames? Or were men's Eros and Thanatos both gratified by the spectacle? These are not questions which may be answered with absolute certainty.

3

Nuns

A Christian woman could not officiate in church. She could not take the sacrament of the priestly order (*ordinatio*) and she was denied the right to preach. As St Paul said:

> Let your women keep silence in the churches: for it is not permitted unto them to speak; but they are commanded to be under obedience, as also saith the law. And if they will learn any thing, let them ask their husbands at home: for it is a shame for women to speak in the church. (I Corinthians 14:34–6)

> But I suffer not a woman to teach, nor to usurp authority over the man, but to be in silence. For Adam was first formed, then Eve. And Adam was not deceived, but the woman being deceived was in the transgression. Notwithstanding she shall be saved in childbearing, if they continue in faith and charity and holiness with sobriety. (I Timothy 2:12–16)

By barring women from religious office, Christianity was continuing the path of Judaism; in biblical times the Hebrew woman took no part in religious service, she could belong neither to the *cohanim* (priests) nor the Levites, and she was allotted a special place in the Temple. But whereas the Old Testament offers no direct reason for depriving women of the privilege of religious officiation, the New Testament did provide justification: the secondary role of woman in Creation and her role in Original Sin. The same arguments served St Paul both to deny the right of woman to officiate and to justify her subjugation to man; and this despite the fact that where grace and salvation were concerned, man and woman were recognized as equal: 'There is neither Jew nor Greek, there is neither bond nor free, there is neither male nor female; for ye are all in Christ Jesus' (Galatians 3:28). The concept of the equality of the sexes as regards salvation was never denied by the medieval Church, but yet it never advocated equality in the terrestrial Church. St Paul's standpoint, as reflected in the above-cited verses, was adopted by the Catholic Church and determined woman's status.

In the third century the deaconesses shared several of the tasks of the deacons, assisting in the baptism of women, instructing women and visiting them in times of sickness, but even in this period these were not priestly duties. Women were unable to advance beyond the level of deaconess, and the position was created in the main in order to ensure observance of maximum modesty in a period of adult baptism. To the extent that this position endured in the High Middle Ages, the number of tasks it encompassed was much more limited than in the third century.[1] At the beginning of the sixth century, Celtic women officiated together with priests in northern Gaul and in Ireland, thus continuing an ancient Celtic tradition within the framework of the Christian Church. The custom was denounced by the bishops and was rapidly abandoned.[2] From then on women officiated only in heretical movements, which were denounced by the Church and excommunicated.

St Paul's theoretical standpoint was developed by theologians and canonists for centuries. The Church Fathers repeatedly described woman as the daughter and heiress of Eve, burdened by the yoke of Original Sin, and as the gateway to Satan. It was she who succeeded in seducing man when Satan had proved powerless to do so, and it was because she deserved to be punished by death that the Son of God was doomed to die.[3] Her role in the annals of mankind was pregnant with catastrophe, and continues to be so, since she is the eternal temptress to the sin of carnality. Once she taught, wrote John Chrysostom in the fourth century, and ruined everything.[4] We find a more dialectical and complex approach in the works of St Augustine, who wrote: 'And the apostle says: And Adam was not deceived ...' (I Timothy 2:14). But the apostle did not say that Adam did not sin. Satan did not believe that men would hearken to him, and hence he turned to woman, the weaker side of the human alliance, knowing that man would succumb to her. Adam was not deceived and did not believe that the serpent's words were true. It was woman who was deceived and believed the serpent, while

Adam succumbed to his wife, the sole human being on earth apart from himself. He sinned with open eyes, but his guilt was no less than that of the woman.[5] Nevertheless, says Augustine, it is only if man and woman are seen as one essence that one can say that woman was created in the image of God. Regarded alone, she is not an image of God, since she was created in the image of Adam, whereas man, even alone, is an image of God. Her subjugation to man is the fruit of her sin.[6]

The description of woman as Eve, mother of all sin, is reiterated in the literature of the High Middle Ages. 'It is not surprising that there still quivers in the descendants of Eve that same spear which the ancient enemy flung at Eve' wrote Peter Damian at the end of the eleventh century.[7] Even in the natural state before the Fall there was no equality between the sexes, writes Thomas Aquinas. The subordination of woman to man is natural, for man, by nature, is endowed with greater logic and discrimination than woman, and even though woman was created in the image, she is inferior to man.[8] (Aquinas also found substantiation for theories of woman's biological inferiority in the biological and medical writings of Hippocrates, Aristotle and Galen.)[9]

But together with these issues, attention was given from the beginning of the twelfth century to the status and role of the Virgin Mary, the Holy Mother. The Church Fathers and the Church councils of the fifth century (Ephesus in 431; Chalcedon in 451) formulated the concept of the virgin who bore the Saviour and the Holy Mother as mediator between the believer and God. But in the twelfth century these ideas spread and were elaborated. All graces are bestowed on mankind through the Virgin Mary, who is free of all sin. The Holy Mother, as Anselm of Canterbury put it, redeemed the sin of Eve: just as the sin which was the source of our loss originated in woman, so too the father of our righteousness and our salvation was born to woman.[10] Anselm stresses the affinity of the Holy Virgin with God the Father, since they have a common son; her affinity with the Son, since she is his mother; and her affinity with the Holy Ghost, through whom she conceived her son.[11] She leads sinners to repent. She works miracles among both Christians and infidels, so as to protect the former and guide the latter to the bosom of the faith. Incantation of her name banishes devils. And above all, she mediates between the believer and her Son. Like Jacob's Ladder, she links between Heaven and earth.[12]

Bernard of Clairvaux composed a lengthy exegesis on the tale of the Annunciation to Mary, devoted numerous sermons to her, and took part in a theological debate on her immaculate conception.[13] The Virgin Mary was pure of spirit, body and life. She is the queen of all virgins, who conceived Christ, who destroyed sin by opening the way to salvation for all mankind. She was the personification of modesty and therefore the Holy Ghost came down to her. She was chosen, and accepted her choice and the suffering it entailed with full acquiescence, and thus was a full partner in the incarnation of God. Just as both sexes played a part in the Fall, thus both took part in salvation. She redeemed the sin of Eve. Holy Mary is the vessel of grace, the mediator between man and God. She is ready to aid all people, and those who are in awe of her Son do not hesitate to approach her, since there is no severity in her.[14] Abélard also devoted a sermon to the Holy Mother, and in a letter to Héloïse he writes of the redemption of Eve's sin by Mary even before Adam's sin was absolved by Christ.[15] Worship of Mary was highly developed in the twelfth century. The Ave Maria became one of the most important prayers, together with the Pater Noster and the Credo. The Holy Mother became one of the central themes of art, sculpture and drama of the age.[16] Songs and hymns were written in her praise – to the radiant mother who bore the Redeemer, to the Mater Dolorosa at the foot of the Cross.[17]

Together with worship of the Holy Mother, there appeared the worship of Mary Magdalene, the repentant sinner. Anselm of Canterbury attributed to her too a mediatory role between man and God: 'It will not be difficult for you to attain whatever you wish from your dear and beloved master and friend.'[18] Before the end of the twelfth century Mary Magdalene appeared as one of the female characters in the *Visitatio Sepulchri* plays.[19] In the twelfth century she was venerated in the Seine and Loire regions, in England and in Italy, and the church of Vézelay (in Burgundy), which was dedicated to her and contained her relics, won renown as a place of pilgrimage. The same was true in the thirteenth century of the church of Saint Maximian.[20] Bernard of Clairvaux lauded her power to inspire repentance and her ability to plead with God,[21] and Abélard writes: 'I have called Mary Magdalene the Apostle of Apostles, for it was she who announced to the Apostles the resurrection of Jesus.'[22]

The development of the concept of the sanctity and special role of the Holy Mother and her redemption of Eve's sin led to partial rehabilitation of woman and reconsideration of her role in the annals of mankind, and brought with it depiction of the image of woman as a believer, faithful, sacrificing and redeeming. Bernard of

Clairvaux described the Virgin Mary as crushing the head of the serpents.[23] Peter the Venerable attributed the very same image to Héloïse: 'You crushed under your heel the Satan always lurking in wait for woman.'[24] But it was Abélard, even more than the two above-mentioned writers, who elevated the image of woman as a reflection of the Holy Mother's image, while Héloïse writes in her letters of the woman as the heiress of Eve.

There were profound psychological factors which led Abélard and Héloïse to develop these two images or two archetypes, but these do not belong within the scope of the present study. In our context it is important to emphasize that the two images had existed long since and were neither original nor unique, although Héloïse and, in particular, Abélard elaborated them in their own way. Whereas Héloïse sees woman as the eternal cause of man's sorrow, from Delilah through Solomon's wives and Job's wife to herself (she depicts herself as the cause of Abélard's catastrophe),[25] Abélard cites the female prophets, holy women and nuns. It was the supplications of women which led to the resurrection of the dead in the Old and New Testament, and the prayer of Clotilde which led Clovis and in his footsteps all the Franks to Christianity.[26] Some of the Jesus' most faithful followers were women,[27] and a woman was awarded the privilege of anointing the Saviour. Christ was conceived by a virgin and born to a virgin. Had the Redeemer so chosen, he could have been born to a man, but he wished to bestow on the weaker sex the glory of his humility.

Yet Abélard was not referring to woman as such, but to the nun alone. The woman who lives a full sexual life, conceiving and giving birth in natural fashion, remains an inferior being, arousing revulsion. This attittude is strikingly evident when Abélard writes: 'The Redeemer could have chosen another part of woman's body to be conceived there and born from there, and not that despised part where other sons of man are conceived and born'. Thus he elevates the female parts of the Virgin which did not function in the way of nature, and thus indirectly but clearly he expresses disgust at the parts of sexual women who give birth naturally. This recalls the cry of the 'continent' in one of the Manichaean hymns: 'I did not cause my master to be born in a contaminated womb.' In that same letter Abélard also writes of virgins of long ago: 'And there were those whose desire to live chastely was so strong that they did not hesitate to deform themselves lest they forfeit their purity which they had vowed to preserve and to reach the bridegroom of all virgins as virgins.'[28]

This same distinction between woman as such and the nun is distinctly evident in the writings of Bernard of Clairvaux. In a letter to a virgin named Sophia who became a nun, he wrote that moral strength was rarer among women than among men, but that a virgin who had taken the vow of chastity had won grace, and was on a different existential plane from other human beings. In the next world, pure and radiant, she will be greeted by her bridegroom. A special place is reserved in the Kingdom of Heaven for virgins and there they will sing and dance before the Lamb. The eye cannot envisage nor the ear imagine the delights which the Master has prepared for her, and already in this world she enjoys grace. She wears rags but she is radiant since the Lord is within her.[29] The same attitude is reflected in a letter to another woman who took the veil. In this epistle Bernard of Clairvaux describes the transition she has undergone in passing from a life lived according to her own will and rules, which is like death, to life according to God. And he concludes by drawing an absolute distinction between the life of the unchaste woman and that of the nun:

> But if you allow the Divine fire burning in your heart to be extinguished, you may be sure that there will be nothing for you but the fire which will never die out. Permit the fire of the Divine spirit to extinguish the lust of the flesh, for if, Heaven forbid, your sacred aspirations which beat in your heart die down because of the lust of the flesh, you will thus consign yourself into the fires of Hell.[30]

We see here acceptance of the female element, the archetype of Jung's subconscious, the *anima*,[31] in the divine world and in the annals of mankind, side by side with rejection of the laws of nature regarding the female reproductive system and the birth process. Hence only the nun, the woman who has not realized her full potential, is accepted, like the virgin goddesses in the Olympic pantheon who alone could serve as a source of inspiration to heroes. This rejection of woman's sexual physiology is more reminiscent of the approach expressed in the Canons of Laodicea (fourth century), which forbade women to enter the sanctuary because of their menstruation, than of Christ's treatment of the woman whose menstrual flow lasted twelve years yet who was permitted to touch him (Matthew 9:20).

But despite the clear distinction between the woman living a sexual life and the nun, no nun was permitted to carry out holy offices, and serve as a priest. Like all other women, the nun was prohibited by canon law from touching the chalice and cloths, burning incense or approaching the altar during Mass. The nun, bride of Christ, could not assist the priest in the holy ceremonies. Like other women, she too was the target of pollution fears, subjected to a code of prohibitions and taboos.[32] How much the idea of a woman priest was considered absurd is illustrated by the custom which prevailed on All Fools' Day. One of the features of this festival was the reversal of customary human and social situations and prevailing norms. Hence, churchmen would march in procession on this day wearing their clothes backwards, or dressed as savages in hides, leaves and flowers, or dressed as women with lascivious expressions and singing lewd songs.[33] The idea of a woman serving in the priesthood was a total reversal of accepted norms, like the thought of a savage as priest. Thus we find a negative common denominator for all women in the Middle Ages. All were deprived of the privilege of holy orders, whether they were of noble origin, of the urban or peasant classes, or nuns. But some women became nuns, and it is this fact which justifies the numbering of women among the praying order.

THE FEMALE ORDERS

There had been a continuous tradition of female monasticism in the Christian Church. Their lives, like those of the monks, were dedicated above all to prayer. Thus women were allotted a place in the praying order, and within that group which held the most elevated position in the ecclesiastical scale of values. This position was allotted in medieval society to those who had voluntarily chosen the most Christian way of life, with the object of worshipping God in the most perfect possible fashion.

Even before monasticism was institutionalized, there were women virgins and widows who lived ascetic lives among Christian communities, and virgins were allotted a special place in the Church from the first centuries of Christianity. This special status was related to the fact that from the infancy of Christianity chastity was regarded not as an obligation, but as a more Christian way of life for both men and women. One passage in the New Testament declares:

> And Jesus answering said unto them. The children of this world marry and are given in marriage, but they which shall be accounted worthy to obtain that world, and the resurrection from the dead, neither marry nor are given in marriage. (Luke 20:34–5)

St Paul wrote:

> I say therefore to the unmarried and widows, it is good for them if they abide even as I. But if they cannot contain, let them marry: for it is better to marry than to burn. (I Corinthians 7:8–9)[34]

Chastity was seen as more Christian not only because freedom from the lusts of the flesh enabled a man to dedicate himself to love of God, and because he was thereby renouncing something for the sake of something else, but also because the ascetic life was an imitation of Christ's. He had chosen a virgin for his mother, a virgin had raised him and he had retained his virgin state all his life.[35] Chastity, which was considered to be a special virtue, was one of the three vows of the monk and of the nun, together with obedience and poverty, with special emphasis on virginity in nuns. The virgin nun was compared with the Virgin Mary, the Holy Mother; she was the bride of Christ, she wore a ring on her finger as a symbol of her mystic marriage to Christ, and her relations with her bridegroom were often described in erotic terms, sometimes inspired by the Song of Songs. It will suffice to cite one more quotation from Abélard's letters to Héloïse: 'I denote you my lady since I must address the bride of my master as my lady ... You have been taken and honoured to share the bed of the king of kings and thus you have been elevated high above all the other servants of the king.'[36]

In popular belief and legend special power was attributed to the virgin. The unicorn, that legendary beast which permitted none to approach him, would rest its head in the bosom of a virgin, and this was the sole way of capturing it, as in one of the poems of the *Carmina Burana*: 'Lo he tames the unicorn through a maid's caresses.'[37] Joan of Arc was a virgin, who, just as the Virgin Mary redeemed Eve's sin, redeemed the sin of Isabel of Bavaria, wife of Charles VI. The latter had brought tragedy on France, the former brought salvation to her country.

Throughout the Middle Ages there were nuns who lived near churches or chapels as recluses or anchorites,[38] but after nunneries were institutionalized, most nuns lived in communities (*coenobium*) in nunneries. The female orders developed in parallel to the orders of monks. Thus, the female Benedictines developed from the sixth century onward, and in the High Middle Ages too most nunneries belonged to this order. Some nuns lived as canonesses in a community, and some left the communities and lived in their own homes from separate prebends like the male secular canons, and they aroused the anger of James of Vitry and others. (The canonesses of

Sienna refused to accept St Catherine when she was young and beautiful, and changed their mind only when smallpox had devastated her beauty.)[39] From the twelfth century new female nunneries came into being in parallel with the monasteries of the new orders. Their objective was reform with the aim of returning to the Benedictine rule in its original purity. Such were the Cistercian and Premonstratensian orders, which lived more strictly ascetic lives than the Benedictines.

In the early thirteenth century the Franciscan and Dominican orders arose, and at the same time there came the Poor Clares, founded by St Clare under the inspiration of Francis of Assisi, and the Dominican nuns who were attached to the Dominicans as a second order. But unlike the Franciscan and Dominican orders, which developed in urban society and whose members served as preachers, teachers and missionaries, the sisters were detached from the outside world like the Benedictine sisters even in the urban nunneries. If they taught, it was in the schools for children attached to the nunneries. Because of the prohibition on leaving the nunnery they could not even succour the poor, and preaching was forbidden to them.

It seems that St Clare did not envisage this type of order, since her aspiration had been to work within the secular world. When she learned of the martyrdom of five Franciscan brothers in Morocco, she expressed the wish to go there and offer up her own life as well. One of her biographers writes that even the nuns who resided with her were dissatisfied at the fact that Francis of Assisi 'imprisoned them forever' (*perpetuo carceravit*). In this way the Poor Clares were deprived from the outset of one of the two important elements of the new orders, namely life according to the apostles (*vita apostolica*) through preaching and working in the outside world. They were also barred from realizing the second ideal of absolute poverty (*paupertas*), but this ideal was short-lived in the male order as well.

The abbess was not permitted to preach to the nuns in public in any of the orders, nor were the abbesses and other senior members of the order permitted to attend the supreme councils and chapters of the order. (For a limited period the abbesses of the nunneries of the Cistercian order held general gatherings of representatives of their nunneries, as in male orders.) In the new orders, the nunneries were under the supervision of representatives of the corresponding male order. In the Benedictine order, the nunneries were subordinate to the bishops of the local diocese.[40] Since in none of the female orders were the nuns permitted to take the sacrament for acceptance into the priestly order, all female orders required the services of male priests. The abbesses were not empowered to receive the nuns' vows, to hear their confession or bless them as did priests.

The authority of the abbess was defined as organizational or ruling power (*potestas dominativa*), and by force of this authority she could demand of her nuns that they observe the rule and discipline in general and could impose punishment on them. In some nunneries the abbesses wielded this authority over male religious functionaries as well. The priests who were accepted in the thirteenth century into the nunneries of the Cistercian order after one year of trial vowed to obey the abbess by kneeling before her and placing their hand on the rule of the order which rested on her knee. But it was emphasized that this authority was in no way judicial, originating in the authority of the 'keys of the Church', and the abbess was explicitly forbidden to judge the nuns within her care or to impose canonical punishments such as excommunication. From this point of view, the status of the abbess resembled that of other women, who, according to canon law, were denied judicial authority. The female judges of biblical times were a tolerated exception, which was out of place in the era of grace following the advent of Christ.[41]

From the inception of monasticism, there were double monasteries. Monks and nuns lived in a separate establishments but in proximity in one monastery with a joint head. These monasteries existed throughout Western Europe, from Ireland to Spain. Some were headed by an abbess to whom both nuns and monks were subordinate. (One of the most famous of these was Whitby Abbey, which was run, in the seventh century, by St Hilda.) There was a great deal of opposition to these double monasteries almost from their inception, the main argument being that there was danger of moral laxity and the dishonouring of monasticism. They were often banned by the resolutions of church councils and papal bulls, but they did not die out altogether until after the end of the Middle Ages. (In the Premonstratensian order, for example, which came into being in the early twelfth century, there were double monasteries in the first few decades of its existence.) Yet the number of such monasteries headed by women was drastically reduced after the Gregorian reform.[42] The order of Fontevrault, founded by Robert of Arbrissel, which established a double monastery under an abbess, was a striking exception in this period.

It is interesting to note that the phenomenon of both monks and nuns being ruled by a woman came to an end precisely in the period when the feminine element in divinity was elevated; when the role of the Holy Mother of God, the mediator without sin, was consolidated in theology; when hymns of praise were sung to the nun, bride of Christ and image of the Holy Mother. This emphasis on the feminine element was not accompanied by elevation of the practical status of women in general, or even of the nun within the religious community. Furthermore, as centralization was increased and the hierarchy was consolidated in the wake of the reform of the late eleventh century, it became more difficult than in earlier periods to accept the status of the abbess who wielded authority over male monks. Stringent supervision was imposed on female monastery heads and on the powers they were granted even in nunneries. If an abbess exceeded the bounds of her authority, the Church bodies responded vehemently. Innocent III, for example, in a letter to the bishops of Burgos and Palencia (later introduced into canon law), expressed his surprise at the fact that some abbesses dared to bless their nuns as did priests, to hear confession and after reading of the Evangelics, even to preach in public. Innocent IV declared, in a papal bull in 1247, that a prioress appointed by an abbot of the Premonstratensian order should no longer be denoted *priorissa* but instead *magistra*, since she was not empowered to exercise judicial authority.[43]

And let us conclude by returning to Abélard, who, in accordance with the request of Héloïse, composed a draft code for the Paraclete priory which she headed. In it he advocated a mixed monastery to be headed by a male abbot. He objected not only to the idea of a double monastery headed by a woman, but even to an autonomous nunnery in which, as he wrote, the very priests who took holy sacraments and to whom the people bowed down, were subordinate to abbesses, this being in violation of the natural order of things. The abbesses could also easily seduce them and arouse forbidden lusts in them. There should therefore be one male abbot appointed over both monks and nuns. Man should be head over woman just as Jesus was head of man and God head of Christ. Abélard again cites St Paul on man's dominion over woman, and in support of his objection to handing over powers to a woman he quotes Juvenal: 'There is nothing as intolerable as a rich woman.'

He continues with a list of the most trite anti-feminine sayings: it is against nature for woman to wield authority; she is domineering by nature and leads man to sin; she is weak by nature and cannot resist temptation; solitude is particularly important for women and the abbess must exercise great caution, since, being a woman, she is easily seduced. The serpent tempted the first woman and, through her, Adam and thus caused the subjugation of mankind as a whole; it was for good reason that the apostle forbade women to wear rich apparel, since their spirit is weak and the lusts of the flesh rule them; silence, which is important in monasteries, is particularly so in nunneries since women are naturally loquacious and chatter when there is no need to do so.[44] These views are a total anticlimax after Abélard's statements about the nobility of the nun, and these bathetic statements are aimed at justifying the subordination of nuns to a male abbot as part of the natural order in this world. The fact that he specifies that the abbot must consult the abbess of the subordinate nunnery and conduct himself as if he were her servant does not mitigate these views.

There can be no doubt that medieval Christian thought revealed an ambivalent attitude to woman, and that this ambivalence was sharpened from the twelfth century onwards with the intensification of the concept of the Holy Mother and the growing worship of her and of Mary Magdalene. Eve-Mary, the sinning temptress or merely the woman who lives a natural, sexual life, is the image of Eve; the nun, bride of Jesus, is the image of Mary. This ambivalence was based on theory and undoubtedly also on the emotion behind the theory. Ambivalence with regard to the opposite sex was not unique to medieval Christian society and found expression in various forms in different societies, but in the sources one can identify only the ambivalence of man's attitude to woman, which was defined in theory, and not woman's ambivalence towards man, which was neither formulated theoretically nor defined in writing. (Though it sometimes emerges from customs and reactions.)[45] But it appears that this emotional and theoretical ambivalence had no practical implications. In practice matters were much more unequivocal. Woman was subordinate to man in the religious community as in society and in the state in general. That same Abélard whose writings clearly reflect this ambivalence demanded obedience to male authority in his rule for nunneries. Thus, when the canonists and theologians discussed the problem of whether women's position as deaconesses in ancient Christianity could be regarded as an order, the debate was totally academic. Even those who saw it as an order did not propose that it be revived. Even the very few churchmen (such as John the Teuton and Raymond Penafort) who believed that the denial of woman's right to serve in priesthood was indeed a fact, but was not founded in law since both man and woman were baptized, did not advocate granting this right to women.[46] The concept of the equality of the sexes on the plane of grace and salvation did not imply equality in the terrestrial church.

THE ATTITUDE OF THE MALE ORDERS TO NUNS

There was no uniformity in the attitude of the heads of the monastic orders towards the nuns who accepted the rules of their order and were affiliated to it or to a parallel female order, although the nuns wanted the orders to which the nunneries were affiliated to accept responsibility for them, and were usually backed by popes in this wish. It is known that there were prominent churchmen who assisted in the establishment of nunneries and instructed the nuns, from St Jerome and St Augustine to St Francis of Assisi and St Dominic. But it was only the new orders with centralized organizations removed from the authority of the diocesan bishops, like those of the Franciscans and Dominicans, which confronted the problem of responsibility for nunneries. The Benedictine order had no organization which encompassed all the monasteries. Both nunneries and monasteries were largely autonomous, and in the sphere of religious offices and law were usually dependent on the diocesan bishops. Sometimes a particular abbot was responsible for the nunneries in the vicinity of his monastery. In this fashion, several nunneries were dependent on the Cluny monastery, and in the double monasteries the female sections were dependent on the male sections. In the new orders, in contrast to the Benedictines, there was a close link between monasteries belonging to the same order, and the leaders of the order were also responsible for the nunneries.

But, in due course, the heads of most orders refused to bear responsibility for the nunneries either for moral reasons or because the organizational burden was too great, for economic reasons or because they did not have sufficient regard for the importance of the nunneries. Several examples may be cited. Thus, in its early days the Premonstratensian order maintained double monasteries. The nuns worked for the monks in weaving, sewing and laundry, and helped to tend the sick in the monastery hospital. They did not usually take part in the joint prayer services and in the choir. Violations of the moral code gradually came to light and the order gained a bad name. In 1137 it was decided to abolish the double monasteries of the Premonstratensian order, and to establish separate nunneries. In the second stage it was decided not to set up new nunneries within the framework of the order, and this resolution was approved by Pope

Innocent III in 1198. Some seventy years later, in 1270, the order passed a resolution against accepting nuns even into existing nunneries, and those already residing there were permitted to join other orders. Some of the Premonstratensian nunneries were disbanded.

The origins of the female Dominicans can be found in the days of St Dominic himself (the first Dominican nunnery was set up in Prouille in 1207), and the male monasteries were responsible for them. But in 1228, under pressure from the heads of the order, the pope absolved the Dominicans of economic responsibility for the nunneries. The Dominican nunneries were not disbanded, and after negotiations it was agreed in 1267 that Dominican brothers should be responsible for instruction and jurisdiction in the nunneries, but they were exempted from material responsibility. On the other hand, it should be noted that in the fourteenth century, particularly in Germany, the Dominican female order underwent an intellectual flowering, and the great Dominican mystics Eckhart, Seuse and Tauler, preached to the nuns.

The Poor Clares nunneries, which corresponded to the Franciscans, were founded in the lifetime of St Francis himself, who maintained close contact with the nunnery headed by St Clare. He visited it and preached there, and drew up the first rule for the nuns. But from the seventh decade of the thirteenth century the Franciscans tried to free themselves from responsibility for the Poor Clares. The pope did not agree to relieve them of the burden, but replaced the head of the Franciscan order and the provincial heads of the order by a cardinal who held responsibility for the Poor Clares, and not all priests sent to nunneries were necessarily Franciscans.

Among the Cistercians, from the first, there was no legal link between the monasteries and the nunneries which adopted the rule of the Cistercian order. Several Cistercian monasteries accepted responsibility for nunneries but most female nunneries of the order remained under the supervision of the diocesan bishops, or else one senior nunnery was responsible for several others. The Cistercian nunnery of Langres in France supervised eighteen other nunneries and convened annual gatherings of representatives of these bodies. In Spain the Cistercian nunnery of Las Huelgas near Burgos was also responsible for a large number of other nunneries. In this manner, for a certain period, the abbesses of these two nunneries enjoyed very wide-ranging authority. On the other hand, the Cistercians who refused for a lengthy period to accept legal and economic responsibility often concerned themselves with the spiritual instruction of nunneries which accepted the Cistercian rule, and of the Beguines.

In short, it may be said that the same contradictory considerations with regard to nunneries were weighed in all the various orders: they were respected and esteemed. Sometimes economic benefit could be derived from taking over the property of nunneries, but at other times the outcome was economic burden, and this was particularly evident in the Franciscan order. In the early days of the order, economic responsibility for the nunneries meant that the friars were obliged to beg alms for the nuns, since the latter were bound to remain in seclusion in their convents, and had no property. The unwillingness of the friars to collect alms for the nuns was one of the reasons why the Poor Clares renounced the ideal of absolute poverty very shortly after the foundation of the order. In this way the nuns were deprived, earlier than the friars, of the second important element of the mendicant orders – absolute poverty. Those nunneries which owned assets may have held out the promise of economic advantage to the order as a whole, but on the other hand they were often involved in financial difficulties which the monks were not anxious to take over. An additional cause of the reluctance to accept responsibility for the nunneries was fear of violation of the moral code by priests of the order and supervisors who visited nunneries. Sometimes the various orders showed themselves anxious to avoid creating the opportunity for this phenomenon.

And, last but not least, just as respect and esteem were often displayed towards the nunneries, there were also manifestations of hostility and contempt towards nuns as towards women in general. When the Marchthal monastery of the Premonstratensian order decided to abolish the female section, the following declaration was issued:

> Since nothing in this world resembles the evil of women and since the venom of the viper or the dragon is less harmful to men than their proximity, we hereby declare that for the good of our souls, our bodies and our worldly goods we will no longer accept sisters into our order and we will avoid them as we do mad dogs.

St Francis of Assisi himself, for all his affinity with the nunnery of St Clare, was opposed to additional nunneries in his order, and on one occasion, commented: 'God has taken our wives from us, and now Satan has given us sisters.'[47] It appears that the distinction between the nun, the image of the Virgin Mary, and other women created in the image of Eve, was sometimes overlooked. But the nuns could not renounce their links with the male orders since the organized post-Reform Church did not permit the establishment of separate female orders.

THE POWERS OF THE ABBESSES

Despite the restrictions imposed on abbesses in general, there were some, particularly in the rich nunneries with extensive land holdings, who wielded considerable powers in various spheres in England, France, the Netherlands, south Italy, Germany and Spain. As estate owners who held land either as full owners or as feudal landlords,[48] the abbesses exercised the same powers as other landlords over the peasants residing on their lands and cultivating them. In the case of extensive holdings, the abbesses usually possessed not only domanial powers (that is to say the powers of the landowner towards those residing on his lands, including jurisdiction in land maintenance affairs, supervision of payments and crops and labour obligations) but also seigneurial rights and governmental powers. The abbesses with seigneurial rights presided over the secular courts of their estates as did other feudal lords; sometimes they also wielded 'higher' juridical powers (*justitia alta*), and in this capacity they were also empowered to try criminal cases and cases involving determination of legal status. With the aid of secular officials they were able, like the abbots who wielded similar powers, to impose fines, to hire professional champions to fight legal duels, and to punish criminals.[49] They approved transfers, sale and lease of land in the areas under their authority, and the establishment of markets and fairs within their borders.[50] In the secular and ecclesiastical courts they litigated on matters pertaining to their property, income and juridical authority with secular seigneurs and Church institutions.[51]

In addition to these secular powers, some abbesses enjoyed extensive powers in the organizational sphere in their own dioceses: they convened Church synods of the diocese, distributed benefices, approved appointments of priests within the borders of the diocese in general and in their own nunneries in particular, and ensured that the churches belonging to the nunnery paid their tithes. These powers, which did not exceed the bounds of canon law, were bestowed on the abbesses of large and prosperous nunneries. Smaller nunneries with financial burdens (and many such existed) held neither land nor the secular and ecclesiastical rights deriving from it.

Within the nunneries the abbesses wielded ruling powers (*potestas dominativa*) and the nuns owed complete obedience to them. Also under their jurisdiction were the priests officiating in their convents, the various men and women servants and the secular sisters (*sorores conversae*), if such resided in the nunnery. In the nunneries of the Poor Clares there were abbesses who were authorized to bear the pastoral staff. In the Cistercian and Dominican orders in the fourteenth century in Germany and Flanders there were some nunneries with forty and more nuns. In the Poor Clares' nunneries there were sometimes fifty to eighty sisters in a nunnery and sometimes even up to one hundred and fifty, and, in contrast, there were very small nunneries with only two or three sisters. In fourteenth-century England, the large Benedictine nunneries housed about thirty nuns and the smaller ones only a handful.[52] In Imperial Germany of the fourteenth century there were Benedictine nunneries with forty sisters, and others with only eight. The nunneries of the new orders were usually supervised by visitations (*visitatio*) of representatives of the order. In Benedictine nunneries the 'visitors' were diocesan bishops or their representatives. There can be no doubt that despite the restrictions[53] the position of abbess offered women the opportunity of exercising organizational and educational talents which in secular society could only be realized by the heiresses of the great fiefs. Daughters of the nobility who wanted to realize their potential, and who were not heiresses, were attracted to nunneries. And thus we reach the question of the identity of the women who entered nunneries and took the vow.

There were undoubtedly women, like men, who entered monastic orders primarily for religious reasons and out of a true sense of vocation. There is no way of assessing for how many of them, and to what extent, other considerations were added to the religious factor. The sense of vocation was undoubtedly often combined with other psychological elements, but this is not a subject for the historian. Even in the case of the saints whose lives were recorded or who are mentioned by the chroniclers it is extremely difficult to assess the complex blend of psychological motives and the intensity of the sense of religious vocation. The very existence of the monastery was an expression of the search for a fuller and more significant religious life than could be lived in the outside world, and a reflection of the desire to flee the world, whether in protest or because of inability or unwillingness to confront it. But together with religious motives, there were also obvious socio-economic factors which played a part in the retreat to nunneries; the religious factor often took second place to say the least.

What were the reasons other than religious motives which led girls and women to enter nunneries? Despite the fact that, in theory, any free individual could enter the service of the secular Church or go into a monastery, and any free woman could enter a nunnery, in practice, and almost without exception, only daughters of the nobility and the bourgeoisie were accepted into nunneries of the Benedictines as well as to those of the newer orders. To the extent that women from lower classes were accepted, it was as lay sisters or as maid-servants. A serf could pay the manumission fee to his lord and send his son to an ecclesiastical school and from there to the service of the Church. There is no record of such a payment being made for the daughter of a serf to enable her to enter a nunnery. Although some of the Benedictine monasteries only accepted sons of certain noble families, and most of the monks were of noble origin, the Benedictine monasteries in general were never exclusively peopled by sons of the nobility; Franciscan and Dominican monasteries took in numerous members of the lower classes.[54]

The main reason why only daughters of the nobility became nuns is that the girl who took the veil was obliged to bring her dowry (*dos*) with her. This was prohibited by canonical law, and church councils often reiterated the ban on this payment, but in vain. It was impossible to root out the custom.[55] Even Peter Waldo, father of the Waldensian movement, in settling his affairs before distributing his estate among the poor, ensured that his daughters would receive their dowries for the convent.[56] The dowry to the nunnery was smaller than that which was customarily given to a secular bridegroom in the upper classes, but daughters of the lower classes were unable to pay even these smaller amounts. Many daughters of the nobility and the bourgeoisie never wed not because of their own unwillingness but because their fathers were unable to provide them with the necessary dowry for marriage to a member of their own class.

In the same way, some of the sons were also unable to take wives. In order to prevent dispersion of family assets, not all the sons would set up their own families. Some sons turned to the Church, others remained unmarried in the secular society, while the remainder wed.[57] But, in contrast to the unmarried woman, the bachelor was faced with several options for activity, whether within the

secular Church or in secular society, and was not obliged to enter a
monastery.

In noble or prosperous urban society, families would sometimes
invest all their savings in a dowry for one of the daughters (usually
the most beautiful), so as to marry into a family with appropriate
status and assets. The remaining daughters were obliged to take the
veil, a situation condemned by the preachers.[58] Nobles and rich
towndwellers preferred to send their daughters to nunneries, since
in these classes the status of nun was considered more respectable
than that of the spinster in secular society. Moreover, in the
nunnery women were protected against the possibility of engaging
in extramarital relations which could bring shame on their families.
Sometimes younger sisters or other relatives joined a nunnery
voluntarily under the impact of an elder sister who had already
taken the veil. Under the influence of St Clare, her mother, aunt and
two sisters all took the veil. But families also directed their
daughters to nunneries where a sister or relative already resided. If
several sisters joined the same nunnery, the younger members paid
less dowry and the older sister could act as their patron and
protector.[59] Just as sons who were to be priests were often sent to be
educated by an uncle who was a bishop, so girls were sent to aunts
who were abbesses. In a will written in London at the end of the
thirteenth century, a father bequeathed annual rent to his three
daughters and their aunt who were all nuns in the same nunnery.[60]
An orphan girl who entered a nunnery brought her inheritance with
her as a dowry.[61]

Many nunneries maintained contact with noble families one of
whose forefathers had been the patron or founder of the nunnery,
and daughters of these families were always accepted into the same
nunnery. In some of the nunneries the position of abbess was
reserved for a daughter of that family and the nunnery was regarded
by the family as part of its feudal estate (this was true of male
monasteries as well). Some nunneries accepted only noblewomen
into their ranks. This was true in Catalonia in the tenth century, in
the Imperial German nunneries, in several nunneries in the Liège
diocese, in the well-known Helfta nunnery in Saxonia, and in most
of the monasteries of Lorraine. The abbesses of these nunneries
were members of the noble founding families.[62] These abbesses were
able to exercise their organizational and educational talents, to
acquire education with greater ease than in the outside world and, if
they so chose, to live fuller religious lives than in secular society.
Some became mystics and saints.

Apart from women who chose the veil for religious reasons, and those sent to the nunnery as an alternative to marriage, illegitimate daughters, or girls who were deformed or backward, were sometimes sent into nunneries. Among men it was often the handicapped son who was earmarked for the monastic life. And just as men who were disgraced were sometimes sent to monasteries as a substitute for prison, so the nunnery sometimes served as a gaol for women who were sentenced to imprisonment for political or personal reasons by rulers, or even by their husbands or relatives who were greedy for their legacies.[63] And – the final point – women who became nuns were to a large extent free of male authority. Some women preferred this liberty to marriage, while others rejected marriage out of a fear which was undoubtedly often fanned by priests, confessors and preachers who inveighed against the sins of the flesh. In one of the troubadour songs written by a woman, two women ask a third, apparently older than themselves, whether it is worth their while to marry, since it is a sorrowful thing to be a wife, and childbirth is painful and mars the beauty of the female body. The older woman replies that it is better for them to wed Him who will not sully their purity since marriage to Him will win them eternal life.[64] This response embodies the religious ideal of chastity, but the motives of the two young questioners are personal-psychological rather than religious.

People of the period were aware that the nunnery sometimes served a young girl as a refuge. In a trial conducted in England in the second half of the twelfth century, the lawyer of one of the parties (in an attempt to prove that betrothal could be annulled) cited Eusebius of Caesarea and St Gregory: a betrothed girl is entitled to prefer the nunnery to marriage even against the will of her fiancé, and the law does not punish such a girl if she flees to a nunnery. The learned jurist cited these facts in support of his case, and chose this argument since it was likely to appeal to the judges.[65] Some widows chose to enter nunneries rather than remarry or remain in the widowed state in secular society. Some married women entered nunneries after separating from their husbands by mutual consent.

In the Middle Ages a girl could become a nun at 14–15, but most entered nunneries as novices at earlier ages, some even as small children (the same as male oblates). St Gertrude was placed in a nunnery at the age of 5. In Italy in the late Middle Ages girls customarily entered nunneries at the age of 9. Parents were not legally authorized to take the vow on behalf of minor daughters,[66] but although girls were entitled to leave the nunnery rather than take the vow when they reached their majority, it is hard to believe that a girl educated in a nunnery and detached from her parents from childhood (and whose dowry had often been paid into the nunnery when she entered) was really able to make a free choice, whatever the law permitted. It is also unlikely that such girls were fired by a sense of religious vocation.

In the lives of the female saints we read of holy nuns who in their childhood had expressed the desire to wed Christ alone and to take the veil. Mechthild of Magdeburg, the thirteen-century mystic who started out as a Beguine, entered a nunnery only as a grown woman, but in her memoirs she relates that she wanted to be a nun from the age of twelve. She confided her religious experiences to her younger brother who later became a Dominican friar. According to the biography of St Douceline, as a small child even before she had learned to read and write and recite her prayers she would go out on to the porch of her father's house, kneel with bare knees on the stones, join her hands in prayer and look up to Heaven.[67] But these are biographies of saints and mystics. It was to the many others, who were placed in nunneries in their childhood without being consulted, that the Dominican Humbert de Romans was undoubtedly referring when he described melancholy nuns whose gloom disturbed the tranquillity of their sisters, or those nuns who were as irritable as dogs chained for too long.[68] Nonetheless churchmen favoured taking novices into nunneries in childhood since they believed that if they were trained as nuns from an early age they would be submissive and would find it easier to accept the demands of the rule of the order. And, in fact, some of the women who entered nunneries only after being widowed, after many years in which they enjoyed the status of great ladies in the outside world, found it difficult to accept authority and sometimes created disciplinary problems for the abbess.

Abandonment of a nunnery was regarded as a grave sin, and a woman who left a nunnery and married was deprived of the opportunity to repent, and was totally excommunicated.[69] There are no precise data on the number of nuns in different countries in the High Middle Ages. E. Power, who analysed data on English nunneries in the second half of the fourteenth and throughout the fifteenth century, came to the conclusion that in this period the number of nuns did not exceed 3500, out of a population of more than two million. (The estimate is that before the Black Death the population of England was about 3,750,000 and that it decreased by some 40 per cent as a result of the Plague.) This number was further reduced during the fifteenth century. In the German Empire there was also a considerable fall in the number of nuns in Benedictine nunneries in the early fifteenth century. On the other hand, R. Trexler's study of Tuscany during the Late Middle Ages shows a large number of nuns in such cities as Florence, Venice and Milan; some 13 per cent of all women there were nuns.[70] It is evident that in the thirteenth and fourteenth centuries large numbers of women sought entry into nunneries. Although some nunneries took in greater numbers of novices than the recommended figure because of this pressure, they could not accept all the applicants. This fact, among others, explains the spread of the Beguine movement, which was religious but non-ecclesiastical, and whose success, like that of female monasticism, derived from a desire for a religious life combined with economic and social factors.

LIFE IN THE NUNNERY

At the beginning of the twelfth century many women joined the new Cistercian and Premonstratensian orders and a minority became affiliated to the Carthusians,[71] and in the early thirteenth century some joined the mendicant orders. In some cases sisters even left the Benedictine nunneries in order to join the new orders which advocated more literal and strict observance of the Benedictine rule and greater asceticism, or the Poor Clares out of a desire to realize the ideal of absolute poverty and of wandering and preaching in the spirit of the apostles. In the early days of the Cistercian and Premonstratensian orders, the sisters engaged in physical labour more than in the Benedictine nunneries, but both monasteries and nunneries soon regressed and adopted the seigneurial way of life which characterized the Benedictine order. The Poor Clares, as we have noted, lived in seclusion within the nunneries from the first, like the Benedictine sisters, and they were also barred from absolute poverty from the outset. (Permission to observe absolute poverty was a special privilege granted to the San Damiano nunnery alone, at the request of St Clare. Later Agnes of Prague also won this privilege.) In the end the Poor Clares' rule scarcely differed from that of the Benedictine or Cistercian nuns. Power's description of the way of life in the English Benedictine nunneries closely resembles that in the nunneries of other orders, excepting perhaps the Carthusian order, which was more ascetic and devoted more time to seclusion. Only a small number of women belonged to this order.

The sisters' day was divided up between prayer, labour and reading, most of the time being devoted to prayer and liturgical hymns, as in the monasteries. The first prayers, Matins and Lauds, were recited from 2 in the morning till dawn and the last at 8 pm. Some five hours of the day were dedicated to work and the rest were divided up between reading and three meals, luncheon being accompanied by recitations and 'sober amusements'. Few nuns were occupied in agricultural labour, and that only in the poorest nunneries and the Cistercian nunneries. In the poorer houses the nuns themselves carried out the household tasks: cooking, laundry, spinning and weaving. Most nunneries were almost self-sufficient where food was concerned, growing their own vegetables, meat and milk products. Bread was baked on the premises and ale was brewed there. Only fish, salt and spices were usually brought in from outside. In the richer nunneries all household chores were done by lay sisters or servant women and the nuns occupied themselves with embroidery, delicate spinning, illumination of books and reading. In addition to the abbess and her deputy there were several other functionaries, like the sacristan who was in charge of the church fabrics and candles, the chambresses who looked after the nuns' clothes, and the cellaress who looked after food, servants and the farm attached to the nunnery and worked directly for the use of the nuns.

The standard of living varied from house to house. The number of maid-servants varied, as did the living conditions and the quality of the food. The rules determined fixed days for consumption of meat and fish, but the quality of these foodstuffs was dissimilar in rich and poor nunneries, and the robes of the nuns also varied. Many nunneries in late medieval England suffered financial difficulties, whether because they lacked sufficient assets or because they did not manage their affairs skilfully. In the instructions issued by bishops in the wake of visitations to both monasteries and nunneries, the abbots and abbesses were forbidden to cut down trees, grant rents or sell property without the approval of the bishop so as to prevent economic deterioration.

The Benedictine (male and female) monasteries in the German Empire in that period also underwent financial problems.[72] Some permitted noble women to pay to live in separate quarters within the nunnery area, sometimes for limited periods, during the absence of their husbands or fathers, and sometimes, in the case of widows, for the rest of their days. According to the reports of bishops who visited monasteries, it seems that these ladies, who continued to dress in high fashion, who kept their lapdogs and servants, invited guests and gossiped with them, had a detrimental effect on the nuns. The bishops tried to prevent this custom of accepting laywomen into the nunneries, but it was generally hard for these institutions to renounce this welcome source of income. From the report of the diocesan bishop of Lincoln after a visit to the priory of Rothwell we learn of a case in which persons unknown broke into a remote nunnery, dragged out a woman who resided there and raped her. The nuns who tried to prevent this deed were cast to the ground, trampled and kicked. The robes obviously did not always serve to protect a woman, but the actual deed was sparked off by the laywoman residing in the nunnery.[73] Married couples sometimes also lived in nunneries. The visiting bishops were particularly scathing about this custom, fearing that it could arouse 'lusts of the flesh' among the nuns.[74]

The nunneries could make only a limited contribution to the secular society of their time. Some nunneries maintained schools and took in both sons and daughters of the nobility and the rich urban class. If the parents or relatives fulfilled their obligations to pay the schooling fees and keep (which they sometimes failed to do), this provided an additional source of income for the house. Since the pupils were selected exclusively from the upper classes, the nunneries made no contribution to educating the children of the poorer strata. Numerically, at least in England, these schools were few, since the smaller nunneries did not maintain them. In the Cistercian nunneries in all countries the sisters were forbidden to teach boys. There were larger numbers of convent schools in Italian towns. To the extent that the nunneries were prosperous, they would distribute alms to the poor, as did the male monasteries. Being secluded in their nunneries, the sisters did not work among the poor, but instead distributed alms to the poor of their neighbourhood, who came to their gate.

In the Early Middle Ages in the double Benedictine monasteries and in the twelfth century in the double monasteries of the Premonstratensian order, the sisters aided the monks in caring for the sick. But, generally speaking, this task was reserved for the sisterhoods established specifically for this purpose, or for lay sisters who lived in religious communities attached to one of the monastic orders as a 'third order'. In the thirteenth century, those sisters who had accepted the Augustinian rule added a fourth vow – to tend the sick – to the three they had already taken. In the early thirteenth century the sick were treated in the famous Hôtel Dieu in

Paris. Nuns were also attached to the order of St John of Jerusalem, and served in hospitals in the Holy Land, Cyprus and various European countries. Of the men and women who joined the Franciscan and Dominican orders in the thirteenth and fourteenth centuries as tertiaries, some also tended the sick. In grants to hospitals in England in the thirteenth and fourteenth centuries, mention is often made of brothers and sisters serving in the hospital: for example, in St Catherine's hospital in London, St Bartholomew's hospital, the Holy Sepulchre hospital, the St Margaret hospital in Gloucester, etc. One should also recall the nuns who laboured in the Hôtel Dieu in Angers from the beginning of the thirteenth century, and those who served in various leprosaria in Western Europe.[75] But in the Middle Ages the nursing profession was not exclusively female (most hospitals were poorhouses and homes for the aged more than hospitals in the modern sense of the word), and women worked there together with men.

We see therefore that in addition to caring for the sick, which was by no means a characteristic occupation of all nuns, the contribution of female orders to society was relatively restricted and in no way comparable to that of monks, both in the intellectual and spiritual spheres and in areas which were closed to sisters, such as leadership of the Church and missionary activity. It should be recalled, however, that the original and primary objective of the monastery was activity aimed at saving the soul of the individual monk or nun, and prayer on behalf of their fellow human beings. Hence it is not true to say that the female orders deviated from their original purpose by failing to make a considerable contribution to society in general. The works of guidance composed for the nuns sometimes state explicitly: do not turn your nunnery into a school (just as Peter Damian objected to the existence of schools in monasteries).[76] The Franciscans and Dominicans took a different path, and engaged in evangelical work, but the women accepted into these orders were never permitted to emulate the monks.

The failure to make a significant contribution to secular society did not constitute a deviation from the primary aims of the nunnery. There were, however, grave deviations from the rule aimed at enabling the monk or nun to realize the primary aim of the order. The degree of deviation differed in the various orders and in various periods. One can ascertain this from the homiletic literature of the period and from a more reliable source, namely the reports of bishops or representatives of orders who visited nunneries and subsequently instructed the abbess to correct the flaws. The homiletic literature of the thirteen and fourteenth centuries accuses the nuns of manufacturing excuses in order to leave the nunnery and meet their lovers.[77] It is too easy for young men to gain access to the nunnery. The nuns behave like ladies and are only interested in their outward appearance. They sing, dance and make merry with the young men who visit them. It is known that in some of the nunneries which adopted the Cistercian rule, and among the Poor Clares, the nuns sometimes kept private maid-servants and private property for their own use.[78] The abbesses sometimes went even further, not only living in separate quarters but also maintaining serving maids who cooked and served them special meals. The lists of wills also reveal that from time to time relatives would leave personal legacies to nuns, in addition to grants to the nunnery.[79]

According to the reports of visitors to both nunneries and monasteries of the Benedictine order in England, the prayer times were not always respected. Nuns and monks tended particularly to appear tardily to the first prayer of the day, at 2 am, and left the chapel before the end of the service on various pretexts. Some would drowse during the prayers, while others recited the prayers in a rapid gabble in order to shorten the service. The impressions of the bishops correspond, to a large degree, to the criticism in homiletic literature where the nuns are accused of vanity, dancing and keeping lapdogs, all these being regarded as unsuitable for the nun. The accounts of the nunneries also reveal the purchase of intoxicating liquor, and outlay on games, torches and musicians on various festivals, all of these being related to activities prohibited to the sisters. Church synods drew up lists of the articles of clothing and ornaments which nuns were forbidden to wear, but to no avail. Fashionable clothing and pet animals (some nuns kept monkeys, squirrels, birds, and above all lapdogs) did not disappear. Church leaders regarded these phenomena as violations of discipline and expressions of the sisters' failure to cast off worldly things. Many nuns were accused of receiving visitors in the nunnery, also a reflection of refusal to cut themselves off from the outside world.

Christine de Pisan draws a picture of life in a French nunnery which illustrates some of the problems and flaws characteristic of the nunneries of the age. It is interesting to note that her description is in no way critical. She describes facts simply, as if all were both normal and desirable. Her picture relates to the Poissy nunnery where her daughter resided. It was founded by Philip IV and was dedicated to the sainted Louis IX. It had the status of priory, and the position of *priorissa* was reserved for the daughter of one the noblest families or even a member of the royal family. According to Christine, the prioress, Marie de Bourbon, told visitors of the strictness of the nunnery's rule. The nuns slept in their robes on hard mattresses. They were beaten if they did not rise in time for morning prayer and were usually not permitted to see visitors except through iron grilles. While the prioress was speaking, Marie de France, the 8-year-old daughter of Charles IV, entered the room. She had been received into the nunnery at the age of 5. The prioress herself lived in separate and most luxurious quarters. Despite the ban on visitors, Christine's daughter spent several hours in complete freedom with her mother and friends. The guests dined together with the lay residents of the nunnery (their gourmet meal of delicacies and wine was served on silver and gold plates). The lay residents with whom they strolled around the grounds showed the visitors their separate and comfortable rooms with attractive beds. The nuns served the lay residents and the visitors during the meal.[80]

Many nuns were accused of leaving the nunnery without sufficient reason. Madame Eglentyne, head of a small nunnery (and hence *priorissa* and not *abbatissa*), who is one of the characters in Chaucer's *Canterbury Tales*, is an example of an elegant nun of courtly manners, toying with a lapdog and glad of the opportunity to leave the nunnery for weeks at a time in order to go on a pilgrimage to the tomb of Saint Thomas Becket (in violation of the orders of the bishops).[81] The reports of the bishops reveal that some nuns, while away from their nunneries, did in fact commit carnal sins, as the homiletic literature claimed.[82] In literature, at least, the possibility of the birth of bastards to nuns is raised. In the Galeran poem (a narrative poem from the end of the twelfth century attributed to Renart) the heroine leaves a cradle in the nunnery to serve any of the nuns who may give birth.[83]

But even if sisters sometimes left the nunnery for more innocent purposes than a meeting with a lover, there can be no doubt that the desire to flee the nunnery at every possible opportunity was an expression of lack of spiritual satisfaction and of ennui. If we compare the reports of visits to monasteries to accounts of visits to nunneries we see that a considerable proportion of the flaws were common to both institutions: unsuitable garments, leave without sufficient pretext and for purposes of meeting with the opposite sex, entertaining guests beyond the permissible degree, granting permission to lay persons to reside in the monastery or nunnery, maintaining private property, consuming alcohol and lax observance of prayer.[84]

Direct charges that nuns engaged in lesbian relations were less common than the charge that monks and priests engaged in homosexual practices. But in instructions to the nunneries, we find hints that the authors were aware of the existence (or the possibility of the existence) of this sin among nuns. In the resolutions of the Church synod in Paris, nuns were forbidden to sleep together and it was stipulated that a light should burn in the dormitory all night, this regulation having already been introduced for monks in the Benedictine rule in the sixth century. In the instructions of the bishops following visits to nunneries in the diocese of Lincoln, the ban on permitting male or female visitors to spend the night in the dormitory is reiterated. In one of the works of guidance for nuns they are instructed to sleep fully clothed and belted. Their detractors accused them directly of lesbian relations. Pierre Dubois (lawyer and political pamphleteer), who favoured reducing the number of nunneries and reforming them, claimed that the implementation of his plan would put an end to several despicable customs, such as acceptance of candidates into nunneries in return for payment (dowries) and the selection of unsuitable women for the position of abbess or prioress, and would abolish certain natural and unnatural sins within the nunneries. A document enumerating the misdemeanours of the Lollards notes that they thought it preferable for girls and widows to wed rather than take the veil. Otherwise, being weak and lacking a true sense of vocation, they committed grave sins such as the practice of lesbianism, bestiality and masturbation with the aid of various instruments.[85]

The English nunneries of the fourteenth century were in a state of cultural decline. Physical labour was carried out in most of them by lay maid-servants. A large proportion of the nuns reached the nunnery without a sense of vocation, and thus the lengthy hours of prayer, uncoloured by spiritual or physical labour, became nothing but wearisome routine. It is not surprising that the nuns became both idle and inquisitive, as Humbert de Romans wrote, and that they tried to amuse themselves, as the visiting bishops noted accusingly.[86] In the case of the more innocent amusements they may have been preferable to depression and irritability. In the absence of the sense of vocation which alone can create inner satisfaction and acquiescence, the forbidden gaiety was the sole panacea to depression. But the cultural and moral decline did not afflict all nunneries in that period. In Germany and the Netherlands the nunneries flourished in the fourteenth century, as did the non-institutionalized movement of women. In Germany in that century female monasticism was part of the contemporary mystical move-ment. The nuns formed part of the audience of the great German mystics, Meister Eckhart and Tauler, and it was they who recorded their sermons in writing.

Copying manuscripts, one of the occupations of the sisters in many monasteries, called for a certain degree of education, and there was in fact a certain degree of continuity in the education of nuns from the beginning of institutionalized female monasticism. Some ac-quired learning before entering the nunnery. Those who entered in childhood learned to read and write and recite their prayers. Most nuns did not know Latin well, and learned the prayers and sections of religious literature by heart; what appeared to be knowledge of Latin was in fact parrot-like repetition. Apart from prayers and hymns in Latin, the nuns in most nunneries studied selected chapters of the Scriptures, writings of the Church Fathers, the lives of the saints and founders of the monastic orders and the translated rule of their order. In the hours allocated for reading, the nuns read these works. It was also customary to read aloud in Latin during one of the meals of the day. The nun who recited to her companions was required to read fluently, and in some of the nunneries there was one sister whose task it was to follow the recitation and correct all mistakes. Since the sisters in most nunneries were educated to a certain degree, they were able to engage in copying and illuminating books. The Cistercian nunneries of Nazareth, near Lierre and La Ramée, were important centres of illumination and calligraphy in the first half of the thirteenth century.

It was universally accepted that nuns were granted a certain degree of education. Even those authors of didactic literature who were violently hostile to women, and opposed their education in secular society, favoured educating nuns.[87] Abélard, who wanted nunneries to be ruled by male abbots, also approved of learning for nuns,[88] and at the end of the thirteenth century the provincial chapter of the German Dominicans decided to appoint learned brothers to teach the nuns, taking into account the education they had already acquired. But in the High Middle Ages the monasteries were no longer centres of learning. In the Carolingian period such monasteries as Fulda, St Gall and St Martin of Tours had been the main focuses of learning, as the Bec monastery had been in the eleventh century. Yet in the twelfth century this role was fulfilled by cathedral schools, and in the thirteenth by the universities and Dominican colleges, which were closed to women, including nuns. In this respect the status of the nun resembled that of women in general. Nonetheless, there were nuns who continued to instruct themselves, with the aid of priests and monks from their own order, and acquired a wider-ranging education than was usually possible for the sisters. Some of these learned nuns became mystics and saints, and their writings have survived to modern times. We will discuss these mystics in greater detail in a separate section, and in the present context we will dwell only on the learning of a few of them.

Mechthild of Hackeborn refers in her writings to the Holy Scriptures, and the works of Origen, St Augustine, Bernard of Clairvaux and Albertus Magnus. St Gertrude openly repents in her writings of the time she devoted to the seven liberal arts and, like many monks, regards herself as having progressed from grammarian to theologian. In addition to her mystic visions, St Gertrude wrote summaries of lives of saints and a book of prayer denoted 'Spiritual exercises'.[89] Both Mechthild and St Gertrude wrote in Latin, and both were members of the Cistercian nunnery of Helfta in Saxony. A third mystic, Mechthild of Magdeburg, who composed the first mystical work in German, also resided in this nunnery. Her book *Das fliessende Licht der Gottheit* ('The Flowing Light of God') strongly influenced German mysticism, but she was less educated than the above-mentioned women scholars.

Hildegard of Bingen, who lived in the first half of the twelfth century, composed a book of visions, wrote theological works and engaged in extensive correspondence with her contemporaries, both secular and ecclesiastical. She also wrote a mystery play, the life of a local saint called Rupert, who gave his name to her nunnery, and a life of an Irish missionary who practised in the Rhineland. Also attributed to Hildegard are a medical work and a collection of musical works, though there is no certainty as to their authorship. She also illustrated some of her writings. In these works and in her visions she made use of scientific knowledge, writing or dictating in Latin. Her writings reveal knowledge of the works of St Augustine, Boethius, Isidore of Seville, Bernard Silvestris, Aristotle and Galen. In the sections on anatomy she cited the eleventh-century monk and translator, Constantine the African, and in depicting the spheres which compose the universe she cited the works of Messahalah. As Charles Singer has written, Hildegard does not distinguish between physical events, moral truths and spiritual experiences. All is seen as the fruit of inspiration and revelation, as in Dante's *Divine Comedy*, but it is possible to trace her sources, just as one can identify those of Dante.[90] The flaws in her writings are an over-abundance of comparisons as a means of establishing *a priori* proof, an attempt to seek the archetype of every thing and phenomenon in this world in the celestial system, and the borrowing of knowledge and views at second and third remove – but all these are typical weaknesses of her time which can be found in the works of her male contemporaries.

We have cited several examples of learned nuns whose literary works have survived them. One could draw up a longer list. There can be no doubt that a talented nun who so wished could more easily acquire an education than a laywoman, and the society of her day accepted her learning without objection. Yet even she was not granted access to institutions of higher learning. The sisters made no contribution to the scholastic philosophy and theology which were the main fruit of the culture of the High Middle Ages, nor to legal and scientific studies. The only sphere in which they made their mark was mysticism. We cannot state with certainty that if institutions of higher learning had been open to them, they would have made an important contribution to scholastic philosophy and theology or science. However since these institutions were closed to them, they were denied the opportunity from the outset.

THE BEGUINES

The Beguine movement was a religious movement, and, therefore, although it was not part of the ecclesiastical establishment, its members can be regarded as part of the order of 'those who prayed'. The movement arose in the thirteenth century and spread through the towns of Belgium, the Rhineland in Germany and northern and southern France. In the main it was part of the religious movement in Northern Europe whose followers sought a significant religious life and wanted to emulate Christ by living lives of chastity, penitence, prayer, poverty and physical labour, and by working among the poor and sick. The women who were attracted to the movement in its early days had not joined the orders of nuns, either because some of them regarded life in nunneries in the early thirteenth century as too soft and easy, or because the existing nunneries could not absorb all the women who sought to join, particularly after the disbanding of the Premonstratensian nunneries and the Dominican renunciation of responsibility for nunneries.

Like other religious movements of the time, the Beguines wanted a less secluded religious life which would offer greater contact with other people. The movement was spontaneous. The first Beguines were drawn almost exclusively from the same social strata as the nuns, i.e. the nobility and prosperous towndwellers, motivated by the same desire for an apostolic life. But gradually the Beguine movement began to offer a socio-economic solution for urban women and girls who could not gain access to the nunneries of their choice (and not necessarily for religious reasons) because they were unable to pay the required dowry. The number of poor women among the Beguines grew particularly in the fourteenth century, against a background of economic crises. The craft guilds were becoming increasingly exclusive and the labour opportunities for women in towns were narrowing, since they were among the first victims of the economic crises. The Beguine movement of the fourteenth century offered them the possibility of working outside the guilds, spinning, weaving,[91] sewing and laundering in their own homes. Some earned their livelihood, particularly in Belgian towns (Liège, Louvain, Bruges, Brussels), by caring for the sick. They sometimes appear on the lists of taxpayers, as in Paris in the thirteenth century.[92] A number of urban schools were maintained by the Beguines. For their devoted and diligent labours they were praised by Humbert de Romans, who cited the 'virtuous woman' of the Book of Proverbs.[93]

As we have noted, the Beguines were a religious rather than an ecclesiastical institution. In the early days of the movement, they lived in their own homes or in the parental household, but donated part of their property to the Beguinage or to the poor and occupied themselves with prayer and charitable deeds. These first Beguines were known as 'the Beguines who dwell in isolation in the secular world' (*Beguinae singulariter in saeculo*). They gradually began to congregate in houses in which they lived a more or less regulated life under the supervision of the mother of the house. Their day was divided up between charity, prayer and work. These were the *Beguinae clausae* (secluded) who lived according to a certain rule which they had chosen. They included girls, married women who had separated from their husbands, and widows. Some churchmen, for example James of Vitry, who were aware of the fact that not all women who so wished were able to join nunneries, and recognized the power of the distaff religious movement, worked on behalf of the Beguines with the aim of winning them papal recognition, supervising them, guiding and instructing them and helping them to a way to support themselves. In 1233 Pope Gregory IX recognized the movement (though not directly) in his *Gloriam virginalem* bull.[94] The parochial organization aided them by allotting them suitable sites where they could set up their Beguinages, and the urban authorities exempted them from payment of taxes. Some of the leaders of the Cistercian and Dominican orders contributed to their spiritual instruction.

But even after at least some of the Beguines began to live 'closed' lives in the above-mentioned houses, and were granted papal recognition, they did not become a Church institution. Their houses were dependent on privileges granted by urban authorities, and in their economic activity they were subordinate to the guild regulations. Furthermore, not only were they not an ecclesiastical or semi-ecclesiastical institution, like the third order of the Franciscans and Dominicans; one might even say that they were never institutionalized at all. They never introduced a regular hierarchy, a uniform rule or a general supervisory system. The Beguines did not take a lifetime vow. They were permitted to leave the Beguinage and to wed. They did not guarantee to distribute all their wealth to the poor or to hand it over to the Beguinage.[95]

Thus we see that from the first this movement offered more scope for individualism than did the institutionalized orders. Some Beguines became influential figures and won great esteem; such was Mary d'Oignies, daughter of a wealthy family, who herself distributed her property to the poor, separated from her husband (out of mutual consent to live chaste lives), and persuaded rich laypeople to give away their wealth and become monks. After her death her sacred relics protected James of Vitry, and she appeared to him in dreams to offer him guidance. There were mystics and saints among the Beguines, such as St Douceline, and the movement in general was distinguished by spiritual vitality until the end of the fourteenth century. But that same individualistic spirit which was not dampened by rules and supervision created situations which the Church establishment could not accept. Some Beguines engaged in translating Holy Scripture into German and French and composed exegeses in the wake of the translations, this being totally prohibited by Church authorities. They even debated questions of faith after reading translations of theological works, again arousing the criticism and reservations of the authorities. A Beguine from Hainaut named Margaret Porete composed a mystical work, *Le Mirouer des Simples Ames* ('Mirror of Simple Souls'), which was denounced as a heretical work, and in 1310 she was burned at the stake. We shall return to her in the next section. Particular anger was aroused by the Beguines who did not live in Beguinages but continued to live in secular society. They were charged with vagrancy, begging, illegal preaching and doctrinal errors. In some cases they were even accused of engaging in prostitution or lesbian relations.[96]

In their mystical experiences, some Beguines approached the borderline of the experience of communion with Christ, which was regarded as pertaining to the sphere of orthodoxy (James of Vitry describes Beguines who were so immersed in ecstasy of love for Christ inspired by the Song of Songs[97] that for years they did not rise from their beds), while others arrived at hysterical erotic experiences. Some found their way into heresy mainly in the spirit of the Joachimite movement and the Free Spirit movement, which sometimes led to total identification with God to the point of annihilation of the self, and subsequent denial of the sacraments as the *conditio sine qua non* for redemption. Others had visions of the third epoch (recalling the epoch of the Holy Spirit of the Joachimites), in which, they claimed, the Holy Spirit would be embodied in a woman.[98] Some were close to the view of the Spiritual Franciscans who were also denounced as heretics.

Despite the fact that in decrees for persecution of the Beguines, the bishops and popes usually distinguished between the Beguines who lived 'in the world' and had strayed into doctrinal error and heresy, and the 'good' Beguines who stayed in their Beguinages, working and observing the orthodox viewpoint, the waves of persecution were often directed at all Beguines indiscriminately. They were persecuted in the second half of the fourteenth century by the Inquisition, together with the heretical movements with which they were often unjustly identified and together with the other non-regular movements which suffered in a period in which voluntary poverty was suspect in the eyes of the Church. The fact that the Beguinages were exempt from taxes vexed the guilds, which placed limitations on the scope of their economic activity for fear of competition. Their field of production was restricted, they were prohibited from using certain tools and they were also banned from selling their products under their own name lest they win a reputation. In the fifteenth century the Beguinages were houses of shelter more than religious institutions and workshops; their residents no longer dealt with theological problems, nor could they support themselves by their own labours. One can sum up by saying that the Beguine movement offered a means of expression for some women in the non-institutionalized religious movement, just as they played a part in the institutionalized orders and in the heretical movements.[99]

The most important contribution of women to spiritual creativity in the Middle Ages was in the sphere of Christian mysticism. One can hardly imagine medieval mysticism without such figures as Angela of Foligno, Bridget of Sweden, Catherine of Sienna, St Gertrude, Hildegard of Bingen, Juliana of Norwich, Mechthild of Hackeborn and Mechthild of Magdeburg.[100] It is not possible, within the framework of a book on women in the Middle Ages, to arrive at any profound analysis of their writings, nor to study in depth the nature of Christian mysticism. We can merely try to examine two specific questions. The first is the special status of women mystics in medieval Christian society. The second is the question of whether their writings displayed any particular features which distinguished them from those of male mystics.

The great female mystics were accorded status and respect which no other women won. Bernard of Clairvaux wrote to the twelfth-century mystic, Hildegard of Bingen:

> We bless the divine grace which resides in you ... How can I aspire to instruct and advise you, who have attained hidden knowledge, and in whom the influence of Christ's anointing still lives. There is no longer any need to instruct you, since it has been said of you that you are capable of examining the secrets of the heavens and discerning, by the light of the Holy Spirit, that which is beyond the knowledge of man. I have the task of asking you not to forget me and those united with me in spiritual fraternity before God ...[101]

Thus Bernard of Clairvaux recognized the sanctity of the mystic, which is unrelated to any official position or priestly rank. This acceptance of a female mystic can be compared to the acceptance of the few female prophets in the Old and New Testaments (Old Testament: Exodus 15:20; Judges 4–5; 2 Kings 22:14; New Testament: Acts 21:9), or recognition of female saints in Christianity whose sanctity rested in their personality rather than in position or title.

The saints (and some of the female mystics became saints) were canonized only after their death, but their particular qualities, whether the gift of prophecy or other traits, were often recognized in their lifetime. One of the chroniclers wrote of Hildegard of Bingen and Elizabeth of Schönau: 'In those days God revealed his power through the weaker sex, in two of his maidservants ... and they were filled with the power of prophecy.'[102] Francis of Assisi believed in the healing powers of Clare, and sent Brother Stephen, whose mind had become unhinged, to her. She made the sign of the cross over him, he lay down to sleep in the place where she was wont to pray, and on the following morning he arose cured.[103] (For some reason, Clare met with less success in attempts to cure the mental illness of several of her sister nuns.)

This distinction between power deriving from personality alone, given as a gift from God, and the authority of rank and title in women was drawn succinctly by Thomas Aquinas: 'Prophecy is not a sacrament but a divine gift ...' (*propheta non est sacramentum sed Dei donum*), since the female sex is unable to symbolize superiority of order, as woman is in a state of subjugation, therefore woman cannot be privileged to receive the priestly sacrament. But since, as regards soul, woman does not differ from man, and is sometimes even better than many men, it transpires that she is able to receive the gift of prophecy and all it entails, but not the priestly sacrament.[104] The female mystics did not dispute the inferior status of women in this world and accepted the concept of woman's secondary role in creation, Hildegard of Bingen wrote:

> When God saw man he saw that he was very good for man was made in his image. But in creating woman, God was aided by man ... Therefore woman is the creation of man ... Man symbolizes the divinity of the Son of God and woman his humanity. Therefore man presides in the courts of this world since he rules all creatures, while woman is under his rule and submits to him.

Just as Hildegard of Bingen accepted the idea of woman's secondary role in creation and her submission to man, she also approved of denying woman's right to serve in priestly office.[105] Disregarding her own femininity she wrote not on her own behalf, but in the name of God. Just as Bernard of Clairvaux accepted Hildegard, she was also recognized by Pope Eugenius III and the Church leaders of the period as well as the great secular figures (including Henry II of England and Eleanor of Aquitaine), and corresponded with them. Her visions were regarded as prophecies, and miracles were attributed to her in her lifetime.

Catherine of Sienna in the fourteenth century was in contact with the great personalities of Church and state and was active on behalf of the return of the pope from Avignon to Rome. During the papal schism, in 1378, she sided with Pope Urban VI. Of the compilations of prayers composed by female mystics, there were some, like the *Exercitia Spiritualia* of St Gertrude, which became very popular. Female mystics who were less involved in contemporary events than Hildegard of Bingen and Catherine of Sienna were also recognized by the abbots of their own orders and their confessors, to whom they sometimes dictated their visions and mystical experiences. The churchmen who wrote about the female mystics emphasized their inspiration and tended to play down their education. Vincent of Beauvais confirmed that Hildegard of Bingen had dictated her visions in Latin but claimed that she had done so as in a dream while inspired, since she was *laica et illiterata*.[106] The churchmen apparently preferred this evaluation, since education was comparable to rank and title, while inspiration could be regarded as a divine gift of the personality. Thanks to this gift the female mystic was a classic example of the deviant who received the blessing of the society in which he or she lives. A woman who intervened in the running of Church and state, instructing leaders in how to act, composing prayers and dictating visions, was a total deviation from the accepted norms.

The female mystics who remained in the sphere of orthodoxy, and who, without exception, were either placed in nunneries as small girls or joined one of the orders or the third order of the Franciscans or Dominicans in adulthood, displayed varying degrees of learning. But none of them acquired extensive theological and philosophical education as did some of the male mystics. The differences in intellectual and educational standard and in literary talent of the female mystics are naturally reflected in their writings.

Like the male mystics in Christian Europe, many of these women were active in the secular world. The religious experiences led to involvement rather than detachment. According to the chroniclers of their lives, many of them displayed in childhood a leaning to the religious life, prayer and meditation, and declared that they would wed Christ alone. Nonetheless in adulthood they became active in various spheres. Hildegard of Bingen, who reacted to all the important events of her time and, in her sermons, denounced the sins of contemporaries, was an abbess. At first she lived in a nunnery near Dissenberg, and later a large nunnery was set up for her and her community of Benedictine sisters at Rupertsberg near Bingen. She established another nunnery near Eibingen which was a kind of subsidiary of her own nunnery. Among other activities, she corresponded with twelve Cistercian abbots in order to dissuade them from resigning their positions. Abbots approached her in order to ask her advice on the moral and organizational situation of their order, and to ask whether they had done anything displeasing to God. In her answer she severely criticized their methods and deviations from the rule of their order. She was also approached on questions pertaining to mysticism, exegesis and theology.[107]

Catherine of Sienna devoted herself for years to caring for the poor and sick and bringing sinners to repentance, and she headed a large community which was part of the Dominican third order. She was also involved in planning the crusade against the Turks and in the struggle between the Florentine alliance and the papacy and, as noted, was active in the campaign to restore the pope to Rome. Bridget of Sweden tried to bring about agreement between the kings of England and France and to prevent the Hundred Years War, and was also involved in efforts to transfer the pope from Avignon to Rome. Mechthild of Magdeburg started out as a Beguine, and in her latter years lived in the Helfta Cistercian nunnery. While a Beguine, she cared for the sick and the poor. The works she dictated at that period to a Dominican brother include, apart from her visions of the divine world and of Hell and the description of her communion with God, calls for reform of the Church in a spirit recalling that of Hildegard of Bingen, as well as criticism of the low morals of all classes. She was so confident of her mission that while still a junior Beguine she did not content herself with condemning the sins of her generation in general terms, but also preached and wrote personal letters of guidance to several churchmen in Magdeburg and its environs.[108]

We noted in the previous section James of Vitry's remarks about Beguines who arrived at ecstatic love of Christ:

> They melted altogether in wondrous love for God until it seemed that they bowed under the burden of desire and for many years they did not leave their beds except on rare occasions.... Resting in tranquillity with the master, they became deformed in body but comforted and made strong in spirit ...[109]

This phenomenon did exist, but it was not characteristic of the important mystics. As E. Underhill has noted, it probably derived more from lack of self-discipline than from a predilection for mysticism. The female mystics too underwent periods of seclusion, accompanied at times by physical weakness, mainly in their younger years, but this was followed by a period of activity, interrupted from time to time by additional periods of seclusion. Such hermit mystics as Juliana of Norwich, who lived as an anchorite, were not typical. Some mystics were responsible for adding feast-days to the Catholic calendar and introducing new methods of worship. The idea of worship of the heart of Christ was developed by Bernard of Clairvaux, but an important contribution was made by St Gertrude and Mechthild of Hackeborn in the thirteen century,[110] and they were responsible for disseminating it among monks and mystics in the thirteenth and fourteenth centuries. (It was defined theologically only in the eighteenth century.) The Belgian mystic Julian of Cornillon, on the basis of her visions, introduced the feast of Corpus Christi in memory of the institution and gift of the Holy Eucharist. This feast was an expression of adoration for the humanity of Christ. It was first accepted by Cistercian, Franciscan and Dominican monks and nuns and among Beguines, and was later approved by theologians and spread throughout western Christianity.[111]

Was there any quality which distinguished the writing of female mystics from those of their male counterparts? Their negative features were usually singled out. Critics noted their excessive sentimentalism, sometimes bordering on hysteria, which found expression in their writings, and their narcissism.[112] G. Scholem has pointed to the strong sentimental element in female mysticism and the autobiographical and subjective nature of their writings. Jewish Cabbalistic thought, on the other hand, is marked by restraint, objectivity and didacticism, because historically and metaphysically it was male mysticism.[113] The works of certain female mystics undoubtedly contain that same strong sentimental element which borders on narcissism and hysteria, and it is true that the authors of didactic Christian mystic literature were not women. But it seems that the path of women in Christian mysticism was determined less by their sex than by the nature of Christian faith in general and Christian mysticism in particular. The focus of the Christian mystical vision was sometimes Mary, sometimes the Trinity depicted in symbols such as light, life and love. Bernard of Clairvaux wrote of love of the Word (*verbum*) as wisdom, justice, truth, good and spirit, as a higher level than love of the Word incarnated,[114] that is to say love of the incarnated God who lived and suffered on earth. But the subject of contemplation in Christian mysticism was God embodied in flesh, the human body of Christ suffering on the cross. Angela of Foligno writes: 'He appeared unto me several times in dreams and waking nailed to the cross and told me to regard his wound ...'[115]

The female mystic was a woman who approached a male God personified in flesh. She turned to him as his bride, his widow and sometimes even his bereaved mother. Mechthild of Magdeburg writes: 'Oh, noble eagle, oh tender lamb, oh burning flame, embrace me. How long shall I remain arid? An hour is too heavy for me and a day is as a thousand years ...' And Angela of Foligno dictated the following: 'As I stood by the cross, I removed my garments and offered him all of myself, I promised him, though afeared, to maintain my chastity always and not to offend him by one of my limbs ...'[116] There is undoubtedly a strong erotic undercurrent in these words. But it should be recalled that the transfer of eroticism from the sphere of male-female relations to relations of man with God was not initiated by women. In the first centuries of Christianity, chastity was already lauded and the Church thinkers and mystics borrowed concepts from the sphere of marriage and various erotic terms to describe the religious experience and the Church establishment.

The female mystics of the High and Late Middle Ages found a ready-made set of symbols. In the third century the Song of Songs was interpreted by Christians as a dialogue between Christ and the Church, and at a later stage it was regarded as a dialogue between the soul and God. Bernard of Clairvaux made a vital contribution to this interpretation. His mysticism was basically didactic, his style is relatively restrained, and he writes in the third person. But he interpreted the Song of Songs as an expression of the yearning of the soul for God and as a mystical epithalamium.[117] Other mystics, including some of the greatest figures in Christian mysticism such as Seuse and Tauler, wrote in the form of a dialogue in which the mystic speaks in the first person. Any critic who interprets the female mystic's vision of spiritual marriage with Christ as a substitute for sexual experience rather than a symbol of spiritual elevation could equally grasp the descriptions of male mystics as representing substitutes for relations with the father, mother or spouse, or as reflections of homo-erotic relations. In a letter to a young noble who joined a monastery, Bernard of Clairvaux wrote:

If you feel the sting of temptation, raise your eyes to the serpent of brass (Numbers 21:8–15) raised above the cross, (John 3:14) and the wounds of the crucified one and particularly his breasts will slake your thirst. He himself will be as a mother to you and you will be as a son to him, and the nails cannot wound the crucified one without reaching your hands and feet through his.[118]

In the thirteenth century Philip the Carthusian wrote in a poem to the Holy Mother:

> You are my father, my brother, my sister, my livelihood and my salvation, in you I shall not be lost. You are my beloved bridegroom, to you I give my virginity, you are my comely bridegroom. My heart yearns for you always. You are my beloved and my friend.[119]

And Raymond Lull in the fourteenth century, in his mystic work *Libre d'amic et amat*, writes:

> You are all and through all and in all and with all. I will give you all myself so that you will be entirely mine and all of me will be yours ... And the beloved replied: I cannot be all yours if you are not all mine; and the lover replied: I will be all yours and you all mine ... The lover and the beloved met and the beloved said unto the lover: there is no need for you to speak to me. Give me a sign with your eyes alone for those are words for my heart – so that I can give you all you ask.[120]

This text recalls the words of Mechthild of Magdeburg, who heard the voice of love saying to her: 'I caught you because I so wished; I chained you, and I am glad that I did so; I wounded you, so that you could unite with me. If I have reigned blows on you, it was so that you would be mine.'[121] According to Christian belief, God became man out of love of man, since as a man He was able to redeem men's sins. God's love for man preceded man's love for God. Hence the emphasis placed on love in Christian mysticism by both men and women; this love is above all the love of God made flesh and man, even if Bernard of Clairvaux saw love of the Word as wisdom, justice and truth as a higher level than love of the Word incarnated.

According to the lives of the saints, some of whom were mystics, there were considerable similarities between the paths of men and women to religious experience: dream by night, a daytime vision, a serious illness. Many sought suffering. They were not content with the inner suffering which was part of the process of purification and liberation from enslavement to the senses and to the world. It should be recalled that in Christianity asceticism was not merely a means of inner liberation. Like poverty, it had mystical value. The

poor and suffering resemble Christ and follow in his footsteps
(*imitatio Christi*). Thus suffering can be idealized and sought after.
Francis of Assisi forced himself to care for lepers and to kiss them,
despite his great revulsion at their appearance and smell. Angela of
Foligno and a sister nun plumbed greater depths of horror when
they drank the water in which they had washed the feet of the
lepers.[122] Both men and women were consumed by sexual fears and,
in their struggle against the wiles of the Devil, shrank from any
contact with the opposite sex.[123] Both men and women, including
some of the greatest monks and mystics such as Francis of Assisi
and Catherine of Sienna, claimed that the stigmata were revealed in
them because of their identification with the sufferings of Jesus on
the cross. In the fourteenth century, against the background of the
spread of the worship of Christ's humanity, some nuns and
Beguines were particularly eager to receive the Eucharist, in which
Christ was revealed to them. (Angela of Foligno: Sometimes I see
the host as if I were seeing a neck or breast in nobility and beauty
exceeding those of the sun and seeming to come from within. In the
face of this beauty I understand without the shadow of a doubt that
I am seeing God – *quod video Deum*.) Some lost all self-restraint
when receiving the sacrament and the heads of the Cistercian order
prohibited participation in the sacrament to those who could not
control themselves. But this phenomenon was also known among
Cistercian monks, and the abbot of Villers was forced to decree that
monks were permitted to receive the Eucharist at the most once a
week.[124]

It should be recalled that the writings of female mystics are not
uniform. Some wrote in relatively restrained style with subtle
distinctions. Mechthild of Magdeburg stressed that the sights she
saw were not external: one cannot comprehend the gift of God
through the natural senses, and those whose spirit is not receptive to
the invisible truth are in error. That which can be seen with the
body's eyes, heard with the body's ears and expressed through the
body's mouth differs from the truth revealed to the loving soul just
as the light of the candle differs from that of the sun.[125] The works of
Juliana of Norwich lack exaggeration and hysteria. She succeeded in
expressing clearly the idea that even the man who arrives at maximal
affinity with God as a result of his own supreme effort and by
divine grace is not annulled, and there is no fusion between him and
God. Her book, parts of which are marked by poetic beauty,
expressed hope and joy that all would end well.[126]

Let us conclude with a work condemned as heretical. This is the work by the Beguine Margaret Porete, *Le Mirouer des Simples Ames*. It will be recalled that she was placed on trial in Paris, refused to defend herself and to answer questions, and in 1310 was burned at the stake. In her work she describes the seven levels of divine grace which bring the soul to communion with God. The soul can only reach the seventh and last stage in the next world. In the sixth stage the liberated soul resembles the angels, nothing dividing their love from divine love. The released soul will find God wherever it turns, even within its own self. It is separated from the virtues, but they are part of it without a struggle. It masters them. It no longer has need of sermons or sacraments or the Church as such.

Nonetheless, Margaret admitted the possibility of salvation by accepted means and it is doubtful whether her work contained more heretical ideas than those of other mystics considered to be orthodox. Her judges did not read the book, with the exception of sections taken out of context, submitted to them by the Inquisitors. Her trial took place at a time of tension and hysteria. The Templars were then being tried, as were various people accused of using witchcraft for political ends. In addition, Margaret was not a nun but a Beguine and, as we have seen, the attitude of churchmen to the Beguines was ambiguous. The interesting point in our context is the fact that although the authoress was burned at the stake, large numbers of manuscripts of the work were preserved in monasteries, and in the fifteenth century it was even thought that it had been written by the well-known Flemish mystic Jan Van Ruysbroeck, who lived in the fourteenth century. In the fifteenth century, then, people could not easily distinguish between the works of male and female mystics.[127] It seems to us that a comprehensive study of the writings of female mystics, and their comparison with the works of male mystics, could substantiate the claim that much that was attributed to the foibles of their sex could in fact be related to the tenets of the Christian faith.

4

Married Women

'Women who prayed', including those who did not take the monastic vows yet chose to live ascetic lives in the shadow of one of the monastic orders as lay sisters, members of the Third Order or Beguines, constituted only a minority among women in the Middle Ages. In the labouring class, in particular, there were women who pursued secular lives and did not marry, whether for economic or personal reasons, or because of a shortage of men in a certain location at a certain time. Some widows did not remarry, but most women in medieval society, as in all societies known to us, were married. One of the central concepts associated with the Middle Ages is monasticism, but there can be no question that the psychological, mental and cultural impact of monasticism and the ideal of chastity on medieval society was greater than the size of the monastic population warranted. Since women had no place in the secular clergy, who like monks were bound by the vows of chastity, the proportion of women who renounced marriage *a priori* was even smaller than the percentage of men who did so.[1]

ECCLESIASTICAL THEORIES ABOUT MARRIAGE

Since the early days of Christianity, chastity has been regarded not as an obligation but as a more Christian way of life. Marriage was permitted by St Paul as a concession to the weakness of the flesh: 'But if they cannot contain, let them marry: for it is better to marry than to burn' (I Corinthians 7:9). Marriage is preferable to adultery and lascivious behaviour, but is not a value in itself, and its objective, according to St Paul, is not procreation. But from a mere concession to human weakness, marriage was transformed by the Church in the eighth century into a sacrament. Thus male-female relations in the framework of marriage (in contrast to all relations outside this framework) were elevated from the sphere of sin to that of sanctity. Since marriage was a sacrament (the sole sacrament which is not administered by a priest but where the parties themselves are ministers), the Church gradually determined the relevant norms, laws and customs. From about the eleventh century, matrimonial affairs were debated by ecclesiastical courts. Churchmen developed a positive theory on marriage, citing several verses of the New Testament in their support.

Nonetheless, the concept of marriage as an inferior way of life to chastity did not disappear, and surfaced directly and indirectly in relation to marriage. The objective of marriage as proclaimed in the preface to the marriage service in the Roman Catholic prayerbook is prevention of sin, procreation and mutual companionship. This is a reiteration of the Pauline concept of the negative role of matrimony, as a means of preventing sinful conduct, together with its positive task, to produce offspring and create companionship between the two partners.

The idea of companionship and love in marriage is mentioned by St Paul, as is the view that the husband is lord and master of his wife: 'So ought men to love their wives as their own bodies. He that loveth his wife loveth himself' (Ephesians 5:28). 'Wives, submit yourselves unto your own husbands, as unto the Lord. For the husband is the head of the wife, even as Christ is the head of the church: and he is the saviour of the body' (Ephesians 5:22–3). A parallel is drawn here between the link between husband and wife and that between Christ and the Church, and is made even more explicit in the following verse: 'Husbands, love your wives, even as Christ also loved the church, and gave himself for it' (Ephesians 5:25). On the basis of several verses in the New Testament (Matthew 5:31–2; Luke 16:18), matrimony was recognized as an indissoluble tie, like that between Christ and his flock.

Concomitantly with this description of marriage as resembling the ties of Christ to the Church, we find the reverse image: of the links between Christ and the Church resembling those between man and wife, and evoking of images from the sphere of marriage and even erotic images to picture the Church establishment and the religious experience. The nun, as we have seen, is the bride of Christ. There was a resemblance between the impressive ceremony (reminiscent of liturgical drama) in which a girl became a nun, and the marriage ceremony. The nun placed a ring on her finger as a symbol of her mystic marriage to Christ, and her relations with her bridegroom were often depicted in erotic terms inspired by the Song of Songs. In the ceremony of investiture of a bishop as well, a ring was placed on his finger, as a symbol of marriage to the Church. St Cyprian's words about the bishop who is in the Church while the Church is in him were understood as referring to an indissoluble marriage tie. In condemning the heretical church, St Cyprian described it as adulterous: the bride of Christ cannot become an adulteress, she is pure and cannot be contaminated.[2] The proponents of the late eleventh-century Reform compared the bishop who obtained his position by simoniacal transaction, or who was imposed by the lay lord, to a bridegroom forced upon his bride, the Church. Because of this coercion the bride has become a whore, and the bridegroom a rapist and adulterer.

In descriptions of mystical experiences erotic terms are used again and again to describe communion with God. When the mystic St Gertrude was asked by a woman who, she writes, wanted to stand before God as a virgin but was defiled because of human weakness, what her fate would be, she replied in the name of Christ:

> If virginity is soiled because of human weakness, but the defiled one truly repents, the stains will be seen by the Saviour as folds of a garment and the repentant one will be gathered to His bosom. But if she is soiled by too many sins, they will be an obstacle to the sweetness of love, just as too many garments worn by the bride are an obstacle to the bridegroom who seeks to embrace her.[3]

In the Church literature of the High Middle Ages, which deals directly and approvingly with marriage, the idea of companionship and love in marriage is reiterated. Peter Lombard, in the twelfth century, explains why woman was fashioned out of man's rib and not out of some other part of his body. If she had been created from his head, this might have suggested that she should rule over him. If she had been fashioned from his legs, this could have been interpreted as meaning that she should serve him. But since she is neither servant nor master, she was fashioned from his rib, so that man should know that he must place at his side as his companion she who was fashioned from his side, and that the ties between them must be founded on love.[4] The same view that woman was made out

of man's rib so as to be his companion and helpmate was reiterated
in the thirteenth century by Humbert de Romans, who goes even
further in describing the primary virtues of woman who, unlike
man, was created within the Garden of Eden, not from the dust of
the earth but from man's rib. At the same time, he echoes the
Pauline concept of the creation of woman for the sake of man,
which justifies man's superiority and dominance.[5]

Thomas Aquinas depicts the marriage tie as a union of hearts
which cannot be sundered. The relations between man and wife are
the greatest friendship (*maxima amicitia*). Since friendship cannot
survive without a certain degree of equality, marriage must be
monogamous, since in polygamous marriage, experience shows that
women are slaves; polyandry is forbidden because of the child's
right to a father. Under the influence of Aristotle, Aquinas emphasizes the naturalness of marriage.[6] The subject of matrimony as a
natural state for man was stressed by those who disapproved of the
celibacy of the priesthood as well. 'The Anonymous of York', in the
twelfth century, expressing his objections to the rule of celibacy laid
down in the Gregorian Reform, based his arguments on the fact that
marriage was in accordance with the laws of nature as determined
by God. In a more humorous spirit, the Englishman Nigel Wireker
wrote in his 'Mirror of Fools' (*Speculum Stultorum*) about a new
religious order more pleasant than all others, since its members
would have female companions. This order had originated in the
Garden of Eden and was founded by God Himself, and the author's
own parents had been members.[7]

But neither the theologians nor the canonists thought that the aim
of sexual relations within marriage was pleasure, and the marital
love of which they wrote had nothing to do with sex. In the first
centuries of Christianity, under the influence of Judaism and Stoic
philosophy on the one hand, and in confutation of the Gnostics and
Manichaeans who condemned sexual relations in general and begetting in particular, procreation was presented as the main justification, if not for matrimony as such, then for sexual relations in
marriage. Disregarding the Pauline justification of marriage as a
curb on adultery, the Church Fathers cited Old Testament verses
which lauded procreation, New Testament verses which could be
interpreted in this spirit, and the laws of nature of the Stoics in
support of their argument. The condemnation of sexual relations for
the sake of pleasure was in accord both with the view that chastity
was a value in itself and with Christian objections to the sexual
morality of contemporary pagan society. Limiting sexual relations

to purposes of procreation offered a partial reply to the Gnostics and Manichaeans.[8]

St Augustine, who exerted a strong influence on the Christian philosophers of the Middle Ages, reaffirms the view that sexual relations which do not lead to procreation and are not undertaken for this purpose are nothing but lust (*concupiscentia*), stemming from Original Sin. As such they are prohibited to Christians. Nothing casts a man down from spiritual heights like contact with a female body. If sexual intercourse is to be tolerated in marriage there must be a reason originating outside the relations themselves, namely the desire to procreate.[9] Gratian, in the twelfth century, wrote that he who was too enthusiastic a lover of his wife was in fact an adulterer.[10] His most important interpreter, Huguccio, under the influence of Gregory the Great, claims that to take pleasure even in sexual intercourse undertaken for procreative purposes is a sin.[11]

In the light of these views, the theologians and canonists prohibited both use of contraception in marital sexual relations,[12] any form of intercourse which could not cause impregnation, and any 'unnatural' intercourse. In the High Middle Ages, as in the third and fourth centuries, the Church was again faced by a dualistic heresy – on the part of the Cathar movement which, like the Gnostics and Manichaeans, denied sexual relations and procreation. In its confrontation with these heretics, the Church again emphasized in its legislation that even married people could be worthy of the next world.[13] Theologians and canonists again cited procreation as the justification for sexual intercourse in marriage.

But these views were not unequivocal. Though procreation was the main justification for sexual relations in marriage from the early centuries of Christianity to the High Middle Ages, the procreation of children was not regarded as a supreme value in itself. In the atmosphere of eschatological tension prevailing in Christian communities in the first few centuries of Christianity, John Chrysostom wrote: 'Marriage was founded after the Fall as consolation for death. Man, who was destined to die, could perpetuate his being through his offspring. The Resurrection vanquished death. The world is full. We are on our way to a better life. There is no need for offspring.'[14] And St Jerome, at the end of the fourth century, in his letter to Eustochium, wrote: 'Let those take wives and procreate who were condemned by the curse of "in the sweat of thy brow shalt thou eat bread and the earth shall produce thorns and thistles", my seed shall bear fruit one hundredfold.'[15] The eschatological fervour gradually waned, but the view that procreation was not a value endured. It found extreme expression (reminiscent of the Manichaean-Cathar outlook) in the twelfth century in the *De Contemptu Mundi* of Bernard of Morlaix, also known as Bernard of Cluny. The author vehemently attacks his contemporaries, both lay people and churchmen, for their lax morals. He condemns woman as 'flesh' (*carno*) in contrast to man who is spirit (*mens*), and as the source of many sins. Matrimony too is condemned. The considerable population growth arouses the author's concern. There are increasing masses of people who lack religious spirit and whose unrestrained proliferation is the consequence of the lusts of the flesh which know no limits.[16]

In the absence of encouragement of procreation, even more moderate writers than Bernard of Cluny, like Peter Lombard and Thomas Aquinas, were able to laud the practice of absolute chastity in marriage (with the mutual agreement of both partners). The supreme example of chastity in marriage were Mary and Joseph, who were married yet celibate. Thomas Aquinas writes: 'As Peter Lombard has said, marriage without carnality is holier.'[17] On the other hand, despite these views, theologians not only justified sexual relations for the purpose of procreation; they sometimes justified such relations on a different ground, that of the mutual obligations (*debitum*) of the partners in marriage. This concept is directly linked with the view of matrimony as a curb on misconduct, and was cited by St Paul: 'Let the husband render unto the wife due benevolence: and likewise also the wife unto the husband. The wife hath not power of her own body, but the husband: and likewise also the husband hath not power of his own body, but the wife' (I Corinthians 7:3–4). Albertus Magnus writes on this subject: 'If one of the partners discovers the lust to sin in the partner, even if this is not stated directly and explicitly, he must act as if he had been asked directly to fulfil the obligation of marriage. He will not be considered to be a sinner thus.'[18] The theologians and canonists usually adopted the same attitude towards men and women with regard to permissible sexual relations. That which was permitted was permitted to both, and prohibitions applied equally to both sexes. Just as celibacy in marriage could only be observed by mutual consent, so if one partner wanted to retire to a monastery, the consent of the other was required.[19] Ivo of Chartres, in a letter concerning the Templars, wrote that a man who wished to join the order must obtain the voluntary consent of his wife, lest he sacrifice others rather than himself.[20]

The very concept of mutual obligations of marriage partners implies recognition of the sexuality of woman, and this is reflected directly and explicitly in the writings of churchmen. Among the questions to the confessant compiled in the eleventh century by Burchard of Worms and included in a manual for confessors, are a series of questions aimed at women. Together with questions as to whether she has used contraceptive devices, whether she has aborted intentionally, and whether she has instructed other women in contraception, there are additional questions relating to sins of a sexual nature: has she engaged in lesbian relations, has she stimulated her vagina with the aid of phallus-shaped objects, has she copulated with beasts?[21] Such questions are reiterated in other such manuals for confessors, including that written by Jean Gerson in the fourteenth century.[22] The authors of the manuals believed that such sexual sins were likely to be committed by women. They were aimed at satisfying her sexual appetites and could have no other aim (whereas sexual relations with a man could be motivated by the desire to carry out his wishes and fulfil marital duties, by submission to pressure or hope of reward). It is immaterial in this context whether or not many medieval women committed these sins. The phrasing of the questions attests to the author's recognition of the existence of sexual desire in women. Thus woman, the eternal seductress of saints and ascetics, does not tempt man only in order to dominate him or to bring about his downfall, but in order to satisfy her own appetites.

The theologians and canonists did not differ from the authors of medical works (most of them churchmen) and from secular writers in their attitude to woman's sexuality. According to the medical beliefs of medieval society, not only was woman possessed of sexual appetites, which derived from her physiology, she even enjoyed intercourse more than man, since she both ejaculated semen and absorbed it. There was also thought to be a close connection between woman's enjoyment of intercourse and conception. Woman produced semen which accumulated in the womb. In order for her to conceive, this seed must be ejaculated, and its ejaculation, which led to conception, was an indication that she had reached a sexual climax.[23] Thus, the logical conclusion would appear to be that the sexual relations which were theologically justified as leading to procreation were those which yielded maximal pleasure for the woman, but the theologians who denied the right to sexual satisfaction did not take note of medical views of woman's sexuality, and the authors of medical works did not delve into the religious and moral aspects of the problem, at least not in the same context.

Secular writers also wrote at length of the sexual desires of women, yet on the other hand we also find in their works criticism of women who do not love their husbands, act sanctimoniously and pretend to be modest.[24] The woman who deprives her husband of sexual relations is, in literature, often part of the image of the bad wife.[25] (In the same fashion Antoninus of Florence also condemned in his sermons those women who dawdled over their nocturnal prayers to avoid fulfilling their marital obligations.)

THE IMAGE OF AND ATTITUDE TO MARRIAGE IN SECULAR LITERATURE

In some secular writings marriage is seen as important and central to human life and to society, and this is reflected in the statement of Walter's men to their lord in the *Canterbury Tales*:

> Save o thing, lord, if it your wille be,
> That for to been a wedded man yow leste,
> Than were your peple in sovereyn hertes reste.[26]

But few works depict marriage as a source of felicity or as based on love, and there are few love tales which end in marriage. In the beautiful thirteenth-century tale of Aucassin and Nicolette, after many vicissitudes, parental objections, natural disasters and much human suffering, Aucassin finds his Nicolette again and takes her to wife.[27] The tale of Marie de France, *Le Fresne* ('The Ash Tree'), also ends in marriage. When the noble origin of his beloved is revealed, the knight weds her. In this story too, marriage and procreation are central to human life and society, and the knight's men threaten to leave him if he does not take a wife and produce an heir.[28] Of the poets, Matfre Ermengaud a troubadour from Southern France, wrote of marriage based on love, in a particular context. Attacking the Cathars, who denounced matrimony, and the poets of courtly love who elevated the ideal of love outside marriage, he argued the possibility of mutual love within the framework of marriage. He described the marriage tie as based not on economic benefit and forced obedience of the wife to her husband but on reciprocal love.[29] Of the authors of didactic literature, some favoured love matches instead of marriages for financial gain, and the author of *De Eruditione Principum* writes: 'Choose yourself a good wife, not the daughter of a usurer, a woman who will be suited to you in age and beauteous appearance.'[30] In one of the manuals of guidance for women composed by a Parisian Goodman (*Ménagier*), and differing from others in that it was written by a man for the guidance of his own wife, the ideal marriage is described as one of companionship and love. When the partners are apart they should both think in their hearts: 'When I see him (or her) I shall do such and such to him (or her), and say such and such to him (or her). The source of their pleasure and joy will be to bring one another pleasure, in love and in mutual obedience.'[31] (Despite these sensitive descriptions the author does not hesitate, in another chapter, to compare the loyalty and obedience of a wife to her husband to those of a dog for its master ...)

And finally, let us cite the words of a woman, Christine de Pisan, on her own marriage. In her didactic works, she wrote at length of the duties of husband and wife (emphasizing the obligations of the latter) in marriage. But more interesting and immediate is her description of her own relations with her husband – a rare picture of marriage by a married person – which she wrote after she was widowed. This is a touching picture of a relationship based on affection, respect and mutual consideration. In one passage she depicts his gentleness on their wedding night, when she was only 15 years old and he a young man of 24. He did not approach her on that night, and apparently wanted to allow her time to become accustomed to his presence. Only on the following day did he kiss her lingeringly and promise her that God created him only to be good to her. During the years of their marriage, the love and affection between them grew until, as she writes, they wished to be one and were closer than brother and sister in good and in evil times.[32] In one of her ballads, Christine again describes the love and loyalty of her husband. He never lied to her. He encouraged her in all she did. When she entertained a friend, she sang, danced and laughed. Why do women complain of their husbands?[33]

In the secular literature condemning marriage we find various ideas developed in classical literature and become a *topos*, such as the idea that the philosopher should be a bachelor. (Boccaccio described Dante's wife, who disturbed his philosophical contemplation, and Petrarch, in a letter of consolation to a friend who had lost his wife, enumerated all the trials of marriage of which he was now free.) We find expressions of archaic motifs which are repeated in different cultures – man's fear of woman's sexuality and suspicion of her magic powers. One of the pupils of Albertus Magnus writes that woman's menstrual blood is injurious to the penis and to any plant she touches. Thomas Aquinas writes that the gaze of a menstruating woman can dim and crack a mirror.[34] From the plague of 1348 to the plagues of the seventeenth century it was believed that lascivious relations harmed man's virility but had no effect on woman.[35] The concepts of secular literature were the fruit of their time and were influenced in part by the attitude of the Church towards marriage and woman. An amusing example of the adaptation of ecclesiastical concepts to secular literature are the remarks which Chaucer attributes to the Wife of Bath, who praises marriage but also quotes its detractors. In her words, with their humorous tone, we can identify a considerable number of ecclesiastical views: virginity is the desired state, but it is better to take a wife than burn with lust; celibacy is a good thing in marriage, but sexual relations are permitted for purposes of procreation (since if marriage disappears from the face of the earth even virgins will no longer be born ...).[36] But sometimes the ecclesiastical influence on the writer is more complex and profound.

Denunciation of marriage is often accompanied by vilification of women, but it is important to emphasize that the defence of marriage did not necessarily entail corresponding idealization of the image of woman, or raising her real status in society, just as its absolute denunciation did not necessarily involve lowering her status. Though Judaism advocated sexual relations and procreation, Jewish women played no part in divine worship and enjoyed no authority in society, either in biblical times or in Diaspora communities; the *midrashim* contain various anti-feminine aphorisms.[37] The Cathars denied marriage, sex and procreation completely, but as we shall see in discussing the heretical sects, women played a part in religious ceremony. But, in retrospect, in Christian culture the condemnation of sexual relations did entail hostility to women. Carnal lust is a sin and sexual activity is accompanied by a sense of guilt; woman is the cause of man's enslavement, to her and to sin. This hostility is reflected in the various kinds of Church literature from the Church Fathers to the later writings of Leo Tolstoy.

An example of denunciation of marriage which did not involve condemning women are some of Héloïse's arguments to Abélard. In the letter known as 'The Story of My Misfortunes' (*Historia Calamitatum*) Abélard describes Héloïse's objections to their marriage and the arguments she cited in order to dissuade him from marriage. Héloïse did not wish to marry because she did not believe that this step would placate the anger of her uncle Fulbert, who had discovered her relations with Abélard; she also felt that it could only harm Abélard's status as a Christian philosopher and teacher and impose burdens on him. According to canon law, Abélard was entitled to take a wife, because he was merely a clerk who had not been ordained, but as a married man he could not continue to teach.

Because of her love and desire for renunciation, she refuses to wed Abélard, and in order to convince him she cites many of the views propounded both in religious literature and in secular works against marriage. Her remarks are not, in the main, original, and reflect more than a personal stand deriving from her own nature and evaluation of their relationship. Her education allowed her to base her arguments on both religious and classical literature.

Marriage, according to Héloïse, is a stumbling block both to the Christian aspiring to communion with God, and to the philosopher. It is a burden and enslavement preventing man from devoting himself to divine work and to philosophical contemplation. St Paul knew this: 'Art thou loosed from a wife? Seek not a wife. But, and if thou marry, thou hast not sinned; and if a virgin marry, she hath not sinned. Nevertheless, such shall have trouble in the flesh; but I spare you' (I Corinthians 7:27–8). The Church Fathers too knew this. If Abélard is not willing to hearken to their advice, she writes, let him attend to the words of philosophers, as did the Church Fathers, who quoted them. St Jerome cited the words of Theophrastus on the vicissitudes and trials of marriage and concluded with the words: 'Can a Christian hear the words of Theophrastus without blushing?' St Jerome also quoted Cicero, who refused to remarry after the death of Terentia, saying that he could not devote the same degree of attention to philosophy and to a wife, and recalled the history of Socrates' marriage to Xantippe.

Philosophy demands all that a man has to give. As Seneca said to Lucilius: 'Philosophy is not a matter for a moment of leisure. We must discard all the rest and concentrate on that alone.' Among the pagans, Jews and Christians there were always those who retired from the world to live lives of asceticism and celibacy. And if they could choose this way of life, is it not Abélard's duty to emulate them? If he is not apprehensive as to his tasks as a cleric and there is no fear of God in his heart, he must at least fear for his image as a philosopher. How would the world see such a marriage? The Church and the philosophers would never forgive her for having enslaved him to one woman, he whom nature created for mankind as a whole. Speaking less eruditely and in a more personal tone, Héloïse asks how a philosopher can contemplate and write in a poor household, amidst the chatter of maid-servants, the sound of lullabies, the cry of babies, and the constant confusion and noise caused by small children.

In the arguments cited, Héloïse does not refer to her relations with Abélard. The same could have been said to anyone living in celibacy and planning to take a wife: celibacy is the proper way of life for the philosopher, as such, and the Christian philosopher in particular. Her words exemplify the idealization of celibacy without demeaning woman. Woman, it is true, is the factor which disturbs the philosopher, but this is more because of the nature of family life than because of her own inherent flaws. Héloïse goes on to speak of the ties between them, and here it is clear that celibacy is not the desirable state and that her objections relate only to marriage. She does not want to break off their relationship, but rather to continue it without marriage. This seems preferable to marriage, and she declares the title of friend to be dearer to her and more dignified for Abélard than the title of wife. She will hold Abélard by force of a love bestowed out of complete freedom, without the pressure of marital bonds, and the long periods of separation will increase the delight of their infrequent meetings. In conclusion, she says that in marriage Abélard would lose all sense of shame and sink forever into the maelstrom of sin.[38] In her references to the delights of rare encounters outside marriage, Héloïse is approaching the ideals of courtly love. Her warning that Abélard will sink into a maelstrom of sin if he marries has a Manichaean-Cathar ring: sexual relations within wedlock are no better than outside it, and as a regular act, they will become increasingly sinful. Héloïse does not cite the source of these arguments.

According to her letters from the nunnery, Héloïse remained loyal to her past. In her first letter to Abélard she writes: God knows that I never wanted anything of you, only you yourself. I simply wanted you, and nothing of yours. I wanted neither the marriage tie nor the status of married woman. It was not my pleasure and aspirations that I sought to satisfy but your own. The title of wife may seem more sacred and binding, but for me the title of friend will be ever sweeter or, if you will permit me to say so, of mistress or whore ...[39] In her second letter she writes bitterly that the wrath of God descended on them after their marriage. God tolerated their misconduct, but when they mended their ways and were legally wed, he laid a heavy hand on them and did not permit the new bond to endure. Abélard, the married man, was accorded the punishment inflicted on adulterers.[40]

In one of his sermons, Abélard repeated some of Héloïse's statements, more bluntly and bitterly than she, and as a general rather than a personal truth. In a sermon on Job 39:5, he distinguishes between the wild and the tame ass. The former, unlike the latter, lives in freedom, far from the society and the concerns of mankind, and without a yoke. He is like a bachelor, while the tame ass is like a married man. Can there be a stronger tie than that between marriage partners? he asks. Is there more burdensome subjugation than that suffered by a man who is no longer master even of his own body? Can there be a more painful life than that of a man who daily suffers in the occupations related to support of a wife and children? Is any life less conducive to worship of God than that of a man who is linked to this world by so many loves?[41]

When we turn from the letters of Abélard and Héloïse to bourgeois literature (whose most familiar form is the *fabliaux* – rhymed stories of humoristic intent, with or without a moral), we no longer find arguments against marriage, but rather descriptions of a negative image of marriage centring on a negative picture of woman. Marriage in this literature, which is mainly satirical, is torture to man, at best because of the objective problems entailed in supporting a wife and children. The husband is described as having been caught in a trap; he carries the burden of the children and the household, which are depicted as pertaining to the woman alone. But, generally speaking, woman's personality plays a central part in creating a hell out of marriage. Sometimes a desire to entertain is evident in this literature, and the descriptions are humorous (and not particularly delicate); and sometimes they deteriorate into cynicism, crudeness and even hostility towards women.

In most satires the married woman is pictured as domineering, deliberately disobeying her husband, quarrelsome, demanding, interested in other men, straying, jealous, making scenes if her husband looks at or greets another woman, lazy, neglecting her home and allowing her servants to be slovenly. She does not hesitate to defend the chambermaid who is her confidante against her husband when he demands that the maid fulfil her duties properly. The married woman is frivolous, capricious, deceitful, sanctimonious, pretending to play the unfortunate victim in order to extract what she wants from her husband. In every argument she is the victor and she leads her husband by the nose. She times her requests skilfully and usually makes them in bed.[42] All this is summed up in the popular saying: 'No man marries without regretting it.'[43] In few of the tales does the wife eventually accept her husband's authority.[44]

In the *Canterbury Tales*, the domineering figure of the Wife of Bath, who wears out her husbands one after another, is balanced by the submissive figure of Griselda, who patiently endures the sufferings and arbitrary trials imposed on her by her husband without questioning him. Between the Wife of Bath's Tale and Griselda's, there is the Franklin's story about Dorigen and Arveragus, which presents a third possibility where neither the husband nor the wife is sovereign in marriage.[45] The tale about Griselda is undoubtedly typical of didactic literature in which the wife's duty of obedience to her husband is emphasized, rather than of the *fabliaux*. The dominant figure in the *fabliaux* is the aggressive woman, like the Wife of Bath, and all the sayings and actions of the female in the *fabliaux* are in total contrast to those of the ideal woman of didactic literature.

Sex plays a vital part in the bourgeois literature dealing with marriage and is represented as one of the sources of enjoyment, while the concept of mutual companionship advocated in ecclesiastical literature finds almost no mention. There is no hint that the purpose of sexual intercourse is procreation, but rather open admission of the existence of sexual impulses and sexual pleasure in both men and women. Marriage gives sanction to sexual intercourse. This point of view is shared by churchmen and authors of bourgeois literature, but they are not referring to the same thing. January, in the Merchant's Tale in the *Canterbury Tales*, says:

> And blessed be the yoke that we been inne
> For in our acts we mowe do no sinne.
> A man may do no sinne with his wyf
> Ne hurte him-selven with his owene knyf;
> For we han leve to pleye us by the lawe.[46]

The Goodman of Paris, in the manual of guidance for his young wife, also speaks of sexual pleasure in marriage, though in more delicate and restrained fashion than Chaucer's January. In his advice to his young wife he describes in detail how she should greet her husband when he returns home: with a smiling face, a lighted fire in the hearth, clean and dry shoes and hose, food and drink, clean and warm bedlinen and loveplay in bed, which he does not wish to detail.[47] He too makes no mention of procreation. As we have noted, these authors attribute sexual appetite to both men and women. Sometimes woman is even accused of having appetites too strong for her husband, but simultaneously she is also accused of trading on her body. In order to get her way, a woman will carry out marital duties which she refuses to perform on other occasions.[48]

We can sum up by saying that bourgeois literature cannot be regarded as condemning marriage, since it is depicted as central to human life, even if its image is negative, and because no alternative way of life is proposed. But this literature is hostile to women. At best the author describes the psychological truth of the bachelor who wanted to be married, and after marrying, wanted to be single again. He sees bachelorhood as synonymous with freedom and woman as responsible for his loss of liberty. It seems fair to assume that if women had written during the Middle Ages, some of them, at least, would have depicted a similar truth (although the possibilities open to them as spinsters were more limited). One author writes of a couple who blame one another for having fallen into a pit from which both long to extricate themselves. At the conclusion of the book, which is a bitter satire on the life of the married man whose lot is fifteen dubious pleasures (the book is entitled *Quinze Joyes de Mariage*), he adds ironically that he could also have written a book about the many injuries done to 'helpless' women.[49] The irony is obvious, since the reference to the helplessness of women comes at the end of a work on the domineering woman who turns her husband into a doormat. The negative image of woman dominates in this literature. Recognition of female sexuality does not necessarily imply respect towards her.

Love outside marriage was lauded in the love poetry written by churchmen, Goliards and poets of courtly love. Their works can be defined, in our context, as writings which condemn marriage without vilifying women. Love poems to youth were written in the Middle Ages in emulation of the classical homosexual poetry, but differed from it in that most medieval poetry of this kind was addressed to girls as well, as witness the following:

> This their reproach: that, wantoning in youth,
> I wrote to maids, and wrote to lads no less.
> Some things I wrote, 'tis true, which treat of love;
> And songs of mine have pleased both he's and she's.[50]

This poetry was written by those clerics and monks who had renounced marriage, and even by leaders of the Church. Homosexuality was known in the Middle Ages first and foremost as a sin of ecclesiastics, and apparently spread in the twelfth century when celibacy was imposed on the priesthood after the Gregorian Reform.[51] There is no way of knowing, however, whether the authors were describing actual experience or were merely emulating the literary forms of classical Rome. In any event, this poetry was written by people who were supposed to be unmarried and untroubled by marital problems. In this context it should be noted that lesbian poetry, one of the expressions of female rejection of the male world of ancient Greece, apparently did not exist in the Middle Ages. We know of only one poem which may have been written by one woman to another. This is a poem by Bieris de Romans written to a woman named Maria.[52]

The Goliards also wrote of love outside marriage, and the love they celebrated was sensuous and close to that of classical pagan poetry. In retrospect we can define them as a wandering intellectual proletariat – I say with hindsight because most of them dreamed of finding a rich patron or winning a lucrative Church prebend, as the Archpoeta wrote: 'Do not think that I am poor because I wish to be.' Just as the ideal of voluntary poverty was alien to them, they also criticized various institutions of society, protested against accepted moral standards, mocked the ideal of virginity and sang the praises of the body and its joys. Their poetry does not speak out clearly against marriage, but their approach to love is direct, fundamental and sensuous. In this poetry, the object of desire is the young girl and the poets do not delve into her sensations and emotions. The Goliards were permitted to take wives, since, like Abélard, they were only clerks, but their poems reveal that they preferred spring, wine, dallying and love to marriage. As Golias confessed:

> Hear me, prelate most discreet,
> Deadly sin I find so sweet.
> I'm in love with dying.
> Every pretty girl I meet
> Sets my heart a-sighing.
> Hands off! Ah, but in conceit,
> In her arms I am lying.
> Much too hard it is, I find,
> So to change my essence
> As to keep a virgin mind
> In a virgin presence.[53]

The problem of the diversified courtly literature is a complex one. Was courtly love envisaged as platonic? How can one reconcile the ideal of courtly love, namely love outside marriage, with the contemporary moral code, both ecclesiastical and feudal? (In courtly poetry the vassal is often the admirer or lover of the wife of his lord.) Did such a way of life exist or was it merely a literary convention? Was it nurtured by women, and did it really elevate the status of women in society? We shall not attempt to answer these questions at present, but will return to them in several contexts. We can merely note that courtly literature is a perfect example of those types of literature which negated marriage without condemning woman. Furthermore, whatever the significance of the veneration of women in courtly literature, there can be no doubt that this literary form elevated woman and love. Love for woman is the source and motive of the heroic deeds of the lover and the realization of his virtues; only through love can he attain moral perfection. This love always exists outside wedlock and has nothing whatsoever to do with propagation. Even the female troubadours who wrote love poetry did not address it to their husbands. As the countess of Dia wrote:

> Know this, that I'd give almost anything
> To have you in my husband's place.[54]

Those of the proponents of the ideal of courtly love who admitted the existence of some kind of love between marriage partners saw it only as love based on duty, whereas courtly love was founded on grace.[55]

MATRIMONIAL LAWS

Matters pertaining to matrimonial law were discussed by ecclesiastical courts, and only from the fourteenth century onwards do we observe the secular courts taking over certain matrimonial matters in most Western European countries. It was the Church which determined which days were prohibited for holding nuptials and the minimum age of marriage (12 for girls and 14 for boys). There were three stages to a properly conducted marriage ceremony: negotiations between the families, betrothal and marriage ceremony at the church door (*in facie ecclesiae*). The Church's representative played a part in the betrothal and in the marriage contract. At the church door the couple expressed their desire to wed and bestowed the marriage sacrament on one another. The bride's dowry as well as that portion of the bridegroom's property pledged to his wife in the event that he died before her were also guaranteed at the church door. It was known as the dower (*dos*) and usually amounted to one third or one half of all his assets. The couple then entered the church to take part in the nuptial mass. When the ceremony was completed a marriage feast was held. Huizinga notes that in all classes nuptial feasts were accompanied by lewd clowning and coarse songs. In the pagan religions the marriage ceremony was regarded as a sacred ritual related to the mystery of copulation. In Christianity the Church transferred the sacred element in marriage to the sacrament and took the mystery to itself; the post-nuptial feast retained only the crudest erotic elements – the remnants of mystery which had deteriorated into lewd games.[56]

Three weeks before the wedding the banns of the future marriage were posted on the church door, to enable any person who knew that one of the partners was already married, or that they were related, to voice his objections. The Church extended the biblical bans on incest as stipulated in the Bible (Leviticus 18) and explained the more stringent attitude according to its own tenets. Between 1065 and 1215 marriage between persons related to the seventh degree was prohibited. A second marriage to a relative of the deceased partner was prohibited. (Thus, in violation of the biblical law, a brother was banned from marrying his deceased brother's widow.) Also forbidden was marriage between persons with spiritual proximity, such as the godfather and godmother of a child. At the fourth Lateran Council in 1215, the bans on incest were relaxed and marriage of blood relatives was prohibited only to the fourth degree.[57]

From the outset the Church banned polygamy both under the influence of Roman law and because of its own conception of the essence and aim of marriage. Under ecclesiastical influence both Lombard and Frankish law recognized the right of a woman whose husband had taken a concubine to return to her parental home.[58] The Church prohibited divorce (unlike Roman and biblical law and in partial contrast to Germanic law). In certain cases it permitted separation. Sometimes it was merely sanctioning separation of property (a mensa), and in other cases it permitted actual physical separation (a thoro). A couple who separated were not permitted to remarry. There was also a possibility of annulling a marriage, if the Church tribunal was persuaded that the marriage had never been valid (ab initio). Marriage could be declared invalid if the partners were relatives to a degree where marriage was banned to them, if one partner was already married, if the partners were coerced into the match, or if the marriage had never been consummated because of the husband's impotence.

The basing of marriage on mutual consent of the couple constituted another additional important difference between ecclesiastical marriage law and Germanic law. Whereas according to Germanic law consent to marriage was given not by the bride but by her protector under whose *mundium* she lived – her father, brother or some other male relative – according to ecclesiastical law it was the consent of the bridal couple alone which rendered a marriage valid. This principle that consent 'made' a marriage (*consensus facit nuptias*) was finally formulated at the end of the twelfth century, largely under the influence of Peter Lombard.[59] It was neither the agreement between the families nor the consummation of marital relations but mutual consent which created the marriage bond. We have already mentioned the analogy drawn between a bishop who bought his position or was appointed under secular pressure, and a bridegroom forced on his bride. In the absence of the consent of the bride/church to the marriage she was comparable to a whore, and the bridegroom to a rapist and fornicator.

Thus although the agreement of the parents was desirable, a marriage was considered valid even if celebrated against the wishes of the parents. Even if the family exerted pressure to separate on a young couple who had wed without permission, it was not possible, by ecclesiastical law, to enforce an annulment or separation. At least from the legal point of view, marriage was evaluated from the point of view of the couple and not from that of the family. The Church evolved a view of marriage which enabled the individual to act against the wishes of his family, of the feudal seigneur or the lord of the manor. But we shall return to the question of to what extent young people of the various classes succeeded in exercising this right bestowed on them by ecclesiastical law, meanwhile noting that although the secular legislator could not make laws which violated ecclesiastical law, secular law often punished those who wed without familial consent, in order to deter the young from such matches. According to the laws of Brabant and Flanders, a girl kidnapped with her acquiescence who married her abductor was disinherited. The same was true according to the laws of Cuenca and Sepúlveda.[60]

The principle of mutual consent as the basis for marriage helps to explain the fact that although the Church demanded that marriages be solemnized in church, after banns had been published, it also recognized marriages celebrated elsewhere with the mutual agreement of the bridal couple, in the presence of witnesses or even without them. These private marriages were known as *sponsalia per verba de presenti* – that is to say in accordance with a statement in the present tense (by the partners that they hereby wed one another). An additional factor in the Church's recognition of such marriages despite opposition was the theological view that it was the partners who bestowed the sacrament of marriage on one another.

In this way the Church was reverting in part to the conception which prevailed in more ancient societies, that marriage was a private matter.[61]

Such private marriages aroused problems. Often, one of the partners would subsequently enter into a second marriage, after which the abandoned partner would appear and question the legality of the second match, leaving the courts to decide which match was valid. If it was proved that the first marriage was the valid one, the second one was annulled even if offspring had resulted, and these were declared to be bastards. The secular authorities urged the Church to declare such private marriages invalid, since they created opportunities for controversy on the legitimacy of offspring, matters of inheritance and widows' rights. Private marriages also made it possible to waive parental consent. The Church once again decided to condemn private marriages, but these did not die out until the end of the Middle Ages. They lingered on mainly among the peasantry, who found it difficult to adapt to the ecclesiastical laws of matrimony, but they were also known among the urban class and, in exceptional cases, among the nobility.[62]

We learn of the proliferation of such marriages and the problems they aroused from the registers of ecclesiastical courts. The registers of the ecclesiastical court of the diocese of Ely between 1374 and 1382 reveal 101 marriages, of which eighty-nine were private. If no one came forward to appeal against the legality of the ceremony, the bridal couple were not punished, nor were they forced to hold a church ceremony. It was usually stipulated that at a suitable opportunity, a ceremony should be held in church. Of the marriages declared invalid, 66 per cent were invalidated on grounds of bigamy. Since sometimes both the first and the second marriages of a man or woman accused of bigamy were private marriages (often held without witnesses), it was extremely hard to determine which of the two was valid. Moreover, the couple often gave contradictory evidence. One partner wanted to prove the legality of the match and the other was anxious to demonstrate its invalidity. It was usually the woman who wanted to prove the marriage legal, and the man who had entered into a new relationship and tried to refute her claims. But sometimes it was the man who submitted the claim. Of six appeals against published marriage banns, two were put forward by men. They claimed that the women who were about to be wed in church had already been married to them in private ceremonies, and that if they now took husbands in church they would be committing bigamy. In one case, the man did not have time to appeal before the marriage was solemnized, and sued the woman after the ceremony. The court accepted his arguments, and the woman, her new husband and her father were excommunicated.

One can cite additional examples from other court registers of the fact that it was sometimes the woman who asked for annulment of a marriage, or who violated the marriage and was taken to court by the man. In one case, a woman claimed in court that her marriage had not been valid since she had agreed with her lips but not in her heart (and this after having borne a child to the claimant). Sometimes wives submitted requests for annulment of marriage as a result of family pressure, but there can be no doubt that the initiative was often their own. Couples who had lived together without marriage also appeared before the courts. One of the partners wished for marriage, and again it was usually the woman. She would claim that the man had promised her marriage, while he would deny this. The registers also record cases of people married twice in church. After a first marriage in his own parish, a man would move to another parish where he was not known and take a second wife. The Church condemned the habit of clerics who married couples with whom they were not acquainted and without proclaiming the banns, but did not succeed in rooting out the custom.

There is no way of knowing to what extent the verdicts of ecclesiastical courts were carried out. If it was decided in a bigamy case that A was the legal husband of B and must therefore separate from C with whom he had been cohabiting, there was no way of ensuring that he did so.[63] In eight out of ten cases in which the court of the bishop of Paris invalidated marriages between 1384 and 1387 the reason cited was bigamy. Four out of eight of those accused of bigamy were women, i.e. had left their partners and remarried. On the other hand, 80 per cent of the claims of non-execution of marriage contracts after betrothal were submitted by women. Women tried to prove that after betrothal they had cohabited with their fiancés, in which case, according to canon law, the betrothal could no longer be terminated. The men tried to deny this.[64]

Can one infer from these registers that people did in fact succeed in exercising the right to carry out a marriage based on mutual consent alone? It should be recalled that marriages which created no problems were never challenged in court, and it may be assumed that these were the majority and were usually arranged by the families. Generally speaking, it can be stated that the nobility were the most limited in choice and that private marriages were much rarer in this class. According to the register of the Paris Parlement in the fourteenth century, particularly strong pressure was exerted on young girls in matches which entailed financial contracts between the families. The pressure on the girls was notably stronger when the matches were arranged not by parents but by other relatives,[65] and coercion was used.

From the correspondence of the Paston family, English gentry of the fifteenth century, we learn of parental pressure on young people to enter into matches advantageous to the family and arranged out of financial and lineal considerations. Though sons were not free to choose either, the brunt of the pressure was brought to bear on daughters. One girl, aged only 20, was promised to an ailing widower of 50. She stubbornly refused to marry him, and her mother beat her mercilessly, lacerating her head. The marriage was never solemnized, not because the girl's intransigence could not be overcome but because the bridegroom's family changed their mind. But there were also different cases. A girl from the Paston family married the bailiff of her father's estate despite parental opposition. The family refused to recognize the marriage and the daughter was banished from the home, but the marriage could not be annulled.[66] Another girl in York was told by her guardian that he would break her neck if she did not marry his son, but she fled and married another.

The court registers also reveal cases in which the ecclesiastical courts permitted couples to separate. Generally speaking only separation of property was permitted, and only rarely physical separation. But in practice the former provided the opportunity to establish a separate household, although in theory the couples were still obliged to fulfil their mutual obligations. It was more often misconduct by the wife than by the husband which provided the pretext for permitting separation, although theologians and canonists demanded mutual fidelity and took an equal view of violation of marriage vows by men or women. Canon law did not insist on separation in the wake of adultery. Husband and wife were entitled to forgive one another, and temporary celibacy was usually imposed on them as penance.[67]

Nonetheless, as we have already noted, separation was sometimes permitted in these cases. Other cases in which separation was permitted were the husband's impotence, the wife's drunkenness, and the husband's harsh conduct (*austeritas*). If the husband squandered joint assets, or if one of the partners was a leper or heretic separation could be granted. The ecclesiastical court often filled the role of marriage counsellor, arbitrator and mediator. If it permitted separation, it often also made the relevant arrangements, such as support for the wife and children.

There can be no doubt that the ecclesiastical courts did not lightly sanction separation. In a certain case the wife requested a separation relating that her husband had attacked her with a knife (in the presence of witnesses) and caused her to flee the house in a distressed condition. On another occasion, he had attacked her with a dagger, wounded her in the arm and broken one of her ribs. The husband claimed that his conduct had been reasonable and aimed at a worthy purpose: to mend his wife's ways. The court did not permit separation and merely demanded of the husband that he guarantee to behave with greater restraint in future.[68] Yet the ecclesiastical court was more lenient regarding separation than were several of the canonists. Some of the latter would not countenance separation even if one of the partners was leprous, and others stipulated that a wife must follow her husband everywhere, and even to prison.[69] The relatively flexible approach of the ecclesiastical courts in comparison with the canonists is an example of the gap which often existed in the Middle Ages between law and actual practice. Secular law (which had no definition of marriage) adopted a similar stand to that of the Church, and jurists specified all those cases where there was insufficient pretext for the wife to abandon her husband's home.[70]

The discrepancy between the self-image of people and their image in the eyes of a partner was as common in the Middle Ages as it is today. One wife speaking of her husband in an ecclesiastical court called him a terrible savage, a sly, dreadful man. The husband described himself as honest, tender, sober, pious, congenial, quiet, peace-loving ('etcetera' added the court clerk). Another husband called his wife disobedient, cruel, dreadful, terrible, restless, noisy, vociferous, disgusting and a virago (the literal meaning of which is a woman who resembles a man). His wife described her own character as 'honest, good, submissive, tender'.[71] A comparison of the number of adjectives used by the couples indicates that in this case at least the women had learned the secret of restraint.

From the fourteenth century onward, several matters of marital status were transferred to secular courts in certain Western European countries. In England such matters as fornication (or the 'incontinent' heiress) and the inheritance rights of bastards were also discussed by secular courts from the twelfth century. In France after the fourteenth century the Paris Parlement dealt with problems of the legitimacy of offspring, fornication, property questions resulting from separation and the rights of widows and their children.[72] Decisions on the validity of marriage and the granting of separation rights remained within the exclusive authority of the Church courts in all countries.

Finally, we noted in the previous chapter the problem of ambivalent attitudes towards the opposite sex. That of women towards men was not recorded in writing (although some men seemed aware of its existence, and the author of the life of Robert of Arbrissel writes that poor and noble women, widows, spinsters, young women, whores and man-haters all followed him).[73] Hostility towards men is reflected in the following cruel story. A woman sought a separation from her husband on the grounds of his impotence. The ecclesiastical court of York appointed seven women to investigate the claim. The women surrounded the husband and tried to arouse him in various ways (all of which the court clerk recorded). When they failed abysmally they roundly cursed him for marrying a young woman deceitfully without being capable of serving her and satisfying her (*deservire et placere*). The decision to send the women to verify the truth of the wife's claim was taken by the court, but they carried out their mission with the utmost cruelty.[74] In England it was also believed that St Uncumber, whose statue stood in St Paul's cathedral, was capable of destroying the husbands of dissatisfied women who brought her offerings of a peck of oats![75]

THE CHURCH AND THE STATUS OF MARRIED WOMEN

Some historians hold that the Church played a considerable part in fostering the inferior status of women in medieval society in general (in addition to denying her the right to holy orders, in contrast to pagan society whose women were permitted to play a part in worship). In order to examine this question, one should scrutinize the role of woman in late Roman society and in pre-Christian Germanic society, and distinguish between the changes which occurred as a result of the adoption of Christianity and those stemming from other factors. This weighty task lies beyond the scope of the present discussion. In the present context it can be said that the ecclesiastical conception of the inferior status of women, deriving from Creation, her role in Original Sin and her subjugation to man, provided both direct and indirect justification for her inferior standing in the family and in society in medieval civilization. It was not the Church which induced husbands to beat their wives, but it not only accepted this custom after the event, if it was not carried to excess,[76] but, by proclaiming the superiority of man, also supplied its moral justification.[77]

In keeping with the view that inequality of the sexes is but a part of the prevailing world order, since on the plane of grace and salvation men and women were equal, Gregory IX (in his legislation of the first half of the thirteenth century) stipulated that if a woman so chose, she need not be buried beside her husband, since burial related to a condition in which she no longer was subservient to her husband.[78] In thirteenth- and fourteenth-century wills, men and women stipulated where they wished to be buried, and despite Gregory's concession, the great majority apparently chose to be buried beside their spouses. If they had been married more than once, they usually asked to be buried beside their first spouse.[79]

THE STATUS OF THE MARRIED WOMAN

'Let not the hen crow before the rooster' says a popular medieval proverb.[80] This was also the view of learned jurists and authors of didactic works. According to the English jurist Bracton, a woman was obliged to obey her husband in everything, as long as he did not order her to do something in violation of Divine Law. He even relates a case in which a wife and husband forged a royal writ. The crime was discovered and the husband was hanged. The wife was acquitted, and the jurist explained that since she had been under her husband's rule (*sub virga sui*)[81] she had no choice but to collaborate with him. We find different versions of the same statement in many of the legal codes of Western Europe in the Central Middle Ages.[82] In England and in France, the murder of a husband by his wife was equated by law to a murder by a subordinate, i.e. of a lord by a vassal, master by servant, or bishop by a cleric or lay/person in his diocese.[83]

Often the jurists or legal experts did not confine themselves to stating the wife's duty of obedience to her husband, and detailed the means which the husband was entitled to adopt in order to extract obedience from his wife or to reform her ways. According to Beaumanoir, a husband was allowed to adopt any measure he considered appropriate in order to reform his wife. He could punish her in any way he chose, but could not injure or kill her.[84] In the legal code of Aardenburg in Flanders in the fourteenth century it is stipulated that the husband may beat his wife, injure her, slash her body from head to foot and 'warm his feet in her blood'. If he succeeds in nursing her back to health afterwards he will not have transgressed against the law.[85]

The right of a husband to beat his wife 'within limits' was generally recognized. If husbands went too far, they were tried and fined and, as we have seen, ecclesiastical courts sometimes sanctioned separation if the husband acted too harshly. The court of Ypres fined a man for stabbing his wife with a knife, even though he claimed that he had committed no crime since the victim was only his wife.[86] One of the Paris courts fined a man for beating his pregnant wife. A baker was fined by the same court for beating his wife until she lost her power of speech.[87]

But we have no way of knowing how many women were beaten by their husbands, did not take them to secular courts and did not appeal for separation to the ecclesiastical courts. There can be no question that there were men who took advantage of the right bestowed on them by the law and by the authors of didactic literature or women who accepted their lot by law and as preached by the learned writers. On the other hand, in medieval society, as in all ages, strong women did not obey their husbands in all things, and in some cases even dominated them. In certain places, men were punished for being beaten by their wives. The husband was seated facing backwards on a donkey, his hands clutching its tail, a humiliating punishment also inflicted on prostitutes and fornicators.[88]

MATRIMONIAL PROPERTY LAWS

By the Central Middle Ages the agnatic principle (affiliation to the paternal family) was well established, after a lengthy and gradual process of acceptance, though the fact that a man was sometimes called after his mother, even when he was a legitimate offspring, reflected this slow pace. When Joan of Arc was asked her name, she replied that she was named Jeanne d'Arc after her father, and sometimes Jeanne Romée after her mother, because in her village girls were often called after their mothers.[89] In noble families, matrimony was a method of linking two lineages and creating alliances. Marriage to a woman from a noble family raised a man's status, and his family ties on the maternal side were also important.[90] The daughter who wed, however, became part of her husband's family and could no longer contribute to her father's family; thus her share in the family inheritance was usually reduced. But every woman brought certain assets with her to her marriage, whether her dowry alone or her share in the family legacy, just as every husband made a certain economic contribution to his new family.

The contribution of the two partners to the marriage was a blend of the Roman tradition, in which the wife provided the dowry, and the Germanic custom, whereby the husband (at least in lesser marriages) paid bride-money.[91] In some European countries, the assets of the couple became their joint property after their marriage for the period of the marriage, while in other countries this was not so. There were also intermediate solutions whereby only assets acquired by the partners in the course of the marriage, and not premarital assets, were regarded as joint property. In any event, immovable property and the income from assets were regarded as jointly shared in almost all cases, and the husband was considered to be responsible for managing the joint property during the marriage. This was stated in the Germanic law of the thirteenth century known as the *Sachsenspiegel*: when a man takes a wife, then by rights of guardianship he takes over all her property, and the wife is adjured to obey him in this as in all other matters.[92]

According to the laws of Brittany, in a case where a husband and wife took a loan and did not repay it as specified, the court officer had to sell the husband's assets in order to repay the loan, since it was considered that women were empty-headed and weak and that all property matters were the domain of the husband, who could force his wife to act as he chose.[93] If the husband was executed, according to the laws of northern France, his seigneur was entitled to confiscate the belongings of the couple; if the wife was executed, the belongings could not be confiscated since the husband was regarded as responsible for all property.[94] The same was true in the case of suicide. If the husband committed suicide, the belongings were confiscated, but not if the wife did so.[95]

In their life together (by law at least), the wife had no power to sell, pawn, transfer or exchange her own property without her husband's consent. She could not make a will without her husband's approval except with regard to her own jewels and clothes.[96] The husband, for his part, could do as he chose with his property, but was not empowered to sell, pawn etc., without his wife's consent either those assets she had brought with her to the marriage or those she had inherited during marriage, or the dower promised her by her husband. In several regions, the right of a wife to approve sale or transfer of joint property was recognized, and it was forbidden to exert pressure on a woman in order to obtain her consent.[97]

Sometimes the court which dealt with transfer of property would question the wife as to whether she had consented voluntarily to the transfer.[98] In a very large number of documents of sale, transfer and bestowal of property the names of husband and wife appear jointly. If the name of the wife appears first, this means that it was her property which was involved.

LEGAL RIGHTS

When an unmarried woman attained her majority she was free of guardianship. She could both appear before the courts and litigate on her own behalf. The legal code of Emperor Frederick II formulated for Sicily declares: We recognize the fact that those who have not yet reached their eighteenth year, both men and women, are minors. When they reach this age, they will be regarded as adults both for purposes of contracts and with regard to legal proceedings and all other matters.[99] The married woman on the other hand was under the guardianship of her husband – in other words she partially reverted to the status of minor, with restricted legal rights. The law generally held that a married woman could not draw up a contract, take a loan, or take any person to court on civil matters without the consent of her husband, not only because the husband managed joint property, but also because of her very status as a married woman. As Beaumanoir wrote, in discussing the possibility that a married woman might take a loan on her own responsibility: 'Since she has entered into marriage, she has no authority from her own will alone.' And in concluding another clause in his code, he sums up: 'The dumb, the deaf, the insane and the female cannot draw up a contract, neither alone nor through a representative, since they are subservient to the authority of others'.[100]

If the husband gave his consent, the wife was permitted to draw up a contract or a will or to take some party to court in person, or through her representative, or else her husband represented her on such civil matters.[101] In the registers of the various courts we find cases in which a wife sued with her husband's consent, and cases in which husbands represented their wives in court. In certain exceptional civil cases the law permitted a wife to go to law without her husband's approval: if the husband had acted in a way which clearly harmed the wife or her property she was entitled to sue him.[102] In addition, if the husband was insane, gaoled, or a prisoner in a distant land without hope of returning, the wife was permitted to draw up agreements and to sue even without his consent.[103] She could also sue as representative of her husband, and court registers record the appearance of women from all social strata in court on behalf of their husbands. In criminal cases, in so far as they related to personal injury to a woman – beating, injury, rape or even verbal abuse – she was permitted to sue even without her husband's consent,[104] and numerous court registers record cases of women suing on these grounds.[105] A married woman trading in her own right was universally permitted to sue without her husband's approval on all commercial matters.

Married women could themselves be sued, and various laws were passed relating to the possibility of exploiting the husband's property in the event that a wife was sentenced to payment of a fine or monetary compensation. According to one of the urban legal codes in England (*Leges Quatuor Burgorum*) a husband could not be obliged to pay a monetary fine exceeding fourpence because of his wife's misdemeanour. An empty-headed woman who conducted herself foolishly without consulting her husband should be punished like an immature child, since she bore no authority for her own actions.[106] Women sometimes exploited marriage laws to their own advantage. A London woman who was summoned to court because of a debt argued that even though she alone had apparently taken the loan, she could not be tried without her husband.[107] She at least succeeded in having the case adjourned.

THE WIDOW

Until the fourteenth century, widows were usually under the protection and jurisdiction of ecclesiastical courts, and only from the end of that century was this jurisdiction gradually transferred to secular courts.[108] Widows were accorded Church protection since they were classified among the oppressed (*personae miserabiles*) whom the Church took under its wing. By granting shelter to widows, the Church was pursuing both the biblical tradition of caring for the widow and the Germanic custom that the widow should be granted special protection because her guardian (holder of her *mundium*) had died and she was now defenceless.[109]

In its early days the Church advocated leaving widows in their bereaved state. St Paul said: 'I say therefore to the unmarried and widows, it is good for them if they abide even as I' (I Corinthians 7:8). The widows who did not remarry, and particularly the older women among them constituted a special order (*ordo viduarium*) worthy of aid and respect, and the deaconesses were recruited from

among them. In the High Middle Ages, widows no longer constituted a special order. Some remained widows and lived secular lives,
others joined monastic orders, whether as nuns or lay sisters, while
many married again (and sometimes even a third time). The Church
solemnized these marriages and did not regard them as a sin.[110] In
justifying marriage in general, as part of its attempt to refute the
arguments of the Cathar heretics, the Church emphasized that even
the marriage of a widow and widower was permissible.[111] Nothing
remained of the Church's original stand on the marriage of widows
and widowers except the rule that clerics of the minor orders (who
were allowed to marry) should not take a widow to wife or remarry
if their wives died.

The authors of didactic literature regarded the remarriage of a
widow as a natural phenomenon. One such author writes that it is
not seemly for a widow to remarry before a year has elapsed since
her husband's death, but that she is not obliged to mourn him all her
life.[112] Francesco Barberino instructs the widow in how to conduct
herself in her second marriage: she should not speak too much
about her first husband to her second spouse; if the first was better,
the second should not be made aware of this; she should not try to
introduce customs which prevailed in her first marriage into her
new household; she should not remarry more than three times.[113]
The elderly Goodman of Paris in his manual of guidance takes it for
granted that his young wife will remarry after his death. Furthermore, he believes that it will reflect on him if her second husband
does not find her a perfect housekeeper and wife, since this will
indicate that he did not instruct her successfully during their
marriage.[114]

Both men and women acted in accordance with the advice of
the didactic writers and entered into second and third marriages
apparently without any sense of guilt. Among the regulations of one
of the fraternities of craftsmen in England there is a clause relating
to the possibility of a member being widowed and taking a second
wife, 'as is customary and natural'.[115] In many wills by men the
writer bequeaths part of his property to his second or third wife
while allocating a certain sum for prayers for the soul of his first
wife and asking to be buried by her side (like the London lady who
was married to two spice merchants, in succession, and asked to be
buried beside her first husband).[116] The remarriage of widows and
widowers often solved the problem of a shortage of men or women
in a certain town or area and reduced the number of men and
women forced to remain in an unmarried state.[117]

Feudal lords sometimes brought pressure to bear on noble widows to remarry, while lords of the manor sometimes exerted similar pressure on peasants' widows, thereby infringing on their freedom. Women were sometimes forced to remarry against their will or, particularly among the nobility, to marry men unpleasing to them. Though remarriage of widows and widowers was accepted, a custom prevailing in various regions indicated the displeasure of the younger generation at such marriages. The young people of the village would assemble under the window of the widow or widower and organize a noisy and discordant musical performance with loud wailing and clashing of cymbals (charivari). This custom is recorded only from the fourteenth century, but may have existed earlier. The main performers in this ceremony were the village bachelors, who were thereby expressing their envy of those who were entering into second marriages while they themselves remained unwed. They were giving expression to the struggle between the generations, particularly in cases where the widow or widower had offspring from the first marriage. The custom was also a reflection of the resentment of those who still lacked a portion of their own in rural communities suffering from lack of land, against those who not only owned land but even increased their holdings by second marriage.[118] It reveals however that society did not differentiate between widows and widowers. The remarriage of a widow was regarded as no more reprehensible or ridiculous than that of a widower. In certain periods there was even a tradition of specially mocking the remarriage of the widower. According to this custom any guest at the wedding could call for a jar of wine for himself, and if it was not brought, the guests would seat the bridegroom on a cart and, to the accompaniment of jeering and cries, pull it along the river and throw him in.[119]

Widows were classified among the *miserabiles* to whom the Church granted protection, but the truth is that a widow who was well provided for enjoyed greater freedom than any other type of woman in medieval society. Once she was widowed she was no longer forced to accept the authority of another and, as Beaumanoir defined it, her full authority was restored.[120] As an adult woman, she did not return to the shelter of her father or brothers, and it may be assumed that her married years had rendered her immune to their possible intervention in her life. In other words, she almost certainly enjoyed not merely legal independence but also a relatively broad degree of freedom in her everyday life. Every widow was guaranteed a livelihood proportionate to the size of her husband's estate through her rights of dower, and this in addition to her own inheritance, if she had such, which came into her possession when she was widowed. By right of the dower, the widow received one third to one half of her husband's assets for her support, and she enjoyed the income throughout her life.[121] On her death the property reverted to her husband's family.

The eleventh clause of Magna Carta stipulates that on the husband's death, the wife's rights should be guaranteed before those of the creditor, whether the latter was a Jew or a Christian. By law of northern France, a wife whose husband sold his property before his death was entitled to claim the property due to her by right of dower from the purchaser and to keep it throughout her lifetime. On her death the property reverted to the buyer.[122] If her late husband had been a bastard and was childless, he could not, by French law, bequeath his fief to his relatives and his seigneur inherited; but the widow's dower was guaranteed even in this case, and only after her death did the property she retained as her dower revert to the seigneur.[123] Neither husband nor wife could bequeath family assets to one another. This ban was established in order to prevent the dispersal of the property of the parties' families. It was possible however to arrive at a mutual agreement whereby the surviving partner inherited the belongings of the deceased spouse (or part of them) as well as property the spouse had acquired during his/her lifetime and which was not part of the family legacy. The widow was free to manage her assets as she saw fit, and in most regions she could act as guardian to her minor sons and daughters, and manage their property.[124] Registers reveal that in all social strata there were women who did in fact act as guardians to their minor children.

To sum up the question of the rights of widows as against those of married women (only in the labouring classes were there unmarried laywomen; in the upper classes almost without exception unmarried women entered the nunnery), it should be recalled that certain restrictions were imposed on women as such, irrespective of their marital status. But there were also differences in the rights of various types of women, deriving from different marital status. The status of the unmarried woman and the widow was not the same as that of the married woman. The legal status of a man in contrast was in no way connected with his marital status. In primitive societies the status of women is often determined on the basis of their physiological development: commencement of menstruation, defloration, pregnancy, parturition, menopause. This was not so in medieval society, where status was based on the superstructure of the civilization, which did not always correspond with the laws of physiology. The bulk of didactic literature aimed at women is dedicated to guiding young girls in how to conduct themselves so as to avoid remaining husbandless, and to instructing married women in how to behave with their husbands.

There is no way of assessing whether more women chose to remarry or to remain in their widowed state. The registers can reveal, at the most, the number of widows in a certain location at a certain time, but this number was not constant, and we cannot tell how many widows listed in the registers later remarried. The widow did not, of course, always enjoy free choice. If there was a shortage of men, she could not marry again even if she wished to do so. Many women married for a second and even a third time in all strata of society, from the high nobility, such as Margaret, countess of Lincoln, to townswomen and peasant women. But some did not take this course, among other reasons because they preferred to enjoy a greater degree of freedom than was available to them in marriage. Quite early in the Christian era, St Jerome recognized that some women preferred to remain widows not because of their desire to live celibate lives and dedicate themselves to religious piety, but out of a longing for liberty (*et quia maritorum expertae dominatum viduitatis praeferunt libertatem*)[125] Thomas of Stitny relates that he once heard his widowed grandmother (whom he describes as a good woman of superior qualities) say; 'Dear God, how is it possible that the reward of widows is greater than that of married women. How much better and more convenient is our situation as widows than as married women.'[126]

It is hard to speak of freedom in the context of nuns in general, but the nun did enjoy liberation from male dominance. Among the noblewomen to whom nunneries were open, there were those who entered nunneries after being widowed, such as Loretta, widow of the earl of Leicester, who became a well-known recluse, or Ella, countess of Salisbury, who became the abbess of an Augustinian nunnery she had founded. An example of a widow who resisted the pressures of her relatives to remarry, and who remained in secular society for twelve years after being widowed, was the mother of Gilbert of Nogent. She managed her household and property efficiently and concerned herself with the education of her children. When her youngest son, Gilbert, reached his twelfth birthday, she retired to a nunnery. (Her husband had died eight months after Gilbert's birth.)[127]

Some of the difficulties which confronted a woman who remained in secular society were described by Christine de Pisan, who
herself preferred to remain a widow. She had to fight hard to obtain
her rightful share in her husband's estate. Influential individuals,
clerks of the court and of financial institutions used delaying tactics.
People gossiped about her when she went to plead with influential
men and hinted that she was seeking their favours and not their help
on behalf of her family. The clerks often treated her rudely and
jested at her expense. Gradually, so she writes, she became more
confident and overcame her fears; her body and voice were stronger
and she was able to work hard in order to support her family.[128]
Many other women undoubtedly felt isolated in their bereavement,
as the old Goodman of Paris wrote in his manual, or else, despite
the greater freedom they enjoyed as widows, were unwilling to
tackle the problems encountered by a woman alone in a man's
world, and preferred to remarry.

WOMAN AS MOTHER

In this section I will discuss the attitude of medieval thinkers and
writers to the woman as mother, and the problem of the attitude to
children in medieval civilization. In the following chapters, I
examine women in various classes in their maternal role.

In few of the contemporary sources do we find mention of
woman as mother. In the literature dealing with marriage (both
didactic works and *fabliaux*), the maternal role of the married
woman is scarcely mentioned, and the same is true of the works of
theologians and canonists. Medieval Christian culture undoubtedly
placed greater emphasis on the roles of man and woman than on
those of father and mother. In theological writings we find some
elaboration of the verse in the New Testament relating to the
function of woman as mother, fulfilment of which can bring her
salvation: 'Notwithstanding she shall be saved in childbearing if
they continue in faith and charity and holiness with sobriety'
(I Timothy 2:15). In canon law, paternal care for offspring is part of
natural law.[129] Theologians also refer in general terms to a man's
duty to provide his children with a religious education, sometimes
within the framework of their discussion of the outcome of
lasciviousness and fornication. The child needs a father who can
give him a Christian upbringing. Lewd and adulterous relations lead
to the birth of bastards who do not know the identity of their

fathers. They are raised by a person who is not their natural father or else grow to maturity without a father.

Even within the family framework, the procreation of children is not a value in itself. Only the provision of a true Christian education can be regarded as a value. To have offspring is good because children can be trained in the worship of God, and not because of the desire of human beings to produce heirs or of the human race to proliferate.[130] Thomas Aquinas stresses that when procreation is referred to as one of the objectives of marriage, the reference is not to the actual begetting of children but to their education. These statements by theologians are in contrast to the views of some of the authors of didactic literature, who wrote that children by bearing their father's name thereby perpetuate his memory and that of his forefathers on earth.[131]

We have dwelt on the elaboration of the worship of the Holy Mother in the twelfth century – worship of the radiant Mother who bore the Redeemer, and of the suffering Mother at the foot of the Cross. In the art of the High and Late Middle Ages the images of the pregnant Mary, of the Holy Mother cradling her infant son in her arms, and of the suffering mother embracing the corpse of her crucified son (Pietà), are among the most prevalent themes of sculpture and painting. Also widespread is the statue of the Holy Mother beseeching mercy for sinners, kneeling by the side of her son in the portals of cathedrals. Many churches were dedicated to her – Chartres, Rocamadour, Ipswich, Walsingham, for example – and pilgrims flocked there. In other churches, chapels were erected to her name. Feast-days were dedicated to the important events in her life. She played a central role in religious drama. She was the patron saint of cities, of guilds and of fraternities. Mariolatry was widespread and highly popular. Nonetheless, the image of the Holy Mother apparently had no impact on the image of terrestrial mothers who bore their children according to the laws of nature.

Even courtly literature, which places woman on a pedestal, did not attribute to her those qualities of tenderness, delicacy and self-sacrifice which are usually regarded as pertaining to motherhood. Woman in courtly literature is not tender. She is adored, and in his love for her the knight attains moral perfection, which, according to the contemporary scale of virtues, is reflected above all in loyalty and courage in battle. But the tasks she imposes on him are often incredibly arduous. She displays no qualities of sensitivity, tenderness, self-sacrifice – all qualities of the Holy Mother. Only rarely do we find in this literature manifestations of dedication and sacrifice on the part of the woman. Seldom do the preachers speak of the love of the mother for her children, as in the case of an English preacher who described the loving mother warming her child in winter, caring for him in sickness, praying for his health, and promising a vow if he recovers.[132]

People of the period often found the mirror of the Holy Mother in the nun, bride of Christ. But this attitude too was not unequivocal, as can be learned from the tale of Ailred of Rievaulx about the nuns in the double Gilbertine monastery of Watton in Yorkshire in the twelfth century. The tale is as follows: a little girl was placed in a nunnery at the age of 4 to be instructed there and eventually take the veil. The child grew into a maiden but revealed no predilection for piety or readiness to observe the rule of the order to which she belonged. Her expression was impudent, her speech unrestrained and her walk lascivious. Eventually she met one of the monks of the order, a particularly handsome man, and they fell in love and met clandestinely every night. After some time the monk fled his monastery and would return nightly to meet with his beloved. When this became known to her sister-nuns, they were consumed by concern for the honour of their nunnery. They wrung their hands and attacked the girl, tearing her veil off. Some of the nuns advocated burning her, others thought she should be skinned alive and some favoured tying her to a post and burning her alive over glowing coals. She was beaten by the nuns and cast into the nunnery gaol. Then one day the nuns discovered that she was in a state of advanced pregnancy, and confusion broke out. They wailed and sobbed, feeling that her disgrace was their own and that all of them would be dishonoured because of her, and once again they attacked her.

When their anger had died down, they debated what should be done. They feared that if the young woman was incarcerated in the nunnery much longer, her cries in childbirth would reveal their shame, but they were also afraid to expel her lest she die of hunger. They therefore ordered her to send a message to her lover and arrange a meeting with him, intending, upon his arrival, to put 'the adulterous whore with her swollen belly' into his hands, 'as the loathsome source of her sin'. They told the monks of their scheme and the latter waited in ambush for him at the destined place of meeting, caught him and beat him with their cudgels. Then they handed him over to the nuns, who had told them of their wish to force him to confess his sin. But the nuns no longer intended to send him off with the girl. They threw him to the ground, secured him with ropes, exposed 'the source of his sin', placed a knife in his hand and forced him to castrate himself. And, as a final act of revenge, one of the nuns thrust the bloody remnants of his manhood into the mouth of his mistress. And the author adds:

> Like the sword of Levi and the jealousy of Phineas was the jealousy and heroism of the nuns. The purity of their sex prevailed and the injustice done to Jesus was avenged by these peerless virgins. It is not the deed they did that I praise but their zeal, not the fact that they shed blood, but the fact that in their zeal they resembled the saints. What might they not do to preserve their chastity, if they did so much to take revenge on its behalf.[133]

This horrific tale does not merely illustrate the depths of perversity to which it was possible to descend in the monastic life, and the role of women in the cruelty which characterized medieval civilization. It also casts light on the image of the nun as envisaged by this learned churchman, known as the St Bernard of the North, who was not distinguished by any particular religious fanaticism. The emphasis is on the zeal of the nuns in observing one of the monastic vows, chastity, which was particularly stringently applied in the case of the nuns. The author was willing to accept the fact that the girl who had conceived naturally aroused nothing but hatred and anger in her sister-nuns; he also condones the measures adopted by the nuns in order to protect the vow of chastity and to punish their transgressing sister. There is no hint whatsoever of the nun as the image of Mary – the personification of good and mercy.

Whether some primitive societies were matriarchal, as several anthropologists have tried to prove, or only matrilinear, there are certain ancient literary works which reflect the clash between matriarchal and patriarchal ideals backed by the gods and goddesses symbolizing each. According to matriarchal ideal, the primary role of the woman is to fulfil her duty as a mother, and the blood tie is the most fundamental and immutable link. Patriarchal principles accord preference to the relations between husband and wife, which take precedence over blood ties and the mother-child link. Despite the slow pace of introduction of the principle of *agnatio* and the continued importance of ties on the maternal side, patriarchal elements came to dominate medieval literature and matriarchal concepts disappeared.[134] In estates literature, almost without exception, the authors stress the wife's duty towards her husband rather than her obligation of caring for her children, and the same is true of didactic literature in general. This literature, which details the ways in which a woman can preserve her sexual modesty, observe her duties to her husband, dress and conduct herself suitably, devotes scant space to her maternal duties. The Goodman of Paris, who goes into extensive detail on the subject of the proper behaviour and dress, household management rules, and ways of pleasing a husband, does not mention the raising of children. He cites them only in order to draw a comparison between step-parents who neglect their children and then wonder why they leave, and the wife who does not care properly for her husband, grumbles at him, does not greet him warmly when he returns home and finally drives him away from home altogether. The stepchildren are merely the analogy, the true subject being the husband and proper ways of caring for him.[135] The fact that the author was elderly and may have had no intention of bringing more children into the world does not explain his failure to mention offspring, since he instructs the young wife in how to treat her second husband, to whom she was likely to bear children.

In the *fabliaux* depicting the bad woman there is generally no reference to her maternal role. She is evil towards her husband, but she is not a neglectful or evil mother, treating her children harshly or domineering them. The children are simply not mentioned. The exception is *Les Quinze Joyes de Mariage*, written at the beginning of the fifteenth century. The author pictures the love and concern of the father for his infant child. The evil wife beats the small child in order to hurt her husband, who loves it. When the husband tries to stop her, she complains that he does not realize what it means to care for children day and night. At night she leaves them to cry and does not approach them, again in order to distress her husband. Sometimes she exploits the child for her own wishes. When she decides to go on a pilgrimage in order to meet her lover en route, she tells her husband of an imaginary illness of her newborn babe and of her desire to pray for his recovery on the tomb of a saint. The husband goes in to see the child, who appears to him to be ailing, and his eyes fill with tears of sorrow and pity. When the husband fails to return from a crusade and the wife believes him dead, she soon finds consolation and, in her second marriage, forgets her obligations towards the children of her first husband.[136] This picture suggests that the evil mother is part of the image of the evil wife, while the husband, with whom the author identifies, is a good and loving father to his children from their infancy. But this description is late and untypical.

The churchmen in their sermons did not specify devotion to children as the first duty of a wife. Worship of God is more important. In one of his sermons for women, Humbert de Romans complains about women who are too deeply involved in worldly matters and remote from worship of God. Some of them concur when their husbands become usurers and thus become accomplices in their crime. Others are too involved in their household affairs, while some devote too much attention to their children, and love them 'according to the flesh alone'.[137]

What is the reason for this dismissal, to the point of total disregard, of the maternal role of woman? Underestimation of the mother's role is undoubtedly linked to the attitude to children in the Middle Ages. Philip Ariès has written of the image of the child as a mirror reflecting and focusing various aspects of contemporary culture: educational works, portraits, methods of instruction. He arrives at the conclusion that the child had almost no place in medieval culture. In medieval iconography the child was viewed as a miniature adult. There are no vivid images of children in the literature of the age. The child is indiscernible among adults of his own class. Ariès finds very few manifestations of emotion towards children. If they survived and grew to adulthood they could contribute to joint ventures and constitute an additional source of power within the family, but there was no existential relationship between parents and children, certainly not in childhood. The nuclear family – parents and children – was not a source of inspiration to poets and artists, because it was a social and moral entity, but not an emotional actuality. The emotional actuality was the lineage.[138] So much for Ariès' view. Let us now try to examine the attitude to children as expressed in medieval literature.

In Church literature children are often depicted as a burden and indirectly also as the cause of sin. It is good to have children, but they sometimes constitute a hindrance to virtuous conduct. Because of them, the farmer does not pay his tithes. Sometimes parents spend their lives in wearisome toil, borrowing and pawning their property, in order to support their children.[139] One of the authors of didactic works writes: 'If you have children, rejoice in them and raise them properly. If they die in childhood, accept your lot. Do not complain and do not regret it overmuch. Think of all the cares which you will spare yourselves.'[140] There is scant reference in medieval literature to children as a source of joy. One of the few who wrote in this strain was Philippe de Novare, who claimed that parents would not exchange their happiness in children for untold wealth. But he emphasized that children were merely a source of spiritual joy for the body, while renunciation of the temporal life for worship of God and spiritual salvation rejoiced the soul.[141]

Eustache des Champs, whose work displays a general tone of pessimism, is particularly gloomy in describing the procreation and raising of children;

> Blessed is the man who has no children, for infants are nothing but wailing and smells, a source of sorrow and anxiety. They must be clothed, shoed and fed. There is always a danger that they will fall and injure themselves or sicken and die. When they grow up they may go to the bad and be cast into prison. They can bring no happiness which can compensate for the fears, trouble and expense of their upbringing. And can there be any greater disgrace than to bring into the world corrupt children? For a man whose limbs are twisted is also perverse in thought – filled with sin and corruption.[142]

The Chevalier de La Tour Landry, in a manual of guidance written for his daughters, declared that one should not rejoice overmuch in the birth of a child, and should certainly not celebrate the birth with lavish ceremony. This could be evil in the eyes of God and lead to the death of the infant.[143] The interesting point in these remarks is that he is not speaking of the evil eye, or of satanic malevolence against the child, but of divine action. The procreation of children is accompanied by a sense of guilt, since children are conceived in sin and distract attention from worship of God. Hence the fear that God, having given, may also take away. This expression of apprehension goes beyond the natural fear of a parent for a beloved child whose survival is threatened or uncertain, a fear which has characterized mankind in all periods. Concern for children in the Middle Ages was well-founded, since the infant mortality rate was extremely high, but, as we have noted, it is divine retribution which is feared and not the Devil's deeds.

The views of the Cathars on procreation close the circle: children are a source of joy, but this joy emanates from the Devil. According to one of the Cathar myths about the tempting of angels by Satan, the Devil lures the Angels with the following words: 'And I will give you a wife who will be your helpmate and you will have a home and children and will rejoice in one child born to you more than in all the peace you have here [in the celestial world].'[144] The medieval Christian viewpoint was not identical with the dualistic stand of the Cathars, who regarded the material world, including the human body, sexual relations and procreation as the work of the Devil. But even in Catholic Christianity we find a dualistic note: emphasis on the gap between body and soul, flesh and spirit, this world and the next. Those who headed the Christian spiritual hierarchy, the monks and the secular churchmen, abstained from sexual relations and procreation. The Church saw procreation as the justification for sexual intercourse but not as a value in itself. Furthermore, though parental duties are stressed, children are often depicted as a hindrance to divine worship and to total dedication to the religious life.

The authors we have cited were mostly churchmen, who neither married nor begot children. A similar attitude to that of male churchmen can be found among women who chose a religious life. St Douceline endeavoured to divest the story of the conception and birth of Christ of any carnal implication. In one of her visions she saw the Holy Mother with a ray of sunlight radiating from her belly with the Infant Jesus at its tip.[145] Angela of Foligno, after becoming a mystic, dictated the following words to the Dominican friar who recorded her visions:

> In that time, by the will of God, my mother, who was a severe obstacle to me, died. Then my husband and all my children died within a brief period. Since I had taken this path (i.e. the path of religious life) and had asked God that they die, their death was a great consolation for me.[146]

There can be no doubt that the view that all men are born in sin was one of the underlying causes of this type of attitude to children in medieval literature, and of the disparagement of the maternal function in this literature. The standpoint of the Church left its mark on lay literature as well. But this literature was influenced by other factors too. The infant mortality in the Middle Ages was extremely high in all classes of society. Many died immediately after birth, many more in infancy. People hastened to baptize their children immediately after birth, since they feared they might die and wanted to ensure that their souls would be saved. These fears are reflected in the words of the writers we have cited. In the Dance of Death, children appear together with adults. It seems that the words of these writers may also have been preparing parents for the eventuality that their offspring might die and offering some kind of consolation. John Wyclif, for example, wrote that mothers who had lost their children should not mourn, since God had done them a 'great mercy' in removing them from this world.[147]

Philippe Ariès claims that not only were these writers preparing the readers for whatever fate held in store, but that parents themselves sought spiritual defences, since they feared excessive attachment to children who had scant chances of survival. To his mind this explains why they did not display emotion towards children – particularly infants – and treated them more as reinforcements of the family strength, if they survived, than as individuals and objects of parental love. Was this in fact true? We will examine this thesis in the following chapters. Ariès also held that an emotional attitude toward little children developed only from the end of the Middle Ages, and then only gradually (reflected in changes in educational methods, in the extension of childhood, in greater focus on the nuclear family as an emotional actuality and on the child as an individual), first in the upper classes and only much later in the labouring classes. In the chapters on women in the various classes, I will examine this viewpoint and try to assess to what extent the writers that have been quoted, most of whom were childless churchmen, could reflect the emotions of parents towards their children. I will also explore whether the attitude to children was uniform in all classes of society.

Since the authors of didactic works did not regard the maternal functions as the primary role of woman they did not generally see fit to cite this particular function as a pretext for denying her the right to fulfil public functions, hold office and acquire education at institutions of higher learning.

VIOLATIONS OF MARITAL LAW

The Church demanded mutual fidelity in marriage, and to the extent that the ecclesiastical courts imposed punishments for adultery, it punished man and woman equally. Yet the adultery of women was cited more often as a pretext for separation than that of men. Ecclesiastical courts imposed on adulterers penitence by fasting, prayer and temporary celibacy, or fines, and even a period in the stocks. But the secular courts also often tried and punished adulterers. Secular legislation on adultery was aimed at restricting to the minimum the individual vengeance permitted by Germanic law. According to the decision passed by King John of England, a man who castrated another for fornicating with his wife had his land confiscated unless it could be proved that he had given the adulterer a prior warning not to approach his home.[148] John's successor, Henry III, stipulated after several brutal cases that only the cuckolded husband himself was permitted to castrate the adulterer, while fathers and brothers of adulterous women were forbidden to take revenge.[149] According to Beaumanoir, a husband who murdered his wife and her lover was acquitted only if he had previously cautioned the lover to keep away from his wife and had later found them together and murdered them on the spot in his rage. A father or brother, however, were prohibited from taking such action. If a husband murdered his wife's lover some time after the deed, he was obliged to prove the latter's guilt; if he could not do so, he was hanged.[150] The same was true of the legal code of Frederick II.[151] According to the laws of Sepúlveda and Cuenca as well, the husband was permitted to murder his wife and her lover only if he caught them in the act. By the laws of Sepúlveda, the wife's relatives were also accorded the same right.[152]

It appears that private revenge for adultery, like private wars, remained the privilege of the nobility alone in the Central Middle Ages. The legislators refer to the possibility of revenge against both the man and the woman caught in adultery, and the chroniclers record cases of cruel revenge against adulterers. Sometimes the husband took revenge only against the lover, while the wife was merely humiliated. Sometimes he avenged himself against his wife, like Fulk Nerra, count of Anjou, who burned his wife Elizabeth alive.[153] There are no records of cases among the nobility where a wife took revenge on an adulterous husband.

The secular courts, like the ecclesiastical courts, usually imposed identical punishments on adulterous men and women, but were sometimes more lenient towards the latter. In some regions a married woman who had intercourse with another man, whether married or a bachelor, was considered an adulteress, while a married man was regarded as an adulterer only if he had relations with a married woman (a relationship with a spinster or widow was defined only as fornication). This more lenient attitude towards men was not influenced by the ecclesiastical outlook or Church legislation, but derived rather from the superior status of man in society in general, and the husband's fear that he might not be able to distinguish legitimate children from bastards.[154] In Reconquest Spain, very stringent punishments were inflicted on Christian women who committed adultery with a Jew or a Muslim. If they were caught in the act, both partners were executed. We find no record of similar treatment of men who committed adultery with Jewish or Muslim women.[155] The Christian man who engaged in intercourse with a non-Christian woman was regarded as having injured and humiliated a woman of another religion, this being permitted and even encouraged in Spain at that time.

We find no uniformity in the punishments imposed by secular courts for the crime of adultery. Some courts were lenient, others strict. Under the legal code of Frederick II an adulterous woman had her nose cut off and was banished from her husband's home. If the husband chose to forgive her, she was not mutilated, but he could not prevent her from suffering a public lashing. The adulterous man was merely fined.[156] In the towns of southern France, an adulterous couple were forced to run through the streets naked and hitched together in humiliating fashion, and were lashed as they ran. It is not clear to what extent these punishments were actually implemented and to what degree they were replaced by heavy fines. The laws of the town of Alais in south-west France stipulated that the specified punishment could not be commuted to a fine, 'and the woman' it was emphasized 'must run first'.[157] There were places in southern France where the seigneur could, by law, confiscate the property of the adulterer and inflict physical punishment on him.[158] In England, punishments were much lighter by royal statutes. According to the Westminster Statute, a woman who left her husband in order to follow her lover forfeited her right to her dower, unless her husband agreed to forgive her.[159] In Brittany too, a husband was empowered to decide whether or not to deprive his adulterous wife of her dower.[160] On the other hand, according to the laws of London, the heads of adulterers were shaved, they were taken to Newgate gaol and then forced to walk through the streets of the city led by a band of musicians to the other side of London, where they were incarcerated in another gaol.[161] In Brabant, the punishment was the same for both sexes – fine, public lashing and the stocks.[162]

On the other hand, in rural areas, in the manors of lay and ecclesiastical lords, we find that the punishment for fornication, adultery and the begetting of bastards was, almost without exception, a monetary fine. In England it was the task of the jurors of manor courts to report to the clerk of the lord of the manor every case of fornication, adultery or the birth of a bastard, so that the fine could be imposed.[163] In almost every case the armerced were the woman or her father. Cases involving bondwomen almost never reached ecclesiastical courts. The fines imposed for the crime of fornication, adultery or begetting of bastards were an additional source of income for the lord of the manor. If the matter was brought before the ecclesiastical courts, sometimes the man was punished as well.[164] In Catalonia the lord of the manor could confiscate half the property of a woman found guilty of adultery. If she committed adultery with her husband's acquiescence, all their property was confiscated.[165] Among the peasants, on the other hand, there were some couples who lived together without marriage. Of fifty couples in the small village of Montaillou in the Pyrenees, where there was no seigneurial demesne, six were unmarried (in other words, more than 10 per cent).[166] But this phenomenon even existed in some English manors with seigneurial demesne, where the peasants were under close supervision and pressure on the part of the clerks of the lord of the manor.[167]

Whereas the Church considered adultery and fornication to be the sin of both men and women, and secular law punished both (though sometimes favouring men), the homiletic and didactic literature is directed, primarily, at guarding the sexual virtue of woman and keeping her from sin. In this literature sexual chastity is considered woman's most important quality, together with obedience to her husband. One author lists a series of evils: a king without wisdom, a master without counsel, a knight without valour, a rich man without generosity, an old man without religion and a woman without chastity.[168] Chastity appears as the most important trait of all women, irrespective of their social class, vocation or marital status. Bartholomaeus Anglicus, who in his didactic work briefly discusses the qualities required of boys and girls, opens his discussion of the latter with the statement: 'The most praiseworthy quality of a girl is chastity.'[169]

We find similar statements in the writings of the anti-feminist Philippe de Novare, and in the works of Christine de Pisan, who came to the defence of women against the accusations of Jean de Meung, author of the second half of the Roman de la Rose. According to Philippe de Novare it is necessary to prevent the development of certain traits in women (profligacy, daring, greed); they should be taught manners and crafts, not for their own good but for one sole objective – to nurture their chastity and prevent the sin of sex. A woman who sins with her body causes greater disgrace to her lineage than a man who commits a carnal sin. In order to be deserving of honour, a man must be courageous, wise, and generous. But a woman is obliged only to be decent in body; then all her flaws will recede, and she will be universally honoured.[170] In her book Le Livre des Trois Vertus, a manual of instruction for women, Christine de Pisan dwells at length on the duty of girls, married women and widows to guard their chastity. They must recall this obligation when they walk or sit, and as for young girls and widows, it is better for them not to mix in male company.[171] Here too, as in other traditional societies, female virtue is the counterpart of male honour.

But in these same manuals in which authors occasionally seem obsessed with woman's sexual modesty, we sometimes find, in complete contradiction of their own exhortations, that when they cite cautionary tales, sexual misdemeanour is no longer the prime sin of woman. Two examples will serve to illustrate this. The Chevalier de La Tour Landry, in his manual of instruction for his daughters, describes the three wives of a knight: one had dozens of dresses, both short and long, and many female ornaments, spent all her life in nurturing her beauty, and was tight-fisted to the poor. She was finally sentenced to Hell-fire. The second, motivated by vanity, painted herself excessively in order to find favour in the eyes of others. She too was sentenced to the nether world. The third committed adultery once with a young man in the service of one of the knights, confessed her sin, and was merely sentenced to Purgatory.[172] There can be no doubt that the author's intention was to explain the importance of confession to his daughters, but the conclusion to be drawn regarding the relative gravity of various sins is enlightening. The elderly Goodman of Paris tells a tale of a wife who deceived her husband with a young man and eventually left home to follow him. Her husband, in order to preserve her good name, told all their friends that she had gone on a pilgrimage to the tomb of St James of Compostela, as she had once promised her father to do, and sent two of her brothers (to whom he had not revealed the true purpose of her journey) to seek her out and bring her home. Her brothers found her miserable and destitute, having been abandoned by her lover (as always happens, added the Goodman), and brought her home. Her husband greeted her joyfully and respectfully in the presence of all her friends. It appears, therefore, that to be tempted into adultery does not necessarily lead to dissolution of a marriage, and that with a small degree of good will, the lapse can be overcome and forgotten.

In the *fabliaux* and courtly literature, as we have seen, fornication and adultery are not considered grave sins. The *fabliaux* depict extramarital relations humorously, usually telling of a woman who cuckolds her husband and betrays him with a young bachelor. The cuckolded husband is the object of mockery, but there is no serious intent in the tale and certainly no strong sense of sin.

In courtly literature, the troubadours' poems are addressed to married women and the courtly romance described forbidden relations between a bachelor or a married man (usually the former) and a married woman, often the wife of his seigneur, thus constituting both adultery and betrayal. According to the conventional interpretation of this literature following the work of Gaston Paris, the troubadours, who serenaded married women of higher social rank than themselves, often their seniors in years, expressed both love for their ladies and readiness to undergo every trial imposed on them so as to win their love. According to this interpretation, Lancelot, for example, as depicted in Chrétien de Troyes' *Conte de la Charrette*, who is the lover of his lord's wife and violates all the moral norms of the age, both ecclesiastical and feudal, is the hero of the tale with whom the audience identify. He is a hero because of his love for and unlimited devotion to his lady. This interpretation arouses two problems. First: how could contemporary readers accept such a total dichotomy between ecclesiastical and feudal ideals and the courtly ideals, and consider a man who was the lover of his lord's wife to be a hero? Second: how could courtly love exist as a way of life at a time when punishments for adultery were particularly harsh in southern Europe and private vengeance was common, particularly within that noble class to whose ladies the troubadours sang? There were undoubtedly noblemen who boasted of their conquests of the wives of others,[173] but none of them would have been willing to be made the victim of similar actions by others.

These problems have led to re-evaluation of the accepted view of courtly literature. J. F. Benton tried to prove that not all courtly romances depict the adulterer and betrayer as a hero. The version of the tale of Lancelot written by Ulrich von Zazikhoven does not condemn Lancelot, but the tale as written by Chrétien de Troyes takes a censorious view of his actions. The disapproval presented is subtle, but nevertheless present. The author leaves Lancelot imprisoned in a tower. Since he wrote in the ironic style of the period he could not censure him directly, but he was implying this and the listeners understood him. Thus, the gap between the norms of some of the courtly tales and the Christian and feudal ideals is narrowed. According to this view, neither the author nor the society of his age were shocked by adulterous conduct, but neither did they regard it as a praiseworthy way of life. Benton dwells on the significance of the word *amor*, love, as used by the troubadours in medieval culture. He notes that during the Middle Ages the word was often used without sexual connotations, and sometimes even had no strong emotional implications. There is mention of *amor* between seigneur and vassal, or between monks in a monastery. The troubadours who serenaded ladies expressed their admiration in courteous terms, but their love was not necessarily interpreted as sexual love or their admiration as sexual courtship. Such courtship on the part of troubadours of lower rank than the ladies would usually have been too fraught with risk. They were not necessarily the lovers or seducers of the ladies of whom they sang in the courts of feudal lords. Thus Benton tries to solve the second problem: how to reconcile the severe punishments inflicted on adulterers with courtly love as a way of life.[174]

All the same, it seems that not all the contradictions can be reconciled. There were contradictions in the medieval attitude towards adultery as towards sex in general. In a large part of the courtly tales the author considers the treacherous adulterer to be the hero. Bourgeois literature did not deliberately foster the ideal of extramarital love, but even in urban society, fornication, adultery and the begetting of bastard children were rife, and the same was true in peasant society. When a peasant woman of Montaillou was asked by the Inquisition court whether she had not been aware that she was sinning when she fornicated with the village priest, she replied: 'At the time it was pleasurable to me and to the priest and therefore I did not consider it a sin and nor did he. Now, I no longer take pleasure in him, so that, if he knew me now, I would consider it a sin.'[175] Here too we find a departure from ecclesiastical norms.

John Huizinga points to the contradictions which marked medieval civilization in various spheres. Among others, he cites Froissart's story about Charles of Blois. This prince lived the life of an ascetic from his youth. As a child he concentrated on his studies and his father tried to dissuade him, since he thought such habits unfitting for a man of war. In due course he took to sleeping on a straw pallet beside his nuptial bed. After his death, it turned out that he had always worn a hair-shirt under his armour. He confessed every evening. As a prisoner in London, he would seek out cemeteries in order to recite the *de Profundis*. His squire refused to join him in prayer, saying that in those cemeteries lay 'those who killed my parents and friends and burned their homes'. When he was released from captivity, he resolved to go on a pilgrimage barefoot in the snow from La Roche-Derrien, where he had been taken prisoner, to the tomb of St Yves at Tréguier. And, in conclusion, Froissart writes: 'As is fitting and becoming, master Charles of Blois died facing the enemy with his bastard known as

Jehans de Blois, and several other knights and squires from Brittany.'[176] Can these contradictions be reconciled?

BASTARDS

The problem of the bastard arose only in the case of unmarried mothers. The illegitimate son of a married woman was usually accepted by the family and considered legitimate in all strata of society, even if there was some suspicion as to the circumstances of his birth. Neither the husband nor the law wished to delve too deeply into such matters, the former for fear of disgrace and the latter since it was extremely difficult to prove bastardy in such cases.[177] Characteristic is the tale told by the old Goodman of Paris: a Venetian woman confessed to her husband on her deathbed that one of her children was not his. The husband, in order to preserve his wife's honour, not only forgave her but also refused to investigate to which of their children she was referring.[178]

According to the outlook of the Church, the bastard was the incarnation of sin, the fruit of forbidden sexual relations whether fornication or adultery, but the Church also preached the sanctity of life and the obligation of Christian mercy, and was violently opposed to abortion and infanticide. Loyal to these views, it was tolerant towards bastards. They were eligible for marriage, and by special dispensation were permitted to enter the service of the Church.[179] Since canon law stipulated the duty of a father to care for his offspring as part of the natural law, even mothers who gave birth outside wedlock were allowed to sue for support for their children in ecclesiastical courts. We do not know to what extent ecclesiastical courts could force the fathers to pay child-support, but on the other hand, agreements were undoubtedly drawn up between parents without need for recourse to courts.[180] Secular laws on bastardy were drawn up under ecclesiastical inspiration, but there were differences between the various regions, particularly as to the right to inherit, to bequeath and to bear the paternal name.[181] The fact that bastardy laws appear in regional, royal and urban codes of law and guild regulations also suggests that the phenomenon was not rare.

Didactic literature echoed the spirit of the law. Francesco Barbarino, in a work directed at women, writes that if a husband has illegitimate offspring it is the duty of his wife to care for them and protect them. The widow was obliged to raise her own children, to pray for the soul of her departed husband, and also to care for his illegitimate children.[182] The Goodman of Paris relates, as an example of ideal conduct, the story of the wife of a Paris lawyer. Her husband had an illegitimate daughter by a poor woman. The child was raised by a nurse, but at a certain stage, the nurse and the father quarrelled and the nurse threatened to reveal the whole story. When the wife learned of this, she came to an understanding with the nurse; when the girl grew up, she entrusted her to a seamstress to learn her trade, and eventually even found her a husband.[183]

As we have noted, bastards were common in all social classes. In the period preceding the Gregorian Reform, many priests had illegitimate offspring, who always took their mother's name. After the reform and the enforcement of clerical celibacy, the number of bastard children of priests apparently decreased, but the phenomenon most certainly did not disappear.[184] We often find in registers of the twelfth and thirteenth centuries the note 'son of a priest' beside the name of an individual.[185] The register of the Lincolnshire court even records a 'lineage' of priests. A nephew came to court to claim the legacy of his uncle, who was a priest and a bastard, son of a priest and bastard.[186] In the Pyrenees region in southern France and Catalonia, priests lived with their mistresses in the fourteenth century even more openly than did their colleagues in the north.[187] Among the indulgences granted in the fourteenth century in France to women accused of murdering their newborn babies, we find one granted to the mistress of a priest. She lived in his house and bore him a child, and he forced her to murder it on birth.[188]

The procreation of bastards was not restricted to the low-ranking rural clergy. John of Salisbury, in his letter to Pope Hadrian, tells of Archdeacon Walkelin, whose mistress bore him a son while he was on his way home to England from a visit to the pope, and who therefore called the child Hadrian. He had now abandoned his mistress, who was again pregnant, but had ordered that if a second son was born, he should be named Benevento, since his father had gone there on a pilgrimage, and if a daughter, that she be named Hadriana. John exclaims: 'What a loyal friend to the Roman Pope. Even in his sins he does not forget him and gives his name to the fruit of his sins.'[189] Nigel, bishop of Ely, who was also an important official of the Royal Treasury, had a bastard son. The son became bishop of London and wrote the work known as *Dialogus de Scaccario*.

In the towns of Italy, southern Spain and Portugal, bastard children were born to slave girls from the east and Africa, and were often given their father's name like legitimate sons.[190] Since the mothers were in any event slaves, there was no deterioration in their status as a result of having borne bastards, and the contrary may even have been true. The regulations and laws of various cities in England and France stipulate the rights of bastards and the restrictions imposed on them as to inheritance and citizenship,[191] and the registers record various cases of litigation involving illegitimate offspring and bequests to them. A lawyer in the Paris Parlement willed a bequest through the courts to his cousin and their joint bastard daughter.[192] A Parisian bourgeois acknowledged his illegitimate daughter, succeeded in having her legitimized, married her to a member of his own class and bequeathed some of his property to her. This aroused the anger and avarice of his relatives, and after his death they succeeded in preventing her from receiving the bequest.[193] The brother of a Florentine merchant brought the illegitimate daughter of his brother, a girl of 10, from Sicily to Florence, regarding it as his duty to bring her up.[194] A London merchant allotted a small dowry (£10), to his illegitimate daughter, but she was lucky enough to wed one of the squires of Richard II.[195] A bastard daughter in Metz left property on her death to her two legitimate brothers.[196]

There were numerous bastards among the nobility as well. John of Gaunt had four bastard children by his mistress. The earl of Salisbury bequeathed a large sum (500 marks) for the upbringing and marrying of his bastard son, enabling the son to enter the prosperous gentry class. John of Gaunt also fought for the legitimization of his bastard children and their acceptance into the peerage.[197] In the French nobility, bastards attained prominent positions at the beginning of the fifteenth century. Some became archbishops or bishops, and held senior political or military posts. This phenomenon can be explained in the light of the fact that the nobility was anxious to recruit as many people as possible from within its ranks to consolidate its position in the face of an increasingly strong monarchy. Even bastards were eligible for this purpose,[198] and this situation endured until the sixteenth century. But it is self-evident that just as conditions sometimes favoured those of illegitimate birth, so any upheaval in society or within the family could undermine their status.

Members of the minor nobility also sometimes recognized their illegitimate offspring. A certain knight bequeathed a fief to his illegitimate daughter; his relatives tried to deprive her of it and the dispute was brought to court.[199] The bastard daughters of townspeople and noblemen apparently enjoyed the same treatment as illegitimate sons, with the exception that among the minor nobility in Franche Comté only bastard sons inherited.[200] In addition, bastard sons of noblemen sometimes became the particular confidants of their fathers, on whose mercies they depended, and served as their faithful assistants and emissaries. The services of daughters could not be utilized in the same way, but fathers usually took their bastard children, both male and female, under their care, and legitimate offspring supported their bastard siblings. In England there were recorded cases of illegitimate daughters of nobles and Church notables whose fathers guaranteed their future as abbesses or prioresses by paying the required dowry and obtaining the necessary dispensation in order to overcome the obstacle of their birth (*defectus natalium*).[201]

There were numerous bastards in the peasant class. A study carried out on the basis of the register of the manor court of Halesowen near Birmingham suggests that in the first half of the fourteenth century the incidence of illegitimacy must have been quite high. Among peasants, there was a clear connection between the economic status of women and the birth of bastards. Most women who bore children out of wedlock came from the poorer strata in the villages. Daughters of prosperous men married at an earlier age and their families could almost certainly supervise their daughters more strictly than could poor families. Some daughters of the poor left home in order to earn a living as agricultural labourers and maid-servants, and thus were faced with greater opportunities for non-marital sexual relations. As court registers show, betrothals were sometimes terminated even though the betrothed couple had already lived together as man and wife. Prosperous families found it easier to compel a man to marry the daughter to whom he was betrothed and thus forestall the birth of a bastard. Even if they did not suceed in forcing him into marriage, it was easier for them than for poor parents to find a substitute husband for their daughter.

The picture which emerges from Halesowen was characteristic of other areas as well. Some of the bastards born to poor girls employed far from their parental homes probably died shortly after birth, but if they survived and their mothers subsequently married, they were accepted into the new family. The rural community in England did not condemn bastards and often even sided with them against legitimate sons who wished to disinherit them. After the Black Death (1348) there was a steep decline in the number of bastards in Halesowen. The general population decreased, land lay fallow, and those who survived found it easier to allocate land to sons to enable them to wed, or dowries to daughters to enable them to find husbands. Though fewer bastards were born, greater numbers of widows gave birth outside wedlock. When there was no longer a shortage of land, widows, however prosperous, were no longer in demand for marriage.[202] In the small village of Montaillou in the Pyrenees in the late thirteenth and early fourteenth centuries, a considerable number of the children were illegitimate. Bastard daughters mostly served as maid-servants and then married peasants, usually the poorest in the village. Some fathers recognized their illegitimate daughters, as they did bastard sons. As in English villages, the mothers were the poorest girls in the village. There is a recorded case of a maid-servant whose bastard daughter was raised by a nurse, and later married a peasant. Another woman who gave birth to bastards was the maid-servant and mistress of a peasant. She hoped that one day he would marry her, a hope which was not fulfilled.[203]

More is known of the fate of girl bastards than that of their mothers. Among the peasants it was usually the mothers who raised bastard children, and sometimes later married members of their class, but not all of them found husbands. In English villages one could find the spinster with a small land holding, which ensured her relative economic independence, who bore children outside wedlock and raised them alone. The Halesowen register lists an unmarried woman named Milicentia who supported herself and her two daughters born outside wedlock by brewing ale, and unmarried Juliana Balle, who supported herself and her bastard daughter by pin-making.[204]

Among prosperous towndwellers and the nobility, there were fathers who undertook responsibility for their illegitimate offspring from infancy. The learned jurist Beaumanoir cites a case in which a grandmother claimed that the illegitimate child entrusted to his father had been handed over to a nurse.[205] The fact that such a case is cited suggests that it was not a rare phenomenon. The Goodman of Paris tells the tale of a father who handed over his illegitimate baby daughter to a nurse. Noblemen (John of Gaunt, for example) sometimes supported their mistresses and their joint offspring. We do not know what fate befell mothers who bore children outside wedlock if the fathers did not acknowledge their paternity. Nor can we guess what happened to such women even if the fathers recognized their obligations if they themselves were not official mistresses and did not succeed in concealing the fact that they had borne a bastard. What was the attitude of their families, and what were their chances of marrying after producing a bastard child? According to Glanville the 'incontinent' girl under guardianship lost her inheritance. In France, a noblewoman who gave birth before marriage was disinherited by law.[206] (There was no corresponding legislation regarding men who begot children outside wedlock.) In England, Henry I's Charter guaranteed the widow's dower as long as she did not commit the sins of fornication and adultery.[207] This legislation ensured the lord against any pressure to accept the girl's or widow's child as his feudal tenant.

It may be assumed that the family endeavoured to marry off the erring daughter or to send her to a nunnery after having separated her from her child. The author of the *Quinze Joyes de Mariage* wrote of a girl who sinned and ran off with a man (he does not specify that she gave birth to a bastard) and, on her return, was married by her parents to a man of lesser rank than her own. It seems likely that this solution was also applied in the case of a girl who gave birth to a bastard. But not all women were of strong enough character to raise a bastard child. From the letters of remission granted in France in the fourteenth and fifteenth centuries we learn of the murder of infants born out of wedlock in rural areas, and the phenomenon is known to have existed in certain parts of Germany and in Florence in the Late Middle Ages.

All the cases of infanticide specified in these letters of remission[208] were committed by women from the peasant class. The murders were sometimes brutal and shocking, the fruit of momentary madness and fear, and in some cases the infant was abandoned to its fate and died. In all the letters the women described themselves as driven by feelings of disgrace and terror. In no case did they cite economic arguments or fears of the difficulties of raising the child. It seems that both men and women did not feel disgraced by the act of engaging in fornication or adultery, but only by its outcome, the bastard child. Characteristic of this approach is the tale which appears in one of the letters of remission, concerning a priest who engaged in a sexual relationship for a year and a half with a woman who lived openly in his house. He began to fear for his honour only when he heard the cry of her newborn infant, and then dug a pit and forced the woman, who was half-mad with grief and pain, to throw in the baby. In another case, a young woman whose parents were too poor to find her a husband entered into a relationship with a man and conceived. Her parents, who suspected her condition, urged her to give birth to the child, but she denied her pregnancy, gave birth in secret and murdered the child.

The same belief that disgrace lay not in forbidden intercourse but in bearing a bastard is reflected in the words of the village priest of Montaillou to his mistress Beatrice Planissol, a member of the minor nobility: 'I do not wish to cause you to conceive as long as your father is living, since this would be a great disgrace for him.'[209] These ethics were based not on a sense of sin of the individual, but on the community's consensus as to what constituted disgrace. (Contemporary studies have shown that even today people find it easier to accept the fact that a girl has engaged in extramarital relations than her delivery of an illegitimate child.) The expression 'because of fear and disgrace' occurs again and again in the arguments cited by girls, widows and married women. The married women justifiably feared the violent reaction of their husbands if they were unable to conceal the true paternity of the child.

Conditions during pregnancy and parturition were intolerable. Most women returned to work several hours after giving birth. Some young girls did not even realize that they were pregnant, and the birth came as a stunning shock to them. They gave birth on the bare ground, and even if the child was born alive, it died soon after. Many women attempted to baptize the child themselves before killing it, thus enhancing the horror of their deed, but it transpires that they were expected to do so. Her baptism or non-baptism of the baby could determine whether or not a woman was pardoned. Some women certainly claimed to have baptized their babies without having in fact done so. If the infanticide came to light and the mother was found, she was sentenced to death by burning or by being buried alive. In the thirteenth century the law differentiated between the first occasion, which could be regarded as an accident, and the second, which proved the woman to be a habitual offender. This distinction was abolished in the fourteenth century, but unpremeditated murder out of momentary rage or neglect continued to be distinguished from premeditated murder. In the latter case the punishment was burning or burial alive. The sentence was often carried out with savagery, particularly in Germany and adjacent areas of eastern France. In Metz in the fifteenth century, the executioners lopped off the woman's hand and tied it to the stake to which she was bound before burning her. After she had suffocated or burned to death, a wooden doll was placed in her arms, and a placard bearing the image of a child was tied round her neck.

The letters of remission were granted on the basis of certain statements under oath: that the accused had already spent two or three years in prison; that her past was blameless; that she had not intended to kill her infant but only to hide it; that she was very young; that she was under pressure from some other person (as in the case of a woman who bore a child to a priest); that she had since repented by fasting and prayer; or that, if her parents had not been barred from finding her a husband by their poverty, she would never have reached such a pass. In one case the accused woman swore that she had six small children and had already spent two years in prison, and if she were to be executed, her children would remain defenceless.[210]

Those women who were afraid to bear the bastards they carried in their wombs were alone in their fear and despair throughout their pregnancies up to the birth and the act of infanticide. From the letters of remission we learn that if the father played any part in the affair, it was by bringing violent pressure to bear on the mother to kill the child, as in the above cited case of the priest; or by violent treatment aimed at bringing about the birth of a stillborn child (as in the case of the husband who mercilessly beat his maid-servant wife who had become pregnant by her master, or the case of the master who beat his maid-servant who refused to admit her pregnancy). Cases in which men helped and supported women did not reach the courts and we have no way of knowing about them.

USE OF CONTRACEPTION

Contraception was known in the Middle Ages as it had been in Greek and Roman times. Through the medical writings of the Romans, and the Greek and Muslim writings translated into Latin, all the contraceptive devices known to the Romans were certainly known in the High Middle Ages. The school of Gerard of Cremona in Toledo translated the medical writings of Avicenna and Rhazes, which mention certain types of contraception known already to Aristotle, Hippocrates and Soranus of Ephesus: various potions distilled from plants, liquids introduced into the womb before or immediately after intercourse, gymnastic exercises which the woman performed after intercourse, and ointments smeared on the male genitals. Also known was 'the act of Onan', namely *coitus interruptus*, as well as 'unnatural relations'. The various contraceptive methods are listed in encyclopedic detail in the medical writings of Albertus Magnus, Arnold of Villanova and other authors whose works were studied in the medical faculties of universities.

Theologians, who dealt at length with the problem of the use of contraception, regarded it as one of the prime sins. Morally speaking, it was considered to reflect unrestrained lust and was as grave a sin as murder and pagan witchcraft. Though associated mainly with fornication and adultery, it was considered to be a particularly heinous sin when practised by married people. Extramarital sex was considered a sin in itself, and abstinence from procreation merely compounded the sin of adultery and fornication. Use of contraception in extramarital relations was preferable to the begetting of bastards, to abortion or to infanticide. As J. L. Flandrin puts it, among theologians who condemned contraception the associative context was apparently as follows: contraception goes with sexual fantasies, pleasure and barrenness; 'natural relations' go with lack of pleasure and fecundity.[211] In actual fact of course the two archetypes of sexual conduct were often confused, and proof of this was the birth of bastards.

Was knowledge of contraception widely prevalent in the High Middle Ages and, if so, was it put into practice? Or, as some Roman Catholic historians have tried to prove, did people refrain from applying their knowledge because of the Church ban?[212] J. T. Noonan, in his comprehensive study of the standpoint of Catholic theologians and canonists on contraception, also discusses the degree to which it was practised in medieval society. In his view, contraception played its part in medieval civilization, but it was not regarded as a socio-demographic threat. It had only a limited impact on demographic stability, which was preserved mainly because of the high mortality rate. Until the fourteenth century, contraception was almost certainly practised only by a minority, particularly in extramarital relations, to prevent the conception of bastards. It was not used extensively for economic reasons, to reduce the birthrate. But the author also stresses that data are not available. For obvious reasons, the issue was not discussed by courts, and the registers of ecclesiastical courts cite no cases in which people were accused of practising contraception. Its use is mentioned in various manuals for confessors, but there is no way of assessing how many people confessed to this sin.

One can only conclude that contraception was not widespread, in the light of several facts cited by the author. Manuals for apothecaries containing information on various therapeutic herbs scarcely mention contraceptive devices, so that one may assume that they were not often sold by apothecaries. Contraception is not mentioned in contemporary literature, even, in those works which condemn common sins. (One exception is the Priest's Tale in the

Canterbury Tales, where the narrator mentions the practice of contraception.) In secular law use of contraceptives is almost never mentioned, although secular legislation reflected the ecclesiastical stand on such matters as homosexuality, for example, so that in some Italian cities the secular fraternities considered it part of their tasks to expose homosexuals in the same fashion as heretics.[213]

As we have seen, theologians classified use of contraception as the most heinous of sins, but canon law does not echo this theological stand. The most stringent punishment it proposed was annulment of marriage, and lesser punishments included physical separation (*a thoro*) or granting the woman the right to refuse to fulfil her marital duties. (We say 'proposed' rather than imposed since as far as we know, neither men nor women were ever charged with using contraception and the laws were never enforced.) In contrast to those relatively lenient punishments, the sentence for homosexual relations or bestiality was burning at the stake after the prisoner had been handed over to the lay authorities. This leniency suggests that contraception was not considered a widespread practice which could endanger society as a whole. The fact that the birth of bastards was not uncommon indicated that even in extramarital relations contraception was not always practised.

Yet certain facts do indicate the limited utilization of contraceptive methods during the High Middle Ages, and particularly in the Late Middle Ages. In the first quarter of the fourteenth century the Dominican theologian Peter Plaude notes that some men have recourse to 'the act of Onan' in order to prevent the conception of more children than they can support. Several preachers reiterated this charge in the second half of the fourteenth century and the first half of the fifteenth. The population registers of the time reveal a considerable discrepancy between the number of offspring in poor families and in prosperous families in both town and country. There were undoubtedly several causes for this phenomenon. The children of the rich were better fed and cared for, and hence more of them survived than among the poor. The rich married younger, and the fertility span of both men and women was more extensively utilized. The rich also probably took greater pains to register their children. On the other hand, it is possible that contraception or *coitus interruptus* were practised by the poor, and that this helped to increase the gap. It is also interesting to note that preachers denouncing bachelors who did not wed for lack of money accused them of fornication, adultery and homosexuality, but not of begetting bastards. The preachers probably exaggerated, but at the same time it is unlikely that all bachelors remained celibate, and if they engaged in sexual relations without begetting bastards they must have been practising contraception. Both ecclesiastical and lay courts tried cases of adultery and fornication which had not yielded offspring, and it may be assumed that some, at least, of the accused had practised contraception.[214]

We can sum up the question of contraception and its implications for women, as follows: consistent with its view that sins against the institution of marriage, like sexual sins in general, were grave transgressions whether committed by men or women, the Church applied the same rules to both sexes where contraception was concerned. But, as can be ascertained from the confessors' manuals, use of contraception was undoubtedly regarded as a specifically female sin, one of the major subjects on which the confessor should question every woman.[215] The ban on contraception affected women more than men. Frequent confinements were exhausting for married women and often endangered their lives. The birth of a bastard (particularly if it was not acknowledged by the father) was harder on a woman than on a man. Sometimes an additional pregnancy could actually constitute a threat to the mother's life, and the Muslim Avicenna discusses at length the problem of use of contraception in such a case. Catholic theologians mostly ignored the problem, and those who mentioned it in passing state that this situation does not justify use of contraception. Nor do the theologians favour granting dispensation to a woman to refrain from her marital duties, though this solution would appear feasible if contraception was forbidden and pregnancy hazardous.

ABORTION

Like contraception, abortion was known both in Roman times and in the Middle Ages. Avicenna lists not only methods of contraception but also various measures which could cause abortion: gymnastic exercises, carrying heavy loads, hot baths and liquids injected into the womb. The Christian opposition to abortion was formulated in the first centuries of Christianity in relation to the theological significance of the injunction to love God and one's neighbour and on the basis of several verses in the Old and New Testament: 'And thou shalt love the Lord thy God with all thine heart and with all thy soul and with all thy might' (Deuteronomy 6:5); 'Thou shalt love thy neighbour as thyself; I am the Lord' (Leviticus 19:18); 'Thou shalt love the Lord thy God with all thy heart, and with all thy soul and with all thy mind. This is the first and great commandment. And the second is like unto it. Thou shalt love thy neighbour as thyself. On these two commandments hang all the law and the prophets' (Matthew 22:37–40). According to the theological interpretation, a man must fulfil these injunctions by bringing a sacrifice to his neighbour just as Christ sacrificed himself for the salvation of mankind. Abortion was an expression of unwillingness to make this sacrifice, and a transgression both against the injunction to love God and the injunction to love one's neighbour.

Following St Augustine, the medieval theologians and canonists distinguished between abortion of a foetus of less than forty days, defined as not yet having been given a soul by God, and abortion of a foetus of over forty days old with a soul of its own; the latter act was regarded as murder. The canonists proposed the same penalty in both cases, usually consisting of several years of penitence. The theological view of abortion as a grave sin was consistent with their view of contraception, while the canonists took a relatively lenient stand on both sins. In the case of abortion, as on contraception, there is no record of any individual actually being brought to trial. It is therefore difficult to know how prevalent abortion was in the Middle Ages. The secular court registers do not record charges of abortion and the subject is mentioned only by theologians and canonists, in manuals for confessors and in secular codes of law. The latter refer to abortion more than to contraception, just as manuals for apothecaries mention abortifacients more than contraceptives. Manuals for physicians sometimes prohibit response to a woman's plea for means of abortion.[216]

Contemporary beliefs linked witchcraft, abortion and prostitution. In Parma in 1233, Gerard of Modena denounced the poisoners who practised magic arts. He accused them of inducing abortions and making their shops into meeting places for purposes of fornication and adultery.[217] Nevertheless it is hard to believe that abortion constituted a socio-demographic threat. The large numbers of bastards reveal not only that use of contraception was not very prevalent, but also that abortions were not widespread. Avicenna, who justified use of contraception by a woman for whom additional pregnancy was hazardous, sanctioned abortion aimed at saving the mother's life. Catholic theologians, who did not acknowledge the right to use contraceptive methods even when a woman's life was at stake, also denied the right to carry out abortion in order to save the mother's life. The sole medieval Catholic theologians who accepted abortion in this case were John of Naples in the early fourteenth and Antoninus of Florence at the beginning of the fifteenth century, and they too only recognized it in the case of a foetus under forty days of age.[218]

If we turn from theology and law to the reality of everyday life, there can be no doubt that abortion was mainly the concern of the woman. It was a female sin, as can be learned from the confessors' manuals (though the means for abortion were sometimes supplied by men who engaged in medicine or sorcery). The ban on abortion, like the prohibition against use of contraception, led to unwanted births within the framework of marriage and the birth of bastards as a result of extramarital relations. Sometimes failure to abort endangered a woman's life. If she did abort, the fear and the emotional and physical suffering were hers alone, and under the hygienic and medical conditions prevailing at the time, the abortion itself was highly hazardous.

5

Women in the Nobility

As we saw in the introduction, most authors of 'estate literature' in the Middle Ages treated noblewomen as a subclass of their sex. Humbert de Romans devoted a sermon to laywomen in general and then separate sermons to various categories of women. The first of these separate sermons is devoted to noblewomen: their lot is a happy one as regards status and riches, he writes, so that more is demanded of them than of other women.[1]

The counterpart of the nobleman (*nobilis vir*) is the noblewoman (*nobilis femina* or *nobilis mulier*). In certain regions in certain periods during the Middle Ages the right to belong to the nobility was handed down on the maternal side, and in other regions at other times through the father. In the High Middle Ages the latter appears to have been more common.[2] The nobleman was also a knight – *miles* – and this word pointed to a status that differentiated him not only from the peasant (*rusticus*) but also from the foot soldier (*pedes*). As a knight, he was a warrior horseman who underwent the ceremony of initiation into the knighthood, which in the High Middle Ages was also of religious significance (so that the initiate became a Christian knight – *miles Christianus*). Knighthood created a common denominator for the different strata of the nobility in most countries of Western Europe.[3] As their name implied, the task of those who belonged to this class, and who were denoted warriors (*bellatores* or *pugnatores*), was to fight. In the literature depicting the sins and omissions of members of the various classes, the heaviest sin of noblemen is non-fulfilment of their function, which is to defend other classes.[4] The brave warrior was a central component of the ideal of knighthood and the name of *miles* predominated over all other designations of the nobleman, since it stressed his military function and image. Though socially divided, all warriors shared the chivalric ethos.[5]

The noblewoman was no warrior in medieval times just as she was never a fighter in any known society throughout history. And as far as we know from anthropological studies of primitive societies, almost every occupation – pot-making, weaving, agriculture, cooking and even child-raising – has been regarded at times as a female occupation, and at times as a task for men. But we know of no society in which fighting was ever considered a female occupation, or where women once constituted the warrior class.[6] Women sometimes defended castles during their husbands' absence. There were heiresses and widows who defended their fortresses, like Donna Jimena, widow of Le Cid, who for more than a year (1001–2) held Valencia, organized the army and beat off Muslim attacks.[7] Of the women who ruled territories, there were some who led their own armies, but one cannot say of noblewomen in general that they were counted among the warriors. Nor did women from other classes fight as infantry or ride as sergeants beside the knights into battle when a summons to service in the host was imposed in a certain area. It was for good reason that to the medieval mind the Amazons belonged in a distant and unknown world, the world of a race of monsters.[8]

The fief was originally granted to a warrior primarily as reward for military service, but in the transition from the Carolingian period to the first feudal era (tenth to eleventh centuries) the fief was no longer granted in return for military service, instead the service was rendered in return for the fief, and the scope of service was largely determined on the basis of the importance of the fief. Be that as it may, military service was the main obligation of the vassal towards his seigneur, from whom he received the fief. It was not feasible for a woman who was not a warrior and could not do military service to hold a fief, and in fact in the early days of the evolution of those ties of reciprocal dependence which entailed granting fiefs (or, as they were previously called, *beneficia*) only men held fiefs. But gradually the right became hereditary, at least *de facto*, and the fief was considered a patrimony; as such, despite the inherent contradiction, it could also be inherited by women.

The contradiction stemmed not only from the fact that the fief was connected with military service, but also from its links with various degrees of ruling powers. Sometimes such powers were granted to those holding fiefs, and sometimes they were seized by usurpation; in the general process of weakening of central power and relaxation of the political ties in favour of personal bonds of interdependence which occurred in the ninth century, even public offices (*honores*) became fiefs and as such were inheritable by women. The woman who inherited a fief which entailed ruling powers, exercised those powers, and in so doing violated the rulings of the canonists and lay legislators, which denied women such rights. Sometimes one clause of a legal code cites the physical weakness and mental limitations of women to justify depriving them of authority, while the following clause specifies ways in which the oath of fealty should be rendered by a woman who inherits a fief entailing ruling powers, and the best way in which lords and ladies can rule their vassals.[9]

The laws of inheritance of a fief varied from country to country in regard to male inheritance as well. Nor was the female right to inherit fiefs equally consolidated in that period in the various countries. In some countries it was established as early as the tenth century, and in others only in the twelfth. It appears that in the Central Middle Ages the right of women to inherit fiefs was recognized in most Western European countries. The rights of sons always took precedence over those of daughters in this respect, while daughters' rights prevailed against males of collateral lines in most regions. In the Central Middle Ages women could inherit fiefs in northern and southern France, in Hainaut, Flanders, west Lorraine, England, several regions of Italy and the kingdoms of Catalonia, Aragon and Castille.[10] In areas in which the principle of primogeniture prevailed, if the oldest child was a daughter, her younger brother inherited; she only inherited the fief if she had no brothers. The remaining sons and daughters, who did not inherit and lived secular lives, were compensated by some endowment.[11] If the daughters inherited, they usually received part of their inheritance as a dowry. If they did not inherit, and married, they received as dowry their endowment. In some fiefs, such as Lorraine, daughters inherited their mother's dowry.

In some areas (such as the royal domain in France), despite the fact that the principle of primogeniture was well established, the eldest of a family of daughters inherited the parental home and was responsible for the entire fief, which was divided up between her and her sisters according to the contract of *pariage* method (which had also applied to sons before primogeniture was accepted). The same was true in England and in some of the fiefs in Lorraine.[12] In other words the archaic custom persisted with regard to inheritance by daughters, but in the case of sons was replaced by the rule that the eldest inherited. In regions in which primogeniture was not accepted, and in which the extended family lingered on among the nobility (Franche Comté for example), the fief was sometimes divided up among the sons alone, and sometimes among both sons and daughters.[13] Here too, as in areas of primogeniture, only some of the sons and daughters were earmarked for marriage, while the remainder were directed to ecclesiastical careers or to monasteries.

The inheritance of a fief by daughters was not an extraordinary occurrence because of the high rate of unnatural death among men of the nobility. A study of ducal families in England in 1330–1475 shows that the average life-expectancy of men at birth was 24 years, and of women 32.9 years. The average life-expectancy of men who survived the age of 20 was 21.7 and of women at 20 was 31.1 years. The source of this discrepancy was the fact that 46 per cent of all men died violently after their fifteenth year: in wars, tournaments or by execution during civil wars. If the violent deaths were excluded from the calculation the discrepancy in life-expectancy was drastically reduced among men and women who reached the age of 20, and the life expectancy of men was even slightly higher. For men at 20 it was then 31.5 years, and for women 31.1. On the other hand, if violent death was taken into account, then in the 20–54 age-group, only 18 per cent of the men survived throughout (i.e. reached the age of 54), while among women of 20–49, 50 per cent lived out the period (i.e. reached the age of 49).[14] A study of families of secular peers in England between 1350 and 1500 shows that 20 per cent of the men died violent deaths, and 25 per cent of them never reached their fortieth year.[15]

In the twelfth and thirteenth centuries, noblemen also went on crusades from which they did not return with the result that the fief was inherited by women. The Castellan Henri de Bourbourg had twelve descendants who reached maturity. Seven of his sons entered the Church, and three sons were killed. The eldest son inherited, and on his death the youngest brother inherited. He had a son and a daughter. The son died in childhood and the entire fief came down to the daughter. (It is not surprising that several suitors competed for her favours!) Another example can be cited from the family of one of the most renowned noblewomen of the Middle Ages, Mahaut of Artois. Her grandfather was killed in battle at Mansura during Louis IX's first crusade, her brother Philip was killed in battle with the Flemish in 1298, her father Robert II was killed in the battle of Courtrai in 1302, and she inherited the county. Inheritances were quite often handed down to daughters in this fashion in total contradiction of the family's intention. Since they were not due to inherit, their fathers often married them off to members of less prosperous families of inferior status to themselves. They inherited when already married, and their husbands subsequently became their partners in managing large estates of great noblemen.[16]

Women owned fiefs not only by right of family inheritance but also by force of their right to part of their deceased husband's property (the dower or *dos* right). We discussed this issue in the chapter on married women. The widow (and because of the low life-expectancy of noblemen who reached adulthood, there were numerous widows) held one third to one half of her husband's property for life by right of dower. In this way fiefs came into the hands of widows who, like heiresses, were obliged to supply the required military service. If the fief entailed ruling powers, they exercised these powers, like Berta of Sweden, widow of Matthew I, duke of Lorraine, who presided over the duke's court, or Beatrice of Brabant, who held Courtrai by right of her dower in the last quarter of the thirteenth century and also presided over the court.[17] When the widows died, the property passed into the hands of their descendants through the husband who had originally left the property, and if he had no progeny, his relatives inherited. The widows swore an oath of fealty to the seigneur and in some areas even to the heir of the fief to whom it would revert after their death.[18] In Metz widows of noblemen who were citizens of the town participated in the political meetings of the nobility.

Women did not only inherit fiefs, they also bequeathed them. It is almost certain that one of the reasons why members of the nobility were sometimes named after their mothers and not their fathers, even when they were legal progency, derives from the fact that they received the bulk of their inheritance through their mothers.[19]

As we have noted, there was nothing unusual in a woman holding a fief. Perusal of the list of vassals of the counts of Champagne and Brie from 1172 to 1361, for example, reveals all the ways in which the fief was held and transferred by women. The registers show women who held fiefs by right of inheritance and gave homage to the count; women who held fiefs by right of dower and gave homage to the count; and men who held fiefs through inheritance from their mothers. There is even a record of a countess who held one fief by right of inheritance, a second by right of dower, and for the third did homage as representative of her brother.[20] The same was true in England. The registers compiled in order to collect the feudal aid mention women who, in the twelfth and thirteenth centuries, held large fiefs directly bestowed by the king, like Isabella de Fortibus, countess of Albemarle, who had dozens of subvassals who held her fiefs; women who held fiefs as subvassals, including some who held fiefs from women, like Haswisia, who held a fief from Johanna de Cyrcester in the hundred of Stanburgh; many women who held parts of fiefs and some who held fiefs by right of guardianship over their sons.[21] The documents of transfer, sale and lease of lands in various regions also indicate the high percentage of land held by women. A considerable proportion of these lands was held as fiefs (the rest as allods). The fact that women held landed property is revealed by Pierre Dubois' plan for the recovery of the Holy Land. He wrote that it was necessary to approach all landowners, men and women, and ask them to recruit money for the warriors. Both married women and widows should be approached.[22]

MARRIAGE AMONG THE NOBILITY

Marital ties among the nobility were based on class, economic and political calculations. Marriage ties with the right family could lead to links between lineages and help to create alliances and agreements. Marriage to an heiress expanded territories, created contiguous areas under the ownership of the same family, and increased its economic and political power. Sometimes such arrangements among the senior nobility even brought about changes in the political map of Europe, as in the case of marriages between royal families. For example, in 1112, as a result of the third marriage of the count of Barcelona, Raymond Berengar III, to Douce, heiress of the county of Provence and several other areas, the counts of Barcelona became the rulers of contiguous territories on the Mediterranean coast from La Roya to the Ebro river.[23] The marriage of Louis VII, king of France, to Eleanore, famous heiress of the duchy of Aquitaine, greatly expanded the domain of the Capetian kings. Her second marriage, after the annulment of her marriage to Louis VII, to Henry, count of Anjou, who became king of England two years later, doubled the land holdings of the Angevin kings on French soil and created an amalgamated land holding in the west of the country. Marriage to an heiress from the middle and minor nobility also entailed consolidation of ties and expansion of territories some degree. If the bride was not an heiress she brought her dowry with her to her marriage.[24]

The mere fact that marriages were arranged by families for class and economic reasons was not characteristic of the nobility alone. Such interests also motivated marital arrangements in the urban class and among the middle-level and prosperous peasantry. What distinguished marital arrangements among the nobility in the Middle Ages was not only the fact that they sometimes involved political interests, but also the fact that the feudal lord could intervene in them. The daughter who inherited the fief or the widow who held it by right of dower could not supply the required military service. Hence, if she married, her husband did so. The lord was therefore anxious to ensure that a suitable and reliable man undertook this task. If the fief entailed ruling powers and the holder married, some of these powers were exercised by her husband. The lord rewarded his vassal for service and loyalty by marrying him to the heiress of a fief. To marry one of his sons to an heiress strengthened the lord's authority. And vice versa: the marriage of the heiress of a fief or a widow who held a fief to the enemy of the seigneur endangered his position. In the light of these facts, the marriages of noble heiresses were arranged not only by the family but also by the lord, sometimes despite fierce opposition from both the girl or the widow and her family.

In areas in which the territory was headed by a strong feudal lord and where a centralized feudal regime existed, as in England, Normandy or Sicily, there was particularly strong intervention on the part of the lord, i.e. the king or duke, in the marriages of the daughters and widows of his direct vassals. The widow, who had freed herself to a large extent from the intervention of her own family, could not escape the intervention of the seigneur unless she paid goodly sums for her freedom. According to Frederick II's code for Sicily, direct vassals of the Emperor were forbidden to take wives or to marry off their daughters, sons and sisters without his approval.[25] In the Coronation Charter of Henry I of England (1100), the lord's right to intervene in the marriages of heiresses and widows is taken as self-evident. The concessions and guarantees apply only to payments and to the avoidance of coercion in marriage.[26] The heiress or her father were forced to pay if they refused to accept the candidate proposed by the lord and were also obliged to pay out money in order to receive the lord's approval of marriage to their chosen bridegroom. As for the bridegroom, he paid the lord for the privilege of marrying the heiress he had chosen.

In this way the marriages of heiresses and widows were one of the feudal sources of income for lords, like wardship, the lord's use of the income of ecclesiastical fiefs while they were vacant, and relief. The payment of such sums caused considerable financial hardship to the young woman and her family, but was often a substitute for coercion and won a certain measure of freedom, if not for the girl herself then for her family. In the case of the widow it was she herself who, as a result of the payment, was free to refuse marriage offers or to wed whomsoever she chose.

Numerous documents have survived from twelfth- and thirteenth-century England recording how the king gave the daughter of one of his noble vassals with all her future inheritance in marriage to another of his vassals. In 1111, Henry I gave a document to Miles of Gloucester, according to which Sybil, daughter of Bernard, was given him in marriage with all the lands she was due to inherit in the future from her parents. The marriage was arranged on the wishes of the father of the heiress, who paid the king for his consent to the arrangement.[27] In 1185, investigators were sent to the various shires to clarify and report on which widows had re-wed and not paid the king, and they were forced to do so.[28] Not only did the king demand payment for the marriage of heiresses, but also his vassals exercised the same right over their own vassals. One vassal argued in court in 1230 that the noble Adam had sold him Emma with her land – in other words he had paid a considerable sum for the right to marry her.[29]

The lord's right to intervene, which constituted the justification for payment, gradually evolved in the thirteenth century into the right to collect money alone. In the fourteenth century the kings of England (and their vassals with respect to subvassals) waived the right to actual intervention and contented themselves with collecting money. In France too, the king was known to intervene in the marriages of heiresses to his vassals. The first marriage of Eleanor of Aquitaine to the French heir (later Louis VII) was arranged by his father, Louis VI, the seigneur of her own father, William X, duke of Aquitaine, who, on his deathbed, entrusted his daughter to his seigneur. In 1215 Philip II of France submitted to the count of Nevers a list of nobles to whom he was forbidden to marry his daughter. One of those on the list was Hugh IV, who later became duke of Burgundy and was then one year old! The legal code of Lousi IX stipulated as law that a vassal was not permitted to marry off his daughter without the consent of the seigneur.[30] According to the legislation of Heinrich IV of Germany, as a condition for her inheritance of the county the heiress of Hainaut was obliged to consult her seigneurs, the bishop of Liège and the duke of Lorraine, before marrying.[31]

There were isolated cases of women who succeeded, despite the intervention of their families and of the seigneur, in acting independently, evading the constraints of the law and overruling the customs of their society to select their own mates. Matilda, countess of Tuscany, for example, fought the Emperor Heinrich IV, together with the reform popes, and in 1080 and 1102 she bequeathed her extensive allodial lands to the papacy. Out of personal choice and political considerations she married the duke of Bavaria, who was many years her junior and the sworn enemy of the Emperor. Eleanor of Aquitaine almost certainly married Henry, count of Anjou, her junior by ten years, out of more than political considerations. After the annulment of her marriage to Louis VII she fled her many suitors by escaping Louis' territory by night with her companions and riding to Poitiers. Two months later she married Henry of Anjou.[32] As regards the gentry, the daughter of the Paston family, despite the efforts of her family to arrange a suitable match for her, and their vehement opposition to her own chosen bridegroom (a bailiff on their estate), married him, at first in private, and later in church.[33] There were apparently exceptions to C. Lévi-Strauss's rule that a woman is always given to her future husband by another man (her father, brother, uncle etc.).

The daughters (and the sons) of the nobility were often betrothed while still in their cradles, particularly among the senior nobility. This was one of the measures employed by noble families in order to evade royal coercion. If the father of the heir or heiress died, they were betrothed by their guardians at a very early age. There were numerous cases of marriages of minors, again mainly in the higher nobility. According to the fifteenth-century jurist Littleton, when a seigneur's daughter reached the age of 7, her father was entitled to demand feudal aid from his vassals in order to marry her off. When she reached her ninth year she was entitled to receive her allotted dowry. In the thirteenth century, Maurice, the third lord of Berkeley, took to wife Eva, daughter of the lord of Zouch. Both husband and wife were 8 years old. Before they reached their fourteenth birthdays they had become parents. Their children married at the same age as had their parents.[34] According to canon law, the minimal age of matrimony for a girl was 12 and for a boy 14. If the lord of Berkeley became a father before he was 14, his marriage must have been consummated earlier than canon law allowed.

On the other hand, Froissart relates a story which indicates that the age of consummation was delayed beyond that specified by law. He recounts that the duke of Berry fell in love with Jeanne, daughter of the count of Boulogne, who was many years his junior. She lost her father while still a child and was placed under the wardship of the Count of Foix, who opposed her marriage to the duke. The duke appealed to his nephew, King Charles vi, to help him to persuade the count to agree to the match. On hearing the story, Charles vi smiled and said: 'And what will you do with a child of twelve?' The duke replied: 'I will guard her for three of four years until she becomes a perfect woman!'[35] It is of course difficult to draw conclusions from isolated and conflicting examples on general customs with regard to consummation of marriages. It is known, in any event, that minors who were married to one another sometimes continued to live apart for several years, with their respective parents or guardians. But there can be no doubt that sometimes actual coercion was used. Richard, earl of Arundel, and Isabella, daughter of Hugh le Despenser, both members of the high nobility in England in the fourteenth century, succeeded after protracted deliberations at various levels of ecclesiastical courts, in annulling their marriage. They claimed to have been married at the ages of 7 and 8 without mutual consent, for fear of their relatives. When they reached adulthood both explicitly objected to the marriage, but were forced, by blows, to cohabit, and a son was born to them.[36] In this case an annulment was obtained, but we do not know how often a couple dared to attempt this (such annulment involving complicated property settlements), and if they did try, how many succeeded, particularly if they had already consummated the marriage, as in the above-cited case.

But not all couples, of course, were married as minors. J. C. Russell, in a study based on registers of feudal inheritances, particularly of royal vassals in England, came to the conclusion that during the reign of Edward i (i.e. at the end of the thirteenth century) the average marriage age for men was 24. Under Edward ii it was 22; under Edward iii, 20. In other words the average age of matrimony fell during the fourteenth century. The age of matrimony for women was slightly lower than for men.[37] According to G. Duby, in northwest France the age of matrimony for men in the twelfth century was the late twenties, particularly among sons who did not inherit. Only marriage to an heiress or the possessor of a dowry enabled them to set up their own homes. First-born sons married younger.[38] A study of ducal families in England in 1330–1475 indicates that the average age of marriage for men was 22, and for women, 17. First-born sons who inherited the estate usually married earlier than their younger brothers.[39] It is clear, in any event, that daughters of the nobility married young. If they were heiresses who had already been allotted a portion of their inheritance in the form of a dowry, they were not obliged to await their father's death in order to marry. If they were not heiresses, their endowment was determined at an early stage and they were married off young. It was also decided at an early stage, as we have seen, which of the daughters would take the veil, and she was dispatched to a nunnery while still a child. One of the characteristics of what J. Hajnal has denoted as the West European marriage patterns in modern times, i.e. a relatively high age of marriage among women, was non-existent among the medieval nobility.[40]

People tended to marry members of their own class, but this was not always possible. Every effort was usually devoted to finding a suitable mate for an heiress, or a suitable wife for the heir. As for the other offspring, compromises were often made. In northern France it was usually the wife who belonged to a nobler family. She married a noble of a lower status than herself either because her parents could not provide her with a dowry big enough for a more satisfactory match, or because of pressure from the seigneur.[41] In Mâcon in the thirteenth century, noblewomen sometimes even married men from other classes, sons of *ministeriales* or of prosperous peasants who preferred marriage to a noblewoman to a large dowry, while noblemen always married women from their own class or a higher one.[42] In England, on the other hand, there were men who took wives from a lower class. Among the gentry more men than women married into the urban class, and some men from the senior nobility even took wives from among the daughters of merchants. In this way some daughters of the urban class climbed the social ladder. An example is Matilda Fraunther of London. Her first marriage was to one of the richest young merchants in London. Her second husband was Sir Alan Buxhill, a courtier, and her third husband was John de Montacute, who later became earl of Salisbury.[43]

Nonetheless, relatives on the maternal side were also taken into consideration in determining social status. Although the principle of affiliation to the paternal branch evolved gradually, both maternal and paternal ancestry were considered in the social assessment of people, and marriage to a woman of higher standing elevated the status of a nobleman; in a purely patriarchal society (the Muslim society of the time, for example)[44] such a marriage did not influence a man's standing. A reflection of the honour accruing to a family from a marriage contracted with a woman from a more prominent family was the addition of the woman's family heraldic bearings to those of her husband, to be engraved on dishes and books, as a sign of the uniting of dynasties. Marriage marked a new stage in life of both men and women. The nobleman became a *vir* only when he took a wife. Prior to that he was considered a *juventus*, even if he married late.

The nobility tried to marry off their daughters at any price and there can be little doubt that the number of unmarried noblemen who continued to live in the secular world was very limited.[45] At the same time, because of the tendency of noblemen to marry members of their own class, they often violated the incest laws. The Church proved itself reasonably flexible here, particularly if the relationship was at third or fourth remove; in return for payment it granted dispensations for marriage.[46] Among the nobility there were also cases of annulled marriages, though these were apparently few. Annulment, like marriage, involved political, class and economic interests. Sometimes a marriage was annulled on the grounds that from the first (*ab initio*) it had been invalid; an example is the marriage of the couple mentioned above, who were forced into the match in childhood. Some noblemen succeeded in ridding them-selves of their wives on grounds of real or fictitious adultery, particularly if they were on good terms with leading churchmen who were willing to collaborate, (at least that is what Gilbert of Nogent tells us). It will be recalled that, according to canon law, adultery did not necessarily justify annulment of marriage. But charges of adultery were apparently sometimes accepted as proper grounds. Acts of vengeance by the husband against his unfaithful wife characterized the nobility more than any other stratum of medieval society. Adultery by a woman was considered not merely an act of infidelity to her husband, but also an offence against the honour of the entire dynasty.[47] Only extremely rarely, apparently, did a noblewoman initiate annulment of marriage. Maud Clifford succeeded in annulling her marriage to John de Neville, Lord Latimer, on the grounds of impotence.

Marriages were annulled because the relationship had been a failure from the outset, or because the man was tired of his wife and desired another woman, or because the new match was likely to bring him greater political and economic advantages, but most marriages endured. What kind of relationships were they? Marriage was not based on free choice in any stratum of medieval society, but the higher nobility were undoubtedly faced with the most limited range of choice of all. They generally did not even enjoy the opportunities given to members of other classes: to reconcile natural predilections and class obligations and to 'fall in love' within the given framework. John of Gaunt no doubt loved his mistress of many years, Catherine Swynford, but he married her only in his old age. The minor nobility enjoyed slightly more freedom of choice, and the men were freer to choose than the women. In marriage, the husband predominated by force of law and with the guidance of homiletic literature. Many women feared their husbands, and some were even beaten by them. Law and custom permitted a man, whatever his class, to bring his superior physical strength to bear against the woman who was supposed to be his helpmate. In one of the Lives of the saints, the author writes of the nobleman Hugh, who hit his wife in the face with his fist until the blood spurted on his clothes.[48] Depression and hostility were the prevailing moods in the lives of some of the nobility, as in the description by a chronicler of the marriage of Margaret de Rivers, as English noblewoman:

> The law married them, love and the marriage bed,
> But what kind of law? What kind of love?
> What kind of marriage?
> A law that was no law, a love that was hate,
> A marriage that was separation.[49]

Sometimes there was love, as in the relationship of Margaret Paston and her husband. Their correspondence reflects the love of this woman, who was unfeeling towards all others (including her daughters), for her husband. Which was more characteristic? We cannot answer this question.

THE NOBLEWOMAN AS MOTHER

Noble families, rich towndwellers and prosperous peasants had more progeny than did the poor. The children of the rich were better cared for and enjoyed better living conditions than the offspring of the poor, and their chances of survival were greater. The rich also married younger, and exploited the fertility span of both men and women to the full.[50] They were probably also more scrupulous in registering the births of their children, and they apparently often took greater care to register the births of sons than of daughters. According to the registers in the families of the dukes and counts of Lorraine, in the twelfth century 64 per cent of the progeny were sons. In the families of other seigneurs and castellans, 72 per cent of the registered progeny were sons. The discrepancy is impossible, and derives from the fact that daughters were given two names, which misled the genealogists; daughters who entered nunneries did not usually appear in family registers; daughters who did not marry well were not registered, and generally speaking less care was taken in the registration of girls.[51]

The number of sons and daughters of the nobility who married and in various ways shared in the division of the family property was restricted by the family for economic and class reasons. In the region of the Cluny monastery in Burgundy, according to the studies of G. Duby, only one out of four or five sons in a noble family would be permitted to marry. The remainder went into the service of the Church, entered monasteries or remained bachelors in the secular world. The daughters who were not destined to wed entered nunneries.[52] Those who set up their own families, on the other hand, did not apparently limit the number of their progeny. Hence there was supervision of the establishment of new families but no control of the birthrate in these families.

In Lorraine, in the twelfth and thirteenth centuries, both among the dukes and counts and among castellans, the average number of children per family was six. In Mâcon in the twelfth century the average was from four to six.[53] In northwest France in the twelfth century, from five to seven children per family on the average would reach maturity. In English ducal families in 1330–1479, where both parents lived through the entire fertility span the average number of offspring was 4.6. But the number fluctuated from family to family. Some 27 per cent of the men in ducal families had no progeny at all, and the same was true of 23 per cent of the women.[54] This meant that fertile families had a very high number of children. The infant and child mortality rate was high in this class too. Some 36 per cent of male babies and some 29 per cent of female infants in ducal families died before their fifth year. Nor did mortality strike all families to the same degree, for the number of progeny varied greatly from family to family. In Mâcon, some families had six children and others none at all. In the family of the counts of Sarrebruck in Lorraine in the thirteenth century, one son had four offspring, the eldest son either had none or none survived to inherit, while the youngest son had twelve children.[55] In England too, in the fourteenth century, there were families where no legitimate children survived to inherit (and they then required their bastards), while on the other hand there are known cases of large families of five, eight or even ten children.[56]

Noblewomen did not usually suckle their children. They kept wet-nurses in their homes, and the wages of the wet-nurse in great families were particularly high. Chroniclers make specific note of mothers who suckled their own infants, such as the mother of Bernard of Clairvaux, who had seven children, all of whom she breast-fed. When children were weaned they were handed into the care of a nurse, and they were usually sent away from home at an early age. The children of many noblemen were sent at the age of 6 or 7 to the courts of other lords to be educated there. Children who were sent to town schools or schools attached to monasteries were usually dispatched there very young, and lived on the spot: in the monasteries, in their tutors' homes or in colleges. Sons intended for the monastic life were also sent to monasteries in early childhood. The fate of girls was similar. Those destined to take the veil were often placed in nunneries as small children, while others who were not earmarked for the monastic life were sent to nunneries to be educated. Others were sent, like their brothers, to the courts of lords, to study good manners and conduct suitable to their class.[57] Of the girls betrothed while still minors, some were sent immediately after the betrothal to live and be educated in the family of the intended bridegroom. In the early thirteenth century, Elizabeth, daughter of King Andrew of Hungary, was betrothed at the age of four to the Landgraf of Thuringia. In the same year she was sent to the palace of Wartburg, and lived there until her marriage, at the age of 14, and subsequently until the death of her husband. (Her marriage was among the happy ones.) When the girls who were not intended for monastic lives completed their education they usually married and never returned to live in the parental home.

The span of childhood was brief, and children were absorbed at an early age into the society of adults. But sons of the nobility enjoyed a period of youth and youthful society which their sisters never experienced. In the twelfth century, the period in which the boy was trained as a warrior (and was known as *puer* or *adolescentulus*) was followed by the period when he was a *juventus*. He had already completed his military training, borne arms and become a knight together with his contemporaries. Now came the period of adventure, the search for tournaments, drinking and carousing. Many met their deaths in this period, and for many it lasted too long, and they continued this mode of living only because they had not yet received estates and could not marry. But there was also liberty and enchantment in this life.[58] Among girls there was an almost direct transition from childhood to marriage, with all it entailed. Even during the brief period in which children lived in the parental home, many fathers were absent for protracted periods: they went on crusades, to war or to serve their king or seigneur.

There can be no doubt that the mother fulfilled a more important function than the father in the life of a small child. The life-expectancy of noblemen, as we have seen, was low. Many children lost their fathers at an early age; their mothers would then act as their guardians, and often defended their rights and jealously guarded their estates. Some of them, by force of their guardianship, exercised the ruling powers inherited by the minor child. Some were forced to repel the attempts of pretenders to the inheritance and to take over the fief by court order, by establishing diplomatic ties and by military action.

Blanche of Navarre, widow of the count of Champagne, Thibaud III, was guardian of her minor son, and ruled the county in 1213–22. She did homage to King Philip II of France and attended his baronial assembly at court in 1213. Blanche repelled a claimant to the county (on grounds of marriage to the daughter of the previous count of Champagne, Henry II) by strengthening her fortifications and making special payments to her vassals to consolidate their ties of fealty. She also conducted negotiations with the pope and the king of France to recruit their support for her son. During her rule she managed the financial affairs of the county with greater caution and wisdom than any of her predecessors or successors. She married her son to the widow of the duke of Lorraine, whose dowry enlarged the territory he controlled. In 1222 she handed the county over to him.[59] In Catalonia, Countess Ermessend, as guardian of her son and later of her grandson, ruled the county of Barcelona, Gerona and Ausone.[60] Many other women who were guardians to their sons who had inherited fiefs, ruled on their behalf and defended their rights. Even if the son was earmarked for an ecclesiastical career, the widowed mother could use her contacts to ensure him of a suitable position and a profitable prebend. According to Gilbert of Nogent, only in the course of time did his mother realize that she had acted in a manner which was not beneficial for the salvation of his soul.[61]

In contrast to the situation in France and Catalonia, English noblewomen did not act as guardians for their sons who inherited fiefs. If there were several children, only those who had not inherited were entrusted to the guardianship of their mother. The heir or heiress was given into the custody of a guardian appointed by the lord, and it was this guardian who arranged their marriages.[62]

There can be little doubt that, like other classes of society, the nobility cared for their children. Their concern was reflected in having them educated as befitted their class, safeguarding their future by finding them suitable posts, allotting them estates, arranging marriages and bequeathing property to them. If the father died, the mother fulfilled all these functions. What was the attitude of noblewomen towards their children? The source material teaches us more about the accepted educational methods and mothers' activities on behalf of their children than about their emotional ties. Here and there we find expressions of the lack of emotional ties, or of fear at bringing children into the world. In the letters of Héloïse to Abélard, for example, their son is never mentioned. Abélard himself mentions in one sentence that after his birth, his parents left him with Abélard's sister in Brittany. But Héloïse, who relates the tale of their love with sorrow, guilt, desire and yearning, never once mentions the child. Her only reference to him is in a letter to Peter the Venerable in which she asks him to try to obtain some kind of prebend for him. He was then a young man in his early twenties.

Nor does Christine de Pisan make any mention of her young children. She, who mourned her dead husband in numerous poems, never writes a word about one of her children who died in infancy. She merely notes the fact of his birth. In writing of her two surviving children, she refers only to their adulthood. She writes of her daughter who became a nun, and describes in detail one of her visits to her together with a group of friends. The main description is devoted to the ride to the nunnery, the landscape and the time she spent with her friends. Very little space is devoted to the daughter herself and her life in the nunnery. But Christine was concerned for her son. At the age of 13, she sent him to be educated in England at the court of the earl of Salisbury, and on his return she arranged for his further education at the court of a French nobleman.

It was apparently during her son's stay in England that Christine wrote *Les Enseignements que je Christine donne à Jean Castel mon fils*.[63] This is a work lacking in originality, and many such were written in the High Middle Ages. A similar work was written by Abélard for his son Astrolabe.[64] The advice in this work is based in part on the writings of Roman classicists and Church Fathers, and partly on folk tales and proverbs. As in other works of this type, no specific reference is made to the particular problems of a boy of 13, and the words of guidance are aimed at a young man and father.

Christine de Pisan was undoubtedly a woman of sensibility, as we shall see in analysing her work, but her writings display few traces of feeling towards her children. She was a responsible mother, worked to support her children and concerned herself with their education, but without displaying affection and tenderness, at least not in writing.

Women sometimes expressed their reservations at the thought of bearing and raising children. In one of the women troubadours' songs mentioned above, the poetess describes two women asking a third if they should marry. Says one: 'Shall I marry someone we both know? or shall I stay unwed? that would please me, for making babies does not seem so good and it's too anguishing to be a wife.' The second says: 'I'd like to have a husband, but making babies I think is a huge penitence; your breasts hang way down and it's too anguishing to be a wife.'[65] In contrast, the German poetess Frau Ava wrote of herself that she was the mother of two children, one living and one dead, both of whom were very dear to her, and in her poems she appeals to her readers to pray for her dead child.

Sometimes a mother was domineering and heavy-handed, as the Paston correspondence shows. Daughters are sent away to be educated and their wishes are not taken into account; husbands are chosen for them irrespective of their own desires; a daughter's objections are dismissed to the point where she is cruelly beaten, and she is sent away all the same. In the Paston family the mothers seem to have treated their sons better than their daughters. They sometimes mediated between son and father, and extended financial aid to sons.[66] In this family the mothers domineered overtly, and this trait was not camouflaged as excessive concern. The children of the nobility apparently suffered more from lack of maternal concern or overt domineering than from the pressures of a frustrated mother who disguised her domineering as excessive mother love.[67] On the other hand, the sources also reveal cases of consideration and sympathy on the part of the mother. In the lives of the saints, many of whom were members of the nobility, the mother often plays a more important role in the education of the child than the father, and is more sympathetic towards him. St Hugh, abbot of Cluny and elder son of the earl of Semur-en-Brionnais, was destined by his father to be a knight, though he showed no proclivity or talent for this life. His mother, unlike his father, understood his feelings and set him on his religious path.[68] According to one of the biographers of Anselm of Canterbury, he was sent in his childhood to a tutor (who was also a relative). The tutor forced him to study day and night and did not permit him to go out to play with other children. The child almost broke down and was returned to his mother completely disturbed. He refused to speak to her or look at her. His mother, filled with sorrow and pain, feared that she might lose him and decided to practise complete permissiveness. She ordered the servants to allow him to do anything he chose, and never to beat him. Some time later he again became a normal and happy child. Anselm never forgot her wise action, her sensitivity and love for him.

Gilbert of Nogent, in his autobiography, written partly under the inspiration of St Augustine, describes his love for his mother and praises her beauty, modesty, piety, strength and concern for him. His father died when the child was only 8 months old, and he writes that it was to the benefit of both that God gave him death. If he had remained alive he would probably have violated the vow he took while Gilbert's mother was suffering in labour, that if the child lived he would be dedicated to the religious life, and would have forced him to take up a military career.[69] (These remarks recall something that Jean-Paul Sartre wrote in his autobiography *Les Mots*: 'If he had lived, my father would have lain down on me and crushed me. Fortunately he died young ...')[70]

In contrast to the prevailing custom, Gilbert, the youngest of the family, lived in the maternal home until he was 12 and studied with a private tutor. The tutor was a dedicated but harsh man who did not spare his pupil, and lacked sufficient knowledge and pedagogic talent. Only at the age of 13 was Gilbert sent to a monastery, after his mother had herself entered a nunnery. There can be no doubt that his ties with his mother were strong, and left their mark on the development of his personality all his life, but in his writings we detect a note of bitterness at the absence of tenderness. His mother, who was an unyielding and pious woman, cared for him but never displayed tenderness or warmth towards him.

Several psychologists have claimed that in a patriarchal society in which the father rules the home, the mother is the ally and confidante of the children. As we have seen, there are more examples of sympathy and consideration on the part of the mother than of the father in the nobility, but we cannot be sure that this was a characteristic phenomenon. Le Roy Ladurie's theory that the images of little adults in the iconography of the Middle Ages do not so much reflect the feelings of contemporary society towards childhood, as express the longing of adult male artists for maternal tenderness and pampering,[71] is far-reaching but not improbable.

Ambivalence in the emotions of parents towards their children and vice versa is a known phenomenon in all periods. (To cite Sartre again: 'To bring children into the world – there is nothing better, but for a man to have children – is a crime! And amidst all the Aeneases who carry their fathers on their backs, I travel from coast to coast alone, and in my heart abhorrence of all those hidden progenitors who continue to ride on their sons, as long as the sons live.')

There were undoubtedly sensitive and loving mothers in medieval times who bestowed warmth and affection on their children. But the social structure and educational system of medieval nobility often precluded the possibility of creating close ties between mothers and children, and sometimes also petrified their natural capacity for love. The registers of the Inquisition court at Pamiers presided over by bishop Jaques Fournier, record the remarks of a witness about a noblewoman from Chateauverdun who was about to leave her home and join the Cathars:

> She had an infant in the cradle and she wanted to see him before she left home. When she beheld him she kissed him and the babe began to smile. She moved away from the cradle in order to leave the room, but retraced her footsteps and again approached the babe. He again smiled, and this happened several times more. She could not leave him. In the end she said to her maidservant: 'Take him out of the room.'

The young woman was burned at the stake by the Inquisition shortly afterwards.[72] This touching story speaks for itself, and concerns a young infant, but we have no way of knowing whether this fond young mother would not have raised him in the customary manner of her class if she had stayed with him – a manner which often distorted normal relationships.

WOMEN'S RULE IN THE FIEF

A woman who inherited a fief whose ownership brought seigneurial powers also inherited the whole scope of authority within her domain, and only the military service due from her was provided by someone else. As we have noted, almost all heiresses, without exception, married, and according to the various matrimonial laws the husband was responsible for the property of the couple and enjoyed its income, and was restricted only by the ban on damaging his wife's property. But despite these laws, it seems that, in most regions, women who inherited such fiefs did not actually forfeit their authority after their marriage. The greatest restriction of the rights of the married woman occurred in England.[73] A woman did not do homage there, but merely swore the oath of fealty.[74] When she married her husband did homage for her fief just as all her vassals did homage to her husband.[75] In Catalonia the husband did homage to the seigneur for the portion of his wife's inheritance which she received as a dowry. For the inheritance which was not part of the dowry she herself did homage.[76] In most of the great territorial principalities in France and the Netherlands, and in western Lorraine, heiresses did homage, and so did women who held fiefs by right of dower. If the heiresses married, their husbands too did homage to the seigneur.

In all regions a clear distinction was drawn between a fief which a man held in his own right and one that he held by right of his wife, and between what he gave as a fief to a vassal of his own and what he gave when acting for his wife. Guy of Thouars, the husband of Constance, countess of Brittany, referred to 'Constance, my wife and the countess of Brittany, into whose hands the county of Brittany came by right of the inheritance and through her to me by means of marriage to her'.[77] In some of the territorial principalities held as fiefs of the king of France, like Flanders, on the death of the countess, holder of the fief, her husband lost the right to the county. Thus Baldwin VIII in 1194 and Thomas of Savoy in 1244 were deprived of the county on the death of their wives, the countesses of Flanders, Margaret of Alsace and Jeanne.[78]

As noted, the greatest restriction of the rights of heiresses was in England, but here too a distinction was drawn between the fief a man held by his own right and that he held by right of his wife, as in the case of Robert de Strodley, who is mentioned in registers drawn up for the purpose of collecting the feudal aid in the 1280s as holder of the village of Shipley in Derby in the name of his wife.[79] In France and the Netherlands, on the other hand, it seems that when territorial principalities which entailed the exercise of extensive ruling powers came into the hands of women, these women exercised their rights not only before they married or when they were widowed (and most outlived their husbands and remarried) but also during their marriages; their husbands cooperated with them. This was true in Hainaut, Artois, Flanders, Brabant, and other seigneuralties in southern France and Catalonia, as well as in Tuscany and Savoy. Beatrice, the countess of Tuscany, ruled Tuscany in 1015–76. Her daughter, Matilda, who has been mentioned in the context of her marriage, ruled Tuscany in 1076–1115. She played an active role, as ally of Pope Gregory vii, in the struggle against Heinrich iv. In the manuscript of her biography (*Vita Matildis*), part of which was composed in her lifetime by Donizone, Matilda is seen mediating between emperor and pope. This was in 1077, when she was 31 years old and widowed for one year.[80] She was also active on behalf of the guilds of her town, Florence.

As examples of the activities of women who inherited territorial seigneuralties let us survey in brief the careers of two women. The first, Mahaut, countess of Artois, married but was widowed after reigning for one year, and therefore, in effect, ruled alone. The second, Jeanne, countess of Flanders and Hainaut, married twice and ruled for part of her.reign as a married woman, but herself exercised extensive ruling powers.

Mahaut of Artois inherited the county from her father in 1302 (her brother was killed in battle with the Flemish in 1298, and her husband Otho was killed in 1303). Throughout her reign she was forced to battle with her nephew, who claimed the county, and she prevailed over him. She crushed all attempts at rebellion by vassals. In 1315 she was summoned to the royal court in Paris, where the count of Flanders was on trial. She forcefully defended her judicial authority against infringement by ecclesiastical institutions, as in her battle against the monastery of St Waast in Arras for judicial power on the question of bastards.[81] The accounts of her bailiffs and of her personal household reveal diligent and organized management of financial matters. All payments were made on the basis of accounts submitted by bailiffs, moneylenders or suppliers. Each account was examined, supervised and marked by a committee appointed by the countess.[82]

Mahaut issued a number of charters to cities in which she not only ratified privileges granted by the counts of Artois, her predecessors, but also determined new legal procedures, determined the method of election of *échevins* (municipal magistrates) and the way in which reports were to be submitted to her. She intervened in internal disputes in towns and after hearing both sides, gave judgment. Sometimes she intervened directly in the election of urban officials and transferred prisoners from town gaols to her own prisons.[83] She also gave judgment on matters related to the textile industry in various towns. In Hesdin, her capital, she set up a cultural centre with a rich library of manuscripts. She was interested in art, and the register of her private treasures reveals expenditure on paintings, sculpture, tapestries and stained glass to decorate her castles. She founded a number of religious institutions and hospitals and regularly gave charity to the poor (which was also scrupulously recorded, like all her other expenditures).

From time to time Mahaut 'entered' one of her towns, that is to say, made an entry at the head of a procession, like a king or great territorial seigneur. The origin of these entries, which were carried out with great ceremony and colour, was the ancient right of the seigneur to pay visits to his vassals. By the fourteenth century they had become demonstrations of political strength in times of peace on the part of the visitor and of loyalty and affiliation on the part of the organizers of the visit, the chief burghers. The burghers, their wives and children participated in the performances put on in honour of the visitor, and took part in the processions.[84]

Jeanne, countess of Flanders and Hainaut, daughter of Baldwin IX, inherited the county in 1206 after the death of her father, who had become emperor of Constantinople in 1204. She was still a minor, and until she reached her majority Philip, marquis of Namur, acted as her regent. She married Ferrand, who in 1214 fell captive to Philip II of France at the battle of Bouvines. Though she signed a treaty with Philip after the battle, her husband was released only in 1227. He died in 1233, and until 1237 she remained a widow. In 1237 she married Thomas of Savoy, who outlived her. On her death he forfeited the right to the county.

Throughout her reign, Countess Jeanne acted to strengthen and develop the administrative apparatus of the county, thereby taking part in the general process (which had commenced in the twelfth century) of improving and consolidating the ruling system of the various principalities. She granted a large number of charters to cities, in which she ratified some of the rights granted by her predecessors, but thereby also imposed on the towns various new laws in different spheres. Among others, she granted charters to Bergues, Furnes and Bourbourg, which included legislation on criminal matters. She reorganized the chancellery of the county and introduced salaried officials. On her instructions, salaried professional judges were appointed to the courts, and presided together with her vassals.[85] She was also active in promoting the textile industry. In 1244 she invited weavers to settle in the town of Courtrai and guaranteed in her own name and on behalf of her heirs not to impose taxes on them.[86] She was the patroness of several Cistercian monasteries and founded several monasteries herself.[87]

If the fief was small and did not entail ruling powers (i.e. its holder did not exercise seigneurial powers, but merely manorial rights), the heiress operated within the same framework as male heirs in this type of fief. An example of this is the announcement found in the archives of Bouches-du-Rhône, inviting all the inhabitants of the village of Cipières to a general meeting to be held in the castle of the lady of Caussol, of whose estate the village was part.[88] The lady of Termonde appears in the registers in connection with an agreement with the hospital of Saint Gille, according to which she granted the hospital a certain area and reserved for herself the right to set up a textile industry there.[89]

Women were also castellans. In Catalonia the noblewoman Guidinild organized her family and henchmen in 1026 to recapture Cervera. After the conquest she built a fortress there and was made ruler of the castellany by Countess Ermessend (whom we have mentioned as ruler by right of guardianship).[90] In England in the thirteenth century, the countess of Aumale maintained the prison at Carisbrooke, and as owner of a gaol exercised judicial powers.[91] A case is also known in England of two women who inherited the post of sheriff (*vicecomes*): the wife of Ranulf Glanville, Bertha, was sheriff of Yorkshire, while Ella, countess of Salisbury, was sheriff of Wiltshire.[92] But we do not know whether they themselves carried out the tasks entailed in this position.

ACTIVITIES OF NOBLEWOMEN IN ASSOCIATION WITH THEIR HUSBANDS

Some women inherited, others held fiefs by right of dower or as guardians of their sons,[93] but most noblewomen brought dowries to their husbands and were their helpmates. Medieval noblemen were absent from home frequently and for protracted periods, and during their absences their wives fulfilled most of their tasks, from managing a large fief to organizing manorial affairs and supervising the peasants who cultivated their lands. As Chaucer wrote of the patient Griselda:

> Though that hire housbonde absent were anoon,
> If gentil men, or othere of hir contree
> Were wrothe, she wolde bryngen hem atoon;
> So wyse and rype wordes hadde she,
> And jugements of so greet equitee,
> That she from heven sent was, as men wende,
> Peple to save and every wrong t'amende.[94]

The *chansons de geste* also reflect the role of the warrior's wife during his absence. Guibourc, wife of the count of Barcelona in the song of Guillaume, manages all the affairs of the seigneuralty during his absence, and after his defeat by the Saracens it is she who recruits soldiers to reorganize the army. Women ruled for several years in Champagne, Brittany and Chartres when their husbands went on crusades. Some women were forced, during their husbands' absence, to defend the castle against the enemy and to repel attacks. In the war between the Scots and the English, the countess of Buchan defended Berwick Castle against Edward 1; he shut her in a cage which he hung over the walls in order to humiliate her.[95] (The ideal of respect and adoration for the lady as propounded in courtly literature was not always observed in real life ...) The countess of Brittany, of whom Froissart wrote that she had the courage of a man and the bravery of a lion, went to battle in 1341 during the absence of her husband, Jean de Montfort, count of Brittany, against the claimant to the county, Charles of Blois. In defending the castle of Hennebont, she organized the women and children to tear out the paving stones and bring them to the defenders on the walls to be hurled down at the enemy. She did not content herself with defending the castle and launched an attack outside the walls, leading her army as far as Brest.[96]

In a smaller fief which did not entail ruling powers, the noble-woman managed all the affairs of the estate: leasing land, collecting rents, receiving reports from her bailiffs, sending surplus crops to market and maintaining buildings. These activities are described, *inter alia*, in the letters of the Paston family. Margaret Paston wrote to her husband about the negotiations she conducted with peasants concerning their debts, and on sales, crops, purchases and legal proceedings at which she appeared as representative of her husband; she also described how she repelled the attack of Lord Moleyns, who claimed some of the Paston lands for himself. The countess of Norfolk also appointed the bailiffs of her husband's estate.[97] Robert Grosseteste composed, for the benefit of Margaret, widow of the earl of Lincoln, a manual of guidance for management of her estate and household, which later came to be known as 'The Laws of Saint Robert' (*Les reules seynt Roberd*), addressed to both the nobleman and the noblewoman. He who conducted himself according to this work, according to the author, would succeed in living off his income and maintaining his property. The book includes instructions on ways of supervising knights, castellans and junior bailiffs, how to entertain guests and the proper seating order at table, all of which the noblewoman was expected to know.[98]

Even when her husband was at home, the noblewoman carried out numerous tasks. Household management was a complex matter, since it included many chores apart from cleaning, cooking and baking. All bread was baked at home, drink was brewed, butter and cheese were made and food preserved. Meat was smoked at home, cloth was woven there and in some manor houses candles were home-made. Those products which were bought, such as wine, fish and spices, required proper storage. Many servants were employed in a prosperous manor house, and even less prosperous families employed large staffs, since wages were low and even those who were not wealthy could afford to keep servants.

One of the tasks of the noblewoman was to supervise the servants to ensure that they carried out all their chores properly. But her task did not end here. Since the nobleman was first and foremost a soldier, and sometimes a diplomat and administrator in the service of his monarch or seigneur, his economic activities were restricted in most of Western Europe, and a sizeable part of the economic burden was carried by wives. In his wedding gift to the Countess Adalmodis, in late eleventh-century Spain, her husband notes what movable property must be given annually to the castellan – in other words this payment is to be carried out by the wife. When a beggar approached a lady (apparently the wife of the Margrave William III of Montfort) who was on a pilgrimage together with her entourage and asked for alms, she replied that she did not have enough for her own needs and the needs of all those who asked of her, i.e. were dependent on her. Here too it seems that it was the wife who was responsible for payments to knights and various officials.[99] In the letter in which Jean de Montreuil lists the grievances of his friend Gontier Cols' wife against her husband, he mentions her complaints against Gontier's profligacy and supports her claim that if it were not for the fact that she managed their financial affairs with care and responsibility, their situation would be atrocious.[100] Christine de Pisan's manual of guidance for women goes into great detail on the correct management of the budget, and advises women to become acquainted with land laws.[101]

Sometimes the wife even carried out her husband's tasks as holder of a certain office. It is not clear whether she did so only in his absence or whether he could simply exempt himself from his duties by imposing them on his wife, this custom being sanctioned by law. According to the statutes of the count of Flanders in the first half of the twelfth century, a resident of St Omer could be summoned in certain cases to pay a fine to the castellan, his wife or his steward.[102] In Catalonia in the eleventh century, the wife of the *vicarii* presided in court like countesses or abbesses who held fiefs.[103] Sometimes women helped their husbands in their political activities as well. The countess of Norfolk organized the election of the knights of the shire to the Parliament of 1455 so as to further her husband's interests.[104]

The sole opportunity open to a noblewoman who did not inherit a fief (heiresses naturally had no difficulty in finding husbands), did not marry and did not enter a nunnery was to serve as companion to a great noblewoman or as governess to her daughters. Ralph de Neville, earl of Westmorland, bequeathed a certain sum in his will in 1424 to each of the noblewomen serving in his household, together with smaller sums which he bequeathed to the serving women.[105]

LEISURE-TIME ACTIVITIES

The well-educated noblewoman was expected to know how to ride (straight-backed, according to didactic works), to breed falcons and release them during the hunt, to play chess and backgammon, to dance, sing, recite poetry and tell stories and, according to several authors of didactic works, even to read romances and poetry. As to the breeding of falcons, according to John of Salisbury at least, women were better at this than men. (He did not think them worthy of praise in this respect, 'since the weaker sex tend more to rapaciousness'.)[106] Riding had a practical purpose; it would be hard to envisage medieval women running a large area or even a manor, going on pilgrimages or attending tournaments without being able to ride. All other occupations were aimed at passing time. Not all noblewomen were given education which covered all these skills, particularly since some, such as singing and dancing, required certain natural talents. But all certainly gained at least a smattering of all of these, and used them to pass their leisure time, particularly if they lived in castles in which social gatherings were relatively frequent.

It is characteristic that courtly literature, which never depicts women as managing territories or manors or carrying out tasks jointly with their husbands, presents the romantic image of the noblewoman who introduces young knights to the mysteries of love, imposes missions on her lover, plays chess, and engages in falconry or embroidery. (Weaving and embroidery were also considered suitable pursuits for the daughters of the nobility.) The looms which the ladies used were apparently light-weight and the cloth woven on them was decorative but not always strong and well-made.[107] Women attended tournaments, one of the main occupations of the knight in peacetime, as spectators only, dressed in their best finery so as to encourage the competitors. Sometimes a knight wore the colours of his lady, who was among the spectators, and ladies often removed their jewels and threw them to the winner of the tournament.[108] Noblewomen accompanied queens and female fief holders when they entered their towns in processions. Sometimes the queen entered the city in a separate procession from the king, accompanied by her noblewomen. After the coronation of Charles v in 1364, the king and his entourage entered Paris, and several hours later the queen entered separately, accompanied by her women.[109]

The urban noblewoman enjoyed a more comfortable life than her counterpart in a castle in a rural area. In the Central Middle Ages castles were large, but none of the inhabitants, including the lords, enjoyed privacy. The lord and his lady slept in one of the upper rooms of the tower, and there was constant traffic on the staircase leading to it. Very close to them slept the soldiers of the guard, and the doors between the rooms were usually open. In the central hall and the rooms it was icy cold in winter, and there were almost no arrangements for bathing. In fact, the women could bathe properly only in rivers in summer. Even the authors of the didactic works never demanded of them that they wash their entire body and usually contented themselves by demanding that they wash face and hands every morning. One author also explains why it is so important to wash the face: 'For people look upon the face more than upon all other parts of the body.' In the southern regions, even the nobility were infested with various types of fleas and lice. Women deloused one another, their lovers, sons and husbands. This task was not entrusted to the maid-servants. It was a ceremony! What would now be considered good manners were not regarded as self-evident by the authors of the didactic works, and they often expounded on proper conduct in basic matters: one should refrain from belching at table, pushing large chunks of food into the mouth, or wiping eyes or nose on the tablecloth ...[110]

In smaller and isolated castles women often suffered long periods of loneliness. Visitors and wandering troubadours did not reach every castle, and when they did arrive it was only at long intervals. The husband was often absent from home. There were relatively long periods when women could not utilize their knowledge of poetry, dance, falconry or chess. Sometimes isolation broke down class barriers. Beatrice Planissol, the wife of the local castellan, who appears in the lists of the Inquisition tribunal at Pamiers, was friendly with the local peasant wives without displaying arrogance or condescension. She had no other women friends.[111]

Some women of the upper nobility, like the men of their class, planned their burial ceremonies as impressive social and religious events. Elizabeth Montague, countess of Salisbury, left large sums in her will to religious institutions, to charity, and for payment to those who would pray and hold masses for her soul. She ordered that the required sum be allotted to buy black cloth for the mourning garments for her entire household (including the servants) and for covering the carriage bearing the coffin, as well as to buy candles and black cloth to be borne by the poor in the funeral procession. She also left detailed instructions as to where the procession should halt for assembly and prayer.[112] Women too wanted to continue to impress the world even after their death!

EDUCATION

Most churchmen who wrote on the subject were in favour of according women in general, and noblewomen in particular, a certain degree of education. The aim was to foster their modesty and religious piety. They should be taught to read their prayers and taught the basic tenets of faith. If they should some day choose to take the veil, this education would help them in their lives as nuns. Several authors of didactic works favoured teaching girls to read and nothing else, so as to enable them to read religious and moral works – they saw no need whatsoever for girls to learn to write.[113] There can be no doubt that the supreme object of study for both sexes was knowledge and love of God. In the case of men, however, secondary objectives were also acknowledged: the nurturing of the intellectual attributes and proclivities (together with material and moral qualities), and training to take a certain place in society and in the state. As for women, the Church writers emphasized the need for only the most elementary of education in order to develop their religious piety on the very lowest plane: to render them modest and chaste.

Only in exceptional cases do these writers cite the need to educate women so as to prepare them to fulfil specific roles: princesses and great noblewomen should be taught to read and write so as to enable them to manage their lands properly when the time came. In this case the defined objective corresponds to one of the secondary

objectives of educating males. Here didactic literature had to reflect
the plain fact that women sometimes headed territorial seigneuralties. Some writers thought it desirable for noblewomen to read tales
of the evil deeds of women in order to draw the proper moral.
Others even permitted women to read tales without moral and
educational argumentation of this type. Durand de Champagne,
confessor of Queen Jeanne of Navarre, wife of Philip IV, states that
it is desirable to educate women and great noblewomen in particular, since education teaches, elevates, consoles and is also a source of
enjoyment.[114] On the other hand, there were sworn antifeminists,
like Philippe of Novare, who in their obsession with chastity totally
denied the need to educate women, even of the noble class, since if a
woman could read she would be able to receive letters from lovers,
and if she could write she could write to them, and so on, thus
bringing shame on her family and on society in general. Nor did the
problem of the salvation of the female soul concern these authors
greatly.[115]

The advocates of female education included two whose arguments were exceptional, namely Christine de Pisan and Pierre
Dubois. Christine de Pisan's writing is of twofold interest, since as
far as we know it is the sole written evaluation of female education
by a medieval woman. She writes bitterly of the fact that she was
given no education in childhood. She was greedy for knowledge and
wanted to learn from her father, but according to custom, though
not justice, girls were not educated. If justice had prevailed, a
daughter would have enjoyed the same education as a son, since the
desire for knowledge existed in girls as well as in boys, and should
be satisfied. Christine's starting point is the ability and desire of a
woman to study and acquire knowledge and her right to do so. The
acquisition of learning is presented as a value and as a vital source of
enrichment and enjoyment for the human spirit. Christine de Pisan
did not fight to extend the rights of women in society and state, and
did not claim that they should carry out all the roles performed by
men. However, out of that same belief that women were capable of
studying and understanding, she condemned the view that there was
no place for women in courts since they were incapable of
understanding and applying the law which they had studied. To her
mind, when women were granted an education, they could do
anything that men did, and even do it better.[116]

Pierre Dubois's plan for educating women was part of his general
scheme for reconquering the Holy Land, which, if carried out,
would lead to French hegemony in both east and west. Women who

were granted an education could carry out tasks in the service of the crusaders and in consolidating Christian-Catholic rule in the east both through their own work and through marriages to sons of the east: Muslims and Christians who belonged to the Byzantine Church or to churches in the east which had seceded from it. Education of women was one of the measures he envisaged to implement his general scheme. The starting point is not the problems of women, nor is his proposal to extend their education aimed at filling a hiatus in their lives or improving their situation in society, but in retrospect Pierre Dubois appears to have believed in their ability to acquire a certain education and to carry out certain functions.

According to Dubois' proposal, schools for girls were to be established in all French provinces, in parallel with special schools for boys, with the objective of training young men and women for service in the east. Young people would study Latin, Greek and Arabic in order to qualify for missionary and organizational work. They would also study medicine, the art of preaching and law. The schools for young women would take in mostly daughters of the nobility. Talented girls from lower social strata would also be accepted, but whereas the sole criterion for the acceptance of boys from lower classes would be talent, girls would need to be beautiful as well. Girls would study grammar, the basic tenets of the Catholic faith, and surgery. Only the most talented among them would also study logic, some of the foundations of the natural sciences, medicine and one foreign language. But even those who studied a wider curriculum would only study those scientific elements with direct bearing on medicine and surgery and in the simplest, easiest and most understandable fashion possible, because of the weaknesses of their sex. Dubois asserted that girls matured faster than boys and reached their peak earlier, and this too because of the inferiority of their natural attributes.

The best female pupils would remain in the school as teachers after having studied more medicine, surgery and the apothecary's art than their companions. The other girls would be sent out to the east on completing their studies. They would treat women and become active among them as missionaries. Some would marry physicians sent from the west and act as their helpmates, but they would be active, in particular, in consolidating French rule in the east by marrying local men. They would be adopted as daughters or grand-daughters by great princes from the west who would settle in the Holy Land, and thanks to their standing, beauty and education would be attractive matches for noblemen and priests from among the oriental Christians and Muslim princes and noblemen. After marriage, they would undoubtedly succeed in persuading their husbands and sons to adopt the Catholic faith. The Muslim women whom they treated and among whom they worked as missionaries would also be glad to adopt the Catholic religion, since according to this faith men were permitted to take only one wife, whereas according to Islam a man could take up to seven wives. These Muslim women would also persuade their husbands to adopt the Catholic faith.[117]

Evaluation of Dubois' scheme is outside the scope of the present study. In the context of the education of women, he seems to regard female education primarily as a means of increasing women's value in marriage, and marriage is seen as a means of disseminating Catholic Christianity in the east. Nevertheless, he did acknowledge woman's talent for study, however limited, and did propose that they might do useful work.

Let us now turn from theories on the education of women to actual practice. Generally speaking, noblewomen were given elementary education. They learned to read and sometimes also to write. They could read prayer books or poetry and tales as advised by some authors of manuals of guidance for women. Some women studied in their own homes with private male or female tutors, others attended schools attached to nunneries, and others were sent to town schools. Héloïse (who may have belonged to the nobility) was educated in the nunnery of Argenteuil, near Paris. In Germany in the fourteenth and fifteenth centuries, for example, daughters of the nobility who were not destined to take the veil were often sent to nunnery schools.[118] The fact that women who entered nunneries in adulthood were required to have a certain degree of education also indicates that noblewomen acquired some learning in the secular world. When several widows of knights killed on Louis IX's crusade appealed to the king to help them and some of their daughters to enter the Pontoise nunnery, the king replied that those of them who were educated would be accepted.[119] Some daughters of the minor nobility studied at small schools run by parish priests. Two of the daughters of Beatrice Planissol attended the school run by the priest in Dalou.[120] Such correspondences as those of the Paston and Stoner families in the Late Middle Ages reveal that women of the gentry could read and write in the vernacular.

There were some women who were exceptionally well-educated, such as Christine de Pisan, who became a writer and educated herself in depth. She read (in French translation) works of history, philosophy, geography, morals and theology and excerpts in encyclopedias from the Holy Writ and the writings of the Church Fathers. She also expanded her knowledge of classical literature by reading translations of Virgil, Horace and Ovid, and was acquainted with the literature of her day, including the writings of Dante in the original. She had no knowledge of science, and could not read Latin. Héloïse was renowned for her erudition in Latin and in both classic and Christian writings.[121] Matilda, duchess of Tuscany, wrote Latin, spoke Italian, French and German, collected numerous manuscripts in her extensive library, initiated the copying of part of Justinian's legal code and helped to found the law school of Bologna. The poetess Marie de France knew English and Latin, in addition to the French in which she wrote. The fables she wrote were translated from English. In her book *Espurgatoire de St Patrice* she based herself on the Roman source, and in the prologue to her poems (*Lais*) she wrote that at first she had intended to translate several tales from the Latin but had subsequently decided to write down the poems she knew.[122]

Many noblewomen were drawn to attractive manuscripts in decorative bindings and purchased them for their libraries, like Jeanne of Valois, sister of Philip vi, and Bonne of Luxembourg, wife of Jean ii the Good. Mahaut of Artois collected a large number of manuscripts in her library, from sacred writings and prayer missals to works of philosophy, law, history, travel, romances and poetry.[123]

Noblewomen contributed to founding of institutions of higher learning (which were religious in nature) and to building churches. Thus they furthered the salvation of their own souls, encouraged learning in the societies in which they lived, and expanded the opportunities for artists. Jeanne of Navarre, wife of Philip iv, for example established the College of Navarre in Paris. The widow of Aymar de Valence, earl of Pembroke, and Elizabeth de Burgh, the lady of Clare, contributed to the establishment of colleges in Cambridge in the fourteenth century. Many noblewomen were patronesses of writers, poets and artists. (We will examine their role below.) A few others also played a part in the spiritual creativity of their age.

Were noblewomen less educated than their male counterparts? It appears that up to about the thirteenth century there was no great difference between the education of men and women in the nobility. The nobleman was not distinguished by his educational level. He was a *miles*, in contrast to the *clericus*, the intellectual of the age. Moreover, it is possible that more women than men dedicated part of their day to reading prayer books and romances of various types. The change to the worse for women occurred gradually from the thirteenth century on, as the universities developed and even those noblemen who were not destined for careers in the Church began to study. Attendance at a university called for some degree of organized prior education, and a relatively organized educational system did in fact evolve for boys. This was not so in the case of girls. Their education was not conducted in the same institutionalized fashion.

The period of academic study came to be recognized as one of the fixed stages in the life of the boy, but not the girl. A fresco in the Doge's Palace in Venice depicts four stages in the life of man: (a) the period of childhood and games, symbolized by boys and girls playing with a windmill, a doll, birds, a toy horse and a rope; (b) the period of study – the boys are learning to read or are holding books or writing implements, while the girls are learning to weave; (c) the period of love, courtship and knightly sport – this section depicts a feast, boys and girls strolling together in a garden, nuptial ceremonies and hunting scenes; (d) adulthood – the jurist and scientist are shown, bearded and dressed in the garments of their professions. As Philippe Ariès has noted, these stages are concomitant not only with the biological stages in man's development but also with social functions.[124] In the 'second stage' the girl has no part in academic study, and consequently woman has no place in the fourth stage, in which men are awarded certain titles (doctor, magister) after completing their studies and begin to fulfil certain functions in society.

One could compare the denial of academic titles to women with their exclusion from ecclesiastical titles or knightly status, since all these titles were awarded ceremonially and empowered a man to fulfil a function which was held in esteem by society. Women might sometimes hold fiefs by inheritance, but they could not win positions on the basis of professional training. At first the discrepancy between the education of women and men was evident mainly within the minor nobility. The sons of great noblemen, as well as the eldest sons of lesser nobility who were to inherit fiefs or were destined for military careers, did not attend universities. Universities were peopled by younger sons of the lesser nobility, by the minor nobility and by orphans.[125] To gain an education gave them access to some sort of career in the Church or in the service of the monarchy and the great nobles. As the universities and other educational institutions, which were closed to women, expanded and spread, and the number of students from the nobility and the urban class increased, the educational gap between men and women grew wider and women became increasingly detached from the life of thought and of action in their society.

A sphere which remained open to women throughout the Middle Ages and in the following centuries was literature. Noblewomen were interested in literature and nurtured it. The reader of Dante's *Vita Nuova* clearly senses that the poet's circle of readers consisted first and foremost of other poets and of noblewomen. Throughout the Middle Ages and later, women were patronesses of writers and poets, from religious authors to poets of courtly romance and lyric. The prayers composed by St Anselm at the end of the eleventh century were sent by him either to his friends in monasteries or to ladies of great piety among the nobility. There can be no doubt that these pious women played a part, together with the monastics, in formulating methods of prayer and religious observance for the individual in his own home. The first prayers which Anselm composed were sent to Adelaide, daughter of William the Conqueror, and the last to Matilda, countess of Tuscany.[126] One poet, Godfrey of Rheims, was so lavish in his praise of that same Adelaide, who was his patroness, that in one of his poems he attributed the victories of her father to fate's desire to make her a princess.[127] She was also the patroness of Hildebert of Lavardin, and there were others of her kind.

The most renowned of the many noblewomen who patronized the authors of courtly romances and poetry was Eleanor of Aquitaine, who was patroness of troubadours in southern France, including Bernard of Ventadour, and her daughter Marie of Champagne, who was patroness of the poet Chrétien de Troyes and of Andreas Capellanus, who recorded the rule of courtly love in great detail. The poets of courtly love proclaimed the names of their lady patrons, praising their beauty, their qualities and their generosity, just as the manuals of guidance for noblewomen instructed: 'Give gifts to poets so that they may make your name known.'[128] The courts of Eleanor of Aquitaine and her daughter Marie were models and inspiration for other courts in Western Europe. Women were also interested in and sensitive to Church music. In fact its critics in the Late Middle Ages condemned it as music intended for women and created in order please them.[129]

One can discern a certain continuity between noblewomen in the High Middle Ages, who nurtured artists and writers, and the ladies who conducted literary salons in the nineteenth century. They served as a source of inspiration, as critics and as readers, and thus made an important collective contribution to the culture of their day. It is customary to claim that since women of the upper classes had considerable leisure time they could devote themselves to the pleasures of the spirit more than could the men of their class. This may be more true of women during the Italian Renaissance, or of the ladies who conducted salons in later centuries, than of noble-women in the Middle Ages, many of whom fulfilled functions and were active in various spheres. There is undoubtedly a greater measure of truth in Simone de Beauvoir's view that because of the marginal place of woman in the world (and her place was always marginal, with variations only of degree from age to age or between countries), the men who sought through creativity to cross boundaries and attain a different world appealed to their support.[130]

It was the Central Middle Ages which bestowed courtly literature on western culture. According to many historians this body of work, more than anything which came before, typified literature written on the inspiration of women, elevating their image and answering their psychological needs. Recent interpretation of courtly literature, on the other hand, emphasizes the inner needs of man to which this literature answered. In the courtly poem or romance, a man seeks the love of a woman, and she responds or rejects him at will. She never succumbs lightly; whether she is responding to platonic love or sensual love it is she who dictates the conditions and rules of the game. The man must court her, act courteously and with restraint. Love in courtly literature is the centre of man's life. In order to win the love of his adored lady he must endure all the trials she imposes on him. This conduct was in complete contrast both to the marriage customs of the nobility, where women were married off for class, political and economic reasons, and to the status of the married woman, who was subject by law to the authority of her husband.

The dictation of the conditions for love by the woman and the subjugation of the lover to his mistress, like a vassal doing her homage, can be regarded as a protest against the existing institution of marriage and in part against the social order in general.[131] Since a considerable number of the courtly poems and romances describe love which is sensual and not aimed at propagation, it also constituted a protest against the sexual ethics of the Church.[132] But most important for the image of woman is the fact that in courtly literature she is not seen as a destructive force; in most of the works, love for a woman is a source of inspiration for heroic action and a factor enhancing all the moral traits of the lover. She holds the fate of her lover in her hand. Neither tender nor forgiving, she imposes on her lover arduous and often arbitrary tasks, but these tasks are regarded as a means of attaining moral perfection; love is a force for good and beauty. Even in those less conventional works, such as some of the versions of the romance of Tristan and Isolde, which express awareness of the clash between love and religious and feudal loyalties, woman is not a destructive factor. Sometimes love is portrayed as a force which can destroy, and the lover loses his ability to fulfil his function in society. But even here woman is not a force of evil. The woman and the man are both swept up by forces stronger than themselves which determine their fate. Their love is forbidden and stolen according to ecclesiastical and feudal norms, but is marked by the almost religious dedication of the lover.[133]

On the other hand, there can be no doubt that courtly literature also responded to the aspirations and needs of male society and to the dreams and sensitivities of the poet and his audience. Just as the feminine element was introduced into western Christianity by fostering the concept of the Holy Virgin's role in history and her mediation between man and God, and by intensified worship of her image, so courtly literature introduced the feminine element into the spiritual world of feudal society. This partial feminization of feudal civilization could not have succeeded as it did if it had not responded to conscious and latent psychological needs of male society. The feminine element opened up for men a path to moral improvement and to full development of their virtue. The perfect knight is a courageous warrior, a Christian, religiously inspired to fight the battle against injustice, and the admirer of a lady. A role is allotted to woman as determinant of the mental and moral discipline whereby he will attain his full *virtus*.

However the classic courtly literature composed by men disregards the development of the full potential of woman by love, and therefore she remains essentially an object, however adored. Furthermore, it often appears as if the situation itself is more important than the beloved object. Only in poems composed by women in the style of courtly love do women cease to be the abstract love object. On another plane, the idea of choosing a mistress answered an inner need in men just as the concept of freedom to select a lover responded to a need in women. For men as well, there were only very limited choices in matrimony, and even if they themselves chose a particular wife, it was usually for considerations other than personal. Others were forced to remain bachelors because they had not been allotted an estate. The idea of sensual love as opposed to the sexual ethics of the Church supplied an inner need in both men and women.[134]

Just as knighthood played a very important part in the first analysis of medieval history in general, so the study of medieval woman devoted considerable attention to the influence of courtly literature. Many scholars seem to have attributed to it a much greater impact on the status of women and the relations between men and women than it actually exerted. It should be recalled that even if this literature reflected a social reality, it was the reality of only a narrow stratum of the female population, namely noble-women. This literature was alien to women in other classes.[135] And even where noblewomen were concerned, the courtly literature had hardly any social effect. It brought no changes in their standing, either *de jure* or *de facto*. The rights which some noblewomen exercised were not granted to them under the influence of courtly literature.

It will be recalled that the veneration of the Holy Mother did not bring about any change in the status of women in the Church, including the nun. None of the authors of courtly literature demanded that women be accorded new status or functions differing from those they already fulfilled in family, society and state, just as none of the theologians who contributed to the definition of the role of the Holy Mother in the salvation of mankind and her place in the celestial array demanded any change in the status of women in the Church. Even the Muslim society of Andalusia, where women's rights were highly restricted, though perhaps wider than those of women in other Muslim countries (and there is no unanimity of opinion on this in research), produced poetry celebrating a love accompanied by suffering which, in its purest form, does not even aspire to win the adored object. This poetry responded to a certain inner need in a purely male society, but did not reflect any desire to improve the status of women in that society.[136]

Courtly literature developed in the twelfth and thirteenth centuries, a period in which external and internal security improved, the standard of living rose and the cultural resurgence known as the twelfth-century Renaissance commenced. Noblemen devoted much more time to social pursuits, and women played an important part in social events which took place in the castle: dancing, games or recitations by poets who accompanied their poetry by music. The relative security and rise in living standards permitted this form of

activity. In addition to the characteristically male forms of entertainment such as knightly tournaments, a new type of leisure-time
activity evolved in which woman was the focus as the patroness of
poets. There grew up a new system of social conduct according to
which the man who acted in knightly fashion towards ladies was
honoured, and this system left its impact on the conduct in society
of the upper classes in Western Europe for centuries. Certain
norms of behaviour developed which were distinguished by greater
respect and courtesy towards women, at least in society. But one
should not exaggerate their impact on the essential pattern of
relations between men and women, and certainly not on that
between man and wife.

Jean de Montreuil, in the above-cited letter to his friend Gontier
Col, lists what he considers the just complaints of his friend's wife
against her husband. She claims that she obeys him in everything
and does not leave her home except to attend church, and even then
only after obtaining his permission, while he is free to come and go,
to play chess or dice. He is not unfaithful to her yet, and fulfils his
marital duties, but with indifference and contempt. As regards the
household expenditure, if she did not take care to manage their
financial affairs frugally, his irresponsible squandering would reduce them to poverty. She herself says:

> This is our fate, we innocent women, to be accursed always by
> men who believe they are above the law, and that everything is
> permitted to them. They are free to do as they choose, like those
> errants who do as they see fit, while as for us, it is enough that we
> look at someone and we are immediately accused of fornication.
> We are not wives or companions, but like slaves or prisoners. If
> they are not given at once all they require, such as clean garments
> or a soft bed, they curse us and insult us. In inns, on the highway
> and in other places which I do not wish to specify, they tear us to
> pieces with their vilifications and insults. They are unfair judges
> who are lenient with themselves and harsh towards others.[137]

This picture of the life and feelings of a noblewoman is remote from
the courtly ideal. One should not regard these complaints as
expressions of excessive self-pity. Jean de Montreuil, who was not
an advocate of women and marriage, accepted them at face value.

The poets lauded their patronesses, but this was the métier they
were paid for, and some of the ladies knew the truth. One of them, a
certain Isabella, who was herself a poetess, places the following
remarks in the mouth of one of her characters, a poet:

> but if I sang your praises
> it wasn't out of love
> but for the profit I might get from it,
> just as any joglar sings a lady's fame.[138]

Bogin even puts forward the idea that poets used the ladies in order to gain access to their husbands. By lauding the lady, they also brought honour to the husband. Like knighthood, courtly love was common to the entire nobility, irrespective of differences of rank within the class. Both great and minor noblemen could identify with the ideas of the poets. As R. Nelli has noted, the ideal of love between a married woman and a young bachelor fitted in with the aspirations of the young wandering knights, those *juvenes* many of whom were bachelors only for lack of choice, because they had no property. It offered a variation on the triangle of erotic relations consisting of the husband, wife and married lover, by introducing a new element, the young bachelor. Andreas Capellanus' statement that 'everyone knows that love can have no place between husband and wife' could easily be accepted by these bachelors.[139]

Platonic courtly love, which does not aspire to attainment of the beloved and is in itself an elevating force (and whose most personal and perfect reflection is in Dante's poetry), did not in actual fact render the erotic life of the nobility more delicate, it merely influenced a style of behaviour. But on the other hand it would not be true to say that it fostered adultery and fornication among the nobility in the Central Middle Ages. We have clear evidence of adultery, fornication and the propagation of bastards in the periods preceding the flowering of courtly love, and sexual morals were no more stringent among the urban class or the peasantry, despite the Church's stand on sexual matters.

At its best, if it did not deteriorate into barren formalism, courtly literature reflected a vision which embodied the illusion of the perfect hero in whom the lusts of the flesh had been transformed into virtue, sacrificing himself for the lady. Like every literature which reflects a dream, it did not mirror reality and only minimally formulated it.

THE FEMININE CONTRIBUTION TO CONTEMPORARY CULTURE

Women's contribution to Christian mysticism was discussed in the chapter on nuns, since all the female mystics whose writings have survived were members of female monastic orders. The female contribution to secular culture is contained in the chapter on noblewomen, since as far as we know almost all the women who composed poetry or prose belonged to this class. There were more poetesses than female writers of prose in the Middle Ages. Apart from Christine de Pisan, and the famous poetess Marie de France, there were noblewomen who wrote poems which, in style and content, are part of the troubadour tradition. M. Bogin has compiled a collection of the poems of eighteen such poetesses in southern France. Héloïse's letters are renowned, of course. In them she describes her relations with Abélard from her own viewpoint and her sensations at the time the letters were written, and they reflect the gradual transition to reconciliation with her destiny as a nun. Her letters are a personal document of the first order, yet anchored in the culture and sensitivities of her time.

Christine de Pisan was the sole full-time female writer in the Middle Ages. She supported herself by writing and was regarded as a 'professional'. She was in contact with contemporary poets and philosophers, such as Eustace Deschamps and Jean Gerson. She dared to come to the defence of women against the anti-feminism of Jean de Meung in the highly popular *Roman de la Rose*, and was the only woman to speak out on behalf of women during the literary quarrel known as the *Querelle des femmes*. She was invited, in her capacity as a writer, to the courts of Henry IV, king of England, and Gian Galeazzo Visconti, duke of Milan. She declined to accept the invitations. Some of her works were written to order, such as the biography of Charles V which was commissioned by his brother, Philip, duke of Burgundy. In the early stages of her literary career she wrote ballads in which she described her brief and happy marriage and mourned her husband's death. She later wrote love poetry, lyrical poems, a manual of guidance for her son, patriotic and homiletic works, political theory and works of philosophy. At the time she wrote these works, she was completing her education and the books she read supplied her with inspiration for her writing. She wrote paeans of praise to French courtiers, some of whom were her patrons (among others, the duke of Orleans), an appeal for peace between members of the royal family directed at Queen Isabel of Bavaria and a lament at the civil war in France. In her old age in a nunnery she wrote a poem in honour of Joan of Arc.

It is interesting to note that in her defence of women Christine was anticipated by the mystic Hildegard of Bingen. It will be recalled that Hildegard never questioned the concept of the secondary role of woman in Creation, and stressed female subordination to man. But she wrote that woman is more tender than man (*suavior*) and that whereas man's sexual lust can be compared to the force of the lion, woman is less lustful and focuses mainly on the desire to bear and raise children.[140]

Despite this impressive list of works by Christine de Pisan and the poems of the female troubadours, the contribution of women to medieval culture was undoubtedly small in volume (with the exception of the mystics). Can one find in this limited body of work a different female viewpoint or different sensitivities able to expand the horizons and experience of readers? We believe that this question can be answered in the affirmative. All the works cited were written in the spirit and style of the age, and the subjects too are characteristic in the main of contemporary literature. Nonetheless, a unique quality does emerge in the love poems written by women, in the way of expression and contemplation of Héloïse, and in some of the works of Christine de Pisan.

The love poems by women are undoubtedly more spontaneous, more personal and less confined within the conventions of courtly poetry than the poems of most male troubadours. They contain few allegories, and reveal expressions of the joys and pain of love. The woman who writes in the first person singular, which is more personal than the first person plural of the male troubadours, is not usually the adored lady allotting tasks to her lover (although the poetesses belonged to that social stratum for which the male troubadours wrote their poems, and some of the poetesses were patronesses of male poets). She is a loving woman, rejoicing in her love and lamenting her disappointments. In Marie de France's poem 'Guigemar', the woman is a tender and loving creature, suffering for her love and through her suffering bringing salvation to her lover. Together with the description of the miraculous and the force of destiny we find a depiction of the psychological motives of the protagonists. Only the love and devotion of the heroine are balm for the wounds of the hero. It is prophesied to Guigemar that: 'thy wound will never be cured, neither by healing herbs, nor roots, nor ashwater nor potions, until it is healed by she who in her love for you bears pain and sorrow, such as no woman before her has known'.[141]

In Héloïse's letters, she bases herself on the ecclesiastical and classic literature which were a source of inspiration and authority for her contemporaries. She presents the familiar image of the woman as the source of evil and cites the common criticism in ecclesiastical and court circles against marriage, but beyond these details we discover a forceful and elemental expression. The frank, merciless introspection as to her past and her life as a nun, the challenge she throws down on God and his injustice, and her yearning for Abélard and desire for contact with him are forms of personal expression which we seek in vain even in the writings of Abélard. Even in his *Historia Calamitatum*, which may have been written as a way of rehabilitating his disintegrating personality as a result of his castration, and of redefining his own identity,[142] the reader still senses the author's desire to preach through *exempla*. There is no trace of this in Héloïse's writing.

Some of the writings of Christine de Pisan are undoubtedly unnecessarily complicated, lacking in originality, and weighed down with allegory. In them she parades all her learning. Even some of the works she wrote in defence of women reiterate the common concepts of pro-female literature: Eve created from Adam's rib and not from the dust of the earth, Christ who was born of woman, etc. Nor did she express any desire for equality of the sexes, but merely sought to defend women who had been treated unjustly by the male authors and to elevate the moral and intellectual image of woman. But nonetheless, her writings contain personal comments and ideas and original concepts which are expressed with simplicity, humanity and wisdom. An example is her advice to older women not to judge younger women too stringently, to forgive them the follies of their years and to remember that they too were once young: 'If there are no longer youthful sins in you, it is not because of your virtue, but because your nature no longer leans to such sins, and since your nature no longer tends to them, they appear so despicable to you.'[143] This is a breath of fresh air after the trite ideas which are reiterated in all the other works of guidance for women.

An illustration of Christine's direct humane approach are her protests against wars and their horrors and the fate of war widows and orphans.[144] It would be hard to find such statements in the writings of men, whose debates on peace and the 'just war' are usually abstract, legalistic and highly erudite, whether based on Christian morality and natural law, or on concepts originating in the ethos of knighthood. (Their like can be found in other works by Christine herself.) An additional expression of her humane approach to life can be found in the fact that in contrast to all other contemporary writers who attribute the fair policy of some ruler towards the Jews to religious piety, Christine de Pisan, in her biography of Charles v, attributed his policy to his humanitarianism: 'He acted justly towards the Jews just as he wished all men to act towards one another.'[145]

As a woman and a writer, Christine de Pisan stood outside the social system, and this helped her to see things from a different angle. To this may be added the fact that from the class aspect as well her place was undefined. She was the widow of a minor nobleman, but inherited neither fief nor any other source of income which could suffice to keep her in accordance with her station in life. She mixed in noble circles and at the royal court, but was not part of them. She was inside and apart at the same time, a fact which also contributed to her unique personal point of view.

Let us conclude with the most interesting of Christine's statements on women, which appears in *L'Epistre au Dieu d'Amours*:

> Women are not as cruel as the men who rule the world, they do not kill, wound, disinherit others, draw up false agreements or cause harm to the kingdom. By nature they are tender, endowed with mercy and grace. Even the worst among them do not cause harm to the world or to the government in their own country.[146]

From all that we know of medieval women it seems to us that this statement implies a certain idealization of woman. Even in her appeal to the queen of France, Isabel of Bavaria, to put an end to the disputes between the princes of France, she appealed to her generosity, mercy and maternal compassion[147] – traits certainly not predominant in Queen Isabel. But her remarks are of great interest. The very depiction of the image of a tender and merciful woman is an exception in medieval culture. As we have seen, these qualities of tenderness, mercy and grace were attributed only to the Holy Virgin. When writers wanted to praise a certain woman, they attributed male characteristics to her, while emphatically denying her feminine traits. They did not always specify in this context what these were (and one never finds great consistency in the enumeration of feminine traits), but they were usually referring to frailty, lack of resolve and inconsistency, rather than tenderness and compassion. In hagiography too, churchmen sometimes wrote that the female saint acted in a masculine rather than feminine fashion (*non mulieriter sed viriliter*).[148] Christine de Pisan defined certain qualities as feminine: tenderness, mercy and compassion, and these qualities are regarded as positive. This emphasis on the desirability of such feminine traits was not only a protest against feudal society and the ethos of the warrior but also opened up the way for liberating men from obsessive masculinity, false heroics and all they implied. Needless to say, these views remained in the sphere of theory, and there too hers was an isolated and unique voice.

Unlike many members of fringe groups who, in their desire to identify with the centre, deny their fellow members of the group, medieval women did not deny the few female creators. The English-Norman poet Denys Pyramus wrote of the great popularity of the poems of Marie de France among the nobility in general and noblewomen in particular. Some women extended their patronage to Christine de Pisan. The manuscripts of her works were purchased by women, among them Valentina, wife of Duke Louis of Orleans, Marie de Berry and Isabel of Bavaria, queen of France. Christine herself, in her defence of women, not only depicted mythological and historical female figures but related to the flesh-and-blood women she knew. She lauded them in her works, as in the tale of the generosity and resourcefulness of Marguerite, wife of Bureau de la Rivière, and listed her female contemporaries in France who, because of their noble qualities, were worthy of entering the *Cité des Dames*.[149]

It is often claimed that it is in the nature of societies based on military organization to drastically curtail the rights of women in comparison to those of men.[150] The feudal society of the High Middle Ages was based on military organization. The upper stratum of this society held fiefs which were originally granted in return for military service, and constituted the warrior class. Can one therefore say that the rights of the women of this class were particularly restricted in comparison to the men's? As we have noted, women did not fulfil the main function of the stratum; they were not fighters, and could not join the alliance of knights. They did not receive knightly education and did not undergo the various stages of initiation into knighthood, nor were they members of the knightly orders, those sacred fraternities of men which developed in the twelfth century. In this way they played no part in the ethos and myth of the nobility.

The roots of the institution of knighthood lay in the sacred rituals of worship of pagan society, and feudal society lent them a Christian flavour; the institution of knighthood outlived the nobility as a fighting force. Even in the late Middle Ages, when the nobility had lost standing as the fighting force, in most European countries the concepts of knighthood and the knightly orders still flourished. Knighthood encompassed the range of ethical and aesthetic values of medieval civilization, and women played no part in it. They played a role only in one of its least vital aspects, the courtly culture, and even then as objects more than subjects. On the other hand, women inherited fiefs, and as such, some of them ruled territories and exercised full ruling powers. In addition, the wives of feudal seigneurs who were not heiresses fulfilled functions at the side of their husbands, who to a large extent left the economic management of the estates to them; they also stood in for their husbands during their absence.

These rights and activities of some feudal women contradict the description of the general class of women in the 'estates literature', and are in conflict with the rulings of jurists; nor did their special status lead to redefinition of the role of women in society in general. The status of feudal women did not resemble that of the mothers, sisters, wives and concubines of rulers who gained influence over government affairs, not only because feudal women were more numerous but because the latter fulfilled no function apart from that of regent, sometimes granted to the mothers of minor heirs to the crown until they attained their majority. They won influence by force of their strong personalities alone. And this is not surprising. Strong, active and power-loving women have always existed, and if they were closely involved with rulers they could realize their aspirations, even though never by virtue of any allotted position or constitutionally vested power.

The standing of feudal women who held fiefs could only be compared to that of queens who succeeded to the crown in later periods (in the Middle Ages no woman succeeded to the throne in Western Europe and actually reigned). As the monarchy gained power in various countries (and the princes grew stronger in Italy and Germany), centralism increased and feudal territories were taken over by monarchs, the number of women wielding ruling powers decreased. The strength of male feudals also waned, but they found places as office-holders in the royal courts, the civilian administration and the army. This path was not open to women. Furthermore, the growth of education among the nobility, acquired at institutions of learning which were closed to women, increased the detachment of women from the life of thought and of action in society. The Civil War and the Glorious Revolution in England in the seventeenth century, the French Revolution and other European revolutions in the nineteenth century did not change this situation. After the power of the landed nobility as reflected in political strength was broken, the representative assemblies were peopled solely by men elected by men until the twentieth century. The universities and other institutions of higher learning did not open their gates to women. It appears therefore that in the society of the Middle Ages, which was based on military organization, some women in the ruling class enjoyed status which was to be unparalleled for centuries to come.

What characterized these women? Christine de Pisan, as we have seen, drew the image of the tender, generous, compassionate woman. She claimed that women never wounded or killed, never disinherited others, never drew up false agreements nor caused harm to the state. Some modern historians have regarded the noblewoman of the Middle Ages as representing polar values to her male counterpart. J. F. Benton regarded the mother of Gilbert of Nogent, who according to her son was pious and chaste, as the representative of the female values of feudal society, whereas the male values of this same society were violence, arrogance, sexual licence and irreligiousness.[151] I do not accept this view. It may have been true of Gilbert of Nogent's mother (at least that is how he saw her), and the pious noblewoman was part of the image of the ideal woman in family myths,[152] but there is nothing in contemporary sources to suggest that women were usually more pious than men, or that they always represented sexual chastity. Sensuality, cruelty and sexual lust, like piety, asceticism and voluntary poverty, existed in medieval society among both sexes. From all we know, religious piety was no greater in nunneries than in monasteries and most nuns were noblewomen. Christine de Pisan was right in claiming that women did not wound and kill like men: the registers of courts indicate the existence of violence among women too, but the number of women charged with murder was undoubtedly very small in comparison with the number of men. Noblewomen did not wound and kill like men because they were not warriors. They certainly caused less damage to the state, because the number of female rulers was much smaller than the proportion of men who took part in government.

One of the chroniclers tells of young widows who appealed to Philip iv of France to put an end to the war in Flanders which had left almost no men unmaimed in France.[153] But those feudal women who held fiefs and exercised ruling powers, ruled like men in a man's world. Their henchmen, the office-holders who were subject to them and the rulers whom they tackled were men, and they adapted to the way of life and scale of values of the male majority, even if some of their basic traits differed from men's (and this is by no means certain). If they were endowed with the traits usually attributed to women, such as tenderness and compassion, these did not find expression in their method of ruling. They battled for their right to rule, like Mahaut of Artois; for the rights of their husbands, like Jeanne, countess of Brittany; and for their sons. They did not hesitate to incite sons against their fathers, like Eleanor of Aquitaine, who supported her sons' rebellions against their father, Henry ii, and it is immaterial that her husband too exercised power both legitimately and illegally and held her in detention for many years.

It is possible that (at least where these women were concerned) the gap between the image of woman in medieval literature, written by men, and her true image was not so great. In the *chansons de geste* the woman encourages her husband to continue fighting even after loss and bereavement. The woman in courtly literature imposes trials on the knight, which are primarily warlike tasks. There is not much tenderness in the lady who sends her lover to fight without a shield. Women were part of medieval civilization and played a part in its cruelty. Women, like men, flocked to watch cruel executions of both men and women. When the mystic, Margery Kempe, was accused of heresy and arrested, an angry crowd of women waved their distaffs threateningly at her as she was led to prison and shouted that she would be burned at the stake.[154] The chroniclers sometimes write of the cruelty of women, including noblewomen, like the wife of the minor lord in Périgord, whose particular cruelty towards other women was depicted by the chronicler Peter of Vaux de Cernay.[155] When heretics were discovered in Orleans, the king's men, by order of Queen Constance, prevented actual acts of vengeance against them without trial, but the queen, in her fanaticism and anger, put out the eye of the heretic Stephen with a stick.[156]

Even if those who thought women to be more pious than men were right, it should be recalled that religious piety in medieval Christian society did not necessarily entail mercy and compassion: this can be learned from the tale of the nuns of Watton or the life of the Beguine Douceline. This saint beat one of her girls until her body streamed blood, for the sin of looking at passing men as she worked, and shouted at her that she would sacrifice her to God.

Would medieval civilization have been different if women had played a greater part, if women had not constituted a marginal group which adapted itself to the ruling majority? This could be asked with equal relevance of all other known civilizations. It is an important question, but not one which the historian as such can answer.

6

Townswomen

Urban society was new in several senses and woman's role in it can be understood only against the background of its unique economic, social and cultural structure. But it is important to emphasize at the outset that women's rights continued to be restricted within the new structure of urban life, although this was no longer a warrior society like the nobility, or a partially unfree society like the peasantry. The town was a place of peace (*locus pacificus*). Peace was essential to its development and its economic activity, which was based on artisanship, commerce and money affairs. It evolved its own ethos, which differed from that of the feudal nobility. Though urban society was a class society from the outset, it abolished the distinctions between freemen and serfs and, legally speaking (in contrast to rural areas), all townspeople were free.

The town arose as a secular corporation, like the guilds which grew up within it and were also secular corporations (excluding the universities), and a stratum of lay officials, notaries and judges developed. A lay society which was not a society of warriors and whose members enjoyed free competition might have been expected to expand women's political rights, but this did not occur. This appears to substantiate the evaluation (based on comparative study of the history of women and their status in society) that woman's status in general and political status in particular in a specific society cannot always be explained on the basis of the economic structure of that society or the degree to which it is democratic. One need only recall democratic Athens in its heyday, where women's rights were restricted even according to the criteria of ancient Greece.

The restriction of the rights of urban women was reflected primarily in the fact that women played no part in running the town. Different forms of government evolved in different towns, some oligarchical, others aristocratic or semi-democratic. But in none, whatever their regimes, did women play a part in government. They were not elected to municipal councils, did not hold positions of authority, and only in exceptional cases did they take part in town assemblies. In this respect the townswoman's lot was no better than that of the peasant woman. However, though women could not fulfil functions in manors and village communities, spinsters and widows in rural areas did attend village assemblies, whereas in town no woman, whatever her marital status, attended such assemblies. The increase in the number of male officiaries and wielders of authority in towns did not bring about a corresponding increase in the number of women who played a part in government. The opposite is true, in fact, so much so that within the framework of the history of women in urban society there is no room for discussion of town government.

In contrast women played an important part in the urban economy. One could scarcely envisage production in the medieval town or its internal commerce without the activities of women. Their role in labour – and there are those who regard it as one of the manifestations of the new urban ethos – was particularly prominent, and won them some place in the guilds of artisans and petty merchants, despite the restrictions imposed on them. The guild which became an ecclesiastical corporation – the university – was closed to them.

WOMEN AS CITIZENS

Women were considered to be citizens of towns, and became such by force of urban property (*burgagia*, as it was called in some towns) which they held either by right of inheritance, through purchase, by right of membership of a guild (in some towns membership of a guild was not only a precondition for permission to work but also for qualification for citizenship), or because they were married to citizens of the town. A man who became a citizen was obliged to pay a certain sum to the community,[1] and sometimes also to the lord of the town,[2] and to take an oath of loyalty to the town. But a female citizen[3] enjoyed only part of the urban privileges. She was entitled to engage in commerce and was answerable only to the municipal courts applying municipal law, at which town judges presided (if the town enjoyed maximal legal autonomy).[4] On the other hand, she did not have the right to elect or be elected to the institutions of government in the town, and in a town which sent representatives to the local or national representative assembly, she was not eligible to elect or represent.

An exception was the participation of women in the mid-fourteenth-century referendum in Provins in the Champagne. In this referendum, which encompassed citizens of the town and the surrounding villages, the population were asked whether they wished to continue to live under the rule of the local officials (*scabini*) of the commune or to become directly subject to the king. Some 1741 town voters and 960 from rural areas, 2700 in all, took part in the referendum, and 350 of them, or 13 per cent, were women. The women voters included widows, married women and apparently spinsters as well. In some cases their occupations were listed beside their names: baker; tavern-keeper, seamstress and cloth-dyer.[5] In several towns, women also took part in the election of representatives to the assembly summoned by Philip IV in Tours in 1308.[6] There were almost certainly other exceptions which are unknown to us, but generally speaking women played no part in urban assemblies and councils.

The rights of a female citizen are comparable to those of the son of a citizen while still dependent on his father. But whereas the standing of the dependent son was temporary, the woman's was permanent.[7] The status of a woman who fulfilled the financial requirements of citizenship was superior to that of the poor townsman who could not become a citizen because he did not own urban property, was not a member of a guild or could not pay the necessary fee for citizenship. But in principle at least, the possibility existed that he might some day become a citizen with full rights.

The laws of inheritance of urban property varied from region to region and even from town to town, but as in the case of the fief and the peasant estate, the rights of sons almost always took precedence over those of daughters, and those of daughters over those of males of collateral lines. In most English towns where the principle of primogeniture of sons prevailed, recognition was given to the right of the other sons and daughters to enjoy urban liberties.[8] If there were no sons, the daughter inherited, and the registers reveal numerous cases of daughters who inherited shops, the rent of urban properties, and land near towns.[9] Sometimes an arrangement was made (as was customary in some rural areas) by which the father transferred his property to his daughter in his lifetime and she guaranteed to support him and supply all his needs as befitted his station.[10] Brothers too sometimes bequeathed property to their sisters, and husbands to their wives in addition to what they received by right of dower.[11] Girls enjoyed inheritance rights very similar to those of sons in most towns in Flanders: Aire, Arras, Douai, Lille, Bruges, Ypres, Saint Omer and also in Verdun, and in Cuenca and Sepúlveda in Spain.[12]

The most drastic curtailment of female inheritance rights was in Italian towns and in Avignon: daughters who wed and were given a dowry received no part of their father's legacy, while in most Western European towns the dowry was merely deducted from their inheritance (just as property which sons received on marriage was deducted from their future legacy). Not all daughters were destined for marriage and some were sent to nunneries to which a smaller dowry was paid than a bridegroom would have received. This curtailment of the inheritance rights of daughters in Italian towns derived not only from fear of dispersal of the family property but also from fear that the property might end up in alien hands in the event that the daughter married a man from outside the town (*propter nuptias extra territoriam*). In Florence it was explicitly stipulated in the contract of sale of a part of a fortress that it must not, through inheritance, come into the hands of a woman. If no male heir could be found it should be sold.[13]

MATRIMONY

There was no outside intervention in the marriage of townswomen as there was in the case of heiresses of fiefs (and hence marriage of minors was much less common among towndwellers than among the nobility). Marriage was decided upon by the families and economic and class interests, and sometimes political calculations determined marital ties. Marriages contracted out of political and economic considerations were common in Italian towns, where matrimony was not merely the linking of two persons, but the coming together of two families. Often the marriage tie symbolized the end of strife and blood feuds between warring lineages of the town's nobility, and the establishment of new political forces.[14] In all European towns marriage was a new stage in the life of both partners. On marriage a man became an adult, bearing responsibility within the society in which he lived. If the girl was an orphan, her guardian married her off with the consent of her relatives. In

London there was a special tribunal whose task was to arrange the marriage of orphans, both male and female, in accordance with their class, when they reached the appropriate age and gave their consent to the marriage.[15]

Some of the authors of didactic works favoured particularly early marriages for prosperous towndwellers, earlier than for knights or peasants. The reason was that the rich burgher who lived a life of luxury was liable to be tempted by the lusts of the flesh, and marriage would provide an outlet for his desires.[16] But in towns, as among the feudal nobility, it was recognized that a man should consolidate his economic standing before establishing a family; and since the opportunities for economic advancement in town were greater than in rural areas, men tended to postpone marriage until they were established. The apprentices as well as the journeymen could not take wives before they attained independence, and it was sometimes stipulated in the contract of apprenticeship that an apprentice could not take a wife during his service.[17] The fourteenth-century English preacher Bromyard, like his Italian colleague, Bernardino of Sienna, denounced the protracted bachelorhood of male towndwellers. According to Bromyard, when he approached the numerous bachelors who engaged in fornication and adultery and asked them why they did not marry, they replied that they would take wives when they had homes to offer them.[18] Economic factors undoubtedly had a greater impact in determining the age for matrimony in men than in women. The remarks of the preachers should be seen against the background of conditions in the second half of the fourteenth century, when the guilds became increasingly exclusive and the promotion from the status of apprentice to hired worker and to independent craftsman was protracted and difficult and entailed considerable financial outlay.

A clear reflection of contemporary awareness that it was often economic conditions which prevented young people from marrying can be found in the *Libri de la Famiglia* by Leone Battista Alberti. He proposes that the maturer and more settled relatives of young people should encourage them, offer them examples and allocate them some part of their own property in order to enable them to set up a family.[19] In London the marriage dowry a bride brought him (in addition to loans from relatives and friends) helped a man to purchase his first goods and qualify as a candidate for entry into the merchant guild. Prospective bridegrooms were also ready to pay a percentage of the dowry, or a certain fixed sum, to a marriage broker in return for a marriage arrangement with the daughter of a

1   Christine de Pisan at her study.

ut sciam quid desit michi.
Ecce mensurabiles posuisti dies meos:
7 sustancia mea tamquam nichilu ante te.

2   The virgin and the unicorn.

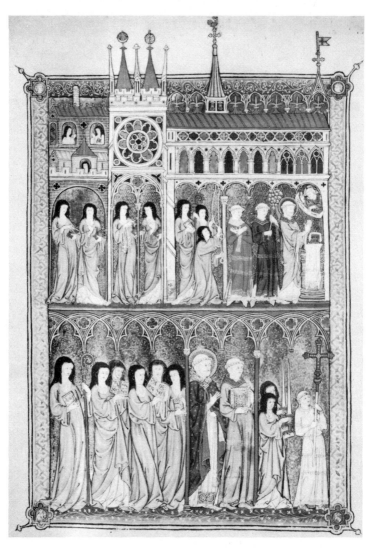

3   Miniature from 'La Sainte Abbaye' showing: (top) the sacristan
pulling the bellrope, the abbess holding her crozier and the celleress
with her keys; and (bottom) nuns in procession.

4   Nuns in the refectory. Poor Clares in the 'Polyptych of the Blessed Umilta' by Pietro Lorinzetti.

5   Saint Margaret.

6   The Virgin and Child with Adam and Eve and the tree of life decorating the base of the sculpture.

7 Scenes of family life: (top) domestic scene,
shepherd sleeping whilst on duty; (bottom)
ploughing and carpentering.

8 Wife-beating.

9 A knight watches a lady in her bath.

10 A midwife hands the mother her baby.

11   Scenes of courtly love from *Manessischen Leiderhardschift*.

12   French ivory mirror case showing a lady
crowning her lover.

13   German ivory
writing tablet showing
a hawking party.

14 'When Adam delved and Eve span,
Who was then the gentleman?'

A fourteenth-century manuscript illumination showing Adam and Eve.

15   Women harvesting, from *Der Jungfrauspiegel*, a twelfth-century German manuscript. The illustration compares, in allegorical terms, the respective benefits of married life, widowhood and virginity. At the bottom are the wives harvesting the field with their husbands: the yield is meagre; in the middle are the widows, who are rewarded with richer crops; at the top are the virgins, whose yield is the greatest of all.

16   Women catching rabbits, from Queen Mary's Psalter, *c.* 1308.

17   Women shearing and weaving wool, from the twelfth-century
Canterbury Psalter.

18   A woman milking a cow.

19 Women carding wool and weaving, from an early
fifteenth-century manuscript.

20   A lady hunting a stag, from Queen Mary's Psalter.

21   A game of chess, from Queen Mary's Psalter.

22 A scene depicting falconry and hunting, from a Franco-Burgundian tapestry dating from the mid fifteenth century.

The most wonderfull

and true storie, of a certaine Witch
named *Alse Gooderige of Stapen hill*,
who was arraigned and conuicted at Darbie
at the *Assises there*.

As also a true report of the strange torments of Thomas
Darling, *a boy of thirteene yeres of age, that was pos-*
sessed by the Deuill, with his horrible fittes and terri-
ble Apparitions by him vttered at Burton vpon
Trent *in the Countie of* Stafford, *and of his maruel-*
lous deliuerance.

23   The torments of witches in hell.

senior member of the guild.[20] The rich delayed marriage while seeking the most suitable match and the highest dowry which could improve their standing even further.

The extent to which the dowry played an important part in the calculations and prospects of the urban businessman in Italy in the later Middle Ages can be learned from the diary of a Florentine merchant which starts in 1391 and ends in 1435. This merchant had four wives, each of whom brought him a considerable dowry. Three of the four died in childbirth or shortly afterwards. All the marriages were connected with new financial projects. Before his second marriage he wrote: 'I had no money but I was about to marry and to receive a dowry. After marrying and receiving the dowry I played an important role in the partnership.' Before his third marriage he wrote; 'I guaranteed to pay 2000 florins in the following way: 1370 florins were still due to me from the previous partnership, the remainder I will receive if I remarry. I hope to find a wife who will bring me a large dowry if God sees fit to bestow it on me.' In May 1403 he took a wife who brought a dowry of 1000 florins, 700 of them in ready cash and 300 from the income of a rural estate. In 1421 he took his fourth wife, who brought a dowry of 600 florins.[21] The problem of the dowry weighed heavily on urban families in general and in those Italian towns in which the bridegroom's contribution to the marriage was very limited in particular. By the twelfth century this contribution was restricted to a certain percentage of the bride's dowry or a fixed sum (which did not increase as time passed, despite the drop in monetary value).

The restriction of the bridegroom's share meant that the widow was also maintained on a relatively small dower. The bulk of the father's property went to his sons on his death, and only a meagre dower was left to the widow. Daughters often inherited this dower when their mothers died. Sometimes the dowry was paid in instalments. Cautious or suspicious bridegrooms postponed bringing the bride home until the dowry was paid in full.[22] According to the regulations of some guilds in England, the guild was required to collect a dowry (for a lay bridegroom or for a nunnery) for the orphaned daughter of a member or for the daughter of a member who could not supply the money himself.[23] Collection of dowries for poor girls was one of the commonest forms of charity.

Wives brought their husbands more than dowries. In England, a woman who was a citizen transferred her right of citizenship to her husband on marriage; he enjoyed this right for his lifetime, and handed it on to sons and daughters of the marriage. In some guilds, such as the bakers' guild in Arras, the daughters of members handed on the right of membership to their husbands if they were members of the same trade.[24]

Daughters of rich townsmen married at a very early age. In Italian towns in the late Middle Ages thirteen was considered the desirable marriage age for a girl. The average age of matrimony for women in Florence and other Tuscan towns in the later Middle Ages was 16–17½; in London, 17. Men married later. In Tuscany the average age of matrimony for men was 27.7–31.2. Many women died in childbirth and their widowers remarried. The second wives were often very young, and the age difference between husband and wife was then even greater than in the first marriage. The third wife of the Florentine merchant mentioned above was a widow of 21 when she married him, having married her first husband at 16. She died in childbirth at the age of 29. In London men married younger, at an average age of 21–26, but they too were older than their wives.[25] Very few of the daughters of the prosperous urban class seem to have remained unmarried without entering nunneries. Daughters of the labouring class probably married slightly later than their more prosperous counterparts. Girls who migrated from villages to towns to work as maid-servants postponed marriage until they had saved up their dowries. The marriages of women who worked as apprentices for female artisans were also postponed until they completed their apprenticeship.[26] As shown by the records of the guilds, there were women of the labouring class who remained unwed without entering nunneries.

In both urban and rural areas the rich had larger families than the poor, as noticed already in a previous chapter.[27] But records of the Late Middle Ages show that the number of progeny in villages was greater than in towns in the corresponding classes. According to the records of the town of Pistoia and the adjacent rural area for the year 1427, the average number of children per prosperous urban family was 2.26; in rural areas, 3.21; in poor urban families, 0.86; and in poor rural families, 1.47.[28] The reason for this difference apparently lies in the higher infant mortality rate in towns in this period; the epidemics of the fifteenth century were very much an urban phenomenon. But despite the lower average number of children in urban families, many women of the prosperous classes bore numerous children, sometimes exhausting the full extent of their biological potential. There are known cases of seventeen births in twenty-two years in prosperous Italian families in the fourteenth and early fifteenth century. Not all the children survived, of course, but there were many large families. Dante's Beatrice, the eldest daughter of Cilia and Folco Portinari, had five brothers and five sisters. Katherine of Sienna was the youngest child of a cloth-dyer, and had twenty-four siblings! In London too there could be as many as nineteen children in a family. The estimate is that ten children were born during a twenty-year span of matrimony.

It is possible that the wives of the rich who, (like noblewomen) employed wet-nurses, conceived again sooner than did poorer women who suckled their own children. But the infant mortality rate was very high. In Pistoia, according to D. Herlihy, 17.7 per cent of the infants died between the ages of 1 and 4; 10.5 per cent between 5 and 9; 8.3 per cent between 10 and 14. This explains why, despite the high birthrate in the more prosperous classes, and the large families, there were some families in which only one male child survived or even none (as appears in certain wills drawn up in London).[29] Of course there were also undoubted cases of barrenness.

Only the urban rich lived in adjacent houses or groups of houses even after marriage and the death of parents. The middle class and the poor were characterized by residence within the nuclear family. This phenomenon of joint or adjacent residence was particularly prevalent in the towns of Italy and southern France, where there was an urban nobility, but also existed in some northern towns such as Metz, Louvain and Paris. The number of persons in households sometimes totalled forty, because in addition to the family members it included the bastards, poor relatives, servants, clients of various types and warriors.[30] The difference between the way of life of a large family and a nuclear family undoubtedly had a stronger impact on the lives of the women of the richer classes. Their lives were more centred on the home than those of the women of the labouring class.

The matrimonial property laws varied from region to region (as we saw in the chapter on married women). In some towns, in Flanders for example, there was greater recognition of a woman's right to the couple's joint property.[31] In other regions, like Italy, only the woman's right to her own property was recognized, i.e. her right to a dowry and to the limited dower promised her by her husband. The rights of the widow and widower also varied from place to place and sometimes even from town to town within the same region. In certain towns, like Cologne, the couple could agree between themselves that the survivor would inherit the deceased spouse's property.[32] In other regions, like Liguria, this was totally prohibited, and if a woman died without leaving heirs her dowry reverted to her family.[33] There were also interim solutions, as in Godmanchester in England, where, if a couple had no progeny, the wife could bequeath half of what she had acquired during the marriage to whomsoever she chose, while the second half came to her husband for life, as his legal right to enjoy the income of the property. Her family property was inherited by her kin.[34] From the wills of the wives of prosperous burghers, in which they bequeathed their personal belongings, we learn of the standard of living and material culture in the bourgeois household. The wills listed clothes, bed linen, furniture and money.[35]

In all towns the widow was entitled to enjoy the fruits of the dower for life, and municipal regulations often safeguard this right.[36] There were towns in which, on remarriage, a widow transferred her citizenship rights to her second husband for her lifetime.[37] In other towns, on the other hand, certain restrictions were imposed on her if she remarried, such as the obligation to leave the house of her first husband.[38] In London the widow kept her dower even if she remarried, but was obliged to renounce any other property bequeathed to her by her husband.[39] According to ancient custom, the widow apparently remained in residence in the house of her first husband because of her children, but by the thirteenth century this was no longer a necessary precondition in all towns for the right to remain in residence. A woman in Bristol permitted her daughter and son-in-law to live with her, but safeguarded herself in the event that the joint residence did not succeed by defining exactly which part of the house belonged to her.[40] According to the laws of Metz, the son of a widow who lived in her home was under her guardianship (*mainburdie*)[41] even if he was married and a father!

In some guilds the widows of craftsmen could transfer their right to engage in their trade and their right to membership to their second husbands if the latter were of the same craft.[42] In the fourteenth century the economic recession and the growing exclusiveness of the guilds as a result of protective legislation increased the eligibility of these widows in marriage. Widows of prosperous merchants were particularly sought after both because of their property and because of the dower their husbands had left them.

We have already discussed the image of marriage in urban society. Urban literature depicts it unattractively; the domineering and cuckolding wife was one of its typical characters. In reality, as in any society where marriages are arranged by families out of economic and class considerations, there were also cases of love matches. A tailor in London married the sister of one of the gentry, on his own testimony 'because of love and the mutual attraction between them long since'.[43] The fact that town merchants, shop-keepers, potters, tailors and shoemakers appeared before the diocesan courts to discuss matrimonial affairs reveals that they sometimes dissolved marital ties or tried to dissolve them so as to enter into new relationships. Some of these new matches were undoubtedly based on love or attraction.[44] The rich were probably more reluctant than the poor when it came to dissolving marriages because of the complicated financial arrangements entailed. Accord-ing to Bernardino of Sienna a husband should teach his wife, improve her, be with her and supply her food and raiment. The wife should be in awe of her husband, serve him, obey him and also reproach him. They owed one another love, respect and loyalty and should observe their marital duties.[45] In the towns of Tuscany, where husbands were usually years older than the young and inexperienced girls they married, the husband undoubtedly enjoyed greater authority over his wife by virtue of his age alone.

There were certainly domineering women (like those depicted in the literature), but the law stipulated the superiority of the husband and was often enforced. A woman in Ragusa, who left her husband's home with all her personal belongings, paid dearly for her action. Her husband charged her before the town council, which found that she had left home with insufficient cause. Several council members tried to persuade her to return home, then they gave her a delay of fourteen hours to return and, in a final attempt, they sent her aged mother to persuade her, but all in vain. (It may be assumed that she had had good reasons for leaving.) She was then imprisoned, her property confiscated, and she was exiled from the town.[46] Urban laws recognized the husband's right to beat his wife, and court records show that some husbands exercised this right.

THE MATERNAL ROLE

In discussing the townswoman as mother one must distinguish between the wives of prosperous burghers and the wives of the labouring class. The former, like noblewomen, did not usually suckle their children, but kept wet-nurses and sometimes sent their infants to wet-nurses in a village and did not see them for long periods.[47]

Francesco Barberino, who explicitly approved of handing

children over to wet-nurses (unlike Bartholomaeus Anglicus and others, who advocated breast-feeding by the mother), offered copious advice to the wet-nurse regarding the physical and emotional development of the child. He advises her on how to swaddle the child (his method confines the limbs so that the child can grow straight ...), how long to nurse him (about two years) and how to wean him. His method of weaning is not particularly gentle, but neither is it sudden and brutal: the wet-nurse should smear her breasts with a bitter but harmless liquid so as to repel the child, and at the same time offer him soft, sweet food, such as bread soaked in milk or apple juice. If the child refuses the food, he should be offered the breast again from time to time. (Some sources counsel much more drastic methods.) He cautions the nurse against all the dangers lurking in wait for the small child, such as pits, horses, rivers, fire, dogs, knives and other sharp instruments, snakes and poisonous plants, and advises against sleeping in the same bed with the child, for fear of overlaying. With reference to the child's emotional development, he writes that the wet-nurse should sing the child tender lullabies, rock him, and if he hurts himself, she should pretend when bandaging his wounds that she is punishing the object which hurt him and comfort him with small gifts.

Apart from the method of swaddling, a modern educator could approve Francesco Barberino's theories, but the question remains why any wet-nurse should choose to act tenderly and patiently towards a strange child given into her care who, at least in part, usurps the place of her own child (unless her own infant has died). At best, if she had an abundance of milk, she nursed both the strange child and her own. If her milk supply ran low, it may be assumed that she first weaned her own child and, under the hygienic conditions then prevailing, thus endangered his life. How could she not feel some hostility towards the other woman's child, even if it was entrusted to her only after the death of her own baby?

It is known that there was a very high mortality rate among infants entrusted to wet-nurses in the fifteenth century, particularly by homes for foundlings, but also by private individuals who handed over their illegitimate offspring. There is no way of assessing the relative incidence of infanticide, neglect or natural death. It seems almost certain that wet-nurses took better care of the children of the rich, who entrusted their legal progeny to them in return for payment, but the phenomenon can also cast light on the treatment of all children handed to nurses. In Tuscany in the later Middle Ages children were sometimes handed from nurse to nurse.

If the mother died, the child was abandoned to the care of the nurse for years. Giovani Morelli relates that his father, who was born in 1335, was entrusted to a nurse. His mother died shortly after his birth and he remained in his nurse's home until he was ten or twelve. His father, who already had grown children, took no interest in him. The nurse was a harsh woman who beat him mercilessly. Even as a grown man he would be overcome with rage when he recalled the nurse who, so he claimed, was the most bestial woman he had ever encountered. This is an extreme, though not necessarily unique, case.

In Tuscan towns, a widow sometimes returned to her parental home and left her child with her husband's family. But in a family where everything was in order the child was usually restored to his parents at the age of two or three. Herlihy and Klapisch accept Philippe Ariès' theory that parents were not greatly attached to their children in their first years of life. They did not accept them into their homes or their hearts. The child's chances of survival were so slim that parents avoided close ties before the age of two or three. It was undoubtedly difficult to become attached to a child who was handed over to a wet-nurse outside the parental home. But it would be hard to draw the conclusion that parents employed defensive emotional tactics with regard to a child whose prospects for survival were poor. It should be recalled that the infant mortality rate was high in later centuries as well when, according to Ariès himself, there were nonetheless closer emotional ties between parents and infants.

When the child returned home he was welcomed, and in Tuscan towns pampered and showered with affection (at least in the prosperous families with which we are acquainted).[48] Did this treatment compensate the child for his early years of detachment from his parents, or did those years leave their mark on him for life? It is hard to answer this question. Honoré de Balzac was handed over to a wet-nurse in a village immediately after birth (his elder brother had died several weeks after birth because his mother did not have enough milk to nurse him herself). Two years later his sister Laura was born and was sent to the same wet-nurse. The two children grew up in her home for four years, detached from their mother. This period left its mark on Honoré for life. As an adult he often declared: 'I never had a mother, I have never known a mother's love.' In the case of Balzac, according to his biographer, this was not an attempt to arouse sympathy but rather a boast emphasizing his uniqueness as an exceptional person, a kind of metaphysical creature.[49] How did the prosperous townspeople of the Middle Ages respond to similar treatment? We have no way of knowing. On the other hand, we learn from the family records of the period and lives of the saints of the affectionate treatment of children of Italian burghers: we read of mothers curling and dyeing their daughters' hair, fathers playing ball with their sons, and children dancing for the entertainment of family and friends.[50] We know of no similar records in Northern Europe. It is interesting to note that one of the characteristic features of the private architecture of the second half of the fourteenth century and first half of the fifteenth in Florence is greater separation between the parts of the home intended for economic activity and directed outwards to the street and those earmarked for the private use of the nuclear family.[51]

Were daughters given less attention than sons? We do not believe that this has been proved. It is obvious that sons were considered a blessing and fathers at least certainly preferred sons. Bernardino of Sienna promised sons who treated their parents with respect that the Lord would reward them with numerous children, particularly sons who in due course would come to resemble their fathers. On the other hand, churchmen repeatedly warned fathers not to smile at their daughters too much (and mothers not to caress their sons excessively). The repeated warnings suggest that this was customary conduct which the churchmen sought in vain to prevent. Surviving children, both boys and girls, were often pampered and were treated with affection and care, at least in the Italian towns of the later Middle Ages. But the span of childhood was brief in this stratum as well, and for girls even briefer than for their brothers. On the other hand, girls usually spent more childhood years and sometimes their entire childhood with their mothers, while many boys were sent away from home at the age of 7 to be educated. Some were sent to town schools or monastery schools, others to serve as apprentices to rich merchants, like Giovanni Boccaccio, who before he reached his adolescence was sent away as an apprentice.

Students of the arts faculty at universities were aged 12–14, or sometimes only 10, when they reached the university, having already attended school away from home. Girls were also sent away from home to town schools or nunnery schools, but more of them studied at home with private male or female tutors. At the age of 12 at the latest their studies ended, and until they wed they remained at home. They married young, and many were wives and mothers by the age of fifteen. Since young men in towns married later than girls, they enjoyed a longer span of youth among their contemporaries and, particularly in Italian towns, sometimes undertook missions for their parents or merchant masters. Among girls there was a very rapid transition from childhood to marriage, with all the responsibilities and duties it entailed.[52]

The mother of an urban saint, like several mothers of saints born into the nobility, treated her son more tenderly than did his father. When the father of St Francis of Assisi, angry at his son for throwing away his money, chained him up in a room of the house, his mother freed him although she must have known that her husband would vent his anger against her on his return, which he in fact did.[53] Among the upper classes in towns, as among the nobility, fathers were sometimes absent from home for lengthy periods. Men travelled away from home in the service of the monarch or the seigneur, and many travelled for commercial and financial reasons. Many children were orphaned of their mothers, who died in childbirth or from disease at an early age, and even more lost their fathers, who had sired them at a relatively advanced age. Because of the low life-expectancy, they did not usually live to raise their children to adulthood. According to D. Herlihy, this phenomenon was pronounced in Florence, where widowers took young wives and died when their children were small, leaving their widows to raise them. The mothers tried to avoid sending children away from home, and sometimes ties of excessive mutual dependence grew up between mother and son.[54] Some children lost both parents in infancy. We do not know at what age Dante's mother died, but it was shortly after she bore him. His father remarried, sired another son and two daughters, and died when Dante was still a child.

In the labouring class women suckled their own infants and raised them alone. The fathers were absent less than men of the merchant and moneyed class. If the parents survived, the ties with their infant children were, for better or worse, enduring and strong, but here too the span of childhood was brief. Children who learned trades became apprentices at an early age, as can be learned from the contracts between parents and craftsmen. In the towns of Northern Europe, the period of apprenticeship was seven years, and the child apprentice lived with the artisan's family. In Tuscan towns apprenticeship began a little later and lasted only three or four years, and some apprentices continued to live in the parental home. Girls of the urban labouring class were also sent to learn a craft under the supervision of the craftsman's wife, as can also be ascertained from the contracts.[55]

In all strata of urban society, people usually ensured the future of their children by giving them an education suited to their station, finding them a position and arranging a suitable match and a future legacy. Sometimes parents among both the labouring and the prosperous class acted harshly and neglectfully. John of Lodi, author of the biography of Peter Damian, writes that the saint's parents, a poor couple from Ravenna, burdened with many children, did not welcome his birth. If the wife of a priest had not taken pity on him and cared for him, and persuaded his mother to give him the breast, he would certainly have died of hunger, since his mother, who apparently suffered from depression, refused to nurse him.[56]

The Franciscan Salimbene, the son of rich notables from Parma, relates that throughout his childhood and youth he could not love his mother because of an incident which occurred when he was a small child and was related to him years later. According to the story, there was an earthquake in Parma. His mother, who feared that their house would be damaged, snatched up his two sisters and went to seek shelter in the home of her parents, leaving him at home. He claimed that she should have concerned herself with him, as a son, more than with her daughters, while she claimed that since they were lighter, she could carry them more easily.[57] One can learn from these complaints by the Franciscan friar something of the relative standing of boys and girls in that world. But it is also illuminating to note the cold calculation of a mother who could abandon one of her children, at best in order to save two others, and the enduring resentment of the son who heard the story later. It may be assumed that it merely strengthened existing feelings of resentment and deprivation.

From the records kept by coroners in England for the use of judges, it transpires that babies and infants often died in accidents caused by insufficient parental supervision. Particularly striking is the number of babies who died in the fires which often broke out in the wooden houses of the period. This source naturally reflects cases of negligence, but occasionally one finds examples of devotion and readiness for sacrifice on the part of the mother. A couple fled a fire, forgetting in their haste to take the baby from its cradle. When the mother realized her omission, she ran back into the flames to save the infant and was suffocated by the smoke.[58]

Labourers did not keep family records, nor were diaries or biographies written in this class which could have taught us something of the attitude of mothers towards their children. As regards the attitude to children in prosperous urban families, let us cite another detail from Balzac's childhood, in order not to draw too severe a contrast between the treatment of children in medieval civilization and in later periods. At the age of 8 Balzac was sent to be educated at an Oratorian congregation school, and he studied there till the age of 15. According to the custom of the congregation, parents could visit only once a year. When he grew up, Balzac swore that his parents never visited him once throughout the seven years of his studies. According to his sister, he imagined this, but she admitted that his mother visited only a very few times and that the school was only forty miles from their home in Tours. For educational reasons his mother deprived him of pocket money during his studies. His health deteriorated to the point where his teachers eventually asked his parents to remove him.[59] Was this an isolated case? As to the scarcity of visits and failure to give pocket money, one may assume so. As to it scarring him for life, this seems unlikely. We do not know how similar treatment affected others who did not write themselves, or whose biographies are unknown. His fellow pupils too might receive visitors only once a year, and the Oratorian congregation school near Tours was not the only one of its kind in Western Europe of the early nineteenth century.

WOMEN'S WORK

In his *Utopia*, Thomas More wrote about the large number of idlers in various societies, in contrast to Utopia, where everyone worked. Among the idlers he includes priests, noblemen and their retainers, beggars and women: 'First there are almost all the women, who constitute half the whole; or where the women are busy, there as a rule the men are snoring in their stead.'[60] But study of the history of women in the Middle Ages reveals that these remarks are in no way applicable to medieval urban society. The role of women in production in medieval towns was considerable, despite the restrictions imposed on them, and this is perhaps the most interesting chapter in the history of urban women. There were occupations in which women played a particularly important part, to the point where they were largely regarded as female occupations, yet they were also engaged in by men, who were never totally replaced in them. Nor was there any undermining of the status of those men who remained active in these occupations. One could not therefore claim that there was a clear division of occupations in towns by sex. Since the women who engaged in certain activities also worked in their own households, they were ruled by two separate rhythms of work: that accepted as 'feminine', characterized by the fact that the work was never-ending and was aimed at satisfying the needs of others, a husband and children, and the 'masculine' rhythm, consisting of alternate effort and rest.

Some women engaged in various occupations within the family workshop as the daughters and wives of craftsmen. It was common to teach girls and women various crafts, and the right of a craftsman to teach his trade to his wife and daughter and to utilize their help was recognized. Many widows continued to engage in their husbands' occupations, and this too was recognized, though various restrictions were imposed by the guild authorities. Had they not learned the trade from their fathers (they often married men who were in the same trade and had been their fathers' apprentices) or their husbands, they could not have engaged in it as widows, and certainly could not have taken their husbands' place in training apprentices. Even in those guilds which prohibited the hiring of women, members were permitted to utilize the services of their wives and daughters.

Women sometimes learned a trade in childhood as apprentices of craftswomen. Some later married men in the same trade and worked with them, some married men engaged in some other occupation and continued to work in their own trade, others never married and continued to follow their trade. Women who worked with their husbands were not usually members of a guild during the lifetime of their husbands, but, if they were widowed, they were permitted, with certain limitations, to continue their husband's trade and to become members of the guild. Spinsters, and some of the married women who worked in trades other than those of their husbands, worked for wages. In some towns, particularly in the spinning and weaving industries, the women were given raw materials and worked at home.[61] Some married women and spinsters were members of guilds. Then there were guilds composed exclusively of women, in which the statutes were drawn up by the women themselves. In the mixed guilds too, women sometimes participated in drawing up the statutes.

We learn of the role of women from the statutes and regulations of the various guilds, from royal and seigneurial decrees, court records and records of taxpayers. We can obtain a preliminary picture of the role of women in urban production by perusing the well-known *Livre des Métiers*, written by Etienne Boileau in the thirteenth century and containing the regulations of the guilds of

Paris at that time. Of the one hundred occupations the author lists, six are occupations in which only female guilds engaged in Paris. In addition, women worked in another eighty of the listed occupations, that is to say in eighty-six of the hundred occupations listed. The occupations which were exclusively female were: spinning silk on a broad loom, production of elegant head-coverings decorated with jewels and gold thread (*chapeau d'orfroi*), and production of decorated purses (*aumonières sarrazinoises*). (A large number of the crafts practised in Paris were connected with fashionable garments.) Spinning on broad and narrow looms was done at home, and the women received the materials from the merchants. They were under the supervision of two male supervisors appointed by the *praepositus* of the merchants of the city, who enforced regulations as to quality, wage rates, conditions for acceptance of apprentices, fines for violations, acceptance of new workers and rest days.[62] The purses makers, like the women who wove silk for head-coverings, were organized in women's guilds whose regulations were determined by the guild members and approved by the *praepositus*.[63]

Many of the other occupations in which women engaged were also connected with clothing: the making of ribbons and bindings, sewing, fur production, hat- and scarf-making, wig-making, work with feathers for decoration and various stages of the textile industry: washing, dyeing, spinning and weaving wool and flax. Women also engaged in sharpening tools, and producing needles, pins, buckles, scissors and knives. They worked as goldsmiths, produced jewelry incorporating natural crystal, and made crystal vases – delicate work which demanded considerable skill. They also worked as barbers. The makers of ribbons, bindings and fringes were members of a mixed guild, where the rights of the widower of a guild member did not differ from those of a widow. If the surviving spouse was in the same trade, i.e. a ribbon and bindings maker, he or she could continue the trade of the deceased spouse as a guild member empowered to train apprentices. Both craftsmen and craftswomen trained boy and girl apprentices. The female crystal workers and makers of needles and pins and other tools used by seamstresses and goldsmiths were members of a joint guild.[64] The wives of weavers who worked with their husbands were considered to be craftswomen like them, and the regulations stipulated that the wife of a craftsman could be responsible for apprentices of both sexes.[65]

The registers of payment of tallage in Paris for the years 1296, 1297 and 1313 confirm and complete this picture of a wide range of female trades. The women mentioned in these records were all working independently in their trades and paid taxes separately. Married women who helped their husbands did not appear in the records, since their husbands paid for them. Among others, the records list the midwife Sara, who was unmarried (though we do not know if she was a spinster or a widow), and a retail trader whose husband Robert was a shoemaker.[66] Note should be taken of the role of women in the guild of embroiderers in gold thread in Paris, who were classified as precious metal workers. Of the four guild officers, one was a married woman.[67] They also played a part in the guild of leather-workers and workers in combinations of leather and metal and leather and wood. The right to work in part of this trade was granted in the days of Louis VII as a monopoly to a widow named Thecia and to her descendants. They processed the leather and made leather belts, straps, gloves, shoes and pouches in which seals, silver, documents, prayer missals and toilet articles were kept.[68] In 1287 the monopoly was again granted to a woman, denoted as Marcelle. The caskets in whose manufacture women played a part were made of combinations of leather, wood and metal decorations. They also made various purses and scabbards for swords and knives. The registers of taxpayers list women as shoemakers and even as metal-workers, but with regard to the latter we do not know whether the denotations beside their names (*forcetière, favresse*) are meant to denote a trade or are merely family names.[69]

Women followed a considerable proportion of the above-mentioned trades in other European towns as well: there were spinners and weavers in Sienna and Perugia;[70] women members of the belt-makers guild in Florence, which was a mixed guild, and of the guild of the flax-weavers,[71] women weavers in Toulouse;[72] weavers and embroiderers with gold thread in Frankfurt, Cologne and most of the towns of Flanders.[73]

In England the women who worked as silk-weavers in London sent a petition to the king in 1368 asking him to order the mayor to restrain a certain Nicholas, who for some time had been hoarding all the raw and coloured silk and other goods, causing a rise in prices and heavy financial damage to the king and to the petitioners whose profession and source of livelihood was silk-weaving.[74] About one hundred years later, in the mid-fifteenth century, within the framework of the protectionist movements which developed in England to defend English production against the competition of imported goods, the London spinners, weavers and seamstresses in silk again appealed to Parliament. These women, who worked at home according to the putting-out system, and who were not registered in guilds, asked Parliament to pass a law forbidding the import of partly or fully processed silk goods into England. They stated in their request that this occupation had provided an honourable livelihood for many women who handed on their skills to others, and now some thousand women were learning the trade. The import of inferior goods from abroad made by foreigners eager for profit could ruin this honourable trade in which women worked, and cause numerous respectable women to be unemployed.[75]

According to the taxpayers register of London in 1319, 4 per cent of all taxpayers were women. Some were rich widows who lived off rent, but they also included women both married and spinsters who worked independently.[76] In York women were members of the hat-makers' guild alongside men,[77] and the same was true in the tailors' guild in Lincoln.[78] In England too, craftswomen, embroiderers and others trained girl apprentices. Sometimes the girl was registered in the contract as the apprentice of both husband and wife, but when a woman worked in a different trade to her husband, it was explicitly stated that it was she who would teach the trade.[79] In York, as also in Paris, there were women members of the guild of leather processers, including women who prepared leather for parchment.[80] In English towns and villages, brewing, which was also done at home, was mainly women's work. The court registers record many cases of women tried for violations of the Assize of Ale, and urban regulations on proper methods of production are often directed mainly at women.[81] The registers of Colchester list a woman named Juliana Gray, who was fined several times not only for transgression of the Assize of Ale but also for selling wine illegally. Despite the charges, she apparently flourished, and on her death bequeathed landed property near the town to her second husband.[82]

In some places, like England and southern Frace, women played a prominent role in the fraternities, those voluntary associations whose members banded together for joint religious and social reasons and which were sometimes affiliated, at least in part, to the guilds. They were not exclusively male clubs, and their membership included women. Women were also sometimes among the founders and the composers of the regulations. The founders of the fraternity of the Holy Virgin, established in 1351 at Kingston upon Hull, for example, included ten men and thirteen women. Ten of the women were the wives of the founders but three were not. The statutes stipulated identical entrance fees for bachelors or spinsters wishing to join the fraternity, and if they married the fee was not increased and the spouse was accepted as a brother or sister. The statutes were signed by the male founders on their own behalf and in the name of their wives, and by spinsters in their own right. This was a legal reflection of the differences we have already noted between the status of married women and that of spinsters. In these fraternities the female members usually enjoyed the same rights to welfare and aid as men. (The only thing forbidden them was to hold wake over a deceased male member of the fraternity ...)[83]

In all European towns women worked as washerwomen, gatekeepers and also as bathhouse attendants.[84] And in conclusion let us note a bookbinder from Norwich,[85] a female book illuminator who worked with a well-known illuminator at Avignon,[86] and another female illuminator in Paris whose work, according to Christine de Pisan, surpassed in beauty anything done by men and whose wage was higher than theirs. Christine adds: 'This is known to me from experience since she did several illuminations for me.'[87] Last but not least, there were women members of the guild of singers and players in Paris, who also took part in drawing up the statutes, led by the king's minstrel.[88]

There were also many women who rented out houses, managed hotels and taverns, and in particular engaged in commerce in foodstuffs both in shops and stalls, in the markets and at weekly or seasonal fairs.[89] Some of them worked alone while others helped their husbands. It seems to have been mainly the wives of petty merchants who helped their husbands in markets and at fairs. They often also came to their aid when brawls broke out with neighbouring stallkeepers at the fair. The records mention women selling poultry, fish and other sea and dairy foodstuffs.[90] In Paris women engaged in trade in cloth and clothing, from old clothes to various garments and to textiles, as recorded in the statutes of the guilds and registers of taxpayers. The latter also list two female money-changers and one money-lender.

In Norwich there was a woman wheat merchant, a trade considered highly respectable,[91] and there were several cases of widows of great overseas merchants who continued their husbands' businesses. The widow Alice demanded of the Guildhall court in London in 1370 half of the cargo of a certain boat which had been seized by the bailiff of Billingsgate as the property of some other person. She brought proof of her claim and the court ordered that the cargo be released and handed over to her. Margery Russell of Coventry, who was robbed of goods to the value of £800 by the Spaniards, obtained permission to seize the cargo of other Spaniards in order to compensate herself. She took a larger quantity than was due to her and the Spaniards lodged a complaint against her. Rose Burford, widow of a rich merchant who loaned a large sum to the king to finance his Scottish wars in 1318, continued her husband's business after his death. When the debt due to her husband was not repaid even after she had submitted several petitions, she proposed to the king that it be repaid in the form of exemption from the tax she was due to pay for wool she wished to export. She was summoned to court to submit her plea, the proposal was examined and her request was granted. There were others of her like, as can be seen from the hundred rolls of 1274, which list among the great wool merchants certain London widows engaged in large-scale trade in wool and other goods, like Isabella Buckerel and others. One woman is even mentioned as the Staple merchant in the days of Edward IV, that is to say the recognized exporter of wool from England to Calais.[92]

As we have noted, these women were widows. Those women who traded independently, on the other hand, and were not continuing the work of deceased husbands, were active mainly in small local trade in garments or foodstuffs. An independent woman merchant who engaged in foreign trade, or even in domestic retail trade, whether a spinster or married woman, was the exception to the rule.[93] It was also usually the wives of petty merchants who worked with their husbands in the markets and at fairs. The wife of a great merchant was more closely confined to the home, there was no economic need for her to work and her husband did not require her help. There were however scattered cases of women who worked without being in financial need. Margery Kempe, who later became a mystic (and whose history is therefore known), was the wife of one of the great merchants in Lynne. Nonetheless she worked, first at brewing and later at wheat-milling. She herself said that she worked because she had leisure time and could not bear for another woman to compare to her in elegance. In other words, her work was an outlet for a desire for activity and brought her an added income which enabled her to acquire the luxuries she wanted. Though she had fourteen children, she was bored and sought an occupation outside the home. This suggests that she did not devote too much time to bringing up her children. We also know of the wife of a London lawyer who owned a shop in Sopers Lane. The silk-making in London was carried out in part by the wives of merchants, who processed the raw material supplied by their husbands.[94]

Some women engaged in retail commerce and were members of the guilds of petty merchants, like the poultry traders' guilds in Paris for example.[95] On the other hand, we have found no record of women members of the great retail merchants guilds, which in effect (though not always officially) constituted the central municipal authority in various towns. In some towns in which the merchants' guild acted as the town council in practice, the right of women to hand on guild membership to sons and husbands was sometimes abrogated, and it was determined that the right could only be inherited from a father or uncle.[96] The right of women to hand on membership of merchants' guilds to husbands, sons and even grandsons was only recognized in towns in which the guild did not constitute the municipal institution.[97] It is characteristic that in Paris women merchants are mentioned in the statutes of 1324 which relate to petty local merchants, but not in the 1408 statutes which deal with the great cloth merchants who were exporters and retail merchants.[98]

The right of women to fulfil functions connected with economic activity varied from town to town. In Paris a woman could not hold the position of measurer of weights.[99] In London, on the other hand, women sometimes held the office of weigher of silk.[100] The assayer of oysters farmed his office to women, but this aroused opposition, 'since it is not fitting for the city because women are not capable of effectively preventing frauds in commerce'.[101]

The female merchants, whether spinsters, widows or married women sued and were sued independently (as *femme sole*). This was to the advantage of the husband, who was thus exempted from responsibility for his wife's commercial activities and their possible outcome, and also bestowed complete independence on the woman merchant even if she was a married woman. This legal independence was recognized in all medieval European towns.[102]

Here and there we find references by the authors of didactic works to women as an urban labour force. Francesco Barberino, for example, writes: 'Let not the woman who sells cheese wash it to make it appear fresh; the women weavers should use all the thread given them with the order and not take any for their own needs.' The author also refers to the professional ethics of servant girls, women barbers, women bakers, tavern-keepers, female haberdashers, and even women beggars.[103] But generally speaking the authors of didactic works concentrated more on the sexual chastity of women and their duties towards their husbands than on their economic activities. The literature of the estates totally obscured the role of women in production in towns.

Women undoubtedly played a considerable part in crafts in town, in petty commerce and occasionally in great commerce. But they were not free to engage in whatever occupation they chose, as men were. Certain guilds were completely closed to them while in others they were restricted. In some guilds it was prohibited to employ women for wages, and in those occupations in which they worked for daily, weekly, monthly or annual wages, they were, almost without exception, discriminated against in comparison with men. In certain guilds unmarried or married women were not accepted, and only the widows of members were taken in, with certain restrictions, to continue the work of their husbands.

It is characteristic that according to a royal decree issued in England in 1364, craftsmen were permitted to engage only in their own crafts, excluding women who engaged in brewing, baking, various stages of production of wool, flax and silk, who were permitted to engage in several trades. The historian who quotes this decree adds that it was issued because medieval society already recognized the 'versatility' of woman, 'the eternal amateur'.[104] But it is doubtful whether this dubious compliment is merited. The truth is that this regulation was issued because not all guilds accepted women and some of those which did take them in imposed certain restrictions. Therefore many women worked at home, the raw materials being provided by entrepreneurs, or worked for wages. They were not recognized as expert craftsmen with full rights in guilds and therefore engaged in several different crafts in order to earn what was needed to finance a household. The law confirmed their right to do so. They did not act out of free choice to answer the needs of their versatility or eternal amateurishness or for lack of the necessary qualifications to specialize in a certain trade.

The following are several examples of bans or restrictions on women from engaging in certain trades. In Paris women were prohibited from working on the carpets known as *tapis sarrazinois*, the argument being that the work was dangerous in general and for pregnant women in particular.[105] In Norwich women were banned from weaving with twine (that is to say weaving types of cloth which required dense weaving) on the pretext that they lacked the physical strength to carry out this work properly.[106] In Ghent the wives of the makers of a certain type of men's hose were banned from working in the trade; they could only supervise the work of hired labourers.[107] The daughters of the leather belt-makers in Paris were allowed to work as independent craftswomen in this craft even if they wed, but were not allowed to teach the craft to apprentices or to their husbands.[108]

The ban against training apprentices often applied also to the widows of craftsmen who were allowed to continue their husbands' work. According to the statutes of several guilds, a widow could complete the training of an apprentice who had begun his service under her husband, but could not take on new apprentices. The widow of a maker of wax candles in Paris in 1399 was forbidden by the jurats to continue working in her husband's craft, the argument being that she was not an expert craftswoman. She appealed to the Châtelet court and the judges accepted her appeal and permitted her to continue working in the craft on condition that she did not work for someone else, did not send labourers to work for others and did not accept new apprentices. If she married a man from outside the trade, she could neither teach him nor their joint children her craft.[109] The same rule applied to women who made prayer beads from shells and coral, and those who worked in crystal and precious stones.[110] In the case of the latter, the pretext cited was that members of the craft could not believe that a woman could become expert in so delicate a craft to the extent where she could teach it to a child.

These are several examples of bans and restrictions on women in guilds. Nor were hired women workers allowed to work in all occupations. According to the statutes of the guild of wool fullers in Lincoln, members were forbidden to use female help in the various stages, apart from their own wives and the servant girls of their wives.[111] The same was true in the guild of belt- and strap-makers in London and the weavers' guild in Bristol. In Bristol it was stated that the employment of hired female labour was responsible for the fact that many men in this trade could not find work and had become vagrants without sources of income.[112] Women's wages were lower than men's, and there were undoubtedly craftsmen who preferred to hire women for this reason. According to G. d'Avenal, in 1326–50 the average wage of women was only 68 per cent of that of men doing the same work. In 1376–1400 their wage was 75 per cent of men's on the average, because after the Black Death there was a fall in the population and a rise in demand for hired labour. All wages rose despite legislation aimed at preventing this, and women's wages were included in the trend. But even in this marginal period, which in general was apparently kinder to surviving urban and rural

workers than the period preceding the 1348 Plague, women's wages
did not catch up with men's.[113] The solution proposed by those of
good intentions who wanted to prevent competition by cheap
female labour was not to employ women. The idea of equalizing
their wages to those of men occurred to no one. In contrast to
women who received daily, weekly, monthly or annual wages,
those women who were paid by the piece for particular products
(strips of woven cloth, embroidered cloth) were not deprived in
comparison with men. This was particularly true in the spinning,
weaving, embroidery and sewing trades, in which women specialized and where there was a demand for their labour.[114]

Why were women excluded from some guilds? An important
historian of the guilds, René de Lespinasse, has reiterated an
argument also cited by historians to explain why women were
burned at the stake rather than hanged, namely sexual modesty.
According to him, attempts were made to keep women out of guilds
mainly because the apprentices lived in the homes of artisans to
mature age. For this reason a widow was forbidden to train
apprentices even if she continued to work in her husband's trade.
But the danger of adultery and fornication existed in the case of the
artisan's wife and daughters as well, and not only that of his widow,
and town craftsmen were well aware of this. An apprenticeship
agreement drawn up in 1371 in the bow-makers' guild in York
stipulated that if the apprentice committed adultery with the wife of
the craftsman or fornicated with his daughter his years of service
would be doubled.[115] The punishment was imposed, but nobody
contemplated abolishing apprenticeship. As we have already seen,
the age did not always consider adultery and fornication to be the
gravest of sins, and sexual modesty was neither the sole nor the
dominant argument cited at the time for restricting women.[116]

In addition to the claim that a woman was not likely to become an
expert craftswoman, we also encounter the argument that certain
jobs, like production of *sarrazinois* carpets for example, were too
dangerous for women, and for pregnant women in particular. But it
is unlikely that this was the true reason for denying the right of
women to work in this trade. They often carried out arduous and
very dirty tasks. The poultry slaughterers and sellers, for example,
sometimes hired women to carry the innards to the walls of the
town, a filthy task which involved carrying heavy weights,[117] and no
voice was raised against their employment in this work. A royal
decree of Jean II of France in 1351 against idlers in Paris stated that
all healthy idlers, whether male or female, who did not wish to

work, should be expelled from the town. If they were caught again, they would be imprisoned; if a third time, placed in the stocks; and if a fourth time, branded on the forehead.[118] Statutes issued in England after the Plague to establish maximum wages for workers stated that any hired worker, whether male or female, up to the age of 60 who was not working for some master must accept work offered for the wage specified in the decree. Any person of either sex who violated this decree would be punished by imprisonment.[119] Court registers reveal that women were tried for contravening the decree, i.e. for refusing to work in return for the specified wage and taking other employment for higher wages.[120] It seems that not only were there no objections to the work of women, not only were they obliged to work in order to support themselves or their families, but in the working classes this was in fact demanded of them by society and state. The objections to female labour arose only when their work competed with that of men and was likely to retrict male activity in that area, or when their occupation brought them status and prestige.

The well-known protectionism of the guilds intensified in the period of economic recession in the fourteenth century, although here the various regulations were not directed against women alone – for instance, the period of apprenticeship was extended. From the status of apprentice, a man rose to that of hired labourer and only after accumulating a considerable sum could he try to gain entry into a guild. Numerous regulations were passed aimed at combating foreign competition and safeguarding the rights of the sons of craftsmen; other regulations were aimed at preventing competition between craftsmen within the same guild. In a previous chapter we mentioned the restrictions imposed on the Beguines in trades in the town. These curbs were imposed not so much because of their sex as because they competed with the guilds.

But, generally speaking, women constituted a large marginal group among craftsmen; such a group, however large, could be cut, and in times of crisis it was the first to be affected. Many poor women joined Beguinages in the fourteenth century precisely because the range of employment opportunities for women in the towns of Flanders and Germany was curtailed in this period. Pretexts were always found for the restrictions. Sometimes the argument was sanctimonious: women should be prevented from working too hard. Sometimes it was a new version of the classic argument of woman's incapacity, cited by jurists who wrote of feminine feebleness of mind and frivolousness. Sir John Fortescue wrote that women lacked the necessary power of concentration to conduct a business,[121] and the authors of the guild statutes cited the inability of women to gain expertise in a craft. The factor of modesty was also sometimes mentioned.

Convincing proof that objections to female labour were voiced when it competed with specialized work which involved a respected status in society, and that the sight of a woman fulfilling a prestigious function was a thorn in their flesh, can be found in the few cases of women who practised medicine, in other words who refused to content themselves with the status of surgeon or midwife and adopted the methods of academic physicians. Throughout the Middle Ages women served as midwives both in towns and in rural areas. (In the period when witchcraft trials proliferated in the fourteenth and fifteenth centuries, some of the accused women were undoubtedly midwives and various kinds of healers who failed to cure their patients.)[122] The daughters and widows of apothecaries and barbers often carried on the trade of their fathers and husbands.[123] There were also female members of the guilds of surgeons, whose members were considered more respectable than barbers and who, apart from practising surgery, also healed skin ailments, swellings and sores. In order to become a surgeon, a man first served as an apprentice as in other guilds. They were experienced and dexterous and could almost certainly provide as much relief as academic physicians.[124] They had their own professional pride and fought for a law to stipulate what types of injuries and sores barbers could treat, insisting that treatment of graver injuries be the monopoly of surgeons.

Royal decrees on the method of work for surgeons issued in Paris in the fourteenth century are addressed to both men and women.[125] In some Italian towns where surgeons were under the supervision of the faculty of medicine, there were women who were licensed to practise surgery. In 1322, on the recommendation of the medical faculty of Salerno university, the court of Charles, duke of Calabria, ruled that Francesca, a married woman, was authorized to practise surgery after having been tested by the representatives of the faculty of medicine. According to the ruling not only did the law permit a woman to practise surgery, but it was even desirable, since for reasons of modesty it was preferable for women to treat women.[126] The fact that women took their place among surgeons and apothecaries can also be learned from a document written in the thirteenth century to guide churchmen who tendered free treatment to poor patients who could not afford the services of academic physicians or even surgeons. The author of the book writes that he collected some of the prescriptions in his book from a woman surgeon and from a female apothecary, the daughter of an apothecary.[127]

Nevertheless women were not permitted to practise as academic physicians. As the universities developed, medical knowledge became an academic subject, but universities remained closed to women,[128] and their medical faculties jealously guarded their privileges. They issued regulations aimed at protecting the monopoly of their graduates and, on their initiative, various rulers forbade the practice of academic medicine by any person who had not studied at a medical faculty and been licensed by its teachers.[129] These regulations and decrees were directed against all those who were likely to practise medicine: barbers, apothecaries and surgeons, both male and female.

It transpires that just as there were men who tried to evade the regulations and to practise medicine without being qualified, so there were women. Of particular interest is the story of a woman named Jacoba, who was tried in 1322 in Paris for practising medicine. According to the indictment she visited, examined and treated her patients in the manner of academic physicians: she took the pulse, tested the urine, let blood, prescribed medicines and purgatives and hot baths. All this she did without being qualified and without receiving a licence from the faculty of medicine. The gravest misdemeanour appears to have been the fact that she examined urine and measured the pulse – a method of diagnosis which was the source of pride and distinguishing feature of academic physicians. All the patients who were summoned to testify spoke in her defence: they praised her dedication and said that in contrast to prevailing custom, she did not demand payment in advance but only after having cured the patient; all of them emphasized that she succeeded where others had failed in curing them. The witnesses for the defence included both men and women.

Jacoba herself pleaded in her defence that the decree banning women from practising medicine had been issued only once, and that before she was born. The decree had been aimed at ignorant women, inexperienced in medicine, and she could not be considered as such since she was skilled in medical science. She also pleaded that it was desirable for women to treat women. Though it could be argued that by the same token it was wrong for a woman to treat men, as she had in fact done, since she had succeeded in healing them this could only be considered a secondary evil. It had prevented the greater evil of the death of patients whom other physicians had not succeeded in curing. But her plea fell on deaf ears. Jacoba was prohibited from continuing to practise medicine and was fined. It seems likely that she paid the fine and returned to her former practice, as she had done a previous occasion.[130]

Like Jacoba, several other women were tried for practising medicine without a permit: Clarice de Rotmago,[131] a married woman; Johanna the convert;[132] Marguerite of Ypres, the surgeon; and Belota the Jewess. They were excommunicated and fined.[133] These women constituted interesting exceptions to the rule. In general, however, medicine, like the other academic occupations which were practised by part of the new urban aristocracy – notaries, lawyers and judges – was closed to women. The criterion for granting the right to practise medicine was not skill or success in treatment but academic study and licensing by the faculty. In the indictment against Jacoba, her accusers did not confine themselves to accusing her of practising medicine without a licence (a crime of which men too could have been accused). They added that women, who were banned from becoming lawyers and giving evidence in criminal trials, should most certainly be banned from treating the sick and prescribing potions and medicines, since the hazards were much greater than those of losing a trial because of ignorance of the law.[134] There can be no doubt that greater opportunities had been open to women in early periods, when certain activities were not yet defined and institutionalized, in marginal periods and even in periods of crisis. Those periods of institutionalization were detrimental to women, and the history of medicine is an example of this.

MAID-SERVANTS

While women were deprived of the opportunity of engaging in more respected occupations, very many of them belonged to the servant class, the lowest of the urban labouring classes. The authors of the literature of the estates, who often glossed over the role of women in urban labour, thought it necessary to classify maid-servants as a separate subclass. Zita of Lucca, who went into service when she was 12 years old and had been a maid-servant in the same household all her life, became the patron saint of servant girls. She is usually depicted with a bunch of keys in her hand.[135] Albert Memmi, in his book L'Homme Dominé, devoted a chapter to women and one to servants.[136] Many women in the Middle Ages, as in later periods, were subjects twice over – as women and as servants.

The number of servants in towns was particularly great. Wages were relatively low, and hence even craftsmen kept servants. In the homes of the great burghers and the nobles there were often dozens of servants.[137] Maid-servants did not appear in the lists of taxpayers because they were too poor to pay the poll-tax, and since they lived in the homes of their employers they were not liable to the payment imposed on the household (*festum*). There can be no doubt that one of the reasons for the large number of women in European towns in the later Middle Ages was the large number of girls who migrated to towns from nearby rural areas to work as servants.[138] Sometimes a girl and a man would arrive in town together to seek their fortune. The Paris court register records such a case. Shortly after the couple arrived in town the girl was abandoned by the man and became a maid-servant. Some time later she married, was later tried for witchcraft, admitted having bewitched her husband and caused him to fall sick, and was executed.[139] Did she really try to harm the man she had married, or was she tortured so cruelly that she was willing to admit to anything? We have no way of knowing the answer.

In his manual of guidance, the Goodman of Paris explains to his young wife in detail how to supervise her maid-servants in the execution of the various household chores. In the burgher household, as in the castle, numerous chores were carried out apart from cleaning, cooking and baking. The war against flies, lice and cockroaches was also no easy task (the Goodman goes into detail on this matter). Some maid-servants tended the domestic animals, cows and pigs.[140] In large towns there was a special mediator (*recomandresse*) who mediated between the maid-servants and the employers and received payment from both parties for her services. In 1350, when the maximum wage for workers in various occupations was fixed in France, the list included the maximum sum to be paid to the *recomandresse* by both sides (1 sou (shilling) and 6 deniers (pence) for a maid-servant, 2 sous for a wet-nurse), and various maximum wages per annum for maid-servants and wet-nurses. The maximum annual wage for a maid-servant who worked only in the house was 30 sous; for a servant who also tended the cattle and pigs, 50 sous; for a wet-nurse 50 sous, and if she kept the child in her own home, 100 sous.[141]

The wage of the servant woman was low compared to that of most urban workers but higher than that of most agricultural labourers.[142] Since she ate at her master's table and lived in his house, she was probably able to save up a dowry within a few years. Withholding of payment was known in medieval towns as it was in

later periods, and servants were sometimes forced to sue their
employers.[143] The wet-nurses of the children of great lords received
higher wages than were stipulated in the regulations, as did some of
the nurses in burgher families.[144]

The authors of didactic works directed advice at servant women,
stressing their obligation to work devotedly and to act properly (a
servant woman should not ape her mistress etc.).[145] Many servant
women were young and the Paris Goodman writes of the frivolity
and inexperience of servant girls aged 15–20. He also advises his
young wife on how to choose a servant woman and how to
supervise her work and conduct in general: before she hires a maid
she should find out where the woman worked previously, and
ascertain from her last mistress whether she was a drunkard or
chatterer or had lost her virtue, for which reason she had been
obliged to leave her last place of employment. She should clarify
and write in the presence of the servant all details about her: name,
place of birth, place of residence of her relatives. If the servant
woman knew that all these facts were known, she would hesitate to
commit a crime or to run away. The mistress should shun the
impudent or servile maid but the shy and obedient one should be
treated like a daughter.

The younger maid-servants should be housed near the room of
the mistress, in a room which did not have a window facing the
street. They should rise and retire at the same hour as their mistress
as an additional means of keeping them out of mischief. If a serving
man or woman fell sick, the mistress herself should nurse them with
care and compassion. In good times they deserved good food and
drink in sufficient quantities, but they should not be given expensive meat or intoxicating liquor.[146] Some employers left bequests to
the maid-servants who worked in their homes as well as to their
men servants.[147] Despite the simple and humane advice of the old
Goodman, it may be assumed that some of the emotional distor-
tions which characterized maid-mistress relations in later periods
and which derived from excessive intimacy, dependence (sometimes
mutual), humiliation and hostility were present in this period as
well.[148]

PROSTITUTES

Like maid-servants, prostitutes were also recognized as a separate
'socio-professional' class. This ancient occupation existed in the
Middle Ages before the great expansion of the towns, and there was

also prostitution in rural areas. In towns it became a profession like any other.

The attitude to prostitution in the Central and Later Middle Ages was undoubtedly determined to a large extent by the stand of the Church Fathers in the first centuries of Christianity. St Augustine wrote: 'If you expel prostitutes from society, prostitution will spread everywhere ... the prostitutes in town are like sewers in the palace. If you take away the sewers, the whole palace will be filthy.'[149] Here we see the expression of the view that prostitution plays a certain part in Christian society and is preferable to the general spread of licentiousness. It is better for a man to make use of the services of a prostitute than to maintain relations outside wedlock with married women or to seduce virgins. Prostitution is a check on adultery and fornication, but its role is like that of a sewage pipe. The prostitute is a contemptible creature not because she poses as a loving woman and has sexual relations with men in return for financial reward, but because her entire life is devoted to the lusts of the flesh (*luxuria*), which are the prime sin. A thirteenth-century preacher adds: The sin of the prostitute is one of those sins which do not cause harm to the sinner herself alone but to others; not only to the property or the body of others but to their souls.'[150]

Essentially loyal to St Augustine's stand, medieval society permitted prostitution, but regarded it as a despicable and inferior occupation. Since it was permitted, it was official and legal. Since it was considered despicable and sinful, those who engaged in it were subjected to humiliating laws. This was clearly expressed in the legislation of Frederick II for Sicily. A woman who placed her body on sale should not be charged with fornication. We forbid any act of violence against her and forbid her to live among decent women.[151]

The supply of and demand for prostitution were great. Apart from the married men who utilized the services of prostitutes, many men never married at all, or were forced to delay marriage for many years after attaining adulthood, while others lived in towns apart from their wives for a lengthy periods. Secular churchmen who did not marry frequented prostitutes, as can be learned from the oft-reiterated regulations banning acceptance of churchmen as clients of brothels (and forbidding monks to bring prostitutes into monasteries). Students in university towns were among the most frequent customers of prostitutes.

The apprentices of artisans and the journeymen were obliged to postpone matrimony until they could open their own workshops.

Many members of the prosperous burgher class also delayed marriage until they were financially settled or until they found a suitable match which could further their ambitions. Apart from these permanent towndwellers who visited prostitutes, there were many men who visited towns for short periods: merchants, pilgrims, people who were sentenced to banishment from their own towns, wandering minstrels, jesters, vagabonds.[152] The farmers who came to town to sell their produce would seize the opportunity to visit brothels. To the prostitutes who worked in towns and those who visited monasteries one should add the camp followers and those who flocked to places of assembly on special occasions, such as the markets, fairs and church councils![153]

As regards supply, women apparently turned to prostitution in the Central and Later Middle Ages for the selfsame reasons for which they have done so in other societies at other times: casual external circumstances, economic factors, emotional reasons deriving from childhood experience, and certainly natural proclivities. As regards the economic factor, it is interesting to note the comment of the Chevalier de La Tour Landry in his manual of guidance for his daughters. He wrote that noblewomen who had a source of income and who engaged in relations with a lover (either a married man, a priest, or a serving man) were several times worse than prostitutes. Many prostitutes had become what they were because of poverty or deprivation or the cunning of their pimps, while noblewomen sinned out of carnal lust alone.[154] There are known cases of prostitutes who were connected with pimps who lured them into prostitution and sometimes also supplied their clients. A considerable part of their income was handed over to these pimps, who terrorized them. Apart from the professionals, unmarried women from the urban labouring class who did not reside with families also engaged in prostitution. Their virtue was suspect from the outset, sometimes justifiably and sometimes without cause. Some married women regarded prostitution as an additional source of income.[155]

The economic recession in the fourteenth century reduced neither the supply of nor the demand for prostitutes in proportion to the size of the population. The opposite was probably true. Women were among the first to be affected by the exclusiveness of the guilds, and while this led many of them, as we have seen, to join Beguinages, others undoubtedly turned to prostitution. Many of those who survived the Plague were better off financially than before, and in the atmosphere of fear of death and 'eat, drink and be merry' which characterized the fourteenth century, the demand for prostitution increased. A woman became a prostitute of her own free will, and no person had the right to incarcerate her in a brothel against her wishes, at least not according to the law. And there were some women who found refuge in the special homes for repentant prostitutes or in the nunneries which cared for such women. (These homes were usually named after Mary Magdalene, the spiritual mother of all repentant sinners.)

In Italian and French towns there were official brothels in the twelfth century, and they are also recorded in England, Germany and Spain from the thirteenth century on.[156] Since prostitution was not considered fornication or adultery in the accepted meaning of the terms, it was the concern, not of ecclesiastical courts but of urban tribunals. The desire to defend prostitutes is clearly evident in Frederick II's legislation, which laid down the death penalty for rape of a prostitute, as for any other type of rape.[157] The urban authorities, through the supervision of brothels, kept a watch on prostitutes and extracted taxes from them for their own benefit or for the seigneur of the town. (These seigneurs included churchmen like the bishop of Mainz, who complained in 1422 that the citizens of the town were trying to rob him of this income which had always been due to the seigneur . . .)[158] They also determined which streets were permitted for their activity. The official brothels were run according to fixed and official regulations. The institutional and official character of prostitution found expression also in Church decrees which stated that it was forbidden to bar a prostitute from attending church on Sundays or Christian feast-days. Prostitutes had their own patron saints (usually repentant prostitutes who had become nuns and saints) like other fraternities organized for religious purposes. There is insufficient evidence in the sources to support the theory that the prostitutes were organized in guilds like other occupations, which had their own regulations, decrees and judges.[159]

Together with recognition and defence of the rights of prostitutes, there were segregationist laws aimed at emphasizing their inferior and despised status. This was reflected first of all in the location of the brothels. The marginal groups and the inferior population groups lived on the outskirts of towns under the walls either inside or outside by the gates, and these areas were also earmarked for the brothels. But in most towns the municipal authorities were forced to recognize additional quarters as permissible areas for the activities of prostitutes. The charters granted by the lords of towns to citizens who wished to set up brothels, and the municipal regulations, reiterate the ban on establishing brothels and soliciting outside the permitted area.[160]

The fact that prostitutes were confined to certain streets undoubtedly reflected the desire to set them apart from all other citizens, but it also expressed the view of prostitution as a profession. Other professions were also concentrated in special streets where artisans displayed their wares, and some authors went so far as to evaluate prostitution as a profession. Thomas Cobham, who composed a manual for confessors in the twelfth century, writes:

> Prostitutes should be counted among the wage-earners. They hire out their bodies and supply labour. It is wrong for a woman to be a prostitute but if she is such, it is not wrong for her to receive a wage. But if she prostitutes herself for pleasure and hires out her body for this purpose, then the wage is as evil as the act itself.[161]

Successful prostitutes rented houses or even owned them. The poorer ones received their clients in the recognized brothels. But despite the regulations it was undoubtedly impossible to confine the prostitutes totally to the permitted houses in approved areas. They solicited customers in the taverns, the bathhouses and the town square, and received their clients in their own homes and in hotels, while the poorest and most degraded worked under the bridges and city walls.[162] Sometimes men or women kept brothels under the guise of workshops, like the procuress in London who ran a brothel camouflaged as an embroidery workshop and supplied girls to all comers and particularly to churchmen. She was punished by being sentenced to the stocks and to banishment from the city.[163]

In addition to being confined to special locations, the prostitutes were ordered to wear distinguishing clothing. They were required to wear eye-catching items of clothing such as red hats, ribbons on the sleeves or sleeves of contrasting colour to their robes. They were forbidden to wear quilted or fur-lined garments like those of noble ladies. The tightening of these regulations reflected a severe attitude, and prostitutes sometimes appealed for permission to tone down these distinguishing signs and to wear the latest fashions.[164] The prostitutes' violations of the regulations were a source of income for the town coffers. Transgressors were fined and their garments confiscated. The costliness of the confiscated items indicates the income and high standard of living of the successful prostitutes. Among the items mentioned are silver jewels, precious stones worn as buttons, and fur garments. Their clothing was an outward expression not only of feminine love of adornment but also of their desire to compensate themselves by lavish display for their inferior status.[165] Sometimes the municipal authorities did not confine themselves to restricting the locations for prostitution or forcing prostitutes to wear distinguishing garments. In Avignon in the mid-thirteenth century, for example, Jews and prostitutes were forbidden to touch bread and fruit set out on display. They were obliged to buy whatever they handled.[166] The Church did not ban prostitutes from attending services, but allotted them special seats.

The most persecuted and humiliated element were the poorer prostitutes who did not work in recognized brothels and were often banished from towns.[167] They formed part of the marginal groups of urban society, the vagabonds, beggars, and criminals, and as court registers show, they were often involved in assault and thievery. Like the other outcasts of medieval society, beggars, criminals and lepers, the prostitutes – probably the poorest and most unorganized among them – were often won over by the religious fervour of individuals or movements. They flocked to the sermons of Robert of Arbrissel in Anjou in the late eleventh century and repented their sins. But the periods of religious fervour, marked by zealous endeavour to reform the world in the spirit of Christianity, were also times of maximum pressure on and degradation of prostitutes. This was true of the activities of the Mendicants in the towns of Lombardy in 1233 and in the days of Louis IX in France, as well as under the Hussites in Prague. Prostitutes suffered, as did heretics, homosexuals and Jews.[168] In general however the attitude to prostitutes in the Middle Ages was undoubtedly better than in the sixteenth and seventeenth centuries, when royal absolutism (which inherited some of the powers of the towns and corporations), the Reformation and the Catholic Counter-Reformation, and fear of venereal disease combined to intensify oppression of prostitutes and render attitudes towards them increasingly hypocritical.

WOMEN BEFORE THE TOWN COURTS

We have mentioned the fact that prostitutes were sometimes tried by municipal courts, but they were not of course the only urban women who appeared in court registers. These registers also reflected the economic activity of women. There are numerous examples of charges against women accused of misdemeanours connected with their work, among them brewing beer in contravention of the regulations (Assize of Ale),[169] selling or pawning good-quality raw silk provided by customers and weaving cloth with poor-quality thread,[170] failure to repay debts, violations of agreements, use of false weights and measures,[171] and stockpiling foodstuffs such as fish and poultry in order to sell them at inflated prices.[172]

An embroiderer was accused of cruelty to a small girl who worked for her as an apprentice. It was her husband who was charged at the behest of the child's father, since the agreement had been signed with him, but the child was apprentice to the wife. She was accused of not having supplied the child's needs and of beating her.[173] Since, according to the regulations of the guilds, 'correction' of an apprentice was accepted practice,[174] the woman must have acted with particular cruelty. A boy who served as apprentice to a townswoman in London complained to the guild authorities that she had stabbed his finger with a needle for no good reason.[175]

We learn of the presence of women in markets and fairs from the squabbles in which they were involved and as a result of which they were charged.[176] The women of the urban labouring class were neither pampered nor bashful. Some were foul-mouthed and quarrelsome and were fined or placed in the stocks for their conduct; some were charged with trespassing or brawling. Women beat other women and sometimes attacked men, either alone or with the aid of their husbands.[177] From regulations issued in Italian towns we learn that the rich burghers and the nobility in towns were not always blameless. In the noble Corbolani family in the town of Lucca in the last quarter of the thirteenth century, all members of the extended family over the age of 16, male and female, were abjured not to raise a hand in anger against one another and not to beat one another with stick or iron.

In Genoa, four men were elected every three months in each quarter of the town as *principales* to manage the affairs of the quarter and keep the peace. In parallel four women were chosen to supervise morals and to settle disputes and quarrels between women.[178] In Paris a burgher's wife was tried for beating her chambermaid in the street for having (so she claimed) seduced her husband. A woman shopkeeper in England boxed the ears of a 5-year-old child who had stolen wool from her shop so hard that she killed him.[179] Men, for their part, acted violently towards women, and many women complained of injury inflicted by males in the street, the market or at fairs.[180] There were women who accused men of rape. A woman named Belon in Paris accused a certain man of having murdered her husband and seduced her. She was found guilty of perjury after admitting she had lied, and was executed.[181]

Female owners of dubious hotels, like their male counterparts, sometimes robbed their customers.[182] A woman was punished for cruel enticement to prostitution and for having aided in the rape of a little girl.[183] Women were also tried for practising witchcraft, for heresy and arson.[184] They were also tried on charges of murder, but as noted already, the number of women sentenced for this crime was immeasurably smaller than the number of men found guilty. Fewer of the urban murders involving women were connected with family than was the case in rural areas. There were also fewer victims of murder among women than among men in towns.[185]

LEISURE

Women played a part in festivals and celebrations in towns, and their presence was felt in the streets. In Italian towns, once a girl reached the age of 12 she was no longer allowed to appear without a chaperone in the street or at family or town celebrations, but once she married she enjoyed relatively greater freedom. Women attended church, and played a part in baptism ceremonies as godmothers and at marriage ceremonies as the companions of the bride. They took part in religious processions (according to the laws of Lille, for example, both men and women who attended the nine-day religious procession in honour of the Virgin Mary were exempt from arrest and legal charges during this period),[186] and they flocked to hear the sermons of preachers in the town streets. Occasionally, like men, they responded to the appeals of the preachers to burn such luxury items as cards, dice and jewellery.[187] In Reggio in Italy women took part in building the Dominican church together with the men.[188]

In the towns of Flanders and France women took an active part in ceremonies held in honour of the entry of rulers into towns, ceremonies which included processions and pageants. The allegorical and mythological figures in these pageants were represented by females.[189] Women attended theatres only as spectators and the female roles were played by boys. They did not participate in the riding tournaments (in Italy called *palio*) which were also held in northern towns, in the ball games often held in Italian towns to open a religious or state ceremony, or in the wrestling matches held aboard boats on the Thames.[190] Women merely wore the colours of one of the competitors just as, like men and children, they wore the symbols of individuals or political factions as an expression of support and loyalty. Thus both men and women in Paris in the fifteenth century wore the colours of Burgundians and Armagnacs alternately.

Women did however take part in the popular games which were not aimed at fostering the traits of the warrior and were not part of the tradition of masculine games. An example is the game customarily played in Padua, a type of spring courtship ritual. The young girls of the town gathered in a wood and cardboard fortress and young men from various towns, dressed in the town colours, besieged them by throwing flowers. On one occasion the girls succumbed and handed over the fortress to the Venetians, who seemed to them the handsomest and finest of the young besiegers. The young men of Padua were enraged, and fist-fights ensued. The young Paduans even tore the standard of St Mark, but the Venetians prevailed nonetheless.[191] On May Day, men, women and children participated in celebrations in towns. In Florence, according to Giovanni Villani, the celebrations were held in the various town quarters. In London, on a fixed date after Easter, a game was held with the participation of men and women. Passers-by, both male and female, were seized by the players, tied up with ropes and obliged to pay a certain ransom in order to be released.[192] Women also attended wrestling matches, cockfights and bearfights.

The women of medieval towns drank in their own homes and in taverns. The old Goodman of Paris instructed his young wife not to employ a drunken servant woman and not to serve male and female servants intoxicating liquor. The preachers denounced drunken women.[193] The Goliards, in their songs of wine, described both men and women at drinking parties and wrote of the girl through whose veins Bacchus had sent a warm and strengthening liquid, so that she was softened and ready for the service of Venus.[194] Some of the drinking parties of the fraternities (*potacio, drinkynnes*) and guilds were attended by women. Some guilds and fraternities had women members, others invited the wives of members to join them in drinking.[195] It should be recalled that beer brewing was one of the occupations followed by many women, and some women ran taverns and thus had close access to drink.

Let us conclude with the bathhouses, which women also attended. Burchard of Worms writes about those who bathed in the bathhouses with women.[196] In late thirteenth-century Paris there were twenty-six hot public bathhouses. The rich had private baths. The public baths enabled men and women in towns to preserve personal cleanliness more easily than in rural areas, and were also a place of entertainment, often of a kind which was not to the taste of the authors of didactic works or of the municipal authorities. The old Goodman had good reason to regard the streets of the city as a place of danger for innocent young women, and ordered his wife to go out only with an elderly companion known for her seriousness and religious piety. The part-author of *Le Roman de la Rose*, Jean de Meung, listed in his cynical fashion all the events to which the lascivious woman would hasten, and the Wife of Bath too described them with unrestrained joy, and no trace of guilt or cynicism:

> That Jankin clerk, and my gossib dame Alis,
> And I myself, into the feldes wente.
> Myn housbond was at London al that Lente;
> I hadde the bettre leyser for to pleye,
> And for to see, and eek for to be seye
> Of lusty folk; What wiste I wher my grace
> Was shapen for to be, or in what place?
> Therefore I made my visitaciouns
> To vigilies and to processiouns,
> To preching eek, and to thise pilgrimages,
> To pleyes of myracles, and to mariages,
> And wered upon my gaye scarlet gytes.[197]

The Wife of Bath speaks of her red dresses. It was not only the preachers who denounced women who adorned themselves and danced. Women who dressed too lavishly and contravened the regulations against excessive luxury of dress (which were very common in the fourteenth century) were charged and fined.[198]

EDUCATION

The education of townswomen was confined to the daughters of the prosperous burgher class, or at the most to the daughters of artisan members of guilds or daughters of petty merchants. Girls of the lower classes were not educated and neither were their brothers. Some male apprentices were sent to school during their term of service to learn reading and writing for several years.[199] Some girls may also have been sent to school during apprenticeship, though we have traced no agreements explicitly arranging this, and we know with certainty only of the vocational training of girls. On the other hand, it is known that there were urban elementary schools where

boys and girls studied together. In 1357 regulations were first issued
in Paris for segregation of the sexes in different schools.[200]

Froissart, who was born in Valenciennes in Flanders, writes of
the mixed school he attended. According to him, both boys and
girls studied Latin. He exchanged apples and pears with the girls.
He also relates how he fell in love with a girl whom he saw sitting
and reading a book under a tree. They read together and she asked
him if he would agree to lend her books. He lent her a book, and
between the pages concealed a love ballad he had written to her, but
she refused to return his love. When they met in the garden and he
tried to persuade her, she yanked out one of his curls in order to
convince him that all was over between them![201] In Paris these mixed
'little schools' as they were called, were supervised by the Cantor of
Notre Dame cathedral, and it was he who awarded teaching licences
to the male and female teachers who taught there. The registers of
payers of the tallage in Paris in the late thirteenth and fourteenth
century mention these women teachers.

Giovanni Villani writes that in 1338 in Florence 8000–10,000
boys and girls learned to read at elementary schools.[202] Children
attended school between the ages of 6 and 12 approximately. At the
beginning of the fourteenth century there was even a woman
teacher in Florence who taught the elements of Latin. Her name was
Clementia; she was a married woman and her title was *doctrix
puerorum*.[203] We learn indirectly of the attendance of girls at
elementary schools in England. In London in 1390 the guardian of
an orphan daughter of a candle-maker paid school fees for her
studies at an elementary school from the age of 8 till she reached 13
and married.[204] E. Power has noted the fact that medical works
dealing with female diseases were translated into English, on the
assumption that literate women would read them themselves or read
them to other women and advise them on their illnesses so as to
avoid the need to consult a male physician.[205] In Germany too there
were elementary schools where boys and girls studied together,
some of them run by Beguines.[206]

In addition to reading the vernacular, all these schools probably
taught the elements of religion, prayers and etiquette. It appears that
Latin was not usually studied in these schools, though Froissart
writes that it was taught in the school he attended. The life of one of
the Beguines mentions that as a child of 7 she attended a *literalis
scholae scientiae*, and the biography of a Cistercian nun notes that as
a child she was sent to be educated by a *magistra liberalium artium*,
but it is hard to guess what the curriculum of these schools

included.[207] Some daughters of the rich burghers, like young noblewomen, studied at nunnery schools without intending to take the veil. These nunnery schools were widespread in Italian towns. Other girls studied under male or female tutors at home. According to the old Goodman's manual, the wife of the rich burgher should learn something of the skills of the noblewoman: riding, parlour games, riddling and how to tell tales. The types of books which the daughters of burghers read are indicated in their wills (though it should be recalled that a book was considered as property, and the fact that a man owned it did not necessarily mean that he had read it). In the last quarter of the thirteenth century Dame Marie Payenne of Tournai bequeathed to her son several books of religion and prayer missals and the tale of the Chevalier du Cygne.[208]

Institutions of higher learning were closed to women: not only the universities and special schools of law, but also the lower schools. In Florence, according to Giovanni Villeni, 1000–2000 boys attended six schools of mathematics to train as merchants; 500–600 boys studied logic and Latin at four schools. From these institutions they moved on to universities.[209] In England some town boys moved up from elementary schools to grammar schools (*escoles generales de gramer*). None of these schools accepted girls. Since a considerable proportion of university students came from the burgher class and the urban-dwelling minor nobility, the gap between the educational level of men and women grew wider in the middle upper class in town, with all this implied.[210]

In evaluating the rights and status of townswomen in comparison to those of the men of their class, one should distinguish between the wives of prosperous burghers and women of the labouring class. The opportunities of the former for activity and self-fulfilment were relatively restricted. They could play no part in running the town and had no role in the municipal ruling institutions, unlike some noblewomen who held fiefs. In contrast to the nobleman, who was a warrior or served the monarch or seigneur, and therefore often left the management of his financial affairs to his wife, the burgher was first and foremost a man of commerce and finance. Economic activity was his occupation, which he did not entrust to his wife. Most wives of rich burghers were responsible only for the management of their households. Very few of them worked during their husbands' lifetime.

It was characteristic that those authors of didactic literature who favoured educating the daughters of merchants to some degree argued that they would need to manage their household accounts and write letters to their husbands and sons, who were often away on business trips, but never claimed that they needed to know how to manage business affairs. Alberti, in his *Libri de la Famiglia*, wrote explicitly that a husband should not discuss business with his wife and should not show her the documents he had signed, or his ledgers.[211] In England, on the other hand, the widows of burghers sometimes continued their husbands' business. The husbands obviously had not followed Alberti's advice, since if they had, their widows would not have been able to succeed them. The widows of rich towndwellers, like widowed noblewomen, acted as guardians to their sons,[212] but this guardianship did not entail fulfilling functions and exercising powers as in guardianship of the heir of a fief.

The wives of rich townsmen also followed the example of noblewomen in utilizing the services of wet-nurses and nurses, and usually their children too left home at an early age. The women of the prosperous burgher class derived no benefit from the urban institutions of learning, despite their physical proximity to them; they could not train there and qualify in the respected occupations of state clerk, notary, judge, advocate or physician, or acquire a higher education for its own sake. Their lot was a happier one only from the socio-cultural point of view, since they could mingle among people and take part in religious life and in cultural events, and thus were less isolated than the wives of petty noblemen in remote castles. The townswoman also had greater opportunities for separate female companionship than the lonely noblewoman. On the other hand, noblewomen who lived in important castles where numerous social events were held played an active part in social and cultural life which was unparalleled in urban society.

When we turn from the prosperous burghers to the women of the labouring class, we find a greater degree of equality in practice between men and women, because of the important role of the woman in urban production and commerce on the one hand, and because a considerable proportion of the men of this class played no part in municipal government and in the institutions of higher learning. Female labour was neither an innovation nor a special privilege. Among the peasant class in the Middle Ages, as in all known agricultural societies, women undertook most of the field tasks and worked in most agricultural branches. The unique factor in female labour in medieval towns was the wide range of occupations in which they engaged, compared to the limited number open to them in later periods. Their role in production accorded them special though not usually leading status in the guilds of artisans and petty merchants, and endowed them with a degree of self-confidence and freedom of movement in urban labouring society. The status of merchant lent a woman legal freedom which other married women did not enjoy. Matrimonial law, however, which was often applied, stipulated the superiority of the male in labouring families, as well as among the prosperous burghers.

The ethos of urban society was not essentially a warrior ethos in which women could play no part. The number of women in towns was great, particularly in the Later Middle Ages, both because girls emigrated to town to work as maid-servants or train as apprentices, because many widows of the prosperous peasant class and the nobility preferred to live in towns and moved there from nearby rural areas, and because there were very many nunneries in Italian towns and Beguinages in Northern European towns.[213] (In Italian towns in the Later Middle Ages in particular, women were often charged with using love charms, namely preparing love philters for men in order to lure them. Was this a reflection of the shortage of men in towns at that time?) Women formed part of the urban work force and held part of the capital.[214] Nonetheless their contribution to the formulation of urban culture was very limited. They played no part in higher culture. They attended town theatres, one of the expressions of urban culture and a source of pride to the guilds, only as spectators.

Violence and crudity were rife in town society, and women did not mitigate them. They were part of a civilization in which acts of cruelty were carried out in public and were a source of savage satisfaction and an emotional outlet for the masses who flocked to watch. We mentioned in chapter 2 the chroniclers' description of the first public hanging of a woman in Paris: the crowds flocked to watch because of the novelty, and women and girls in particular came.[215]

Urban literature is marked by expressions of contempt and hostility towards women. This satirical genre, which attributes ugly traits to women, indicates perhaps that urban women were strong and domineering. As far as we know, the townsman did not take revenge on his adulterous wife as the nobleman did, and in those towns in which degrading public punishments were imposed for adultery and fornication, they were usually imposed on both men and women. But this literature also indicates what kind of female image amused medieval urban society, and that image was by no means shaped under the influence of women, or in order to please them. Courtly literature undoubtedly answered the psychological needs of noblemen, but the image of women fashioned there also appealed to women. Women encouraged the poets who propagated this image, and served both as their critics and their inspiration. Courtly poetry laid down certain norms of conduct marked by greater delicacy and respect towards women, at least in public. The birthplace of the literary salons of a later era was in the courts of the noblewomen and not in the homes of the townswomen.

7

Women in the Peasantry

The role of peasants in the management of society and realm in the Middle Ages was very limited. Only occasionally did prosperous peasants play a part in the regional framework on behalf of the central regime or the feudal lord, or participate in elections to local or national representative assemblies. But there was local organization in villages. Meetings and court sessions were held, and office-holders and functionaries were elected by the village assembly or nominated by the lord of the manor.[1] There were also certain functionaries who were neither appointed by the lord of the manor nor elected by the peasants, like the parish priest (who was not officially appointed by the seigneur, or at least not by him alone) or the village notary.

Women fulfilled none of these functions, and their part in the local assemblies was limited. They could not hold the office of village notary, scribe of the manorial court or parish priest. The meetings where attendance of village landowners was compulsory were attended only by unmarried or widowed female landowners. Married women who owned their own land were represented at the meeting by their husbands, although the decisions taken were binding on all landowners without exception. In the small village of Cravenna, in Piedmont, for example, it was decided in 1304 that the lord was not entitled to transfer or sell lands on which peasants resided without the consent of all the villagers, both men and women. But this applied only to women who were widowed or unmarried and were householders.[2] And even those women who attended assemblies and court sessions could not fulfil functions there: they could not serve as jurors, or as guarantors for the appearance of some other person at a trial, or serve as chief pledge for the tithing groups which existed in England to stand pledge for the fulfilment of one another's duties towards the public authorities. (Needless to say, all these were duties enforced to ensure public discipline but they were a source of power and standing in the community as well.)

For a woman to fulfil any official function in peasant society was an exception even rarer than for a noblewoman to fulfil a function by virtue of holding a fief. One of the exceptions which can be noted in the early fifteenth century was the election of women in Halesowen, near Birmingham, to the post of ale-taster. This was a respected office in the village community, and those who held it were empowered to impose fines on those found guilty of brewing ale in contravention of the assize. The fact that women were elected to this post may be explained against the background of the decimation and internal migration of the population in this period. It will be recalled that periods of crisis were times of relative improvement in the status of women. On the other hand, as in all classes of society throughout history, there were sometimes women among the peasantry who were gifted by strength and qualities of leadership and attained the leadership status by force of personality alone, without being allotted any official position. Agnes Sadler of Romsley, a married woman, headed the peasants who, in 1386, objected to an increase in the labour services by the seigneur and demanded the abolition of villeinage. Like the other peasants, she refused to appear before the royal judge who summoned her, was outlawed and disappeared without trace.[3]

Peasants sometimes rebelled in the Middle Ages, but not in order to change the status of women. During the Peasants' Revolt in England in 1381, the peasants emblazoned on their banner: 'When Adam delved and Eve span, who was then the gentleman?', but they were expressing thereby their protest against a social order which granted excessive rights to members of the upper classes, and not against the inequality between the sexes.

INHERITANCE RIGHTS

The structure of the peasant family, like the customs of land inheritance, differed from region to region. Certain regions were characterized by the nuclear family: father, mother and progeny. In some of these regions the family property was not divided up

among all the offspring, but was inherited by the oldest son
(primogeniture), or the youngest (ultimogeniture); the family also
allotted some portion to those children who did not inherit.
Daughters were allotted a dowry and sons were endowed in order
to enable them to marry and set up their own home. In other
regions, such as Mâcon in France, the land was impartible and was
held by all the offspring, who cultivated it jointly. At the end of the
twelfth century, the sons of peasants who owned allods held the
landed property jointly; after the father's death, at least some of the
married sons and sometimes also one of the married daughters
continued to live together, and the partnership endured for several
generations.[4] In the Orleans-Paris region the property was divided
up among those descendants who remained in the village. Those
who left and were endowed while the parents were still alive had no
further claims. Similar inheritance customs existed north of the
Orleans-Paris region as well, in Amiens, in some of the regions of
Germany (at least up to the thirteenth century) and in Switzerland.
In Brittany, Maine and Anjou, the land was divided up among all
the male offspring, and the same was true of Normandy.[5]

In the Haute Ariège region, near the Pyrenees, the family
property was not divided, and neither were there fixed inheritance
customs. The father chose his heir arbitrarily. In the small village of
Montaillou in Haute Ariège, only one of the children inherited the
property, but for a certain period, even after the heir married, some
of his brothers and his widowed mother or father continued to live
with him. These brothers who had not inherited gradually left
home. When the old father or mother died, only the nuclear family,
the heir, his wife and children, remained in the home,[6] and the same
was true of other villages where the inheritance was impartible.
Tuscany in the early fifteenth century was characterized by the
extended family. The family property was not divided up among the
progeny and was cultivated jointly by the parents, at least some of
the married sons, and sometimes also the father's brother. As in
Mâcon, the partnership continued for several generations, as long as
all those concerned could subsist from the same property. The
Tuscan system was typically patrilinear. Daughters received a
dowry and moved to their husbands' homes.[7]

In the light of the different inheritance laws and the different
structure of the peasant family in various regions, the inheritance
rights of peasant daughters also varied. Generally speaking, it may
be said that in most regions daughters too inherited, but almost
without exception the rights of sons took precedence. In other

regions, daughters were totally excluded from the inheritance and their dowry was their entire share of the family property, even if they had no brothers. In the regions where primogeniture was practised, if the eldest child was a daughter her younger brother took precedence in inheritance rights. In ultimogeniture regions, the older brother took precedence over the younger sister. In regions where the property was not divided and there were no fixed inheritance customs, like Haute Ariège, where the father himself chose his heir, he selected a son and not a daughter. But if there were no sons, the daughter usually inherited (except in those areas where she was totally excluded from the inheritance).

Court registers of manors in the Midlands list not only daughters who attained their majority and inherited land but also minor daughters whose landed inheritance was under the custody of some other person, who cultivated it until they reached their majority.[8] If the bridegroom of an heiress was poorer than she, he was often integrated into her family and took her family name. Daughters who inherited land bequeathed it to their descendants, and in some regions, if a man inherited land from his mother, he took her name.[9] In regions where primogeniture or ultimogeniture was practised, families not only endeavoured to allot something to those sons who did not inherit, but also tried to provide a dowry of some kind for daughters to enable them to wed. Lands added in one way or another to the original family holdings were divided up among those descendants who had not inherited. There was blatant discrimination against daughters in rural areas of Flanders, Normandy and Tuscany.[10] In the southeastern regions of England too, the land was divided among the sons, and the daughters inherited only if there were no sons.[11]

MARRIAGE

Marriage in peasant society, as among other classes, was arranged by the families. Among prosperous families in particular, economic calculations and considerations of prestige prevailed in the selection of a partner for a son or daughter, and people aspired to marry members of their own, if not of a higher class. In regions where there was a seigneurial demesne the lord of the manor intervened in the marriage of a widow, an heiress or the daughter of a serf. The lord of the manor sometimes exerted pressure on an heiress to marry in order to ensure the service due to him on the demesne, but generally speaking there was no need of this. Heiresses had no difficulties in finding husbands and married in any case.

As for the daughter of the serf, there was no interference in her choice of a mate, but the lord of the manor extracted the fine due to him, generally from the bride's father. Sometimes the woman herself paid, or if she was a widow who brought her husband land, it was he who paid the fine, which was known as 'merchet' and was one of the distinguishing features of the unfree peasant. In certain regions, the same sum was demanded for marriage to a man from the same manor as for marriage to someone out of the lord's jurisdiction. In other areas, as in most of Germany, and certain manors in England, for example, a higher sum was extracted for the right to marry off the manor.[12] According to the manorial customs in several regions, if an unfree peasant woman married a man from elsewhere and moved to his village, some of her progeny (usually half) were considered to be the serfs of the lord of her home manor and he was entitled to demand that they move there. The legal status of the progeny of such a mixed couple was defined in most parts of Western Europe according to the standing of the mother. This usage appears in the custumals in several regions,[13] but there is no way of knowing if in practice and until what period lords of the manor in all the above-mentioned regions exercised their right. Nor do we know at precisely what age children left home and moved back to the manor of their mother's lord.

Certain stages existed in properly conducted marriages in the peasant class which also characterized marriage in other classes: negotiations between the families would be followed by betrothal and a marriage ceremony at the church door. But as we saw in the chapter on married women, private marriage, despite all the problems it entailed, was prevalent in the peasant class. It was particularly characteristic of poor families where marriage did not involve complicated financial arrangements and parents were unable to impose their will on their children. In Haute Ariège in the late thirteenth and early fourteenth centuries there were cases of Cathar marriage. In the presence of witnesses the Cathar *Perfectus* proclaimed the marriage of the couple and gave them his blessing. These marriages were based not only on local, but also on religious endogamy, as E. Le Roy Ladurie has noted.[14] Local endogamy characterized most regions, and in most villages it was not possible to observe the ban on incest to the fourth degree. In small villages of several dozen families it was impossible to observe the ban if people married within the village. In many cases the inhabitants did not know to whom they were related to this degree, since family genealogies were not recorded and surnames were not fixed.

Among peasants as in other classes, marriage was an important stage in the lives of young people and symbolized the transition to the new status of householders. The English word, husbandman, reflects this view clearly. The individual was provided with the opportunity to become a person of consequence. He could now beget children, who would help him one day, and the number of his relatives and friends would increase. On the other hand, there can be no doubt that the economic burden on a family when its sons and daughters wed was heavy and burdensome. The daughter was given a dowry; the son, if he did not inherit, was allotted some holding in order to enable him to establish a family. If the property was not divided up, then whenever one of the sons married, the number of individuals living off the same plot increased. In prosperous families married daughters were given plots of land, and sometimes a house or household possessions, money or a farmyard animal. In Provence peasants sometimes borrowed money in order to provide their daughters with the best possible dress as a dowry, namely one fashioned from woollen cloth from Courtrai.[15] If bridegrooms were promised a dowry, they insisted on receiving it in full (as in other classes), like the bridegroom in the manor of the Bec monastery in Northamptonshire who sued his father-in-law for not handing over the dowry he had promised. He demanded compensation of thirty-five shillings. The father-in-law admitted only to his promise to supply a coat worth five shillings.[16]

Marriage among peasants, therefore, as in other classes, was essentially a family, social and economic affair, but within the given framework there was a certain degree of freedom of choice for young people. If the marriage was unhappy, the partners did not always reconcile themselves and sometimes changed partners. A first private marriage was sometimes followed by a second marriage in church, or else marriages were solemnized in church twice, on each occasion with a different partner in another parish. Sometimes people simply abandoned their partners and lived without wedlock with another partner. These phenomena suggest fluctuations in affection, love and attraction, indicating that some people followed the dictates of their own hearts. A strong desire to leave a marital partner also suggests a search for love or companionship in marriage, so that if these were absent, an attempt was made to dissolve the tie. The register of one of the courts of an English manor in 1301 records the case of a farmer named Reginald. With the approval of the lord of the manor, he gave his wife Lucy land and a house in his possession on condition that she did not enter his courtyard or cross the threshold of his home! It was also stipulated that if Lucy tried to infringe their legal separation the agreement would lapse and be null and void.[17]

There can be little doubt that previous ties were sometimes dissolved in favour of new ones for utilitarian reasons and under family pressure, but this was certainly not always so. As we saw in the chapter on married women, it was sometimes a woman who abandoned her first husband for the sake of a new relationship, and the first husband who tried to prove to the ecclesiastical court the indissolubility of the marriage. It was also sometimes utilitarian motives which led women to seek separation, as in the case of a free woman who discovered that her husband was a serf, something she had not known when she married him; she asked for dissolution of the tie.[18]

From a rare source on the peasant society of the late thirteenth and early fourteenth centuries – the records of evidence submitted to the Inquisition tribunal at Pamiers, presided over by Bishop Jacques Fournier, researched by E. Le Roy Ladurie – we learn that peasants in this region distinguished between liking (*diligere*) and loving passionately (*adamare*). A man who agreed to marry a girl who was proposed to him said that he liked her and therefore agreed to the proposal. The village bailiff, Bernard Clergue, described his love for the woman he wished to wed, and who in fact became his wife, as passionate love. Their families were related and both had Cathar tendencies, but by marrying her he renounced a larger dowry which had been offered him. He spoke of his love for her both before and during his marriage. A choice existed within the given framework which families accepted. However the women who used the term 'passionate love' in their testimony were referring to lovers and not to husbands. Love apparently led to matrimonial initiative on the part of men but not of women, at least in Montaillou. In successful marriages husbands conversed at length with their wives. Endogamy of religion and conscience resulted not only from the search for security (a Cathar was safer from the informers of the Inquisition court if his wife and her relatives were associated with the Cathars), but also from the fact that men wanted to find a companion with whom they could share Cathar beliefs.[19]

One should not, of course, idealize relations between marital partners in peasant society. The husband ruled the household and the property, even if most of it consisted of his wife's inheritance.

He was restricted by the need to obtain her consent to the sale of her property or any other activity related to it, as also of the dower guaranteed her on marriage out of his property, and the courts often checked whether her consent was obtained without coercion,[20] but this did not prevent him from ruling his household. As E. Power has noted, peasants read neither the ecclesiastical literature relating to women and marriage nor urban literature, but they listened to the sermons of their priests and heard the wandering minstrels who propounded the idea of the superiority of man and mocked women.[21] Peasants often beat their wives cruelly, and court registers record cases in which they made assaults so savage that they threw knives or other tools at their wives and accidentally killed their babies in the process.[22] Many women had good cause to fear their husbands.

Yet there were also manifestations of love and affection, which we come across even in the records of the manor courts. In one village in England, a peasant tried for fishing inside his lord's enclosure pleaded in his defence as follows: 'Sir, my wife fell sick and she has been lying in her bed for the past month and there is neither food nor drink that she is willing to taste. And then her soul yearned for a perch and she sent me to bring just one fish . . .'[23] Women often nursed their husbands (who were their seniors) with great devotion when they grew old and sick, and refused to leave the sickbed when asked to do so in Montaillou by the Cathar Perfect.[24]

According to Le Roy Ladurie, whereas the young wife in the Haute Ariège region was under her husband's authority and did not enjoy respected status in society, an older woman, even if she were not widowed, was to a large extent free from her husband's authority. Her standing was superior to that of the young woman, and her grown children respected and consulted her. A man reached the height of his power at the early age of 25–30, and at 40 was still in his prime. After 40 there was a gradual decline. His prestige and status in rural society did not increase with old age – rather the contrary. Women, on the other hand, as soon as they ceased to be sexual objects, gained status: 'The cessation of menses brought an increase in authority.' In other words, the standing of a woman in this society was determined to a large extent, as in primitive societies, by her physiological stage. But it should be recalled that even in Montaillou, the sons of widows who reached their majority became the householders, and their mothers lived with them, and not the opposite, despite the widow's right of dower.

In the Tuscany region the evil eye (*mal occhio*) of the old woman was feared as liable to cause harm to infants. Here too, when the sons of a widow reached their majority, her standing deteriorated and they became masters of the home. A man attained the peak of his status in Tuscany at the age of 60 (if he survived to this age), and only rarely did he renounce his status as head of the household in favour of his son or younger brother.[25] As far as we know, in the Late Middle Ages it was not necessarily the young and beautiful women, those who were regarded as sexual objects and sources of temptation, who were charged with witchcraft, but often older and lonely women. The status of the older woman too was not unequivocal.

The daughters of peasants usually married young, like girls of other classes in the Middle Ages, irrespective of whether the dowry constituted their entire share of the family property or whether they inherited. Sometimes similar arrangements were made between fathers and daughters as between fathers and sons: the father handed over the estate in his lifetime to his daughter, who guaranteed in return to keep him and supply all his needs.[26] If the daughters did not inherit, they were allotted their dowry when young. One should not compare the peasant society of the Central and Later Middle Ages to those of Sardinia or Ireland in the twentieth century. In the latter societies, longevity is widespread and children are obliged to await their inheritance for many years; in addition a larger number of progeny survive and it is not possible to supply all of them with the means required for setting up their own households. Many are forced therefore to postpone marriage. In the Central and Later Middle Ages, on the other hand, because of the high mortality rate a smaller number of progeny survived and the life expectancy of parents was lower. According to the studies of M. M. Postan and J. L. Titow, the average further life-expectancy at 20 in the Winchester estates at the end of the thirteenth century and the first half of the fourteenth (up to the Black Death) was 20 years. According to Z. Razi, in Halesowen in the same period the average life-expectancy at 20 was another 25–28 years.[27] It appears therefore that, as in other classes, medieval peasant society was not characterized by the West European marriage pattern of female marriage at a relatively advanced age, i.e. in the late twenties.[48]

On the other hand, like other classes of medieval society, the peasants were aware of the need for a man to have adequate means to set up a family. They simply had to be content with little. In England a cottage and several acres of land sufficed, and the same is true of other regions of Western Europe. The offspring of prosperous peasants were more likely than children of the poor to remain in their home villages, since they could find a livelihood there. The offspring of the very poor were forced to emigrate and seek their fortunes elsewhere. The sons and daughters of the more prosperous peasants married younger than their poorer counterparts. In the period following the Black Death, when land lay vacant and it was easier to purchase property than before, the average age of marriage dropped in some regions. According to the Halesowen records, the average age of matrimony for males in the period after the Black Death (1349–1400) was 20, and for women lower. Some 26 per cent of girls married between 12 and 20.[29] In Montaillou at the end of the thirteenth century and the beginning of the fourteenth, i.e. in the period preceding the Black Death, girls also married young, although this was an impoverished mountain region. There are recorded cases of girls who married at 14, 15, 17 and 18. Men took wives at approximately 25.[30] In the rural region adjacent to Pisa in the first quarter of the fifteenth century, the average age of marriage for men was 26.3–27.1 years, and for women 17.3.[31]

The great majority of village girls married, and the girls who did not marry in rural areas were usually from the poorest sections of the population. It was they who emigrated from their villages to work as serving girls in towns or as hired agricultural workers in other villages, and they who were the most likely to engage in extramarital relations and bear bastards. Some of them eventually settled permanently in villages and brought up their bastard children alone. Others married, as we saw in a previous chapter. With the men of their class, they constituted the lowest rung of the peasant society, but it was the women who shouldered the burden of bringing up the illegitimate offspring. There were probably also cases of women who never married and lived in the homes of married brothers, helping with the household chores and agricultural work.

The number of children in prosperous peasant families was larger than among poor peasants. In Halesowen before the Black Death the average number of progeny per peasant family was 2.8, while the average in prosperous families was 5.1; in less prosperous families it was 2.9, and in poor families 1.8. The same ratio between the economic status of a family and the number of progeny characterized families in other estates in England too.[32] After the Black Death the average number of children per family was lower, despite the relatively improved economic standing of the survivors, because of the high infant mortality rate in the epidemics which broke out after the Black Death. The average in Halesowen dropped to 2.1 children per family.[33] In Mâcon in the twelfth century, farmers who held allods had five or six children on the average.[34] In Montaillou, which, as we have noted, was a poor mountain village, there were families with two, four, five, six and even eight children in the late thirteenth and early fourteenth centuries. The average number of births per family was 4.5. Even a prosperous family, if it produced eight children that survived, could not supply land to all of them. In one such family it is known that one of the sons became a woodcutter and another a shepherd. In Montaillou, as in English villages, and in the rural area near Fribourg in Switzerland, there also was a drop in the average number of children per family after the Black Death.[35] In the rural area near Pistoia, according to 1427 records, the average number of children in the most prosperous family in the village was 3.21, as against 1.47 in the poorest family.[36]

As noted above, the larger number of children in richer families resulted from the greater exploitation of the fertility span and from the fact that the children of the richer peasants had a better chance of survival. Did some of the poorer peasants try deliberately to limit their families? A Franciscan preacher of the fourteenth century, Alvarus Pelagius, accused peasants of refraining from intercourse with their wives for fear of conception of additional children whom they would be unable to support because of their poverty.[37] It was in this period, as we saw in a previous chapter, that preachers first condemned the use of contraception for economic motives, whereas previously they had only denounced its use in the context of adultery and fornication.

THE PEASANT WOMAN AS MOTHER

Very little is known from chronicles and didactic works about the peasant woman in her maternal role. When the chroniclers wished to depict the relations between mothers and children they described noblewomen and their progeny, and not the peasant class. It is also hard to gauge what the ideal was in the peasant class. Educational manuals were intended for the nobility or the richer urban class, in general, and not for peasants. Court registers reveal only the exceptions to the rule, but what was the norm? We know that peasant women suckled their children and raised them themselves. The span of childhood was brief. Children began to work at an early age and thus were partially integrated into adult society, the girls among the women and the boys among the men. Shared labour was also a means of education and transmission of traditions.

In villages in which there was a demesne, children worked from an early age not only in the parental farm but also for the lord of the manor. Other children worked as hired labourers for more prosperous farmers. A decree issued in England in 1388 stated that a boy or girl under the age of twelve who were working regularly as carters or behind the plough (i.e. driving the beasts and guiding them) or in any other agricultural labour should continue in this work even after reaching the age of 12 and not commence any other work or occupation. This meant that before they were 12 years old, these children were working for wages. Guarding the sheep, cattle or geese was a task entrusted to children in most regions.[38]

When they were not working, the village children were relatively free to sing, dance, play and associate with their contemporaries, as can be learned from Joan of Arc's tales about her childhood in the village of Domrémy on the River Meuse. Some peasant children, like members of other classes, were sent away from home at an early age. Some were sent to work as apprentices to artisans in towns; others were sometimes sent to shepherds to learn from them how to tend the sheep far from home, but there can be little doubt that most peasant children spent their childhood with their parents, unlike the children of the nobility and many of the offspring of towndwellers.

Records drawn up by coroners in England for the use of judges (which we mentioned in the context of urban workers) list deaths of numerous babes and infants in rural areas as a result of carelessness. Babies were often left to the care of an older brother or sister or a disabled grandmother who did not care for them in the proper fashion. Babes in cradles died in fires. Older children who could walk and were naturally inquisitive but lacked the necessary motor skills died by drowning in wells, pools and rivers, and particularly from burns and wounds caused by playing with sharp instruments. The number of accidents dropped markedly after the age of 4. The children developed motor control, learned to behave cautiously and were apparently no longer left at home but accompanied their parents to work.[39] The number of accidents recorded is not inconsiderable, but it should be recalled that these records make no mention of those families which succeeded in raising their children without incident.

The accidents in themselves indicate that often care was inadequate, but do not necessarily suggest that there was no emotional relationship between parents and infants or small children. The

court records do not note the reaction of parents to tragedies, but
the authors of the lives of the saints do. In this source we find
hundreds of records of parents turning to the saints for help in cases
of accident, as well as of their offspring's illness or deformity. There
are tens of cases in which it is clear that the children involved were
very small infants – from a few weeks to 5 years old – and the
reaction of parents to the loss of an infant was often violent grief.[40]

Few literary works describe relations between parents and children among the peasants. In *Piers Plowman*, by William Langland
(who was apparently a churchman of the minor orders, married and
with a daughter), the author, writing of the poverty of the peasants,
describes the problems of supporting numerous children. There is
no trace of the bitterness discernible in many of the didactic works
discussed in a previous chapter. Children are central to family life,
but are also a heavy burden.[41] In two of the literary works
describing peasant families, the author speaks of parental love.
Hartmann von Aue's poem *Der Arme Heinrich* ('Poor Heinrich'),
written in the late twelfth century, depicts a young peasant girl who
is ready to sacrifice her life to cure the lord of the manor of leprosy.
Her parents raise an outcry when they learn of her intention. Only
after they realize that her mind is made up, and after she asks their
pardon and expresses her love and gratitude to them for all she owes
them, do they agree to allow her to do as she wishes. But they are
prostrated with grief and sorrow, and act like people who have lost
their reason for living.[42]

In the thirteenth century poem on the peasant Helmbrecht (*Meier
Helmbrecht*), we also find loving and devoted parents. Their son is
rebellious, denies the class into which he was born, and despite all
his parents' attempts to dissuade him, he becomes a robber in the
company of robber-knights. Eventually he is caught, his eyes are
put out and one of his arms and legs amputated by order of the
lord's bailiff. Blind and crippled, he is brought to the parents' home.
His father refuses to accept him and calls to the boy who leads him:
'Take this horror away from me.' He tells his son: 'Betake yourself
you faithless boor in greatest haste forth from my door; your
suffering is nothing to me.' 'But the mother,' writes the poet, 'who
was not as hard as he passed out as to a child a crust.'[43]

These are literary descriptions, but perusal of the testimony
submitted to the Inquisition tribunal at Pamiers in the early
fourteenth century offers a rare opportunity of learning something
of the attitude to children in peasant society from the mouths of
peasant men and women themselves. This evidence attests to strong

emotion, love and concern for the small child among the farmers of Montaillou, countering Ariès' theory of lack of affection for small children in medieval society, as E. Le Roy Ladurie has already noted. The peasant women suckled their own children, unlike many noblewomen and women of the prosperous urban class. The child was breast-fed for one or two years, and the primary and basic care was therefore warm, close and direct. The poorest and most degraded of the girls of the village, Brune Poucel, who bore a bastard child, agreed only very reluctantly when her neighbour urged her to bring her baby to a woman living in her house who had surplus milk to suckle him. She feared that the milk of a strange woman would harm the baby.[44] The mother of a bastard girl, who worked as a servant girl and hired labourer, transferred her baby from one nurse to another when she changed her place of employment so as to be close to her.[45]

When children died, their mothers wept and mourned them. Neighbours who visited the mourners tried to comfort them by telling them that the dead were in a better place than the living, that the soul of the child would enter the body of the next child the bereaved mother would bear, or that the dead child was privileged before his death to join the alliance of the Cathar faith (i.e. to receive the *consolamentum* on his deathbed), so that the salvation of his soul was assured. But like all words of consolation throughout history, these did not relieve the pain of loss and bereavement. A mother who mourned her daughter, and whose neighbour tried to console her by speaking of salvation of the soul replied that she was glad that her daughter had entered into the alliance of the Cathar faith, but that as much as she had mourned her, she would continue to mourn her even more (*quod bene plus doleret de morte filie sue quam faceret*).[46]

The most illuminating of the testimonies as to the attitude to small children is the following: a Cathar couple had a daughter not yet a year old named Jacotte. The child sickened and was about to die. The parents found a Perfect who, in violation of all the principles of the Cathar faith, was ready to grant her the *consolamentum* before her death, although she had not yet reached the age of understanding, so as to ensure her soul of redemption. After the infant received the *consolamentum* she was forbidden to drink milk (the Cathar Perfects abstained not only from eating meat but also from all animal foods, such as eggs and milk products). This meant that the child was doomed to die of hunger. The Perfect and the father left the house after the father said: if Jacotte dies she will become an angel of God. The mother remained alone with the infant and could not bring herself to observe the ban which condemned her to starvation. She gave her the breast. When this became known to the father and their Cathar friends they were angered and reproached the woman. According to the wife, after this her husband withheld his love from her and the infant for a lengthy period. The child survived another year and then died.[47]

A very similar case of a mother refusing to starve a baby of three months is also cited in the evidence.[48] These expressions of love and strong ties to small children completely contradict the view that people in the Middle Ages were not attached to small children as individuals. The ties between peasant parents and children were not usually severed at an early age, since, as already noted, most peasant children remained at home until maturity. Fathers were not absent from home for long periods. Parents regarded their children as a working force providing help for the future and security for their old age. As one of the Cathars said: 'From a legal wife you will have sons and daughters who will serve you in your old age.'[49] After the death of his son, a villager said: 'On the death of my son Raymond, I lost all I had. There is nobody who can work for me.'[50] But this in no way ruled out love.

Together with the manifestations of love and affection for small children, there are also examples of love and devotion to older children. A poor daughter who lived in the same village as her parents was helped by her mother who loaned her tools and a farm animal.[51] A daughter of one of the most prominent families in the village, the Clergue family, married a man from another village, fell sick and was brought back to her parents' house, where she remained for three years until her death. Her parents spent most of their money on medication for her. On her deathbed she received the *consolamentum*. For adults, it was the custom that after receiving the *consolamentum* on a sickbed, they not only abstained from forbidden foods but also condemned themselves to death by starvation (*endura*), but the mother said: 'If my daughter asks me for food or drink I shall give it to her.' The mother was spared this. The daughter asked for nothing and died on the following day.[52]

A boy of 15 lay dying and asked for the *consolamentum*. The mother, who feared the Inquisition informers, was afraid to bring a Perfect to the house to grant the dying boy the *consolamentum* and said: 'It is enough that I am about to lose you for I have no other son but you. There is no need for me to lose all my property because of you ...' – harsh and calculated words. But the son continued to plead, and his mother gave in and summoned the Perfect.[53] When one of the villagers tried to dissuade a neighbour woman from admitting to the Inquisition tribunal her affiliation to the Cathars, he said to her: 'Foolish and arrogant woman, if you confess, you will lose all your property, you will extinguish the fire of your hearth and your children, with anger consuming their hearts, will beg for bread ...'[54] There were, of course, less sympathetic kinds of behaviour too, even among the villagers of Montaillou, whose testimony we have cited. A Cathar mother from the village plotted, with several other Cathars, to kill her Catholic daughter Jeanne by throwing her over a cliff.[55] But have not modern totalitarian regimes also fomented strife, hostility and total distortion of family relations, as did the Inquisition in the Middle Ages?

As in other periods, property was a source of dispute, and there were selfish parents who preferred their material interests to the good of their children. A widow in England was left with a young son and three daughters. She was more anxious to remarry than to marry off her daughters, and did in fact marry twice more after the death of her first husband, the father of her children. Her third husband did all he could to take over the share of one of his stepdaughters in the family inheritance. Another daughter of the same family bore an illegitimate child, almost certainly because her mother did not give her a dowry and she was unable to marry. Another widow fought tenaciously over her inheritance with her four children. One of her daughters also bore an illegitimate child.[56]

Didactic literature cautions children against doing injustice to their elderly parents. In one of these works we find a peasant version of *King Lear*: a father divides up his property in his lifetime among his sons and they insult him and treat him unjustly. There are no tales cautioning parents against harsh and unjust treatment of their children. Still, though the attitude of churchmen towards the begetting and rearing of children was by no means unambiguous, preachers admonished negligent and ill-intentioned parents, and priests reminded their parishioners of their duty to bring up their offspring in a Christian way. The biblical reward for respect towards parents is long life. The late thirteenth-century author Robert Mannyng of Brunne tells a tale aimed at cautioning children that if they do not honour their aged parents and care for them, their own children will treat them in the same fashion.[57]

There were cases of demented mothers who murdered their children in moments of insanity. In England a woman was charged for beating her 10-year-old son to death in an attack of rage. Another murdered her 2-year-old daughter and forced her 4-year-old son to sit on red-hot coals. The court attributed their actions to insanity.[58] But one finds similar stories in the European press of today. In the wake of the Montaillou study, E. Le Roy Ladurie proposed that Philippe Ariès' theory be reversed. According to Ariès, it will be recalled, a warmer attitude to children evolved gradually only from the end of the Middle Ages. The change commenced first among the upper classes and only much later among the labouring classes. According to E. Le Roy Ladurie, the opposite is true. Love and warm affection for children characterized the peasant class in the Middle Ages, and only much later did similar attitudes evolve in the upper classes.

It is important to recall that parents whose attitude to their children is warped have existed throughout history and exist today in all classes, despite the great focus on children which characterizes our society. The outcome of this warped attitude is basically similar in various civilizations. It is not easy to decide which aspects of a maternal attitude are primary and which are the result of a certain socio-cultural pattern.[59] But according to evidence submitted to Jacques Fournier's tribunal, it seems that in the peasant society of Haute Ariège the social structure and educational system had a less detrimental effect on the natural maternal instincts than among the nobility. It is difficult to arrive at generalizations from the testimony of one isolated region and it is possible that there was a difference between peasant societies in northern and southern Europe (from extant sources at least, it appears that there were instances of affection towards children in Italian towns which have not been found in northern towns). But there can be little doubt that the picture which emerges from Montaillou moderates and at least partially undermines Ariès' theories.

THE WIDOW

No clear-cut difference can be laid down between the average life-expectancy of men and women in rural areas in the Middle Ages. In Halesowen in 1343–95 the female mortality rate was higher than the male, probably because of some epidemic to which women were more vulnerable. In the rural area near Pistoia, according to records for 1427, the numerical gap between the sexes increased with age. At 20 the sex ratio between men and women was 105 to 100; at 50 and over it was 109 to 100; at 60-plus there were

117 men for every 100 women. In the central mountainous region, in a poverty-stricken region with harsh living conditions, the sex ratio at 60-plus was 125 to 100. The gap was undoubtedly also caused by the migration of elderly and prosperous widows to towns, but this was surely not the sole reason. On the other hand, the number of widows in many rural areas was undoubtedly great, because women married younger than men, and their older husbands were likely to die before them. According to a study of ten manors in the Midlands in England in 1350–1450, some 14 per cent of all landholders were women, the great majority of them widows. Only some 5 per cent were spinsters.[60] According to J. Z. Titow, in the first half of the fourteenth century in the Glastonbury monastery manors and the manors of the bishoprics of Winchester and Worcester, the percentage of widows was between 9 and 15 per cent.[61]

As in other classes of society, the rights of peasant widows were safeguarded by ecclesiastical and secular law and custom; these rights were reflected primarily in laws relating to the dower and to guardianship of offspring. The right of dower was not uniform in all areas. Generally speaking, the widow received one third to one half of her deceased husband's landed property as a dower for her lifetime. As an exception to the rule, in certain regions such as Emley Castle she received all the land. There were places where if she remarried she lost her right to the dower. This was the case in Bucksteep in Sussex, where by right of dower the widow kept half of the land while the other half was inherited by the youngest son. If she remarried, she forfeited her land. But in most regions, the widow could continue to hold the dower even if she remarried. She also inherited one third of the household belongings. (One third was divided up equally among sons and daughters, and one third could be bequeathed to whomsoever the property owner chose. Generally speaking it was bequeathed for alms to one of the churches.)

If the deceased was a serf, the lord of the manor, by right of heriot (another characteristic toll upon the serf, in addition to merchet) could also take a portion of the estate; in money, in beasts or in tools. The priest was entitled to collect from the estate all money owing in tithes. If the wife died first, and if she and her husband had a joint child, the widower in most regions continued to hold her land for his lifetime; only on his death did it revert to the heir. If they had no joint progeny the land reverted on the wife's death to her relatives. If a man married a widow, and she died, some of her estate came into his hands, and the majority was inherited by the children of her first marriage.[62]

Many widows maintained their dower without interference, but others were forced to battle their dead husbands' relatives in the courts for their rights. The registers of the King's Ripton manor record the case of a widow who sued thirteen persons and whose case was tried several times. (Unfortunately we do not know the outcome).[63] The dower, which accounted for a considerable part of the property, deprived the heirs, and widows sometimes entered into disputes with their offspring justifiably or without good cause (as we saw in the previous section). It was particularly when widows remarried that the heirs tried to obtain all the land. Most widows acted as guardians to their children. Manor court registers record numerous cases of women paying for the right to act as guardians after the death of their husbands, and handing over land to the heir when he attained his majority.[64]

Some widows did not remarry and cultivated their holdings alone. In regions with demesnes, they also laboured on the demesne, sometimes with the help of hired labourers. Others waived the right to their estates, whether as inheritances or held by right of dower, in favour of one of their children who guaranteed, in return, to keep them. A widowed peasant woman who gave up her property to her son took care to list in the agreement between them the quantity and type of pulses and corn crops which he should supply to her each year, and the amount of coal and the sum of money due to her each year. The son also guaranteed to build a separate house for his mother: a wooden house, 30 feet long and 10 feet wide (inside the walls) with three doors and two windows. If he did not honour his obligations, the contract stipulated, he would be obliged to pay her financial compensation.[65] Other widows remarried. They were sought after mainly if they were heiresses or if, according to the custom of the region, they retained a considerable part of their late husband's property as a dower which would not be forfeited on remarriage. It is characteristic that after the Black Death, when the population was decimated and land fell vacant, the demand for widows dropped. A peasant could more easily obtain land in order to establish a family, and families could provide their daughters with adequate dowries. This was the period in which the number of widows who bore illegitimate children increased, as we have seen.[66]

In places with a demesne the lord of the manor sometimes exerted pressure on the widow to remarry in order to ensure the supply of service and labour due to him, and it happened that the widow paid the lord for permission to postpone her second marriage.[67] Pressure was also sometimes exerted on peasants of the manor to marry widows. A widow named Agatha on one of the English manors was proposed as wife to two peasants, but both refused her! One of them was even willing to pay a fine in order to exempt himself from the duty. The second was sentenced in court for refusing either to marry her or to pay the fine.[68] One can compare the customs which served the function of marriage taxes on peasant widows to those which prevailed among the nobility: pressure by the feudal seigneur or lord of the manor on the widow to remarry; payment by the widow for the right to marry whomsoever she chose; payment of a fine for the offence of marriage without the lord's approval. And in both classes there was demand for the hand of the widow who was an heiress or who held land by right of dower. Several of the widows of Montaillou chose a unique way of life under unusual conditions after being forced to flee their village because of the persecution of the Inquisition. They settled together in Lerida and ran their household communally.[69]

The woman who enjoyed the greatest freedom in peasant society in most regions was the strong landowning widow, like her counterparts in other classes. Property brought status and strength, even though there was the control of the lord and his agents. The widow was free of the supervision of a husband and of her relatives, particularly if she did not live with one of her sons. But many widows in peasant society, again like widows in other classes, preferred second marriage to solitude and the independence it granted.

FEMALE LABOUR IN VILLAGES

In medieval peasant society, as in all known agricultural societies, women were employed in most of the agricultural tasks. If daughters or wives, they worked on family farms; if widows and spinsters, they managed their own holdings. In manors with a demesne they helped to provide the services demanded by the seigneur and laboured on the demesne. If they were widowed or unmarried they were responsible for supplying all the services which those holding a tenement in the manor were required to give. Many women worked as agricultural labourers and servant girls in the homes of lords of the manor and of prosperous farmers. Illuminations in books and stained-glass windows in cathedrals depict the role of women in agricultural work. Together with illustrations of agricultural dormancy in the winter months and of the numerous spring festivals, there are pictures showing women separating wheat from chaff, bringing drink to the harvesters, helping to slaughter pigs and spinning. Literary works which describe peasant life also depict female characters working in the vegetable garden or the field, tending farm animals or fulling cloth.[70] Historical literature once attributed to the peasant woman responsibility for household and the kitchen garden alone, i.e. indoor work. Field and pasture labour were attributed solely to men. Pasture was in fact a male domain, but women played a considerable part in field work.

The household chores and work in the kitchen garden included cleaning, cooking, drawing water and bringing it home, stoking the hearth, bringing wheat to the nearest mill for milling, cheese-making, tending animals and work in the vegetable plot by the house. Ale was brewed by women not only for home consumption but also for sale. Spinning and weaving were also among the female chores. In sheep-raising areas, they spun and wove the wool. In flax-cultivating areas they used the flax for their work. Generally speaking, women also carried out all the other stages in producing the cloth, such as fulling and dyeing. Only the most prosperous peasants spurned home-made cloth and bought more expensive cloth in markets and at fairs. Spinning and weaving were also among the typical household duties of women serfs for their masters, the lords of the manor.[71]

Of the field labours, women took part in weeding, hoeing and sowing pulses. They worked at the harvesting itself, tied the sheaves, separated wheat and chaff and collected the hay. In English villages it was the man who guided the plough as it turned the sods while the woman spurred on the beasts with her goad and guided them, as in Langland's description in *Piers Plowman*. If a harrow was used to separate wheat and chaff, it was the woman who goaded the farm animal. The court registers of one of the manors list a farmer who was charged with cutting the reins of the horse harnessed to the harrow while the peasant woman Christine was harrowing.[72] Joan of Arc attested at her trial that not only had she worked in her parents' home, spinning and sewing exemplarily, but had also ploughed with her father.[73] This evidence was repeated twenty years later by the people of her village to the interrogators who came to the village to reassess the trial. In wine-producing regions women took part in the vintage. In several estates in

Leicester in the second half of the fourteenth century, when the labour force was small because of the decimation of the population, hired female labourers even carried and scattered the manure and engaged in thatching. The world of the shepherds who wandered long distances with their flocks, as in the Pyrenees, was exclusively male, but in England women also washed and sheared the sheep.[74]

Among the women tenement holders there were some who not only held land by inheritance or dower but also purchased it themselves, as emerges from the court registers confirming the sales.[75] This meant that they were able to hold land, cultivate it and fulfil all the obligations this entailed. An example of an independent woman was a peasant woman from Montaillou, who, as a Cathar, was forced to flee her village for fear of the Inquisition. She moved to San Mateo in the Tarragona region and succeeded in purchasing a house and farm there which included a vineyard, a mule and a herd of sheep. In a small workshop in her home she dyed wool. In the busy harvest season she worked as a hired labourer with her children. Apart from this success, achieved honestly, she also increased her property by cheating a relative who had entrusted his herd of sheep to her. She cheated him of the price of the wool and of the hides of 150 sheep. This classic combination of initiative, energy, diligence and readiness to cheat others ensured her of success.[76]

As against those women who flourished through their labours, cultivated their property and fulfilled all their obligations, there were others who collapsed under the heavy burden, like a widow from Newington in Oxfordshire who declared in court that she was powerless (*impotentem*) to keep the land and was therefore handing it over to her grand-daughter and her husband, who had guaranteed in return to keep her and provide all her needs;[77] or like the peasant woman whose son guaranteed to build a house for her.

Peasant women sold surplus agricultural produce in the markets and at fairs.[78] Certain tasks, such as tending poultry or piglets, and work in the dairy, which included butter-making, cheese-making (including salt-cheese, which was singled out for special mention) and churning cream, were considered mainly female chores, although men also engaged in them. In one of the manuals of advice on correct estate management (*Husbandry*) it was stated that if the overseer of the dairy was a man he should carry out all the tasks done by a woman overseer, and most of the instructions in the manual regarding dairies and directed at women; the same is true of other such manuals.[79] Apart from work in the dairy itself the task of the dairy overseer included sifting and winnowing of various types of pulses and grains. Not only instructions on dairy work are directed at women; manuals on other agricultural labours too, refer to both male and female workers.[80] And from the royal statutes fixing the maximum wage for workers in the fourteenth century we learn that women engaged in all agricultural labours. Moreover, in regions with silver and lead mines, it was the women who rinsed the lead in troughs and passed it through filters.[81] They also sometimes cut stone for mending roads.[82] If there existed division of labour by sex in medieval rural society, it applied to men alone. Household and home farm work was not done by men, whereas almost all field work was also carried out by women, who carried out household and auxiliary chores as well.

Women's wages, almost without exception, were lower than men's. The author of the *Husbandry* clearly states that even in an estate without a dairy it is worth employing a woman to tend the animals and carry out the sifting and winnowing, since her wage is lower than a man's. Several examples will suffice to show the differences between male and female wages. According to an ordinance of Jean II of France in 1350, the wage of pruners in vineyards was fixed at 2 shillings and 6 pence a day from mid-February to the end of April. The wages of diggers were 2 shillings a day for the corresponding period. The best female workers in the vineyards were paid 12 pence a day.[83] Women therefore earned half the wage of a digger and less than half that of a pruner. According to an ordinance issued by Richard II of England in 1388, the wage of a dairy worker was 6 shillings a year. This corresponds to the lowest wage for men, that of the swineherd and the ploughman. The wage of the carter and shepherd was 10 shillings a year.[84] The tasks of the dairy overseer were numerous. The work demanded a certain degree of expertise and called for supervision of the auxiliary workers. The authors of manuals on estate management listed the traits required for these tasks: cleanliness, responsibility, honesty, scrupulous care of instruments.

So much for the ordinances determining wages. The records which attest to the actual wages paid (not all records yield this information, since they often list the overall sum paid to hired labourers without detailing how much was paid for each type of work) show that the wage of the female dairy overseer corresponded to the lowest wage paid to men. In the Beauchamps manor of Emley Castle in 1366–7 her wage was 5 shillings a year, corresponding to the wage of the man who spurred the beasts during the ploughing and of the swineherds and oxherds. The wage of the carter and shepherd was 6 shillings a year. In the manor of the bishopric of Worcester the woman in charge of the dairy received 7 shillings and a certain amount of grain every six weeks. The lowest wage of a male worker was 8 shillings and the same amount of grain, given to him every twelve weeks.[85]

According to the studies of E. Perroy, women's wages were particularly low in France even after the Black Death. Because of the general ruin which followed the war conducted on French soil, the fall in production was greater then the decrease in the labour force. Since the demand was small the pay was low.[86] According to J. G. d'Avenal, the average female wage in France in 1326–50 was only 68 per cent of the male wage for the same work. In 1376–1400 women earned 75 per cent of the male wage, in other words their pay increased, but did not catch up with that of their male counterparts.[87] In England, on the other hand, there are several examples from the period following on the Black Death of equal daily wages for men and women in the busy seasons. In Minching-hampton in Gloucestershire in 1380 the harvesters and binders of sheaves received 4 pence a day. In nearby Avening women received the same wage for equal work, i.e. 4 pence a day.

There can be no doubt that the hired labourers taken on for a particular urgent job exercised greater bargaining power than regular workers, and among the latter there was in fact a gap between the wages of men and women.[88] This is an additional example of the temporary rise in the status of women in marginal periods. In England, in contrast to France, the labour force decreased proportionally more than the scope of production, since the war was not conducted on English soil. The wages of workers and women in particular rose.[89] But one should not exaggerate the importance of this marginal period. Equalization of male and female wages was not a widespread phenomenon, not even when labourers were taken on for a particular job. In one of the Leicestershire manors a woman named Alice received 1 shilling for goading the oxen for twelve days. In other words, her wage was a penny a day, with the addition of food. On the other hand, a male harvester received 1 shilling and 4 pence for eight days' labour, that is to say 2 pence a day, with food. Alice therefore earned only half as much as the harvester.[90]

Poor women in rural areas worked as servant women as well. Some worked for families, others as maid-servants and sometimes mistresses of parish priests or prosperous peasants. Some hoped that their employers would marry them some day (like one of the servant women in Montaillou), but this hope was not always fulfilled.[91] There were women who ran taverns or inns or sold wine to peasants,[92] and sometimes they prospered to such an extent that they were able to lend money at interest.[93] Women worked as midwives, and in rural areas which professional healers never reached, they also engaged in medicine, like Na Ferrena of Prades d'Aillon, who was consulted as an expert on eye diseases.[94]

Court registers reveal that women enjoyed the right to hold land, whether by inheritance or by right of dower, and indicate the efforts they made in exercising their rights; we read of women who purchased new land for cultivation, of women serving as custodians of their offspring, and of their violations of matrimonial law. The registers also cast light on charges against women and the reasons why both men and women took others to court. The gravest offences were tried before the seigneurial or royal courts, lesser ones before the manorial courts. Peasants who owned their own land were tried only before the former. The charges listed in registers of both types of court partially reflect the role of women in rural labour, their relations with their own sex and with men, their degree of self-confidence and their role in violent crime. When women were charged, it was usually their male relatives who pledged their appearance in court and were fined if the woman did not appear for the trial on the date specified. Women, it will be recalled, could not stand pledge.[95]

In English villages, as in towns, numerous women were charged with offences against the Assize of Ale, such as selling ale without allowing the 'taster' to check it first, selling in utensils which had not been checked for measure by the authorities, selling ale of low quality or for a lower or higher price than the official rate, or selling before or after the approved seasons. Fines were imposed so frequently that they could be considered a tax more than a fine. The fact that such large numbers of women were charged with these offences indicates what an important role they played in production.[96] Women were charged with trespassing by sending their cattle to graze in areas belonging to others and with lopping off tree branches in the lord's forest without permission. They were also accused of raising the hue and cry without justification, which indicates their involvement in events around them.[97] Sometimes they trespassed not only by sending their cattle to graze illegally, but by invading neighbouring property in the wake of exchanges of insults or blows.

Both women and men were charged with insulting language and with assault. A woman of the manor of King's Ripton sued a man for beating her, breaking a trunk and throwing her out of her home, but the jurors attested that these were not the true facts, and she was fined for bringing false charges.[98] Since women's participation in brawls and in exchanges of insulting language was not a rare occurrence, the accepted legal phraseology relating to such charges refers to women as well, as do the regulations relating to the Assize of Ale.[99] Among the commonest insults hurled by women at one another were the terms 'whore' and 'witch' (*vocando ipsam meretricem et sorceram*).[100] In so violent a society as that of the Middle Ages, the frailer physique of a woman was a clear disadvantage, but this limitation did not render all women retiring and submissive, either in rural or in urban regions, as we have seen. On the other hand, among the peasants, as in other classes in that period, the number of women in the violent criminal class was very small. Christine de Pisan was right in noting this.

Women of the poorer strata were charged with petty theft, mainly foodstuffs, household goods and clothing. Sometimes they were charged with receiving stolen goods, particularly those stolen by a male member of their own families. Very few were charged with murder. Of those so charged some committed the act alone, but most acted together with a member of their family. Others were accused of the murder of their husbands in collusion with a lover. There were also women members of gangs of habitual criminals who murdered for gain. Women killed with knife, spade or axe, instruments with which they were acquainted from the household and from field work. They were not skilled in the weapons of war. In the rural areas of Bedford, Bristol, Kent, Norfolk, Oxford, Warwick and London in the thirteenth century, only 8.4 per cent of all those charged with murder were women. According to registers of the courts of Norfolk, Yorkshire and Northamptonshire, in the fourteenth century, before which mainly rural inhabitants were charged, only one woman was charged with a criminal offence for every nine men. Women accounted for only 7.3 per cent of those sentenced for murder.

As in towns, women in rural areas constituted only a relatively small proportion of the victims of murder. A study of the villages of the above-mentioned regions in the thirteenth century shows that only 20.5 per cent of the victims were women.[101] (Infanticide by mothers in rural areas of France and Western Germany has already been mentioned in a previous chapter.) When the lord of the manor used coercive force against his tenants, women too were sometimes amongst the victims. In 1282, when the canons and servants of the abbey of Halesowen broke into the house of one of the villeins in order to put him into the stocks, his pregnant wife, who probably tried to resist his arrest, was beaten to death.[102]

There was distinct though informal separate contact among women in rural areas, in both work and leisure: at the flour mill, by the well or the stream, during spinning and weaving, in leisure-time conversation. The young women of the village could simply stroll together. But we know of no uniquely female entertainments, the counterparts of men's activities. In Montaillou the men played chess and dice games, and on some evenings met together for joint meals and community singing accompanied by flute music. There are no records of similar female leisure-time activities. Their separate sociability was reflected in conversation at work and rest, in mutual aid and perhaps also in walks together. Conversation by the hearth was popular among the peasants of Montaillou, and women took part (or at least were present), sitting together on a separate bench.[103] From time to time minstrels or wandering actors would reach the villages, or more frequently the markets and fairs, and both men and women attended their performances. Humbert de Romans, in preaching to poor village women, cautioned them against these wandering minstrels (*trutanni goliardi*), who might exploit their interest and gullibility.[104]

Peasant women, like townswomen, drank with the men at home and at taverns. It will be recalled that some taverns were also run by women. It was with good cause that among the places which the lord of the manor should dissuade the peasants from visiting needlessly, the manuals of guidance on manor management list taverns at markets and fairs as well as wrestling matches and nocturnal entertainments held in honour of various occasions.[105] One poet listed the spinning equipment and items of clothing which women were willing to pawn in order to buy ale. (Most of the items of clothing mentioned belonged to their husbands.)[106] Weddings and other celebrations were naturally opportunities for extensive drinking.

On the various holidays, which were many (Walter Henley, author of *Husbandry* accepts without question eight weeks of holidays each year),[107] both women and men celebrated. Festivals were linked to seasons of the agricultural year and the Christian calendar, and some involved a blend of ancient pagan customs and

Christian custom. In England on the eve of Hockday the women of the village seized the men and did not release them until they paid ransom, and on the following day it was the turn of the men to capture the women. We learn about some of the festivals from the bishops' bans. On May Day in some English villages the most beautiful girl in the village was chosen as Queen of the May and was garlanded with flowers; this was prohibited by the bishop of Worcester. Young boys and girls danced together despite repeated bans by churchmen. Sometimes the dancing was held in the church square, and sometimes it was part of the celebrations during nocturnal festivals which also included singing and games. On the evening of the first Sunday of Lent, the dance of the Brandon was held in some European villages. This was a nocturnal festival in which men and women went out with lighted candles to the vineyards and fields, danced, sang liturgical songs and uttered incantations against pests which harmed trees.[108] This recalls the fairy tree in Joan of Arc's village, Domrémy, under which young men and women danced, sang and drank.

Several preachers enumerated among the particular sins of women the fact that they did not listen to sermons in church but chattered among themselves.[109] Did women in fact treat the sermons lightly and chatter more than men, or was prattling one of the fixed components of the image of women, which preachers could not renounce? It is hard to assume that women displayed less religious piety than men. In Montaillou it was the men who sometimes uttered apostasy, expressing hatred of the clergy who exploited and impoverished the peasants by taking tithes not only from the crops but also from the flocks.

Few Christian saints were born peasants, but among these few, several were women. A thirteenth-century peasant woman named Margaret of Cortona was mistress of a nobleman and bore him a son. After the death of her lover she renounced all worldly things and chose the worship of God. She joined the third order of Franciscans, did acts of charity and tried to bring sinners to repent. She spent her last years as a recluse. Margaret was canonized only in 1728, but was recognized as a saint immediately after her death by the people of her village.[110] In Hartmann von Aue's poem *Der Arme Heinrich*, as noted above, the heroine is a very young peasant girl who is willing to sacrifice herself for the leprous lord of her manor. She is willing to sacrifice her young life without a struggle, since she contemplates the eternal life awaiting her. Her readiness for sacrifice brings about a change of heart in the knight. He accepts his fate and refuses to accept her sacrifice. It is then that the miracle occurs and he is cured of his leprosy.

In Montaillou it was the women who sat in vigil with the corpse (of men as well) until the burial, and in the absence of a sexton prepared the corpse for burial, washing it and dressing it in its shroud. If the relatives of the deceased observed archaic customs, such as clipping one of his nails and a lock of his hair to keep in the home so that the blessing would not depart from it after his death, women took an active part in the ceremony.[111] Christianity did not succeed in rooting out these magic ceremonies in which the women played a part even in more ancient cultures.

Peasant women and men did not write letters or keep diaries which could reveal something of their way of thinking or mentality. The few literary works describing the world of peasants were not written by the peasants themselves. What is known we know mainly from the outside: organization and activities. Only indirectly do the sources allow us a glimpse of the inner world of members of this class, which constituted the great bulk of the population of Europe in the Middle Ages. A few peasants were educated in the schools run by parish priests, which could enable them to play a part in the manor administration, the seigneurial system or the realm, or to become parish priests in their turn. Some became monks and acquired some learning within the monastery. In southern France there were even prosperous peasants who reached universities.[112] But we know of no peasant woman who gained an education. Joan of Arc, whose family were not poor, learned from her mother the basic tenets of Christian faith and the most important prayers: Ave Maria, Pater Noster, Credo, and no more.

The fact that peasant girls were not educated had less bearing on their standing in their own society than the exclusion of women from institutions of higher learning had on noblewomen and townswomen. The great majority of men in peasant society were uneducated. Essentially it was not lack of education which precluded women from holding office within the manor of the rural community, whether in the seigneurial or the state system, just as lack of education was not the factor which closed the Church to them. Medieval society never wanted women to hold office, but the lack of education denied them any opportunity from the outset and in retrospect provided justification for the denial of their right. Acquisition of education by a peasant man enabled him to step outside his class, but this possibility was not open to women.

Certain anthropologists have cited the method of division of labour between the sexes in the dawn of civilization as one of the central factors in the inferior status of women in all known historical societies. Leadership was connected with fighting, hunting, boat- and house-building. Women played no part in these activities. If we return to the description of the triune society of the Middle Ages, a functional society of Worshippers, Warriors and Workers, we see that the women of the labouring class played the fullest role in the functions of their class. Women took the veil but no women took holy office, not even the nuns. Some women inherited fiefs and exercised ruling powers, but noblewomen did not fulfil the warrior function, and held office or exercised ruling powers only as individuals.

The closest to the peasant women (and in the division of society into three functional orders, the workers are peasants) were women of the urban labouring class, but nonetheless women played a much more limited part in urban than in rural society. The distinguishing features of the town were not only production and petty trade but also foreign trade, financial dealings and institutions of learning where women played no part. In rural society, on the other hand, as we have seen, women played a part in almost all agricultural activities, and there was very little division of labour by sex (exluding building and woodcutting, which were carried out by men alone). However, the source of the discrimination against the medieval peasant woman lay not only in her class but also in her sex. Her rights were not equal to those of the male peasant. The working role of rural women gave them a certain degree of self-confidence and freedom of action, as it did to women of the urban labouring class, but men wielded the power in society and in the family as in other classes. The almost total absence of division of labour by sex did not result in equality between the sexes, either because, from the outset, it was not (or not solely) the division of labour which caused discrimination against women, or because in the process of the development of human society, this discrimination became anchored in law and custom, in the organization of state and society, in religion and in woman's literary image in the various societies.

Essentially (with certain exceptions which we have discussed) those authors were correct who depicted women in medieval society as a separate order. Certain public and legal rights were denied, and certain legal concessions due, to women as women, just as in some countries women, as women, were executed in a certain manner. The rights denied to women in church were denied them because they were women, irrespective of their class. And in summing up these chapters on the women of various classes we see that in no class were the rights of women equal to those of their male counterparts – a negative common denominator for the women of all classes.

8

Witches and the Heretical Movements

Many women joined the heretical sects between the beginning of the spread of heresy in Western Europe and the end of the Middle Ages. The chroniclers took pains to stress this fact, not only in order to tell what happened, but often by way of denigrating the worth and aims of the heretics. The mere fact that women responded with enthusiasm to the sermons of a heretic was enough to prove his utterances ignorant, if not an actual deviation from orthodoxy and a sin. (That women were also among the faithful audience of the orthodox preachers could be overlooked.) Some of the heretical sects gave women the right to preach and officiate in church, which was undoubtedly a violation against the Scriptures and canon law. In their attacks against the heretics, Catholic writers also ascribed to them sexual transgressions, and promiscuity became a regular feature of the stereotyped heretic in the chronicles, and even in some of the Catholic polemical writings. Naturally, women had to be included in these descriptions of heretical debauchery.

Nevertheless, the chroniclers were certainly correct in stating that many women joined the heretical movements. This can be gathered from the letters of churchmen, from manuals of inquisitors that were designed for internal circulation, and from the records of the Inquisition. As early as 1028, Radulfus Glaber ('The Bald'), describing a heretical group in Piedmont – a group that might be described as proto-dualist – tells of a countess who joined it. The community included men and women of the peasant class. They were moved to a large extent by the same aspirations as the Reform movement of

the eleventh century, advocating chastity, renunciation of property
and bodily asceticism, and opposed to incontinent and simoniac
priests and their concubines.[1] In the early twelfth century there
were many women, and many prostitutes, among the followers of
Henry of Le Mans, at the very time when many prostitutes
followed Robert of Arbrissel, listened to his sermons and repented.
Whereas the orthodox solution for these women was for them to
withdraw to one of the homes for repentant whores, Henry of Le
Mans proposed that they should marry his disciples, once they had
cut off their hair and burnt their fancy clothes and jewellery. He
also decreed the abolition of the dowry.[2] At that time women were
also flocking to Tanchelm (a wandering preacher) in the Netherlands, and somewhat later to Arnold of Brescia, in Italy.[3]

In the twelfth as in the eleventh century, women belonged to
various proto-dualist groups, that is to say groups whose precise
doctrines and rites cannot be ascertained, but to whom are ascribed
some of the beliefs and customs of the Cathars, as well as ideas
which had previously been introduced by Henry of Le Mans, Peter
of Bruys and others. The existence of such groups was recorded in
Soissons, Périgueux, Rheims and elsewhere.[4] The writers mention
matrons, prostitutes and nuns as belonging to them. Ralph of
Coggeshall mentions a woman of Rheims who was well versed in
the Scriptures (with an erroneous interpretation) and a sharp
disputant. It is known that there were women among the pseudo-
Amalricians, the early thirteenth-century vulgarizers of the doctrine
of Amalric, who were accused of antinomianism. It was charged
that they claimed that the Holy Spirit was incarnated in them, and
maintained that 'all is one, because all that exists is God'. Being
incarnations of the Holy Spirit, they could no longer sin, and were
therefore in no need of the sacraments.[5] Others joined the ranks of
the pseudo-Joachimites, the vulgarizers of the doctrine of Joachim
of Fiore.

In 1300 the court of the Inquisition ordered the exhumation of
the remains of a woman named Gulielma, who had died in 1281.
According to the inquisitors, she had been worshipped by her
followers as an incarnation of the Holy Spirit. They also believed
that her helpmate, a woman named Manfreda, would become pope,
and would bring about the conversion of the Jews and Muslims, and
a new era for mankind. As pope she would create women cardinals,
too.[6] Reference has already been made to the episode described in
the annals of Colmar, of a beautiful and eloquent young woman
who came to baptize women in the name of the Father, the Son and

herself. In contrast to the prophetic utterances of women mystics who remained within the bounds of orthodoxy, hers were excoriated as heretical, and after her death her remains were disinterred and burnt at the stake. The pseudo-Apostles, a movement that flourished briefly in Italy in the thirteenth century, believed in absolute poverty in emulation of the Apostles, and engaged in prophecy, inspired by the teaching of Joachim of Fiore. This movement also counted women among its members, and a woman called Margaret closely assisted its leader Dolcino. She had been a nun, and left the convent to follow Dolcino. In 1307 these two with another disciple were burnt at the stake.

There were also women among the so-called 'Brothers of the Free Spirit', to whom, as to the pseudo-Amalricians, was attributed the belief in their absolute identification with the deity, and resultant inability to sin. It does not appear to have been an organized sect, but a few scattered groups only. It is also not clear if they were all as promiscuous and licentious as they are described by the chroniclers, or if they were not in fact much closer to the orthodox mystical movement of the Late Middle Ages. Among the women who belonged to the 'Brothers of the Free Spirit' there were Beguines as well as laywomen. Some clustered around male leaders, while others underwent mystical experiences in solitude.[7]

In 1372 a woman by the name of Jeanne Daubenton was charged before the Parlement of Paris with being one of the leaders of a group known as the *turlupins* (the members of the group referred to it as the Society of Paupers), to which were ascribed beliefs and customs resembling those of the 'Brothers of the Free Spirit'. She was burnt at the stake.[8] We saw in a previous chapter how the Beguines who were close to the Spiritual Franciscans were charged with heresy. There were women among the Waldenses and Cathars from the inception of these sects. The records of the court of the Inquisition at Pamiers from the first quarter of the fourteenth century show that just before the final extirpation of the Cathars in southern France, there were still many women among them, and the same is true of the Waldenses. There had been women in the very first groups that followed Peter Waldo in the last quarter of the twelfth century, and they remained present in the sect through the centuries. (This is the only heretical movement that began in the High Middle Ages and was never entirely destroyed but survived into modern times.)

When in the late fourteenth and even more in the fifteenth century, Lollardy changed its character as an intellectual heresy with its centre at Oxford university and became a popular belief among the lower middle classes, peasants and artisans, many women joined its ranks.[9] Women also flocked to the Hussites. One Anna Weiler, the companion of the Hussite preacher Frederick Reiser, was burnt with him at the stake.[10] The Taborites recognized the right of women to leave their husbands and sons to go to the hills, or to one of the five towns that were the centres of their movement. They did not seek to revolutionize society or the relations between the sexes altogether, here and now, though they did expect far-reaching changes to take place at the end of time: 'Then women shall bear children without travail, and men also will bring forth children, virgins shall give birth without male seed as did Saint Mary, and the mutual duties of husbands and wives will be made null.'[11]

We cannot discuss the position of women in each of the sects mentioned. About some of them there is scant and fragmentary information, and some were short-lived. Just as the few, and hostile, sources do not allow us to determine to what extent these sects really diverged from the Roman dogma, if at all, or in what ways their rites differed from the Catholic, so it is difficult to ascertain their exact attitude to women, and the rights women actually enjoyed in these communities. I have therefore chosen to concentrate on the place of woman in the theology of the two major heretical movements in the High Middle Ages, the Waldenses and the Cathars, as compared with her real rights in their communities. Concerning the first sect, up until the fourteenth century the only sources available are Catholic; about the second, there are some Cathar sources extant too.

THE WALDENSES

We have noted that there were women Waldenses as early as the last quarter of the twelfth century. Catholic chroniclers and polemicists denounced the Waldenses for preaching, men and women alike, without proper authority. With the establishment of the court of the Inquisition, male and female Waldenses were equally persecuted.[12] The Catholic writers noted the presence of women in the Waldensian community, yet on the whole they did not attribute lascivious behaviour to this sect as much as they did to others, though they did not always refrain from making such charges – part of the stereotype of the heretic – against it too. Writing at the beginning of the thirteenth century, Burchard of Ursberg said:

'What is so disgraceful about them is that men and women walk together on the roads and frequently remain overnight in one house, and it is said that sometimes they sleep in one bed – and all this, they vow, they were instructed to do by the Apostles.'[13] Waldensian women could be Perfects (*perfectae*), that is to say, belong to that class of the adherents who followed all the religious precepts of the sect, including chastity and the renunciation of private property. Female Perfects, like men, could preach and conduct the religious services: prayer, the blessing of the bread in the communal meal, and administration of the sacraments. This was described by a Catholic writer in the thirteenth century: 'Not only do their laymen presume to administer the sacrament of the Mass, but it is known that even their women presume to do this.'[14] Other women belonged to the class of 'Believers' (*credentes*); some were married and others, single or widowed, lived together in a hostel (*hospicium*) run by the Perfects. In the fourteenth century, when the Waldensian movement had become fully established (albeit clandestinely), in some of its communities women were deprived of the right to preach and conduct religious services. In other communities they apparently retained these rights.[15]

Did Waldensian theology assign to women a different place than in Catholic orthodoxy? As far as is known, the Waldenses did not develop a new general theology of their own, nor a particular one concerning woman's role in the celestial hierarchy or in the story of the redemption of mankind. In the beginning, the Waldenses called only for poverty and a way of life based on the Apostles – that is to say, wandering and preaching (*paupertas; vita apostolica*). Nor were they strictly speaking, an anticlerical group, because to begin with they did not criticize the Church establishment or the clerical mode of living, and they asked the pope for permission to preach. Permission was not given, and they went on preaching nevertheless, and were consequently proscribed, excommunicated and outlawed. They gradually formed a number of separate communities, and evidently adopted some of the doctrinal deviations of other heretical movements in southern France and Italy, finally diverging from Catholic orthodoxy also by way of their literal interpretation of the precepts of the New Testament. Their rites too, on some points, varied from the Catholic.

Waldo himself had been a wealthy burgher, and so were some of his earliest followers. Only a propertied person can discard his possessions and voluntarily elect poverty. But as the community grew it was joined chiefly by members of the lower middle classes, peasants, shepherds and artisans. They did not have an educated leadership and did not evolve a new theology. Characteristically, when a Waldense was asked by the judges of an Inquisition court if he believed that women would be resurrected in female bodies, or that everyone would be resurrected in male bodies, he replied that each would be resurrected in his own sex (*quilibet resurget in sexu suo*). This was an orthodox statement of faith, unlike the belief attributed to the Cathars, and which was in fact popular in the lower classes, that all would be resurrected in male bodies.[16] In Peter Waldo's statement of faith, wherein he rejected the prevalent heresies of his time, especially those of the Cathars, he declared *inter alia* that Jesus was 'true god from the Father, was true man from his Mother, having true flesh from the womb of his mother and a rational human soul ... born of the Virgin Mary by true birth of the flesh'.[17] The Waldenses who came after him never abandoned this Catholic belief. On the other hand, they never exalted St Mary mother of God. It is doubtful if all the Waldenses celebrated her feast-day and if they all accepted her prayer, the Ave Maria.

Certain testimonies given before the court of the Inquisition show that some Waldenses even questioned Mary's role as mediator between the believer and God.[18] There is no doubt that, as a whole, they neither stressed nor promoted her role and her worship. In this way they reduced the function of the feminine element in the celestial hierarchy as compared with its place in Catholic theology, especially from the twelfth century on, when the latter enlarged the idea of the role of the Virgin, mother of God, the mediator between Him and man. The Waldensian ritual was generally characterized by extreme simplicity, and the worship of the Virgin, in particular, was reduced to a minimum. It is therefore impossible to explain the greater rights of women in the Waldensian community on the basis of a theological change concerning the function of the feminine element in the celestial hierarchy or the redemption of mankind.

What, then, was the reason for the wider rights of women in the Waldensian community? It seems to have been caused by two factors: (a) the return to the New Testament and the consequent emphasis on the spiritual equality of all Christian believers, including women; (b) the fact that it was a persecuted fringe community, which naturally made for relatively greater equality among the members, including women. Catholic polemicists, in disputing with the Waldenses, quoted all the texts which the heretics did not refer to, and from which could be deduced a prohibition of women preachers; they took great care to avoid contending directly with the texts used by the Waldenses. When they could not avoid them, they applied their own interpretation to those texts, holding, of course, that they could not be used to justify women's right to preach.

The best example of this style of disputation may be found in the book of the Premonstratensian Abbot Bernard. The fourth chapter is devoted to the denial of the right of laymen to preach, and the eighth to a similar denial with respect to women. The method used in both chapters is the same: quotations from the Scriptures denying the right of laymen to preach (in the fourth chapter) and of women (in the eighth); quotation of the verses used by the Waldenses to justify preaching by laymen and women; a refutation of the interpretation placed by the Waldenses on the said verses; and, in conclusion, the prohibition of such preaching. With respect to women, the author quotes the texts referred to previously in the chapter on nuns (Ephesians 5:22–3; I Timothy 2:11–12; I Corinthians 11:3–15; Genesis 3:16). The woman sinned first and caused Adam to sin; the head of the woman is the man, for whom she was created; she must be silent and not usurp authority over him. Preaching by women was also a violation of the canon law established as early as 398, at the Church council in Carthage.

According to Bernard, the Waldenses based their justification of women's preaching on the Epistle to Titus, chapter 2, verses 1–3:

'But speak thou the things which become sound doctrine. That the aged men be sober, grave, temperate, sound in faith, in charity, in patience. The aged women likewise, that they be in behaviour as becometh holiness, not false accusers, not given to much wine, teachers of good things.'

But, he says, their interpretation of these verses is erroneous: it is not written that the women are to teach the public, but only to give their children correct behaviour. Equally erroneous is the Waldensian reliance on the reference to Anna, the daughter of Phanuel (Luke 2): this Anna had been an old woman who fasted and prayed to God for many years, and was granted the gift of prophecy, but it was nowhere stated that she taught in public. The gifts of the spirit are manifold, and prophecy differs from the right to preach (*Igitur aliud sit donum prophetiae aliud sermo doctrinae*).[19] So much for the Premonstratensian author. The distinction between function and title and the divine gift to a person has been discussed in the section on women mystics in Chapter 3.

It seems, therefore, that the Waldenses' return to the New Testament, which they translated into the vernacular of their various countries, was one of the reasons for their granting these rights to the women in their communities. The Waldenses' choice of quotations from the Scriptures was of course selective. It is not known whether they also relied on chapter 3, verse 28, in St Paul's Epistle to the Galatians: 'There is neither Jew nor Greek, there is neither bond nor free, there is neither male nor female, for ye are all one in Christ Jesus.' At any rate, the polemicists who disputed with them made no reference to this verse. But whether this means that the Waldenses made no use of it, or that it would have been difficult to refute an argument in favour of women preachers based on this particular text, we cannot tell.

The granting of rights to women in their religious communities was not a central objective of the Waldenses. Rather, it was part of their general broadening of the rights of the laity, their narrowing of the gap between it and the priesthood, and their rejection of the Church hierarchy – all of this relying on Scriptural authority. It is significant that even William of Occam, the fourteenth-century nominalist philosopher, while criticizing the regime of the Church hierarchy, and claiming the right of the laity to participate in the Church's general councils, also called for greater rights for women in the Church, including the right to participate in councils.[20] Then again, the Waldenses, as a deviant, persecuted, marginal group, maintained relatively greater equality among its members than in the Catholic community. Such a group needs the active consent of all its members, and this precipitates the collapse not only of class divisions but also of the divisions between the sexes. The Perfects, male and female, abjured all private property as well as marriage. The woman who became a Perfect did not belong to a family, that is to say, to an economic unit subject to the authority of a husband and father.

As we have already noted, in the fourteenth century certain Waldensian communities deprived women of the right to preach and serve in church, as part of a broader process of institutionaliza-tion and of limiting the preaching rights of the laity. The pheno-menon was to repeat itself in the Protestant sects in seventeenth-century England. These also began by abolishing the distinction between clergy and laity, including women, and were persecuted by Church and state; in the end, they recoiled from the logical consequences of acknowledging the spiritual equality of men and women. By the Restoration the Dissenters no longer upheld such equality in the earthly congregation.[21]

THE CATHARS

As Catharism spread through all social classes in southern France, it was also adopted by women of all classes. Many of these belonged to the middle and higher nobility. There is no doubt that one of the factors that facilitated the great expansion of the movement in southern France was the support it received from the great nobles. But whereas men of the higher nobility merely extended their sympathy and support, or, at best, became Cathari Believers, many women of that class received the *consolamentum* in their lifetime and became Perfects. Some were widows, others had been separated from their husbands. There were women of such families as de Puylaurens, Laurac, Mirot, Mirepoix, and the like. Esclarmonde, the sister of the count of Foix, and widow of one of the great lords of Gascony, became a Perfect and regularly took part in disputations between Cathars and Catholics. According to the chronicler Guillaume de Puylaurens she so aroused the ire of the Catholic cleric at one of these debates that he addressed her with the words: 'Madame, go home and spin threads. It is not meet for a woman to take part in a religious discussion!' Her brother was only a sympathizer of the Cathars.

During the twelfth and at the beginning of the thirteenth century, when Catharism existed openly in southern France, women sometimes resided together in a house, designated by the Catholics 'Heretics' Home' (*Domus haereticorum*). These houses were often established by Cathari noblewomen. The inmates, like those of the Waldensian hospices, were girls and women who belonged to the class of Believers, receiving the instruction of the Perfects. Most of these houses included workshops, clinics and schools. As Catharism went underground, it survived mainly in the villages, where many peasant women joined it, as we have seen in the discussion of the peasant society of the Haute Ariège. Women played an especially important role in transmitting Catharism to relatives and the younger generation. During the twelfth century they also sometimes acted as wandering missionaries.

Women could not serve as deacons or bishops in the Cathari community, but these were in any event mere administrative functionaries and did not stand higher in the religious hierarchy than other Perfects (in contrast to the custom in the Catholic Church whereby only bishops or higher ecclesiastics could administer the sacraments of ordination and of confirmation). As Perfects women could preach, bless and administer the *consolamentum*. In general, women Perfects gave the *consolamentum* to women, and men to men. But in the absence of male Perfects, a female one could administer to men also.[22] All Perfects were admired by the Believers, who expressed this feeling by making them a ritual curtsy (*melioramentum*), signifying their adoration of the Holy Spirit which was upon them. Male and female Perfects alike practised complete chastity, owned no property, ate no meat nor any other animal product, and lived a life of extreme simplicity and austerity. Sometimes they also engaged in manual labour.[23]

What place did the feminine element have in Cathari theology? The Cathars minimized the function of the Holy Mother. Some held that she had been an angel from heaven; if she were an angel, then the materialization of Jesus was entirely illusory. (This belief, known as Docetism, was already prevalent among the Gnostics in the second century.) Others held that she was a flesh-and-blood woman, in whose body Jesus had dwelt, without taking anything from her.[24] In either case, the Cathars held that she had not really borne God (*Dei Genetrix*). According to the two Bogomil texts which were accepted by the Cathars, 'The Secret Supper' and 'The Vision of Isaiah', Jesus entered Mary's body via her ear: 'Then I descended and entered her by way of her ear and exited by way of her ear.'[25] Thus Mary was a woman through whom Jesus passed but from whom he did not receive anything. In testimonies given by Cathars in courts of the Inquisition, they reiterated this idea with even greater emphasis. In the words of one of the witnesses:

> God did not receive human flesh from the Blessed Mary, nor did she give birth to Him, nor was she the mother of God ... It is improper to suggest and to believe that the Son of God was born of a woman and was contained in such a lowly thing as a woman.[26]

According to other evidence given before the court of the Inquisition and to the inquisitor Moneta Cremona, the Cathars believed that Mary was an angel from whom Jesus did not take anything. In support of this belief they quoted, among other texts, chapter 2, verse 4, of the Gospel According to St John, the much-interpreted Woman, what have I to do with thee?' According to the Cathars it means: 'What have I taken from you? – Naught.' (*Quid de tuo sumpsi? – Nihil.*)[27] Angel or woman, there is no question but that in the Cathari belief St Mary played a secondary and instrumental role only. And as it negated the idea of the voluntarily God-bearing virgin, by whose consent there came the incarnation of God for the redemption of mankind, so her role as the mediator between the believer and her Son was also absent

from their creed. (The Cathars rejected the very concept of mediation between the faithful and God. The only mediator between the
soul of the believer and God was his own Spirit.) Needless to say,
she was also entirely absent from their rites. Thus there was no
feminine element in the celestial world of the Cathars, and woman
played no part in the salvation of mankind.

But whereas the Cathars rejected the role and function of the
Holy Mother as perceived by the Catholics, they did retain in their
own special frameworks – if not in the theology, then at any rate in
their myths and popular beliefs – the image of woman as the
temptress and corrupter, who is also a creature inferior to man.
According to the 'Secret Supper', Eve's soul derived from a lower
heaven than Adam's, and was thus further removed than he from
the source of goodness and light. In one of the Latin translations of
this text (the so-called 'Vienna Version'), Satan created the body of
man and ordered an angel of the second heaven to enter and inhabit
it. Later he created another, female, body and ordered an angel of
the first heaven to inhabit it. In the other Latin version, that of
Carcassonne, Satan has an angel of the third heaven enter the body
of Adam, and of the second the body of Eve.[28] In both versions the
serpent seduces Eve and mates with her.[29] In certain myths which
were widespread among the Cathars as popular beliefs, and described in testimonies they gave before the courts of the Inquisition,
Satan also tempted the angels by presenting before them the image
of a seductive woman. The myth sometimes concludes with God
declaring that, in punishment for her role in bringing about the
downfall of the angels, woman will not enter His kingdom; in other
myths the woman is one of the temptations offered by the Devil to
the angels in addition to fields and orchards, silver and gold and
other riches of the visible world.[30] Some Cathars believed that the
souls of women who reached paradise would be unable to enter it in
female bodies, and that therefore they would take on male forms.[31]
In the fourteenth century, one of the last Cathari Perfects in
southern France even blamed Peter's thrice-repeated denial of
Christ on the voice of a woman.[32]

Earlier, in the chapter dealing with woman as mother, mention
was made of the Cathari myth concerning the temptation of the
angels by the Devil, who offered them offspring, that would bring
them happiness greater than any in the heavenly world.[33] This myth
can be understood in terms of the Cathars' absolute rejection of
sexuality and procreation, as a result of which they sometimes
viewed the woman as a Satanic creature, even in the material world

which is wholly evil. The greatest misfortune which could befall a woman was to die in pregnancy, for pregnancy came from the Devil, and the soul of a woman who died in that state could never be redeemed.[34] Thus, not only was the feminine element totally absent from the process of the salvation of mankind, and from the mediation between God and His faithful, but in the myths and popular beliefs of the Cathars woman was indeed inferior to man and had a share in the downfall of the angels.

And yet, matters were not so cut and dried. Side by side with these myths it is possible to discern in the Cathar doctrine a certain neutralization of the sexes, based on the following premises. First, that the very existence of sexes is a creation of Satan, and thus part of the order of things in this world, the world of matter and evil; the true Lord God did not create the sexes, and at the time of the redemption He would undo the difference between them. The second premise was the belief in metempsychosis. Souls – or most of them – were destined to be reincarnated again. Only the soul which, while living in this world, attained the level that permitted it to become a Cathari Perfect would not continue to be reincarnated, and having once died, would become one with its Maker. But most souls were fated to undergo many more incarnations, and so long as they did, they would alternately assume male and female bodies.

This is how the creation of the bodies by Satan is described in 'The Secret Supper': 'When the angels saw the different [male and female] forms of the bodies in which they were imprisoned, they wept.'[35] The Devil then compels them to have sexual relations. Evidence for the belief that with the Redemption, when the souls return to their origin, the sexual difference would cease to be, may be found in several testimonies given in the courts of the Inquisition. One defendant testified: 'The souls of men and of women were identical, without any difference between them. The difference between men and women is in the flesh, which was created by the Devil. Once the souls shed their corporeality, there will no longer be any difference between them.' These yearnings for the androgynous being are found not only in the popular beliefs of the Cathars, but also in the dualistic movements of the early centuries and in John Scotus Erigena.[36] The Cathari belief in metempsychosis is disclosed in testimonies given before the courts of the Inquisition, as well as in Catholic polemics, and in the most important Cathari theological text to have come down to us, 'The Book of the Two Principles' (*Liber de Duobus Principiis*).[37]

Chastity, as we have seen, was of paramount value among the Cathars, as may be gathered not only from the Inquisition records but also from the Cathari texts which have survived. Even the authors of the Catholic polemics against them admitted that the Cathari Perfects were as chaste as they vowed to be. A willingness to marry was one of the signs of repentance and return to Catholicism. Thus the phrase, 'took a wife', or 'was married', often recurs in describing Cathars returning to Catholicism.[38] In Cathari texts the elevation of chastity as a supreme value is an outcome of the cosmic and metaphysical rejection of sexuality. In the Cathari text known as the 'Manichaean Treatise' (*Tractatus Manicheorum*), chastity is defined as the way of the Perfects, who do not take wives, and avoid the temptations of the flesh, fornification and procreation, all of which are of this world, the world of evil. Among other authorities, the author quotes the words of Jesus in the Gospel According to St Luke 20:34–5: 'The children of this world marry and are given in marriage. But they which shall be accounted worthy to obtain that world and the resurrection from the dead, neither marry nor are given in marriage.'[39] In the two texts which describe the Cathari ritual, the value of chastity is also emphasized. God is entreated to judge the sin of the flesh and to be merciful to the flesh, which was born of corruption.[40] Virginity and chastity are the approved way, and they bring man closer to God.[41] The Perfect who is free from sexual desire in this world is on a different existential and ontological plane from the rest of mankind. He will require no more incarnations, and once dead, his soul will return to its source.

This represents an even sharper contrast between the man who lives a sexual life and he who practises celibacy – or, among women, between the one who has a sexual life and procreates, and the nun – than we have seen in the writings of Bernard of Clairvaux and Abélard. But the Cathars were more consistent than either Bernard or Abélard. As we know, although the Catholic thinkers made a distinction between the nun and those women who led a sexual life and bore children, and although they praised the former as the bride of God and the reflection of St Mary, none of them proposed that nuns be given the right to become priests and serve in church. The Cathars made one law for men and women. Having received the *consolamentum*, the woman Perfect became, like the man, a vehicle of the Holy Spirit, and like the man could officiate as priest of the congregation.

We may conclude, therefore, that neither the Cathars nor the

Waldenses granted rights to women in their religious communities because of a strong female principle in their concepts of the celestial hierarchy and the process of human salvation. Very likely the neutralization of the sexes in the Cathari belief was a contributing factor where the community was concerned, as the return to the New Testament was one of the reasons in the case of the Waldenses. Both movements were marginal (though numerous in southern France and Italy), and from the time of the Albigensian Crusade on were implacably persecuted. We have already noted that it is in the nature of marginal groups to maintain relative equality among their members, including greater equality between men and women. Thus even the general run of Cathari Believers practised greater equality than did the Catholics. Cathari marriage was not a sacrament; the consent of the two parties was enough, and divorce was also allowed. (Both Henry of Le Mans and Peter Bruys had already favoured this view.) The very undertaking of marriage by a Cathari couple, especially during the times of persecution, represented a stronger link than would be found in a Catholic marriage, and the Cathars encouraged Believers to marry among themselves.[42] This was the conscientious endogamy that E. Le Roy Ladurie wrote about. The possibility of divorce also gave women a measure of freedom.

We have seen that sexual promiscuity was a regular part of the stereotype of the heretic. (To this day demagogic attacks on any group frequently include accusations of sexual misconduct).[43] It is true that the Cathars did not transform the relations of men and women within the marriage from the sphere of sin to the sphere of sanctity by means of a marriage sacrament, as did the Catholics. Much has been written about the neutralization of sin in the Cathari belief – which meant that sexual congress within the framework of marriage was no less a sin that outside it – and about their opposition to procreation. Theoretically and logically, it might be concluded from this that everything was, *ipso facto*, permitted. Nevertheless there is no more evidence for lascivious behaviour among the Cathars than among the Catholics. In preceding chapters we have seen that men and women of all classes often wandered from the sexual path approved by the Church. This was the reality, even if we discount the description of courtly love as a way of life. Contemporary Catholic sources hardly ever deny the high morality of the Cathari Perfects, who served as examples and models to others (which, to put it mildly, could not always be said of the Catholic clergy). They certainly did not encourage the Believers to fornicate, and there is no evidence anywhere that the neutralization of sin promoted extramarital relations among the Cathars.

Did women join the heretical movements as a way of rebelling within the given system? (During the High and Late Middle Ages the heretical movements were part of the given system, even though the Church fought against them by every means. Certainly they were neither created by women nor, basically, for them, nor were they sustained by women alone.) If we answer the question in the affirmative, it would mean that women joined these movements because they offered greater rights and a more respected status than did Catholic society, as well as greater freedom from male authority. Doubtless, this was one of the reasons for their joining, but it would be simplistic and inadequate to fix on it as the only motive.

In a preceding chapter, while dealing with the subject of nuns, we noted the difficulty of analysing the delicate and intricate complex of various personal factors, combined with a religious vocation, that led men and women to enter convents. It is not an easy matter to determine whether a woman took the veil owing to a religious vocation, or because she wished to escape the world she feared; whether she chose the nunnery from love of God, or from fear of marriage, from unwillingness to bear children, or the desire to escape an unhappy marriage, or, if she was a widow, to evade a second union about to be forced on her; whether she elected to enter a convent because she yearned for a meaningful religious existence, or because there she was freed from male authority and could express herself in work at a particular function. We also noted the economic and family considerations (one daughter given in marriage, one to the nunnery) which led women to take the veil. All these factors must be considered again when we try to discern the motives of the women who joined the heretical movements, despite the fact that life in the heretical community did not offer the relative security and peace they could find in a convent.

The easiest factor to study is that of family economics. Maids and widows resided in the Waldensian *hospicium* and, especially, in the Cathari *Domus haereticorum*. Life in these houses offered a personal and economic answer to the problem of poor widows without family, and girls who could not be married because their families lacked the means to give them a dowry, but could not enter a Catholic convent, either on account of their poverty or because the existing convents could not take in all the women who sought to enter them. The Cathari and Waldensian houses served the same purpose as did those of the Beguines, and like the Beguines, Cathari

women ran schools. The German Dominican Jordanus censured the
parents who sent their daughters to be educated at those schools,
where they might become heretics.[44]

Yet he must beware of overestimating the importance of the
economic factor in the adherence of women to the heretical
movements, including the Waldensian and Cathari. Some of the
heretics did not succeed in establishing communities. Henry of Le
Mans, Tanchelm, and Arnold of Brescia criticized the existing
Church establishment, and developed ideas about the true religious
life, but they did not establish communities in which women
enjoyed a special status or in which they could find an answer to
their material and personal problems. Nor did the Lollards, whose
movement lasted for nearly 150 years – from the last quarter of the
fourteenth to the second half of the fifteenth century – live in
communities, and their organization was generally rather loose.
Nevertheless, there were women followers in these movements.
Many women who belonged to the Cathari class of Believers did
not live in the special houses, but were married and lived ordinary
family lives, listening from time to time to the sermons of the
Perfects, participating in those rites which were open to Believers,
and wishing to receive the *consolamentum* on their deathbed. The
noblewomen who joined the Cathars certainly did not do so in
order to solve their economic problems, and the same is true of the
nuns who joined the heretical movements.

What did those women seek who turned to the heresies for
reasons other than the need for relative economic security? Was it a
more meaningful and profound religious life than they could find in
the Catholic Church, or a relative freedom from male domination?
It is not easy to answer this question, which also applies to the men
who joined the heretical movements. Did they seek, above all, a
religious life in which they as laymen would have a greater share
than they could in the Catholic Church at that time, following the
eleventh-century Reform which had failed to satisfy? Or was it
primarily a kind of protest against the social order in general? Some
of the heretics aimed their attacks directly at the Church establishment and the mode of life of its selfish, incontinent and greedy
clerics. Others, such as the Waldenses, neither criticized nor
attacked, at least not at the beginning, but their choice of a life of
complete poverty and wandering was, in effect, a protest against the
social order of which the Church was a part. Gradually, the
Waldenses and the Cathars formulated their opposition to the oath
(and in the Middle Ages all undertakings were sealed by oaths), to

the existing law, to seigneury, to coercion and to war – albeit neither the Waldenses nor the Cathars fought to abolish these things. They were social deviants, not rebels.

The Lollards denied the right of the Church to own possessions under any circumstances. Only a just priest might own property. A sinful priest might not, nor should he receive the tithe. Other movements which were denounced as heretical, from that of Arnold of Brescia to the Hussites, also incorporated ideas of social and political change with their endeavour to achieve a religious trans-formation. Both elements were no doubt present in the following of the heretical movements, but it does not seem possible to determine which of them predominated; the same is true of the female following, even though the protest of the women differed from the men's. What the women chiefly protested against was their inferior status in the Church, in society and in the family. In the Waldensian and Cathari communities women, whether Perfects or mere Be-lievers, enjoyed a position of greater respect than in the Catholic Church. Other heretical movements did not enable women to perform clerical functions in their churches, but they too opposed the existing ecclesiastical, and thereby, partly, the entire social order.

The Lollards sought to narrow the gap between the laity and the clergy, and favoured a more active participation of women in the religious life. Women did not perform clerical functions among the Lollards, but their right to read the Scriptures in the English translation was upheld, and they were encouraged to learn portions of the sacred texts by heart. The Hussites, too, sought to raise the position of the laity in the Church. Their demand to administer to laymen the Eucharist in both kinds – that is to say, both the bread and the wine – was an attempt to reduce the difference between laity and clergy. They, too, made use of the vernacular (Czech) in reading the Scriptures. Therefore, even in these movements women had a greater share than in the Catholic Church and, as a result, a higher status in the community as a whole. But we must not overlook the actual will to live a meaningful religious life that would satisfy religious feelings of people in the religious society of the High and Late Middle Ages. Men and women went to the stake for their beliefs, and most of them could have saved themselves by recanting and repenting. (Only a person who recanted and re-pented, relapsed and again recanted and repented, was liable to be burnt at the stake.)

Even Albert Camus, who denied that people would die for an

ontological concept, did not preclude the possibility that they would die for ideas. (And how could he, seeing that all human history shows that they do?) And if ideas are worth dying for, how much more so religious beliefs. Thus no one can pinpoint the decisive motive for the willingness of women to die at the stake. Was it their fidelity to their faith and their conviction that after their agonies they would win the kingdom of heaven; was it fidelity to their fellow heretics, with whom they had lived in joint devotion, some of whom had already died for the faith or been sentenced to life imprisonment; or was it a supreme expression of protest against the existing form of society and the world and the situation of women in them?[45]

THE WITCHES

The theory of witches, in its peculiar West European connotation, that is to say, of the witch as the Devil's ally, appeared only towards the end of the Middle Ages. The great witch-hunts took place in the sixteenth and seventeenth centuries, not in the Middle Ages. Thus in a book dealing with the situation of women in the High and Late Middle Ages it might have sufficed to describe the attitude towards women who were accused of practising witchcraft in the pagan sense of using magical means to cause harm (*maleficium*). The text known as 'The Witch Hammer' (*Malleus Maleficarum*) – in H. Trevor-Roper's words, the *summa* of demonology, upon which all witch-hunters, Catholic and Protestant alike, relied for 200 years – was composed in 1486, later than the chronological limit of the present work. The reason for including a short discussion of the witch as the Devil's accomplice is that some of the ideas expressed in the *Malleus*, including those that concern women, summarized concepts which had been developed in ecclesiastical literature of the Middle Ages. Before we discuss the place occupied by women among the persons who engaged in witchcraft, or were accused of engaging in it, we must briefly survey the history of the attitude towards these people in the Middle Ages, and the evolution of the theory of witches.[46]

Let us start with witchcraft in the sense of using magical means to do harm to another (*maleficium*), or even to dominate the environment and the forces of nature. In the Middle Ages, as in ancient Germanic society or the Greek and Roman world, some men and women engaged in witchcraft and some were wrongfully accused of doing so. People believed in the existence of good and evil magic: by means of certain actions and the uttering of certain formulas the magician expected to obtain an automatic result. Secular law forbade the use of evil magic. According to the Salic, Frankish and Ripuarian laws, a person who caused another man's death by means of magic had to pay the 'man price' (wergild) to the victim's kindred. Men and women were accused of using witchcraft to cause illness, sterility, impotence, the deaths of persons or animals, storms and floods to destroy harvests. Such accusations crop up in Icelandic, Swedish, Alemanni, Lombard, Visigothic and Bavarian sources. Men and women were accused of bewitching members of the Merovingian and Carolingian royal families. The sons of Louis the Pious by his first wife accused his second wife Judith of using evil magic against them, their intention being to prevent her son Charles from sharing in their inheritance.[47]

To begin with, secular law was concerned with preventing the harmful applications of witchcraft, but gradually, under the influence of the Church, the very practice of it was banned, because it was a form of paganism, like the worship of trees and sacred springs, and other surviving pagan customs.[48] The Church in those days viewed witchcraft as a form of idolatry, because like idolatry witchcraft had recourse to demons. Thus it was deemed necessary, in the process of evangelizing Europe, to uproot witchcraft together with all other pagan vestiges. But on the whole the Church took a more lenient view of the practitioners of witchcraft than did the secular law, perhaps because it wished to win over the recently converted population without applying too much pressure, or because it accepted the position of some of the Church Fathers concerning the unreality of witchcraft.

That position had been clearly expressed in a text known as the 'Episcopal Canon', attributed to the Council of Ancyra in 314, but which appears for the first time in a ninth-century collection, and its origins remain obscure. In the eleventh century it was included by Burchard of Worms in his manual for confessors, also by St Ivo of Chartres in his *Decretum* and later by Gratian. According to this text, whosoever believes in witchcraft is as one who relapses into pagan beliefs and accepts as real the delusions wrought by Satan; and whosoever holds pagan beliefs is as one who worships demons. Witchcraft is unreal, Satan and the demons do exist, but men cannot perform sorcery with their help, this being merely their imagining, and only a fool believes that that which takes place in the spirit also occurs in the body.[49] It should be noted that equating the sorcerer with the worshipper of demons was only the authors' Christian interpretation of things – it was not said that witches believed themselves to be demon worshippers, much less the allies of demons or of the Devil.[50] According to the 'Episcopal Canon' the punishment for practising witchcraft was to do penance for two years – the penance being imposed not for the act itself, but for believing that one could do magic. If witchcraft is unreal, that means that the acts themselves were unreal. And though even before the fourteenth century there were clergymen who believed in the reality of witchcraft, as for example Gilbert of Nogent,[51] the dominant position of the learned clergy was a complete rejection, on behalf of Christianity, of the popular belief in witchcraft.

That there was such popular belief – both passive, i.e., the belief that one has been harmed by witchcraft, and active, that one can perform witchcraft – cannot be doubted. Mobs were known to do summary and extremely cruel justice to persons suspected of sorcery, but the Church did not encourage such persecutions. It did not open proceedings against them for the good of the public, as the courts of the Inquisition did with the heretics. A person who accused another of sorcery and failed to prove it was liable to severe penalties. On the other hand, the penalties imposed by the ecclesiastical courts upon those who had been found guilty of sorcery were generally nothing more than to do penance, or at worst to be expelled from the diocese. Clergymen were known to protect suspected sorcerers from the fury of the mob.[52] It seems that until the fourteenth century there was not a great number of court cases involving witchcraft.[53]

From the thirteenth century onwards there was a marked growth of ideas on the Devil, and speculative elaborations on the subject were developed mainly in the Franciscan and Dominican schools. Gradually the attitude of the Church towards persons who engaged in sorcery began to change. In the fourteenth century it began to view witches as the Devil's accomplices, and to believe in the reality of witchcraft. This view of sorcery as an alliance with the Devil may have developed from the clerical understanding of 'ritual magic'. Or it may have stemmed from the attribution to heretics of magical dealings with the Devil. Scholars who studied astronomy, astrology, chemistry, alchemy and medicine, such as Ceco d'Ascoli, or Arnold of Villanova, sometimes experimented with the 'ritual magic' by which the sorcerer bound the demons to his will. Those who did so were not accused of being in a pact with the Devil, but only of invoking demons, which was in fact prohibited. The Church, and only the Church, might act against the demons, whereas these sorcerers invoked them to their service. The ecclesiastics knew that the sorcerers were not worshipping the demons, but merely calling upon them (*invocatio*) in the name of God, to come and do their bidding, but the very dealing with them was considered a sin.[54]

It may be, as N. Cohn maintains, that the view of witchcraft as a pact with the Devil grew out of the conception that 'ritual magic' entailed the invocation of demons. As for the heretics, by the early twelfth century certain sects in Western Europe were believed to be engaged in sorcery in complicity with the Devil.[55] The heretic who deviated from Catholic orthodoxy was believed to have overturned all the accepted norms of conduct. This meant that he chose evil over good, that is to say, abandoned God to worship the Devil. But during the thirteenth century the practice of sorcery and the pact with the Devil were not categorized as a separate and distinct heresy. As late as 1257 Pope Alexander IV, responding to questions of inquisitors concerning the limitations of their authority and the procedures they should adopt, decreed that they must concentrate on the exposure of heretics only. Only those persons might be prosecuted for engaging in witchcraft who were clearly also given to heresy. The researches of R. Kieckhefer and N. Cohn show that prior to 1435 there were only isolated cases of people being accused of being in league with the Devil. Generally speaking, people accused of sorcery were charged only with causing harm by such means.

The theological and judicial definition of a witch, male or female, as well as the creation of the witch's stereotype, came about only in the last quarter of the fifteenth century. Two decisive stages in this process were the bull of Pope Innocent VIII of 1484 (*Summis desiderantes affectibus*) and the publication of the work by two German inquisitors, Jakob Sprenger and Heinrich Institoris, known as 'The Witch Hammer' (*Malleus Maleficarum*). A witch is one who is in league with the Devil and denies Christ, baptism and the sacraments. Since the person in question is himself, or herself, baptized, these actions constitute a Christian heresy. The witches forgather on the 'Witches Sabbath' to worship the Devil, celebrate the 'Black Mass', perform Satan's rites, and engage in vile orgies including child murder and cannibalism. The witch acts individually, yet is a member of a society of witches. According to the authors of the *Malleus Maleficarum*, the Devil can work his will directly, but prefers to do so by the intermediary of the witch. It offends God to see evil done by his own creatures, and the Devil desires this offence. The witch also causes harm to men, to livestock and to crops.

This juxtaposition of harmful doings and Devil-worship characterizes the theory of witches in Christian Western Europe. For some ecclesiastics, however, the harm done by the witches became a secondary matter compared with their complicity with the Devil – in fact, the former came to be seen as an outcome of the latter. To the best of our knowledge, this is a peculiarly West European Christian phenomenon. In all historical and primitive communities in which charges of witchcraft were brought, the emphasis was always on the damage caused by the sorcerers. Even in those societies where, according to anthropologists, the witch was viewed as a person naturally endowed with a certain power (as distinct from the idea of magic as a skill anyone might acquire), what was stressed was the danger and the harm caused by the witch.[56]

When the practice of witchcraft was defined as a form of heresy, the prosecution of the practitioners changed from the accusational system to the inquisitorial. It was no longer up to the plaintiff to prove the guilt of the accused: the defendant had to prove his or her innocence. It ceased to be an issue between plaintiff and respondent, and became the concern of society acting in self-protection. The method of the courts of the Inquisition was adopted by most of the ecclesiastical and secular courts in their prosecution of persons accused of practising withcraft. The authors of the 'Witch Hammer' suggest promising amnesty to the accused if they confess, but add that it is not necessary to keep the promise, and there were judges who acted on this advice. The questions asked were based on the demonological literature and on the admissions made by defendants in previous trials. These questions, which were often asked after torture or the threat of torture, received the expected answers.

Men and women did engage in sorcery in the Middle Ages – they practised healing by magic, prepared various love-potions, and shaped wax images of persons who were to be harmed, to be pierced with pins and hidden under the victims' thresholds. The popular belief in magic and its power was widespread, and Christianity never succeeded in uprooting it entirely. But the belief in the alliance with the Devil and all that it entailed was an invention of learned churchmen, and was gradually implanted in the minds of the masses. Some elements were taken from folk beliefs and incorporated in the ecclesiastical stereotype, as for example the ideas of the flying witch, of her ability to go through closed doors and to transform herself into an animal, and so on.[57] The study of R.

Kieckhefer shows that before 1500, when a person was accused of practising witchcraft, it was usually claimed that he – or she – had made people fall ill, caused impotence or sterility, stopped a cow's milk from flowing, and similar allegations, but there were no charges of complicity with the Devil or membership of a diabolical society. After a few days of questioning the accused would also confess to being in league with the Devil. In Kieckhefer's opinion, not all the churchmen who held this view of the witch were psychotic or neurotic. They obtained this definition on intellectual, rather than psychological grounds. By developing the idea of the pact with Satan they exchanged the magical interpretation of witchcraft for a theological one: sorcery is real because it is the work of the Devil, whom God allows to exist.

It was difficult for the ecclesiastics to accept a causality which was neither entirely natural nor entirely supernatural – in other words, to accept magic as an independent reality. The Church, to be sure, had its own officially-approved magic, such as having the priest carry the consecrated Host around a field, to protect it from storms or to bless the crop, but it was not defined as such.[58] The doctrine of devilish pacts was transmitted from the schools of higher learning to the courts, and thence down to the masses. Possibly, too, the Church took a strong line with the sorceress because their magic competed with her own, and the witch jeopardized the status of the priest as the exclusive manipulator of supernatural forces. It may be that the reason it all happened when it did is that the plagues and terrors they spread stimulated the practice of witchcraft, and the Church felt threatened. H. Trevor-Roper suggested that the inquisitors took up the persecution of witches because the worst heretics, the Cathars, had been wiped out, and the Waldenses had gone underground, and the courts of the Inquisition wanted a reason for continued existence.

There can be no doubt that there were psychological and sociological reasons for the proliferation of charges of witchcraft. Anthropologists explain such a phenomenon in a given society at a given time as an outcome of interpersonal relations and states of tragedy and catastrophe. Some historians have applied these interpretations to the problem of witchcraft in certain periods and places.[59] But there must have been certain intellectual premises which made possible both the accusations and the active belief on the part of some people in their power to practise witchcraft. The intellectual premises for the existence of sorcery in complicity with the Devil in Western Europe were supplied by the Church, which proceeded to make the witch its principal scapegoat. It was also the Church which for hundreds of years cultivated in Christian society a certain image of the woman. When the doctrine of witches as Satan's allies evolved, this image made possible and justified bringing such charges mainly against women.

According to H. Kieckhefer, during the years 1300 to 1500 two thirds of the persons accused of practising witchcraft were women.[60] In the period 1300–30 there was a considerable number of trials in which members of the higher classes were accused of using witchcraft for political ends, and the number of women defendants was relatively low, though they were not entirely absent. Some were accused of instigating the act – as for example the Irish noblewoman Alice Kyteler – others of collaborating with the instigators, or of acting professionally, for a fee.[61] One of the female accused was a Beguine who had been greatly honoured at the court of Philip iv on account of her predictions. She was charged with attempting to poison the king's brother, working in the service of the Flemings, but was eventually exonerated. Among the women who were accused of being instigators in witchcraft trials was Mahaut of Artois, whom we discussed in a preceding chapter as the heiress of a fief who exercised extensive political powers. She too was exonerated.[62] Women were not accused of performing the 'ritual magic' for which scholarship was required and which, as we have seen, was practised chiefly by learned men.

With the proliferation of charges of complicity with the Devil, in the second half of the fifteenth century, the proportion of women defendants increased. Out of 300 persons accused of witchcraft in Savoy, between 1415 and 1525, we know the sex of 103 only; eighty-eight were women. In Tudor and Stuart England as well as in southwest Germany, west Switzerland and Belgium, women constituted the overwhelming majority of defendants in these trials.[63] Why? Women have often been charged with practising sorcery in other societies, too, all of them ruled by men. This was true in many of the primitive societies,[64] as well as in ancient Greece and Rome and among the early Germans. In the biblical injunction, 'Thou shalt not suffer a witch to live', witch is in the feminine gender (Exodus 22:18). And in the *Mishnah* it is stated: 'Many wives – much sorcery.' It is not certain whether women did in fact practise witchcraft more than did men, and if so, to what extent. Among the Junja of Africa the definition of the respective social roles of men and women is such that witchcraft is viewed as a legitimate means in a struggle when used by men, and as a horrible expression of capriciousness and inherent wickedness when used by women. There was no reaction to male sorcery at all, whereas women paid cruel penalties for the same thing.[65]

But to return to Europe during the period 1300–1500. What sort of women were accused of engaging in witchcraft? Their age is not recorded. In so far as their marital status is known, most of them appeared to have been married. Some practised magic healing and were skilled in the use of medicinal herbs; some were failed midwives and healers.[66] Miscarriage was frequently attributed to witchcraft, as we have seen. Some were prostitutes, or old procuresses.[67] Women known to be sexually promiscuous were also liable to be accused of witchcraft. Some women were accused by former lovers who had taken other wives. Some were accused by neighbours, male and female, with whom they had been on bad terms or had actually quarrelled. Some were accused of using sorcery for their own purposes, and some of doing so for others, for a fee.[68]

It should be noted that women were frequently accused by women. We have already seen that one of the derogatory names most commonly used by women against women was 'whore and witch'. (Here it is worth noting that a Junja woman, when asked by the anthropologist why women were witches, replied: 'Because we are bad.' She then went on about how the quarrels of children lead to rows among their mothers, about the frustrations of a barren wife, and the envy felt by a poor woman at the sight of the fine possessions of another.)[69] If it is still necessary to prove that there was no sect of witches, which existed as a form of protest against masculine domination, this should do so.[70]

Many of the defendants were women of the lower classes. Even the authors of the 'Witch Hammer' noted the fact that witches were not wealthy: they did not reap much benefit from their pact with the Devil, and the reason for it was that Satan, wishing to offend God, sought to obtain their services for the lowest price. It expressed his defiance of the Lord and his contempt for the persons he bought. Their indigence was also explained as a precaution against being too conspicuous.

Some witchcraft charges laid against women could be explained in much the same terms as the charges against men. People often interpreted failures and misfortunes as the results of a spell laid on them. B. Malinowski gave it a broader definition: magic is the answer to the sense of despair men and women feel in a world they cannot control.[71] Others have already noted that the most convenient explanation for failure and catastrophe is the one that permits direct and effective action. And so men and women were accused of causing death, disease, loss of property, and failure. The person accused was often the object of the projected feelings of fear, rage, greed and cruelty which animated the accuser and made him feel guilty. Almost in every case there was some previous connection between plaintiff and defendant, and not infrequently the defendant had had the moral advantage over the other. K. Thomas noted that in seventeenth-century England, people who felt guilty about refusing to give alms to beggar women consequently charged them with being witches. If most of the defendants were women, it was because they were the most impoverished, and the most dependent on the help of neighbours during that period when the traditional social structures were disintegrating, and with them the systems of mutual aid.[72] Similarly, it was a case of projected guilt feeling when a man accused his abandoned mistress of being a witch. Or a man who could not give vent to his rage against a more powerful person, who had done him wrong, would transfer his feelings to a supposed witch and make her his scapegoat. And just as prostitutes and procuresses were charged with engaging in sorcery, so were men on the fringes of society – beggars, vagrants, itinerant singers.

Some of these people, male and female, did in fact engage in sorcery. A book of magic was found in the possession of a man who was a vagrant, gambler and thief.[73] In 1460 in Artois an itinerant singer, an itinerant painter, a former mercenary soldier turned vagrant, and a few whores, were convicted of sorcery and burnt at the stake.[74] The insane were likewise natural objects of such charges; especially, we may conjecture, the types of madmen who frequently provoke latent aggression. Lonely and helpless old women would boast of possessing magical powers, as a way of winning the only kind of attention and respect they could hope for from society. Some did more than boast, but actually took up occult practices, because they were too weak to deal with people in any other way. Men and women consumed with hatred for the people around them, and feeling guilty about it, might take up magic and even believe that they had made a connection with the Devil.

In the Christian society of those days, to desire evil was to be seduced by the Devil. This was the subjective truth for the people of the age. We are also familiar with a certain type of person who, under investigation, confesses to things he did not do, even without the threat of torture. Some of the plaintiffs no doubt believed quite sincerely that they had been bewitched; others coldly resorted to extreme accusations so as to dispose of rivals; still others were pathological liars. All these explanations are applicable equally to men and women. Why then did women constitute two thirds of the accused witches, when their position in society was far from dominant, and when causes of tensions and conflicts which might lead to allegations of witchcraft were at least as common between man and man, as between man and woman or woman and woman?[75]

Psychologists have explained this fact as arising from the distrust and resentment felt by the man for the woman (this, in societies dominated by men). Such distrust and resentment, it is said, often originate in the child's relations with its parents. Freudian theory has it that man fears woman in sexual connection: he entrusts her with the sexual member and gives her his seed, and by this act he endows her with his vital energy, whereas she can castrate him. Fear of castration is rooted in infantile guilt feelings. However, men are also attracted to women, and this is the source of the ambivalence. Fear and resentment on the one hand, attraction on the other. There is also a masculine fear of the woman's life-giving power, for whoever can give life, can also take it away.[76] The ambivalence is reflected in various myths which derive from the collective subconscious. There we find the archetypes of the positive mothers – Demeter, Isis Astarte – and their polar opposites, the destroying mothers – Kali, Gorgon, Hecate.

The image of woman in Christian literature has been discussed in preceding chapters. The story of Creation in the Book of Genesis also reflects the ambivalent attitude to woman. Christianity set Mary as against Eve. But whereas in the pagan myths there are archetypes of good and evil virgins, as well as good and evil mothers, Christianity has an archetype of a virgin-mother. St Mary is a mother, but one who bore a child in contravention of the laws of nature. This is not a positive fertility mother. A woman who lives a sexual life, who conceives and bears children in the natural way, cannot be a reflection of St Mary. Nor can old women, who in the past lived sexual lives and bore children the natural way.

As we have seen, Christian literature depicts woman as having been created inferior, as the mother of all sin who played a disastrous role in the story of mankind, the eternal tempter and seducer. In Christianity, desire for a woman not only makes for masculine dependence upon her, but is a sin in itself, and one which became the main obsession of many churchmen. Thus, woman became a projection of man's sinful desire. Indeed, one ecclesiastic saw fit to revile woman even in justification of the prohibition against homosexuality. In his gloss to Leviticus 20:13 ('If a man also lie with mankind as he lieth with a woman, both of them have committed an abomination, they shall surely be put to death, their blood shall be upon them'), Anselm of Laon states that the male sex is characterized by spiritual powers and perfect inherent qualities, which is why men must avoid feminization in speech or deed. To do so is a sin that calls for the death penalty.[77]

Art emphasized the association of woman and the Devil. A carved capital at the abbey church of Vézelay, in Burgundy, depicts Satan playing upon a woman as upon a musical instrument. And at the abbey church of Moissac a woman is shown with serpents hanging from her pendulous breasts, a toad over her genitals, and the Devil overseeing her torments. In medieval art lust was always personified by a woman, who is either beautiful or shows traces of past beauty, is either being punished or has been punished. She needs no symbolic trapping – her body is itself the symbol of lust. In the twelfth-century cathedral of Autun there is a carving showing a demon seizing a woman by the shoulders, while a snake twists about her body and sucks at her breast.[78] Unlike the theological writings, which were known only to few, religious art was familiar to all classes of society, in addition to which they were also exposed to the sermons of preachers denouncing sinful woman.

We do not know the ratio of women among persons who practised witchcraft, or who were accused of practising it, in the period prior to the fourteenth century. Churchmen, at any rate, even before the formation of the theory of the witch as the Devil's ally, viewed women as peculiarly given to witchcraft. In the eleventh century, Burchard of Worms' manual for confessors described women as especially inclined to believe in the reality of witchcraft. Men are asked if they believe that women are capable of flying, of causing harm, etc.[79] In Humbert de Romans' textbook for preachers, in the chapter devoted to poor women in the villages, the author notes that women 'are prone to witchcraft'.[80] Other preachers also attributed this inclination and practice to women.[81] Belief in witchcraft, both passive and active, was doubtless a constant in the Middle Ages. But were women in fact particularly prone to sorcery, especially the most defenceless among them? Or could it be that in rural society women were often the healers and midwives, and as such were particularly vulnerable to these accusations? We can answer neither these questions nor the question about the ratio of women among the accused prior to the fourteenth century.

In any case, it is plain that once the doctrine of the witch as the Devil's accomplice had been established, the ratio of women among the alleged witches increased, and that it was the accepted image of the woman which provided the intellectual foundation and justification for these charges. The authors of the *Malleus Maleficarum* had only to sharpen that image somewhat, and could use for their authorities earlier churchmen from John Chrysostom to Bernard of Clairvaux. (For the deprecation of woman they were also able to quote the classical Roman authors.) In Part I, Question 6, of the 'Witch Hammer' the authors explain why a greater number of witches is found in the fragile feminine sex than among men. In brief, it is as follows: woman is naturally weak and inclined to extremes. She knows no moderation. When ruled by a benevolent spirit she is most virtuous (*optima*), and when ruled by a malevolent spirit she is most evil (*pessima*). There have been virtuous women in history (Deborah, Judith, Esther, Clotilde), but most women are lustful, impressionable, credulous, garrulous, and cannot keep a secret. Their credulity makes it easy for the demons to persuade them. Their susceptibility causes them to be easily swayed by the evil spirits. They are intellectually inferior to men and lack self-discipline.

Woman is more carnal than man, and imperfect from creation. She is weak in the faith, as her name suggests – *Femina* being made up of *fe* and *minus*. It was Eve who seduced Adam and brought about the Fall. Women are animated by jealousy and vindictiveness, as shown by the stories of Sarah and Hagar, Rachel and Leah, Hannah and Peninnah, Martha and Mary. Feminine jealousy was likewise the cause of the disagreement between Moses and Miriam. Through the malice of women kingdoms were destroyed: Troy through Helen; Judea through Jezebel and her daughter Athaliah; Rome through Cleopatra. How far a woman may go in envy and vengeance may be learned form the stories of Joseph and Potiphar's wife, and of Medea and Jason. She is a liar by nature, and her voice, like the song of the sirens, entices only to destroy. She is moved by pride (*vanitas*) which is expressed in worldly vanity. Being weak, 'they find an easy and secret way of vindicating themselves by witchcraft'.

But woman's chief vice is carnal lust, which is insatiable, and which is incalculably stronger than the man's. Thus vanity and carnal lust are the principal causes that make women succumb to the Devil and his demons. Those women are most inclined towards witchcraft who are given to the vices of ambition and lust, and especially adulteresses and fornicatresses. Women being the great majority of sorcerers, it is only proper that this heresy be named the heresy of witches rather than of wizards.[82] Thus far the authors of the 'Witch Hammer'. It should be kept in mind that in Christianity the Devil is a male figure, while his demonic servants appear in both male and female form (*incubi, succubi*), which permitted the authors to give rein to their diseased sexual imaginations. (The title of the chapter is 'Concerning Witches who copulate with Devils'.)

Even when, in the second half of the sixteenth century, John Weyer denounced the belief in the reality of witchcraft, saying that it derived from Devil-inspired delusions (his faith in the existence of the Devil and demons was unshaken), he repeated some statements of the authors of the 'Witch Hammer': Satan is a cunning enemy, who seduces mainly members of the weaker sex, who are inconsistent, easily waver in the faith, are impatient, malicious, melancholy and have no control over their feelings and instincts. The persons most apt to believe in the reality of witchcraft are foolish and mentally unstable old women.[83]

The image of woman, as accepted and developed by churchmen in the Middle Ages, affected her position in society and the attitudes towards her, as we have seen throughout this book. Once the theory of the witch as Satan's ally was developed, this image, sharpened by the authors of the *Malleus Maleficarum*, permitted her special persecution. Deeply rooted psychological factors, as well as the specific social ones which affected Europe at that time, gave rise to the allegations of witchcraft in general, and against women in particular. But the ecclesiastical doctrine was the point of departure for these accusations, and the mighty Church establishment was relentless in pursuit of the accused – for the 'cause of the faith' (*negotium fidei*) – and encouraged their persecution by the secular authorities.

There was another image of woman in medieval civilization, that of the Virgin Mary, of Jesus' faithful female attendants and other Christian saints. We find the image of the wife who is also a companion and a helpmeet to her husband; the adored mistress of the courtly romances, for love of whom men were moved to goodness and beauty; the virtuous woman of the Book of Proverbs; or, now and then, the devoted mother, such as the barefoot peasant woman who is seen combing her small boy's hair in the Magdalen chapel at Vézelay.[84] However, it is evident that the opposite image was not only more emphasized and developed, but that during the great witch-hunts it affected reality directly and viciously.

Notes

FOREWORD

1 E. Power's article was a breakthrough in the history of women in the Middle Ages: E. Power, 'The position of women' in *The Legacy of the Middle Ages*, ed. C. G. Crump and E. F. Jacob (Oxford, 1926), pp. 401–33; also published from her literary remains was E. Power, *Medieval Women*, ed. M. Postan, (Cambridge 1975).

2 S. Shahar, 'De quelques aspects de la femme dans la pensée et la communauté religieuses aux XIIe et XIIe siècles', *Revue de l'Histoire des Religions* CLXXXV (1974), pp. 29–77.

3 See C. Erickson and K. Casey, 'Women in the Middle Ages: a working bibliography', *Medieval Studies* XXXVIII (1976), pp. 340–59; *The Role of Woman in the Middle Ages*, ed. R. T. Morewedge (New York, 1975); *Cahiers de Civilization médiévale, X-XIIe siècles* XX (1977); H. H. Kaminsky, 'Die Frau in Recht und Gesellschaft des Mittelalters' in M. Kuhn and G. Schneider (eds), *Frauen in der Geschichte* (Dusseldorf 1979), pp. 295–313.

4 Since published as Z. Razi *Life, Marriage and Death in a Medieval Parish: Economy, Society and Demography in Halesowen 1270–1400* (Cambridge 1980).

CHAPTER I

1 See among others, H. Hacker, 'Women as a minority group', *Social Forces* XXX (1951); A. Montagu, *The Natural Superiority of Women* (New York 1970), p. 29.

2   J. Le Goff, *La Civilisation de l'Occident médiéval* (Paris 1904), pp. 319−27; G. Duby, *Les Trois Ordres, ou l'Imaginaire du féodalisme* (Paris 1978), pp. 11−17.

3   Humbert de Romans, *De Eruditione Praedicatorum* (Barcelona 1607): chs XLIII−LI, Ad mulieres religiosas quascunque; XCIII, Ad omnes mulieres; XCV, Ad mulieres nobiles; XCVI, Ad mulieres burgenses divites; XCVII, Ad famulas divitum; XCIX, Ad mulieres pauperes in villulis; C, Ad mulieres malas corpore sive meretrices.

4   Etienne Fougères, *Livre de Manières* ed A. A. Heutsch, *La Littérature didactique du Moyen-Age* (Halle 1903), pp. 42−5.

5   See J. Huizinga, *The Waning of the Middle Ages* (New York 1954), pp. 145−6.

6   See R. Mohl, *The Three Estates in Medieval and Renaissance Literature* (New York 1962); B. Jarret, *Social Theories of the Middle Ages, 1200−1500* (Boston 1926), ch. 3.

7   *Chronicon Hugonis Abbatis Flaviniacensis*, Monumenta Germaniae Historica, Scriptores (MGHS), vol. VIII, p. 384.

8   Geoffrey Chaucer, *The Canterbury Tales*, ed. W. W. Skeat (Oxford 1947), p. 308.

9   See E. McLeod, *The Order of the Rose. The Life and Ideas of Christine de Pisan*, (London 1975), pp. 133−5; C. C. Willard, 'A 15th century view of woman's role in medieval society. Christine de Pisan's "Livre des Trois Vertus"', in R. T. Morewedge, ed., *The Role of Woman in Medieval Society* (New York 1975).

10 Philippe de Novare, *Les Quatre Ages de l'Homme*, ed. M. de Fréville (Paris 1888), p. 10.

11 R. Lakoff, *Language and Woman's Place* (New York 1975), pp. 40−1.

12 Quoted by C. Petouraud, 'Les léproseries lyonnaises au Moyen Age et à la Renaissance', *Cahiers d'Histoire*, VII (1962), p. 440.

13 F. L. Lucas, *Tragedy in Relation to Aristotle's Politics* (London 1930), pp. 114−15.

14 E. Auerbach, *Mimesis. The Representation of Reality in Western Literature* (New York 1957), p. 120; about the literature of the Middle Ages, ch. 6−10.

15 See K. Millet, *Sexual Politics* (New York 1969).

16 Bernardus Silvestris, *De Mundi Universitate duo libri, Sive Megacosmos et Microcosmos*, ed. C. S. Barach and J. Wrobel (Frankfurt 1964). Concerning the work and the sources used by

the author, see E. R. Curtius, *European Literature and the Latin Middle Ages* (New York 1953), pp. 108–13.

17 H. Huizinga, *The Waning of the Middle Ages*, p. 156; E. Neumann, *The Great Mother. An Analysis of Archetype* (London 1955), pp. 176–7, 331.

18 'In precedenti anno, venit de Anglia virgo decora valde pariterque facunda dicens se Spiritum Sanctum, incarnatum in redemptionem mulierum, et baptisavit mulieres in nomine Patris et Filii ac sui.' *Annales Colmarienses Maiores*. A – 1301. MGHS vol. XVII, p. 226.

CHAPTER 2

1 R. Mohl, *The Three Estates in Medieval and Renaissance Literature*, p. 341.

2 'qui non possunt nec debent nec solent esse in servitio domini Regis in exercitu nec aliis servitiis regalibus'. See F. Pollock and F. Maitland, *A History of English Law* (Cambridge 1898), vol. I, p. 485.

3 About unconscious ideology see D. J. Bem, *Attitudes and Human Affairs* (Belmont, California, 1970), pp. 89–96.

4 *Coutumier d'Artois*, ed. A. F. L. Tardif (Paris 1883), p. 121; *La Très ancienne Coutume de Bretagne*, ed. M. Planiol (Rennes 1896), pp. 126, 186.

5 J. T. Rosenthal, *Nobles and the Noble Life. 1295–1500* (London 1976), pp. 26–7.

6 For example: 'quod propter hoc si ipsa mulier, non debeat repelli ab hujis modi successione et quod officium facere poterat per interpositam personam.' (If it is a woman, she should not be removed from the succession because of this and she can fulfil the office by some interposed person.) *Les Olim ou Registres des Arrêts*, ed. A. A. Comte Beugnot (Paris 1842), vol. I, p. 417.

7 *Ordonnances des Roys de France*, ed. M. Secousse (Paris 1736), vol. IV, p. 173.

8 *Le Livre de la Taille de Paris, l'an 1296*, ed. K. Michäelsson (Göteborg 1958), pp. iii–xviii; *Le Livre de la Taille de Paris, l'an 1297*, ed. idem (Göteborg 1962), p. x; *Le Livre de la Taille de Paris, l'an 1313*, ed. idem (Göteborg 1951), p. xviii. In the year 1296, 776 women paid the tax; in 1297, the number was 1177; in 1313, 672.

9   S. Thrupp, *The Merchant Class of Medieval London* (Michigan 1968), p. 168.

10   J. C. Russell, *British Medieval Population* (Albuquerque 1948), pp. 150–6.

11   *Recueil de Documents relatifs à l'Histoire du Droit municipal en France des Origines à la Révolution*, ed. G. Espinas (Artois 1943), vol. III, p. 214.

12   *Memorials of London and London Life*, ed. H. T. Riley (London 1868), p. 108.

13   P. de Beaumanoir, *Coutumes de Beauvaisis*, ed. A. Salmon (Paris 1899), vol. I, §190; vol. II, §1287.

14   Rosenthal, op. cit., p. 125.

15   P. de Beaumanoir, op. cit., vol. I, p. 484.

16   Pollock and Maitland, op. cit., vol. I, pp. 484–5.

17   J. Gilissen, 'La Femme dans l'ancien droit belge', *Recueils de la Société Jean Bodin* XII (1962); G. Rossi, 'La femme en droit italien', ibid; *Liber Augustalis or Constitutions of Melfi, Promulgated by the Emperor Frederick II for the Kingdom of Sicily in 1231*, ed. and trans. J. M. Powell (New York 1971), p. 100.

18   *Magna Carta*, §54, in W. Stubbs, *Select Charters and other Illustrations of English Constitutional History* (Oxford 1921), p. 299.

19   Y. Brissaud, 'L'infanticide à la fin du Moyen-Age, ses motivations psychologiques et sa répression', *Revue historique de Droit français et étranger* L (1972); 'Emmeline la duchesse matronne jurée du Roy et la nostre', *Registre criminel de la justice de St Martin des Champs à Paris*, ed. L. Tanon (Paris 1877), pp. 43, 64, 82, 132, 139, 147, 159, 188; 'bonnas mulieres et legales matronas', *Très ancienne Coutume de Normandie*, ed. E. J. Tardif (Rouen 1881), p. 40.

20   L. Tanon, *Histoire de la justice des anciennes Eglises et Communautés monastiques de Paris* (Paris 1883), p. 356.

21   J. Bellamy, *Crime and Public Order in England in the Later Middle Ages* (London 1973), p. 13.

22   *Borough Customs*, ed. M. Bateson (London 1904), vol. I, p. 185. *Calendar of Select Pleas and Memoranda of the City of London, 1381–1412*, ed. A. H. Thomas (Cambridge 1932), p. 51.

23   *Visitations of Religious Houses in the Diocese of Lincoln*, ed. A. H. Thompson, (Horncastle 1914), p. 113.

24   *Leet Jurisdiction of the City of Norwich during the 13th and 14th Centuries*, ed. W. Hudson (Selden Society, London, 1892), p. 51.

25 Pollock and Maitland, op. cit., vol. I, p. 484.

26 *Calendar of Wills. Court of Husting*, ed. R. Sharpe (London 1889), pp. 675, 677; *Year Book of Edward II*, vol. V (Selden Society, London 1910), p. 10.

27 M. Goodich, 'The politics of canonization in the 13th century. Lay and mendicant saints', *Church History* XLIV (1975). About the testimony given by women to the committee appointed by the pope to prepare the canonization of Elizabeth of Thuringia, see A. Vauchez, 'Charité et pauvreté chez Sainte Elizabeth de Thuringie d'après les actes du procès de canonization', in M. Mollat, drc., *Histoire de la Pauvreté (Moyen-Age–XVIe siècle)* (Paris 1974), pp. 163–4.

28 P. de Beaumanoir, op. cit., vol. I, §824; *Les Olim ou Registres des Arrêts*, vol. I, p. 420; *Year Book of Edward II*, vol. V, pp. 134–5 and note 1.

29 *Liber Augustalis*, pp. 24, 26.

30 H. Thienne, 'Die Rechtsstellung der Frau in Deutschland', *Rec. Soc. Jean Bodin* XII (1962).

31 H. Dillard, 'Women in Reconquest Castille. The Fueros of Sepúlveda and Cuenca', in *Women in Medieval Society*, ed. S. Mosher (Pennsylvania 1976), p. 81.

32 Pollock and Maitland, op. cit., vol. II, p. 494.

33 *Liber Augustalis*, pp. 26–7.

34 *Registre criminel de la justice de St Martin des Champs à Paris*, pp. 44, 159; *Registre criminel du Châtelet de Paris*, ed. H. Duplès-Agier (Paris 1864), vol. I, pp. 55–61.

35 R. Nelli, *La Vie quotidienne des Cathares du Languedoc au XIIIe siècle* (Paris 1969), p. 82.

36 *Year Book of Edward II*, vol. V, p. 111 and note 2.

37 R. Herschberger, *From Adam's Rib*, (New York 1948), pp. 15–27.

38 J. B. Given, *Society and Homicide in 13th Century England* (Stanford, 1977), pp. 48, 117, 134–49.

39 B. A. Hanawalt, 'The Female Felon in 14th Century England', in *Women in Medieval Society*, pp. 125–40; B. A. Hanawalt, 'Childrearing among the lower classes of later medieval England', *Journal of Interdisciplinary History* VIII (1977), pp. 15–16. Notes about other recorded crimes committed by women appear in the chapters about women in town and in the peasantry.

40 J. L. Flandrin, 'Mariage tardif et vie sexuelle', *Annales Économies, Sociétés. Civilisations (Annales ESC)* XXVII (1972), pp. 1356–9.

41 P. de Beaumanoir, op. cit., vol. II, §1956; W. S. Holdworth, *A History of English Law* (London 1909), vol. II, p. 373 and note 3.

42 *Liber Augustalis*, p. 145.

43 H. Thienne, op. cit., pp. 373-4.

44 J. W. Bosh, 'La femme dans les Pays Bas septentrionaux', *Rec. Soc. Jean Bodin* XII (1962).

45 Hanawalt, 'The female felon in 14th century England', p. 136.

46 Y. Bougert, *Cours d'Histoire de Droit pénal* (Paris 1966-7), p. 330.

47 *Ordonnances des Roys de France*, vol. IV, p. 48.

48 *Registre criminel du Châtelet de Paris*, p. 351; R. B. Pugh, *Imprisonment in Medieval England* (Cambridge 1968), pp. 103, 357-8; *The Paston Letters*, ed. J. Warrington (London 1956), vol. I, pp. 75-6.

49 *Ordonnances des Roys de France*, vol. V, p. 673.

50 This distinction between the modes of execution of men and women does not always appear, for example the legislation of Louis IX. See *Recueil général des anciennes lois françaises* ed. Jourdan, De Crusy and Isambert (Paris 1822-30), vols I-II, p. 400.

51 Examples of the execution of women by burning at the stake or burial alive can be found in Tanon, *Histoire de justice des anciennes Eglises*, pp. 30-1, 334, 364, 447; *Registre Criminel de St Martin des Champs*, pp. 43, 220; *Registre Criminel du Châtelet de Paris*, vol. I, pp. 268, 327, 363, 480; vol. II, pp. 60, 64, 337, 393, 436-7. About execution by these methods for the crime of infanticide, see Y. Brissaud, op. cit.

52 Jean Chartier, *Chronique de Charles VII*, in L. Tanon, *Histoire de justice des anciennes Eglises*, p. 33.

53 G. Rossi, 'La femme en droit italien'; E. Poullet, 'Histoire du droit pénal dans l'ancien duché de Brabant', *Rec. Soc. Jean Bodin* XII (1962).

54 Y. Bougert, op. cit., p. 76.

55 P. Viollet, *Le Droit du XIIIe siècle dans les Coutumes de Touraine - Anjou* (Paris 1881), p. 164. Viollet quotes Wilda, ibid.; Y. Brissaud, op. cit., pp. 248 note 78, 256, note 88.

56 J. C. Schmidt, 'Le suicide au Moyen-Age', *Annales ESC* XXXI (1976), pp. 1-3, 5.

57 See J. Huizinga, op. cit., pp. 11-12.

58 See note 52.

CHAPTER 3

1 J. C. Davies, 'Deacons, deaconesses and the minor orders in the patristic period', *Journal of Ecclesiastical History* XIV (1936). About the limited role of the deaconesses according to Thomas Aquinas, see Aquinas, *Summa Theologica* (Rome 1894), vol. V, p. 197.

2 A. Borst, *Les Cathares* (Paris 1974), p. 251; E. S. Duckett, *The Gaeway to the Middle Ages, Monasticism* (Ann Arbor 1963), pp. 65–6. About the state of woman in canon law, see R. Metz, 'Le statut de la femme en droit canonique médiéval', in *Rec. Soc. Jean Bodin* vol. XII (1962), pp. 62–3.

3 Tertullian, *De Virginibus velandis*, Patrologia Latina, ed. J. P. Migne (PL) vol. II, cols 899–900.

4 Works of Chrysostom, in *Select Library of the Nicean and Post Nicean Fathers*, ed. P. Schaff (Buffalo 1886), vol. XII, pp. 151, 222.

5 St Augustine, *De Civitate Dei*, PL vol. XLI, col. 419.

6 St Augustine, *De Trinitate* PL vol. XLII, cols 1002–3; *De Genesi ad Litteram*, PL vol. XXXIV, col. 450.

7 Peter Damian, *De Sancta Simplicitate*, PL vol. CXLV, col. 695.

8 Thomas Aquinas, *Summa Theologica*, vol. I, pp. 717–18.

9 About woman's biological inferiority, see, among others, Gallenus, *Oeuvres*, ed. and trans. C. Daremberg (Paris 1854–6), vol. II, pp. 99–101; M. T. d'Alverny, 'Comment les théologiens et les philosophes voient la femme', *Cahiers de Civilisation médiévale, X-XIIe siècles* XX (1977).

10 Anselm of Canterbury, *Cur Deus Homo*, PL vol. CLVIII, col. 364.

11 'Anselm de Cantorbéry', in *Dictionnaire de Théologie catholique*, ed. A. Vacant, E. Mangenot and E. Amann (Paris 1927).

12 Gilbert of Nogent, *Histoire de sa Vie*, ed. G. Bourgin (Paris 1907), *L.I.C.* 26. See also *Miracula Beatae Mariae*, Ms de XIIe siècle, Bibliothèque Nationale, Paris, fonds latins 3177, fol. 137 V°, 147 V°; Rutebeuf, *Oeuvres complètes*, ed. A. Jubinal (Paris 1839), vol. II, p. 1; Jehan Bodel, *Li Jus Saint Nicolai*, ed. L. J. N. Monmerqué (Paris 1832).

13 St Bernard, *Opera secundi curis Domini Joahannis Mabillon* (Paris 1690), vol. I, *Epistola CLXXIV*, pp. 169–70.

14 St Bernard, *De Laudibus Virginis Matris, Homeliae*, ibid., vol. I, pp. 735, 737, 750, 996, 1005, 1006, 1012, 1066, vol. II, pp. 695, 722.

15 Peter Abélard, *Epistola VII*, PL vol. CLXXVIII, col. 243; *Sermo V, In Purificatione Sanctae Mariae*, ibid., col. 419.

16 K. Young, *The Drama of the Medieval Church* (Oxford 1933), vol. II, ch. 24.

17 Jacopone da Todi, *Stabat Mater*, ed. L. M. Guffroy (Nancy 1880).

18 St Anselm, *Oratio ad Sanctam Mariam Magdalenam*, PL vol. CLVIII, col. 1010.

19 K. Young, op. cit., vol. I, *Visitatio Sepulchri*.

20 V. Saxer, *Le Culte de Marie Madelaine en Occident* (Paris 1959).

21 St Bernard, *Opera*, vol. I, p. 899, vol. II, pp. 1046–50.

22 Peter Abélard, *Epistola VII*, PL vol. CLXXVIII, col. 246.

23 St Bernard, *Opera*, vol. I, p. 738.

24 'vetusti anguis ac semper mulieribus insidiantis caput atque ita elides, ut nunquam ulterius contra te sibilare audeat.' *The Letters of Peter the Venerable*, ed. G. Constable (Cambridge, Mass. 1967), vol. I, letter 115, p. 304.

25 Héloïse, *Epistola IV*, PL vol. CLXXVIII, col. 195.

26 Peter Abélard, *Epistola III*, PL vol. CLXXVIII, col. 190.

27 Peter Abélard, *Epistola VII*, ibid., col. 228.

28 ibid., col. 256. The line from the Manichaean hymn is quoted by J. T. Noonan, *Contraception. History of its Treatment by the Catholic Theologians and Canonists* (Cambridge, Mass., 1965), p. 112.

29 St Bernard, *Opera*, vol. I, *Epistola CXIII*, p. 121.

30 ibid., *Epistola CXIV*.

31 C. G. Jung, *Zentralblatt für Psychotherapie*, IX (1963), pp. 259–74. For an analogy between the Jungian archetype and Christology, see P. Evdokimov, *La Femme et le Salut du Monde* (Paris 1958), p. 193.

32 R. Metz, 'La Femme en droit canonique médiéval,' pp. 105–7; about the accentuation of the danger of female sexuality at the time of the eleventh-century Reform, see R. I. Moore, 'Family, community and cult on the eve of the Gregorian Reform', *Transactions of the Royal Historical Society (TRHS)* XXX (1980), pp. 49–69.

33 J. Heers, *Fêtes, Jeux et Joutes dans lá Société de l'Occident à la fin du Moyen-Age* (Paris 1971), p. 126.

34 See also Revelation 14:4.

35 Peter Damian, *de Caelibatu Sacerdotum*, PL vol. CXLV, col. 384; Thomas Aquinas, *Summa Theologica* (Rome 1899), vol. II-II, pp. 985–6.

36 Peter Abélard, *Epistola V*, PL vol. CLXXVIII, col. 199.

37 'Capiatur rinosceros Virginis amplexu', *The Goliard Poets*, ed. F. Whicher (New York 1949), p. 166.

38 About a Benedictine nun who wanted to become an anchorite after having lived in a community of nuns, see *Visitations of Religious Houses in the Diocese of Lincoln*, ed. A. H. Thompson (Horncastle 1914), p. 113.

39 'Chanoinesse' in *Dictionnaire de Droit canonique*, ed. R. Naz (Paris 1942), vol. III, cols 488–500. About the canonesses in Lorraine who did not live in a community, see M. Parisse, *La Noblesse lorraine, XI-XIIIe siècles* (Paris-Lille 1976), pp. 418, 431. For Tuscany in the later Middle Ages, see D. Herlihy and C. Klapisch, *Les Toscans et leurs Familles* (Paris 1978), pp. 580–1. About St Catherine, see *ActaSanctorum*, April III (Paris-Rome 1866), pp. 879–80.

40 'Abesse' in *Dictionnaire de Droit canonique*, vol. I, cols 62–71; S. Roisin, 'L'Efflorescence cistercienne et le courant féminin de piété au XIIIe siècle', *Revue d'histoire ecclésiastique* XXXIX (1943), pp. 367–8.

41 *Corpus Iuris Canonici*, ed. A. Friedberg, vol. I (Leipzig 1789) Decreti Pars Secunda, Causa XXXIII, q. V cols. 1254–6.

42 M. Bateson, 'Origins and Early History of Double Monasteries', *TRHS* XIII (1899) pp. 137–198; M. Barère, 'Les monastères doubles au XIIe et XIIIe siècle', *Académie royale de Belgique, classe de Lettres et des Sciences morales et politiques*, Mémoires Sér. 2, XVIII (1923), pp. 4–32.

43 E. W. McDonnell, *The Beguines and Beghards in Medieval Culture* (New York 1969), pp. 104, 343.

44 Peter Abélard, *Epistola VIII*, PL vol. CLXXVIII, cols 256–326, especially cols 260–1, 272, 275, 276, and *Historia Calamitatum*, ibid., col. 178. See also T. P. Maclaughlin, 'Abélard's rule for religious women', *Medieval Studies* XVIII (1956). Since it has never been definitely proved that the letters are a fraud, we may take letter VIII as expressing Abélard's views about female monasticism. An attempt at disproving the authenticity of the letters has been made, *inter alios*, by J. F. Benton, 'Fraud, fiction and borrowing in the correspondence of Abélard and Héloïse', in *Pierre Abélard, Pierre le Vénérable: les courants philosophiques, littéraires et artistiques en Occident au milieu du XIIe siècle* dr. R. Louis (Paris 1975), pp. 469–511. See also J. Monfrin, 'Le problème de l'authenticité de la correspondance d'Abélard et d'Héloïse', ibid. pp. 409–24.

45 K. Horney, 'Distrust between sexes', in *Feminine Psychology*, ed. H. Kelman, (New York 1967), pp. 107–18.
46 R. Metz, 'La femme en droit canonique médiéval', p. 99.
47 E. M. McDonnell, op. cit., pp. 101–14, note 44; J. Moorman, *The Franciscan Order from its Origins to the Year 1517* (Oxford 1968), p. 35; M. Barlière, 'Les monastères doubles', p. 26 and note 43. About the attitude of the religious orders towards the nuns, see H. G. Grundmann, *Religiose Bewegungen in Mittelalter* (Darmstadt 1961). The monastery of Marcigny-sur-Loire was at the head of fifteen feminine subject convents: see P. Cousin, *Précis d'Histoire monastique* (Belgium 1956), p. 233.
48 For an example of an abbess who held the convent's landed property in full ownership, see *Inquisitions and Assessments Relating to Feudal Aids: 1284–1431* (prepared under the superintendence of the Deputy Keeper of the Records, London 1849) (Mendeln-Klaus reprint, 1973), vol. I, p. 31; for one that held them as a fief, ibid., vol. II. p. 247.
49 As formulated for example in a case concerning judicial rights at the time of Louis IX in France: 'pronunciatum est quod alta et basa justitia in terra remaneat abbatisse et conventum supradictis'. *Les Olim ou Registres des Arrêts*, vol. I, pp. 328–9.
50 See for example the charters confirmed to the bourgeois of Caen by the abbesses of the Holy Trinity: *Le Bourgage de Caen*, ed. L. Legras (Paris 1911), pp. 405, 413, 422.
51 *Le Droit coutumier de la Ville de Metz au Moyen-Age*, ed. J. J. Salverda de Grave, E. M. Meijers and J. Schneider (Haarlem 1951), vol. I, pp. 581–3; *Les Olim ou Registres des Arrêts*, vol. I, pp. 711, 1254–73; H. Regnault, *La Condition du Bâtard au Moyen-Age* (Pont-Audemer 1922), pp. 136–7.
52 E. Power, *Medieval English Nunneries* (Cambridge 1922), pp. 1–3; E. W. McDonnell, op. cit., p. 93; J. Moorman, *The Franciscan Order*, p. 407; A. Bouquet, 'Les Clarisses méridionales', *Cahiers de Fanjeaux* VIII (1973); F. Rapp, 'Les abbayes, hospices de la noblesse: l'influence de l'aristocratie sur les couvents bénédictins dans l'Empire' in *La Noblesse au Moyen-Age*, ed. P. Contamine (Paris 1976).
53 'Abesse' in *Dictionnaire de Droit canonique*, vol. I, cols 67–79; R. Metz, 'Le statut de la femme en droit canonique médiéval', pp. 99–103; S. Roisin, 'L'efflorescence cistercienne', pp. 366–8.

54 E. Power, *Medieval English Nunneries*, p. 14; N. F. Rapp, op. cit., pp. 315–38; N. F. Cantor, 'The crisis of western monasticism 1050–1130', *American Historical Review* LXVI (1960–1), p. 48 and note 3.

55 See E. Power, *Medieval English Nunneries*, pp. 21–4.

56 *Chronicon Universale Anonymi Laudunensis*, MGHS, vol. XXVI, p. 447.

57 G. Duby, *La Société au XIe et XIIe siècle dans la Région mâconnaise* (Paris 1953), pp. 8, 418–21.

58 D. Herlihy, 'Vieillir au quattrocento' *Annales ESC*, XXIV (1969).

59 R. C. Trexler, 'Le célibat à la fin du Moyen-Age. Les religieuses de Florence', *Annales ESC*, XXVII (1972), pp. 1329–50.

60 *Calendar of Wills. Court of Husting, London 1258–1688*, p. 126.

61 *Memorials of London and London Life*, p. 535.

62 Examples: E. Power, *Medieval English Nunneries*, ch. 11; A. Lewis, *The Development of Southern French and Catalan Society* (Austin 1965), pp. 250–1; M. Parisse, *La Noblesse lorraine, XI-XIIIe siècles*, pp. 429–38.

63 This custom was condemned by authors of didactic literature and by preachers, as well as by some abbots. See Vincent of Beauvais, *De Eruditione filiorum nobiliorum*, ed. A Steiner (Cambridge, Mass., 1938), p. 128; R. G. Owst, *Literature and Pulpit in Medieval England* (Oxford 1961), p. 263; P. Riché, 'L'enfant dans la société monastique', in *Pierre le Vénérable, Pierre Abélard*, pp. 692–3; E. Power, *Medieval English Nunneries*, pp. 31–3.

64 *The Women Troubadours*, ed. M. Bogin (London 1976), p. 144.

65 *The Letters of John of Salisbury 1153–1161*, ed. W. J. Millor and S. J. and H. E. Butler (Nelson Series, 1955), pp. 230–1.

66 *Corpus Iuris Canonici*, ed. A. Friedberg, vol. II (Leipzig 1881), Decretalium Gregorii IX, Lib. III, Tit. XXXI, cols 571–2.

67 P. Morel, *Offenbarungen der Schwester Mechthild von Magdeburg* (Regensburg 1869); J. Ancelet-Hustache, *Mechtilde de Magdeburg 1207–1282* (Paris 1926), p. 65. See also E. W. McDonnell, op. cit., p. 87; C. Carozzi, 'Une Béguine joachimite, Douceline soeur d'Hugues de Digne', *Cahiers de Fanjeaux* X (1975), p. 184. The attribution of inclination to the

religious life from childhood to the saints-to-be is very common in the *Vitae*. As regards girls see *inter alia: Acta Sanctorum*, April II, p. 791; April III, p. 874; May III, p. 181.

68 Humbert de Romans, *De Eruditione Praedicatorum*, p. 187.

69 *Corpus Iuris Canonici*, vol. I, Decreti Pars Secunda, causa XXVII, q. I, col. 1051.

70 E. Power, op. cit., pp. 1-3; F. Rapp., op. cit., pp. 318, 322-3; R. C. Trexler, 'Le célibat à la fin du Moyen-Age'.

71 About women joining the Carthusian order, see Gilbert of Nogent, *Histoire de sa Vie*, ed. G. Bourgin (Paris 1907), bk. I. Ch. 11, p. 35; about the 'Poor Clares' in southern France, see A. Bouquet, 'Les Clarisses méridionales', *Cahiers de Fanjeaux* VIII (1973).

72 *Visitations of Religious Houses in the Diocese of Lincoln*, vol. I, p. 32; N. F. Rapp, op. cit., p. 337.

73 *Visitations of the Religious Houses in the Diocese of Lincoln*, vol. I, pp. 107-8.

74 ibid., p. 53.

75 'Hospitals', *The Catholic Encyclopedia*, vol. VII; J. Riley-Smith, *The Knights of St John in Jerusalem and Cyprus 1050-1310* (London 1967), pp. 240-2; *Memorials of London and London Life*, p. 488; *Records of the Corporation of Gloucester*, ed. W. H. Stevenson (Gloucester 1893), pp. 49, 109, 112, 367, 372, 376.

76 See, for example, *The Ancrene Riwle in La Littérature didactique au Moyen-Age*, ed. A. A. Heutsch (Halle 1903), p. 62; see also P. Riché, op. cit. pp. 692-9.

77 R. Mohl, *The Three Estates in Medieval and Renaissance Literature*, p. 352.

78 J. Moorman, op. cit., pp. 409-10.

79 *Calendar of Wills. Court of Husting*, vol. II, p. 218. Ralph de Neville also left a certain sum for his Poor Clare nieces, and another sum for their convent, see J. T. Rosenthal, *Nobles and the Noble Life, 1295-1500* (London 1976), pp. 184-5.

80 M. McLeod, *The Order of the Rose. The Life and Ideas of Christine de Pisan*, pp. 54-5.

81 Geoffrey Chaucer, *The Canterbury Tales*, pp. 4-5. For an analysis of the character and the historical background, see M. Power, *Medieval People* (London 1951), pp. 71-95.

82 See, e.g., *Visitations of Religious Houses in the Diocese of Lincoln*, vol. I, pp. 54, 82-6.

83 The poem is quoted in H. Regnault, *La Condition de Bâtard*

au Moyen-Age, p. 28.

84 *Visitations of Religious Houses in the Diocese of Lincoln*, vol. I, pp. 24, 26, 30, 53, 54; L. Delisle, 'D'après le registre d'Eude Rigaud', *Bibliothèque de l'Ecole de Chartres* XXV (1846), pp. 495 f. For the Imperial monasteries in Germany, see F. Rapp, op. cit.; for the monasteries in Tuscany, D. Herlihy and C. Klapisch, op. cit., pp. 580–1.

85 M. Goodich, 'Sodomy in ecclesiastical law and theory', *Journal of Homosexuality* I (1976) pp. 427–33; *Visitations of the Religious Houses of Lincoln*, vol. I, p. 24; *The Ancrene Riwle*, p. 62; *The Rule of Saint Benedict*, ed. J. McCann (London 1952), p. 70; Pierre Dubois, *De Recuperatione Terre Sancte*, ed. C. V. Langlois (Paris 1891), p. 83. The text including the accusations against the Lollards in old English and Latin was published by H. S. Cronin in *English Historical Review* XXII (1907), pp. 294–304.

86 Humbert de Romans, op. cit., p. 187.

87 Philippe de Novare, *Les Quatre Ages de l'Homme*,   25; Humbert de Romans, *Sermones* (Venice 1603), p. 97.

88 Peter Abélard, *Epistola VIII*, PL vol. CLXXVIII, col. 309f.

89 *Le Héraut de l'Amour divin. Révélations de Sainte Gertrude* (Paris–Poitiers 1898), pp. 9, 101.

90 C. Singer, *From Magic to Science* (New York 1958), pp. 199–239. For a general description of the education of nuns, see L. Eckenstein, *Women Under Monasticism* (Cambridge 1896). See also R. Lejeune, 'La femme dans les littératures française et occitane du XIe au XIIIe siècle', *Cahiers de Civilisation médiévale* XX (1977), p. 202.

91 *Documents relatifs à l'Histoire de l'Industrie drapière en Flandre*, ed. G. Espinas and H. Pirenne (Bruxelles 1929), vol. I, pp. 42, 307, vol. II, p. 401.

92 K. Michäelsson (ed.), *Le Livre de la Taille de Paris de l'an 1296*, p. 158; *Le Livre de la Taille de Paris de l'an 1297*, p. 5.

93 Humbert de Romans, op. cit., pp. 201–2.

94 S. Roisin, op. cit., pp. 337–42.

95 For an example of a Beguine who sued about certain properties, see *Le Droit coutumier de la Ville de Metz au Moyen-Age*, vol. I, pp. 17, 57, 59, 173.

96 M. Goodich, 'Sodomy in medieval secular law', *Journal of Homoxexuality* I.

97 Jacques de Vitry, *Vita Mariae Ogniacensis. Acta Sanctorum*, June IV, pp. 637, 677–9.

98   R. Nelli, *Dictionnaire des Hérésies médiévales* (Toulouse 1968), p. 66.

99   The most important research works about the Beguines which we have used are E. W. McDonnell, *The Beguines and Beghards in Medieval Culture* (New York 1969); H. Grundmann, *Religiöse Bewegungen im Mittelalter* (Berlin 1935). On a Beguine who was declared a saint, see C. Carozzi, 'Une Béguine joachimite: Douceline soeur d'Hugues de Digne', *Cahiers de Fanjeaux* X (1975) pp. 169–201, and 'Douceline et les autres', *Cahiers de Fanjeaux* XI (1976) pp. 251–67. On the schools run by the Beguines, see E. W. McDonnell, op. cit., pp. 273, 383. For the heresies attributed to the Beguines, see Bernard Gui, *Manuel d'Inquisiteur*, ed. G. Mollat (Paris 1964), vol. I, pp. 81–108.

100 They are all covered in E. Underhill, *Mysticism* (New York 1955).

101 'Congratulamur gratia Dei quae in te est ... Diceris enim caelesta secreta rimari et ea quae supra homines sunt spiritu sancto illustrante dignoscere ...'; Saint Bernard, *Opera*, vol. I, *Epistola* CCLXVI, p. 331.

102 E. W. McDonnell, op. cit., p. 282.

103 J. Moorman, op. cit., p. 37.

104 Thomas Aquinas, *Summa Theologica*, vol. V. Supplementi tertiae partis, q. XXXIX, art. I, p. 197.

105 'Homo enim plenum opus Dei est ... Femina enim opus viri est ... illaque in disciplinatu illius existens ei subdita est': Hildegard of Bingen, *Liber Divinorum Operum Simplicis Hominis*, PL vol. CXCVII, col. 885. See also Hildegard's *Liber Scivias* L. II, visio 6, ibid., cols 545–6.

106 E. W. McDonnell, op. cit., p. 377.

107 P. Salmon, *L'Abbé dans la Tradition monastique* (Sirey 1962), p. 73; S. Roisin, op. cit., pp. 346–9.

108 J. Ancelet-Hustache, op. cit., p. 262; *Acta Sanctorum*, April III, pp. 868, 986.

109 'Cum Domino suaviter quiescentes, quanto spiritu confortabantur, tanto corpore infirmabantur': Jacques de Vitry, *Vita B. Mariae Ogniacensis*, p. 637.

110 *Le Héraut de l'Amour divin. Révélations de Sainte Gertrude*, vol. I, pp. xvi–xviii.

111 E. W. McDonnell, op. cit., p. 305.

112 S. de Beauvoir, *Le Deuxième Sexe* (Paris 1949), ch. 24.

113 G. Scholem, *Major Trends in Jewish Mysticism* (New York

1941), pp. 37–8.

114 St Bernard, *Opera*, vol. II, *Sermo XX*, pp. 62–6.

115 St Angela of Foligno, *Le Livre de l'Expérience des vrais Fidèles*, ed. J. Férre and L. Baudry (Paris 1927), p. 12.

116 J. Ancelet-Hustache, op. cit., p. 217; St Angela of Foligno, op. cit., p. 10.

117 St Bernard, *Opera*, vol. II. *Sermo I*, pp. 1–5.

118 ibid., vol. I *Epistola* CCCXXII, p. 299.

119 Brüder Philipps des Kartäusers, *Marienleben*, in *Erzählende Dichtungen des Späteren Mittelalters*, ed. F. Böbertag (Berlin 1886), p. 46.

120 Ramon Lull, *Obras*, ed. D. Jeronimo Rosello (Palma 1886–7), *Libre d'amic et amat*, pp. 89–90.

121 *Offenbarungen der Schwester Mechthild von Magdeburg*, ed. P. Morel (Regensburg 1869), vol. I. ch. 3.

122 St Angela of Foligno, op. cit., pp. 104–6. About St Francis, see Thomas de Celano, *Vita Prima* (Rome 1880), C. VII, p. 21. St Catherine of Sienna did the same thing: *Acta Sanctorum*, April III (Paris-Rome 1866), p. 902.

123 M. Goodich, 'Childhood and adolescence among 13th century saints', *History of Childhood Quarterly* I (1973) pp. 285–309; C. Carozzi, 'Une Béguine joachimite', p. 177.

124 E. W. McDonnell, op. cit., pp. 310–19.

125 J. Ancelet-Hustache, op. cit., pp. 96–8.

126 *Revelations of Divine Love recorded by Julian Anchoress at Norwich*, ed. G. Warrack (London 1901), chs 5–6.

127 R. E. Lerner, *The Heresy of the Brothers of the Free Spirit in the Later Middle Ages* (California 1972), pp. 2, 71–7, 74, note 35, 200–8.

CHAPTER 4

1 J. Hajnal, 'European marriage patterns in perspective', in *Population in History*, ed. D. V. Glass and D. E. C. Eversley (London 1965), pp. 118–19, 123.

2 St Cyprian, *Epistola* LXIX, PL vol. IV, col. 406, and *De Unitate Ecclesiae*, ibid., col. 502.

3 *Le Héraut de l'Amour divin. Révélation de Sainte Gertrude*, vol. I, pp. 352–3.

4 Peter Lombard, *Sententiarum libri quatuor*, PL vol. CXCII, cols 687–8.

5 Humbert de Romans, *De Eruditione Praedicatorum*, p. 271.
6 Thomas Aquinas, *Summa Theologica*, vol. IV, p. 546, vol. V, pp. 249–58, and *In Decemi Libros Ethicorum Aristotelis ad Nicomachum*, ed. P. F. Raymundi. M. Spiazzi O.P. (Turin–Rome 1949), p. 452.
7 E. R. Curtius, *European Literature and the Latin Middle Ages*, p. 123.
8 J. T. Noonan, *Contraception*, ch. 3.
9 St Augustine, *Soliloquiorum Libri Duo*, PL vol. XXXII, cols 878–80.
10 *Corpus Iuris Canonici*, vol. I cols 1128–9.
11 J. T. Noonan, *Contraception*, pp. 148–94.
12 'Fornicarii sunt, non conjuges qui sterilitatis venena procurant': *Corpus Iuris Canonici*, vol. I, col. 1121. About sexual relations which are 'against nature', see J. T. Noonan, *Contraception*, pp. 223–7.
13 See the legislation of the Fourth Lateran Council: Mansi, *Sacrorum Conciliorum collectio* (Florence 1759), vol. XXII, cols 981–2. The paragraph about the legitimacy of marriage in Peter Valdes' Profession of Faith, is an example of the attempt of the Church to discredit the heretic's attitude toward marriage, see C. Thouzellier, *Catharisme et Valdéisme en Languedoc à la fin du XIIe et au début du XIIIe siècles* (Paris 1966), pp. 28–9.
14 Quoted in J. T. Noonan, *Contraception*, p. 83. See also E. Patlagean, 'Sur la limitation de la fécondité, dans la haute époque byzantine', *Annales ESC* (1969), pp. 1353–69.
15 'meum semen centena fruge fecundam est': St Jerome, *Lettres*, ed. J. Labourt (Paris 1949), *Epistola* XXII, *Ad Eustochium*, p. 128.
16 Y. Dossat, 'Les Cathares d'après les documents de l'Inquisition', *Cahiers de Fanjeaux* III (1968), pp. 100–1 and note 156.
17 Thomas Aquinas, *Summa Theologica*, vol. IV, p. 253.
18 J. T. Noonan, *Contraception*, pp. 284–5.
19 *Corpus Iuris Canonici*, vol. I, cols 1250–3; vol. II, cols 579–87.
20 'nec sacrificium offers de tuo, sed de alieno ...'. Ivo of Chartres, *Epistola* CCXLV, PL vol. CLXII, cols 251–2.
21 Burchard of Worms, *Decretorum Libri viginti* PL vol. CXL, cols 971–2.
22 J. J. Flandrin, 'Mariage tardif et Vie sexuelle', *Annales ESC* XXVII (1972), pp. 1356–9. On the negation of woman's

sexuality, see Havelock Ellis, *Little Essays of Love and Virtue*, (London 1930), pp. 102–15.

23 *Tractatus Henrici de Saxonia, Alberti Magni discipuli, De Secretis mulierum* (Frankfurt 1615), p. 51. For more about the ideas of theologians of woman's lust, see M. T. Alverny, 'Comment les théologiens et les philosophes voient la femme', *Cahiers de Civilisation médiévale X-XIIe siècles* XX (1977), pp. 123–5.

24 Etienne Fougères, *Livre de Manières*, in A. A. Heutsch, *La Littérature didactique du Moyen-Age* (Halle 1903), p. 43.

25 *Les Quinze Joyes de Mariage*, ed. F. Fleuret (Paris 1936), pp. 59–63.

26 Geoffrey Chaucer, (ed. Skeat) *The Canterbury Tales*, p. 355.

27 *Aucassin et Nicolette*, ed. M. Roques (Paris 1936).

28 Marie de France, *Lais*, ed. A. Ewert (Oxford 1965), pp. 35–48.

29 R. Nelli, 'Catharisme vu à travers les troubadours', *Cahiers de Fanjeaux* III (1968), p. 193.

30 B. Jarret, *Social Theories of the Middle Ages, 1200–1500* (Boston 1926), p. 78.

31 *Le Ménagier de Paris*, ed. J. Pichon (Paris 1846), vol. I, pp. 92–4.

32 Christine de Pisan, *Le Livre du Chemin de Long Estude*, ed. R. Püschel (Geneva 1974), pp. 4–5.

33 *Oeuvres poétiques de Christine de Pisan*, ed. M. Roy (Paris 1886), p. 216.

34 *Tractatus Henrici de Saxonia, Alberti magni discipuli, De Secretis Mulierum* (Frankfurt 1615), p. 51; Thomas Aquinas, *Summa Contra Gentiles* (Rome 1924) L. III, c. 103, p. 446.

35 J. N. Biraben, *Les Hommes et la Peste en France et dans les pays européens et méditerranéens* (Paris 1976), vol. II, p. 39. About the fear of woman, see H. R. Hays, *The Dangerous Sex* (New York 1964).

36 Geoffrey Chaucer, *The Canterbury Tales*, pp. 292–3.

37 In support of marriage: Yevamot, 63, Tosafta Yevamot, 88. Examples of statements condemning women: 'The most admirable of women is possessed by witchcraft' (Sofrim, 41); 'He who follows his wife's directions falls into Hell' (Baba Mezia, 59); 'A woman is a sack of dung and her mouth is filled with blood and all pursue her' (Shabat, 152).

38 Peter Abélard, *Historia Calamitatum*, PL vol. CLXXVIII, cols 130–2.

39 Héloïse, *Epistola* II, ibid., cols 184–5.

40 Héloïse, *Epistola* IV, ibid., cols 193–8.

41 Peter Abélard, *Sermo* 33, *De Sancto Joanne Baptista*, ibid., col. 582.

42 See, for example, E. Faral, *La Vie quotidienne au Temps de Saint Louis* (Paris 1938) p. 147; *Les Quinze Joyes de Mariage*, ed. F. Fleuret (Paris 1936).

43 P. Maranda, *French Kinship, Structure and History* (Paris 1974), p. 100.

44 See, among others, *De Sire Hain et Dame Anieuse*, cited in E. Faral, *La Vie quotidienne au Temps de Saint Louis*, pp. 152–3.

45 G. L. Kittredge, 'Marriage discussion in the Canterbury Tales', in J. J. Anderson, ed., *A Collection of Critical Essays* (New York 1957), pp. 61–3. In his opinion the tale of Dorigen is the compromise approved by Chaucer.

46 Geoffrey Chaucer, *The Canterbury Tales*, p. 402.

47 *Le Ménagier de Paris*, vol. I, p. 169.

48 *Les Quinze Joyes de Mariage*, pp. 11, 59–60, 66–7.

49 ibid., p. 131 and epilogue.

50 'Virginibus scripsi nec minus et pueris. Nam scripsi quaedam quae complectuntur amorem; Carminibusque meis sexus uterque placet.' Quoted in E. R. Curtius, *European Literature and the Latin Middle Ages*, p. 115.

51 M. Goodich, 'Sodomy in ecclesiastical law and theory', *Journal of Homosexuality* I (1976), pp. 427–33.

52 M. Bogin, *The Women Troubadours*, p. 75.

53 *The Goliard Poets*, ed. G. F. Whicher (New York 1949), p. 109.

54 M. Bogin, op. cit., p. 88.

55 A. A. Heutsch, op. cit., p. 65.

56 J. Huizinga, *The Waning of the Middle Ages*, p. 110.

57 On incest in primitive societies see M. Mead, *Male and Female. A Study of the Sexes in a Changing World* (London 1950), pp. 33–4, 198–200. On the Christian view, see St Augustine, *De Civitate Dei*, PL vol. XLI, cols 457–60; Thomas Aquinas, *Summa Contra Gentiles* (Rome 1924), L. III. c. 125, pp. 477–8; *Corpus Iuris Canonici*, vol. I, cols 1425–36.

58 On Frankish marriage law, see F. Ganshof, 'La femme dans la monarchie franque', *Rec. Soc. Jean Bodin* XII (1962).

59 About the attitude of Gratian and Peter Lombard, see 'Marriage', *Dictionnaire de Théologie catholique*, vol. IX, 2; see

also J. Imbert, *Histoire du Droit privé* (Paris 1950), p. 56.

60 E. Poullet, *Histoire du Droit pénal dans l'ancien Duché de Brabant* (Bruxelles 1866), vol. I, pp. 324–8; Heath Dillard, 'Women in Reconquest Castille: the Fueros of Sepúlveda and Cuenca', in *Women in Medieval Society*, ed. S. Mosher-Stuard (Pennsylvania 1976), pp. 79–80.

61 On private marriage, see R. H. Helmholz, *Marriage Litigation in Medieval England* (Cambridge 1974), pp. 22–34; 'Clandestinité', in *Dictionnaire de droit canonique.*

62 For ecclesiastical legislation, see *Corpus Iuris Canonici*, vol. I, cols 1104–6; Mansi, *Sacrorum Conciliorum Collectio*, cols 1035, 1038–9. One example of a case of private marriage in the nobility may be found in *The Letters of John of Salisbury 1153–1161*, ed. J. Millor and S. J. Butler (London 1955), pp. 267–71 and Appendix VI. For condemnation of private marriage in the fourteenth century, see J. Myrc, *Instructions for Parish Priests* (London 1868), pp. 7, 27.

63 M. M. Sheehan, 'The formation and stability of marriage in fourteenth century, England. Evidence of an Ely register', *Medieval Studies* XXXII (1971), pp. 228–63; and see R. H. Helmholz, op. cit., pp. 60–1.

64 J. P. Lévy, 'L'officialité de Paris et les questions familiales à la fin du XIVe siècle', in *Etudes d'histoire du droit canonique dédiées à Gabriel le Bras* (Paris 1965), vol. II, pp. 1265–94.

65 J. M. Turlan, 'Recherches sur le mariage dans la pratique coutumière (XIIe-XVIe siècles)', *Rev. historique de Droit français et étranger* CCXVII (1957), pp. 477–528.

66 *The Paston Letters*, ed. J. Warrington (London 1956), vol. I, letters 28, 81, 82, 227, vol. II, letters 290, 406, 407, 424.

67 *Corpus Iuris Canonici*, vol. I, cols 1116–17.

68 J. P. Lévy. op. cit.; R. M. Helmholz, op. cit., p. 105.

69 J. T. Noonan. op. cit., p. 282; G. Imbert, *Les Hôpitaux en Droit canonique* (Paris 1947), pp. 186–8.

70 See for example P. de Beaumanoir, *Coutumes de Beauvaisis*, vol. II, 1627–29, 1634.

71 R. H. Helmholz, op. cit., pp. 105–6.

72 J. M. Turlan, op. cit., pp. 510–11; *Le Droit Coutumier de la Ville de Metz au Moyen-Age*, vol. I, p. 401.

73 *Vita B. Roberti de Arbnissello*, PL. vol. CLXII, col. 1053.

74 R. H. Helmholz, op. cit., p. 89.

75 K. Thomas, *Religion and the Decline of Magic* (London 1973), p. 29 and note 4.

76 'ne ultra modum conjugalem verberet eius uxorem . . .' in J. P. Lévy, op. cit.

77 For the opinion that the status of women deteriorated under the influence of Christianity, see D. M. Stenton, *The English Woman in History* (London 1957), pp. 11–12, 30. For the view that Christianity improved women's status, see P. Guichard, *Structures sociales 'orientales' et occidentales dans l'Espagne musulmane* (Paris 1977), pp. 81–4. According to G. Duby, women's property and inheritance rights were restricted in eleventh-century Mâcon; but was it under the influence of Christianity? G. Duby, 'Lignage, noblesse et chevalerie au XIIe siècle dans la région mâconnaise', *Annales ESC* (1972), pp. 803–23.

78 R. Metz, op. cit., p. 91; and according to Thomas Aquinas: 'vincula matrimonii non se extendit ultra vitam in qua contrahitur'. *Summa Theologica*, vol. V, p. 253.

79 *Calendar of Wills. Court of Hustings. London 1258–1688*, ed. R. R. Sharpe (London 1890), vol. II, pp. 3, 336.

80 F. Maranda, op. cit., p. 100.

81 F. Pollock and F. Maitland, op. cit., vol. II, p. 406.

82 *La Très ancienne Coutume de Bretagne*, ed. M. Planiol (Rennes 1890), 222; *Le Livre de Droit de Verdun*, ed. J. J. Salverda de Grave and E. M. Meijers (Haarlem 1940), p. 28.

83 P. de Beaumanoir, op. cit., vol. II, § 1965; W. S. Holdsworth, *A History of English Law*, vol. II, p. 373 and note 3.

84 P. de Beaumanoir, op. cit., vol. II, § 1631.

85 E. Poullet, *Histoire du Droit pénal dans l'ancien Duché de Brabant*, p. 145.

86 J. Gilissen 'La femme dans l'ancien droit belge', in *Société Jean Bodin*, vol. XII (1962), pp. 290–1.

87 L. Tanon, *Registre criminel de la Justice de St Martin des Champs à Paris*, pp. 143, 189.

88 'Asinus', in Du Cange, *Glossarium Novum ad Scriptores Medii Aevi* (Paris 1776).

89 M. Bloch, *La Société féodale* (Paris 1939), vol. I, p. 214. On the slow consolidation of the *agnatio*, see G. Fourquin, *Lordship and Feudalism in the Middle Ages* (London 1976), pp. 59–60; D. Herlihy and C. Klapisch, op. cit., p. 532.

90 About the importance of the relationship through the mother, see P. Guichard, op. cit., pp. 95–6; about the special ties with the maternal uncle, G. Duby, 'Structure de parenté et noblesse. France du Nord IX-XII siècles', in *Miscellanea*

mediaevalia in memoriam J. F. Niermeyer (Groningen 1967), pp. 149–65.

91 D. Herlihy, 'The medieval marriage market', *Medieval* and *Renaissance Studies* VI (1976). In fourteenth-century Venice, women contributed from their property not only to raise dowries for their daughters but for other female relatives as well: see S. Chojnacki, 'Dowries and kinsmen in early Renaissance Venice', *Journal of Interdisciplinary History* I (1975), pp. 571–600.

92 *Der Sachsenspiegel*, in O. Stobbe, *Handbuch des deutschen Privatrechts* (Berlin 1884), vol. IV, p. 76.

93 *La Très ancienne Coutume de Bretagne*, p. 290.

94 P. de Beaumanoir, op. cit., vol. I, § 930.

95 *Ordonnances des Roys de France*, ed. M. Secousse (Paris 1734), vol. V, pp. 619–20.

96 About a woman's right to will her clothes and jewellery without her husband's permission, see *Le Droit coutumier de la Ville de Metz au Moyen-Age*, vol. I, pp. 279, 290; about women's wills: S. Chojnacki, op. cit.; examples of women's wills: *Calendar of Wills. Court of Hustings*, vol. I, pp. 11, 15, 20, 209–10, 428. (Some of the wills were made by married women, others by widows.)

97 See, e.g., P. de Beaumanoir, op. cit., vol. I, § 622, vol. II, §1330.

98 See, e.g., *Calendar County Court, City Court and Eyre Rolls of Chester 1259–1297*, ed. R. Steward Brown (Aberdeen 1925), p. 18.

99 *Liber Augustalis*, p. 99.

100 P. de Beaumanoir, op. cit., vol. II, §1054, §1796. In English Law: F. Pollock and F. Maitland, op. cit., vol. II, p. 403.

101 *Liber Augustalis*, pp. 66–7; P. de Beaumanoir, op. cit., vol. II, §1288.

102 *Liber Augustalis*, p. 100.

103 P. de Beaumanoir, op. cit., vol. II, §1330, 1378.

104 *Recueil général des Anciennes Lois françaises*, vol. I, p. 546.

105 See, e.g., L. Tanon, op. cit., p. 144; F. Maitland, ed., *Select Pleas of the Crown* (London 1888), p. 28.

106 P. de Beaumanoir, op. cit., vol. II, §1796; F. Pollock and F. Maitland, op. cit. vol. I, p. 482; *Le Droit coutumier de la Ville de Metz au Moyen-Age*, p. 268; M. Bateson, ed., *Borough Customs* (London 1904), vol. I, p. 223.

107 A. H. Thomas, ed., *Early Mayor's Court Rolls, 1218–1307*

(Cambridge 1924), p. 149.

108 According to the custom of fourteenth-century Verdun, a widow could be sued by the town court: *Le Livre de Droit de Verdun*, pp. 48-9, 59.

109 In Frankish legislation, inspired already by Christianity, the king is the protector of widows: *Recueil général des anciennes Lois françaises*, vol. I, pp. 26, 53.

110 On the right of widows to remarry in canon law, see *Corpus Iuris Canonici*, vol. I, cols 1111-12. See also R. Metz, op. cit., pp. 91-5.

111 Mentioned in the profession of faith of Peter Waldo: see C. Thouzellier, op. cit., p. 29.

112 *Der Waelsche Gast*, in A. A. Heutsch, *La Littérature didactique du Moyen-Age* (Halle 1903), p. 54.

113 ibid., pp. 113-14.

114 *Le Ménagier de Paris*, vol. I, pp. 166, 168.

115 T. Smith, ed., *English Gilds* (Early English Text Society (EETS), London 1870), p. 159.

116 *Calendar of Wills. Court of Hustings*, vol. I, pp. 18, 421, 452, 672, 673, 680, 684, 685, vol. II, pp. 65, 319.

117 J. Hajnal, op. cit., pp. 128-9.

118 C. Gauvard and A. Gokalp, 'Les conduites de bruit et leur signification à la fin du Moyen-Age, le charivari', *Annales ESC* XXIX (1974), pp. 693-704.

119 S. Luce, *Histoire de Bertrand du Guesclin et son Époque* (Paris 1876), p. 65.

120 P. de Beaumanoir, op. cit., §1335.

121 According to paragraph 7 of Magna Carta, the widow is entitled as her *dos* not to a third of what her husband had when he married her, but to a third of what he had before his death, unless it was explicitly agreed otherwise. In France, according to Beaumanoir, from the reign of Philip II onwards she was entitled to half of what he had when he married her. By the legislation of Louis IX she got only one third. According to the laws of Verdun she got half. See Magna Carta, 7, in W. Stubbs, *Select Charters and other Illustrations of English Constitutional History* (Oxford 1921), p. 294; P. de Beaumanoir, op. cit., vol. I, §445; *Le Livre de Droit de Verdun*, pp. 1, 73.

122 P. de Beaumanoir, op. cit., vol. I, §432.

123 *Recueil général des anciennes Lois françaises*, vol. I, p. 484.

124 For the woman's right to be guardian of her children, see *La*

Très ancienne Coutume de Bretagne, pp. 384, 433–4; P. de Beaumanoir, op. cit., vol. I, §629, 631; P. Viollet, *Le Droit du 13 siècle dans les Coutumes de Touraine-Anjou*, vol. I, ch. 21; W. Stubbs, op. cit., p. 118. Examples of women who were actually appointed as guardians for their children will be dealt with in the chapters dealing with women in the different social classes.

125 St Jerome, *Lettres*, ed. J. Labourt (Paris 1949), vol. I, *Ad Eustochium*, p. 125.

126 Quoted by F. R. Du Boulay, *An Age of Ambition* (London 1970), p. 108.

127 Gilbert of Nogent, *Histoire de sa Vie*, L. I. C. XIII.

128 E. McLeod, op. cit., pp. 33–5.

129 R. H. Helmholz, op. cit., p. 108 and note 124.

130 Thomas Aquinas, *Summa Theologica*, vol. V, p. 251; J. T. Noonan, op. cit., pp. 279–82.

131 Philippe de Novare, *Les Quatre Ages de l'Homme*, ed. M. de Fréville (Paris 1888), §79, p. 46.

132 J. Heers, op. cit., p. 102. G. R. Owst, *Literature and Pulpit in Medieval England* (Oxford 1966), p. 34.

133 Aelred of Rievaulx, *De Sanctimoniali de Wattun*, PL vol. CXCV, cols 789–96. Some scholars interpret it as if it was the nun who was forced to castrate him: see G. Constable, 'Aelred of Rievaulx and the nuns of Watton: an episode in the early history of the Gilbertine order', in *Medieval Women*, ed. D. Baker (Oxford 1978), p. 208 and note 9.

134 See E. Fromm, *The Forgotten Language* (London 1952), ch. 7, pp. 169–201 (includes also the main theories about matriarchy).

135 *Le Ménagier de Paris*, vol. I, pp. 169–70.

136 *Les Quinze Joyes de Mariage*, pp. 53–4, 110, 157.

137 Humbert de Romans, *De Eruditione Praedicatorum*, p. 274.

138 P. Ariès, *Centuries of Childhood. A Social History of Family Life* (New York 1962).

139 R. Mohl, op. cit., p. 347.

140 A. A. Heutsch, op. cit., p. 151.

141 Philippe de Novare, *Les Quatre Ages de L'Homme*, pp. 81–2, 46–7.

142 Quoted in J. Huizinga, *The Waning of the Middle Ages*, p. 35.

143 *Le Livre du Chevalier de La Tour Landry*, ed. M. A. Anatole de Montaiglon (Paris 1854), p. 169.

144 *Registre de l'Inquisition de Jacques Fournier 1318–1325*, ed. J.

Duvernoy (Toulouse 1965), vol. III, 251b, p. 130.

145   C. Carozzi, op. cit., p. 193.

146   'Et factum est, volente Deo quod illo tempore mortua fuit mater mea que erat mihi magnum impedimentum; et postea mortus est vir meus et omnes filii brevi tempore. Et quia inceperam viam predictam et rogaveram Deum quod morerentur, magnus consolamentum tum habui.' Angela of Foligno, *Le Livre de l'Expérience des vrais Fidèles*, ed. J. Ferré and L. Baudry (Paris 1927), p. 10.

147   *Select English Works of Wyclif*, ed. T. Arnold (London 1871), p. 199.

148   F. Pollock and F. Maitland, op. cit., vol. II, pp. 484–5.

149   Matthew Paris, *Chronica Majora*, ed. H. R. Luard (Rolls Series (RS), London 1880), vol. 57, 5, pp. 34–5.

150   P. de Beaumanoir, op. cit., vol. I, 933–4.

151   *Liber Augustalis*, p. 147.

152   Heath Dillard, op. cit., p. 81.

153   J. Benton, 'Clio and Venus: an historical view of medieval love', in *The Meaning of Courtly Love*, ed. F. X. Newman (New York 1968), pp. 19–43.

154   An example of the increasing severity towards men accused of fornication or adultery may be found in the legislation of the town authorities of Parma in 1233. This legislation was passed to meet a moral reform inspired by the Dominicans. M. Vauchez, 'Une campagne de pacification en Lombardie autour de 1233', *Mélanges d'Archéologie et d'Histoire* LXXVIII (1966), p. 534.

155   Heath Dillard, op. cit., pp. 85–6.

156   *Liber Augustalis*, p. 145.

157   *Les Olim ou Registres des Arrêts*, vol. III, pp. 688, 1484.

158   J. Benton, op. cit.

159   F. Pollock and F. Maitland, op. cit., vol. II, pp. 395–6.

160   *La Très ancienne Coutume de Bretagne*, p. 91.

161   Quoted from the Liber Albus in R. W. Robertson, 'The concept of courtly love as an impediment to the understanding of medieval texts', in *The Meaning of Courtly Love*, ed. F. Newman (New York 1968), p. 2.

162   E. Poullet, op. cit., vol. I, p. 327.

163   In some regions the fine paid by bondwomen for adultery, fornication or the birth of a bastard was called leyrwyte, in others there existed a special term, childwyte, for the fine for the birth of a bastard. See J. Scammel, 'Freedom and marriage

in medieval England', *The Economic History Review* Sec. Ser. XXVII (1974), p. 526; Z. Razi, *Life, Marriage and Death in a Medieval Parish: Economy, Society and Demography in Halesowen 1270–1400* (Cambridge 1980), p. 64; *Select Pleas in Manorial and other seignorial Courts*, vol. I, p. 162; H.E. Hallam, *Rural England 1066–1348* (Glasgow 1981), pp. 257–9, 263.

164 P. Vinogradoff, *Villeinage in England* (Oxford 1892), p. 154.

165 P. Bonnassie, *La Catalogue du milieu du Xe siècle à la fin du XIe siècle* (Toulouse 1975), vol. II, p. 826.

166 E. Le Roy Ladurie, op. cit., p. 242.

167 *Select Pleas in Manorial and other Seignorial Courts*, p. 8.

168 R. Mohl, op. cit., p. 123.

169 Bartholomaeus Anglicus, *Liber de Proprietatibus Rerum* (Strasburg 1595), L.VI., C. VI – *De puella, f.b.r.*

170 P. de Novare, op. cit., pp. 14–21, 49–50.

171 E. McLeod, op. cit., ch. 13.

172 *Le Livre du Chevalier de La Tour Landry*, pp. 105–13.

173 *Les Chansons de Guillaume IX duc d'Aquitaine 1071–1127*, ed. A. Jeanroy (Paris 1927), pp. 8–13.

174 J. F. Benton, op. cit.; D. W. Robertson, op. cit.

175 '. . . quia hoc sibi et dicta sacerdotis placebat.' *Registre de l'Inquisition de Jacques Fournier*, vol. I, p. 302.

176 J. Huizinga, *The Waning of the Middle Ages*, pp. 184–5.

177 F. Pollock and F. Maitland, op. cit., vol. I, p. 398; *Bastardy and its Comparative History*, ed. P. Laslett, K. Oosterveen, R. Smith (London 1980), pp. 7–9.

178 *Le Ménagier de Paris*, pp. 182–5.

179 On Church legislation concerning the bastards, see 'Bâtard', in *Dictionnaire de Théologie catholique*, col. 2558.

180 R. H. Helmholz, op. cit., p. 108.

181 See, e.g., *Recueil général des anciennes Lois françaises*, vol. I, p. 848; *La Très ancienne Coutume de Bretagne*, pp. 258–61, 479, 506; F. Pollock and F. Maitland, op. cit., vol. II, pp. 397–8; M. Bateson, *Borough Customs*, vol. II, p. 135.

182 A. A. Heutsch, op. cit., p. 113.

183 *Le Ménagier de Paris*, pp. 182–5.

184 Aelred of Rievaulx, the Cistercian abbot, who was born in 1109, was the son of a priest who himself came of a long line of married, learned and respectable priests. *The Life of Ailred of Rievaulx by Walter Daniel*, ed. M. Powicke (London 1950), p. xxxvi.

185 'Nicholaus filius sacerdotis', in W. O. Ault, 'Village assemblies in medieval England' in Album Helen M. Cam, *Studies Presented to the International Commission for the History of Representative and Parliamentary Institutions* XXIII (Louvain 1960), vol. I, p. 15.

186 *The Earliest Lincolnshire Assize Rolls, 1202–1203*, ed. D. M. Stenton (London 1926), pp. 69, 105.

187 E. Le Roy Ladurie, op. cit., pp. 138–40.

188 Y. B. Brissaud, op. cit., about a priest's mistress and their descendants in Colmar: *Annales Colmarienses Maiores*, MGHS vol. XVII, p. 231

189 *The Letters of John of Salisbury*, p. 25.

190 J. Heers, *Le Clan familial au Moyen-Age* (Paris 1974), pp. 75–6.

191 *Beverley Town Documents*, ed. A. Leach (Selden Society, London 1900), p. 11; Heath Dillard, op. cit., p. 81.

192 H. Regnault, *La Condition juridique du Bâtard au Moyen-Age* (Pont-Audemer 1922), p. 124.

193 M. Harsegor, 'L'essor des bâtards nobles au XVe siècle', *Revue historique* CCLIII (1975), p. 349.

194 D. Herlihy and C. Klapisch, op. cit., p. 577. For more examples in Italy, see *The Society of Renaissance Florence. A Documentary Study*, ed. G. Brucker (New York 1971), pp. 40–2; *Acta Sanctorum*, April I (Paris-Rome 1866), p. 516.

195 S. Thrupp, *The Merchant Class of Medieval London* (Michigan 1968), p. 263.

196 *Le Droit Coutumier de la Ville de Metz au Moyen-Age*, p. 265.

197 J. T. Rosenthal, op. cit., pp. 34–91.

198 M. Harsegor, op. cit., pp. 348–9.

199 H. Regnault, op. cit., p. 123.

200 J. Heers, op. cit., p. 82.

201 E. Power, *Medieval English Nunneries*, p. 31.

202 Z. Razi, op. cit., pp. 65–71, 138, 139. On the incidence of bastards in thirteenth-century Rickinghall in Suffolk, see R. Smith, 'A note on network analysis in relation to the bastardy-prone subsociety', *Bastardy and its Comparative History*, pp. 240–6.

203 E. Le Roy Ladurie, op. cit., pp. 61, 73–4, 76, 78, 91.

204 Z. Razi, op. cit., p. 70.

205 P. de Beaumanoir, op. cit., vol. II, §1813.

206 *Recueil général des anciennes Lois françaises*, vol. I, p. 380.

207 W. Stubbs, op. cit., p. 118, §4.

208 These remission letters were accorded by the royal chancery, and were a remission of the punishment meted out to the culprit had she been lawfully judged and condemned. They were accorded on force of written evidence by the judge, following his inquest. They include many details concerning the accused and the circumstances of the murder or abandonment of the baby.

209 *Registre de l'Inquisition de Jacques Fournier*, vol. I, 43ab, pp. 243–4.

210 Y. B. Brissaud, op. cit., pp. 229–56. One case in England is described in B. A. Hanawalt, 'The female felon in 14th century England', *Women in Medieval Society*, ed. S. Mosher-Stuard (Pennsylvania 1976), p. 130. For another case in France, see M. Harsegor, op. cit., p. 347. For Louis IX's legislation, see *Recueil général des anciennes Lois françaises*, vol. I, pp. 401–2. About the different reaction to non-marital sexual relations and the birth of a bastard: C. Vincent, *Unmarried Mothers* (New York 1961), pp. 3–5. In England, as far as it is known, the cases of infanticide were rare: see B. A. Hanawalt, 'Childrearing among the lower classes of late medieval England', *Journal of Interdisciplinary History* VIII (1977), p. 9. For Florence: R. C. Trexler, 'Infanticide in Florence: new sources and first results', *History of Childhood Quarterly* I (1973–4), pp. 98–116.

211 F. L. Flandrin, 'Contraception, mariage et relations amoureuses dans l'Occident chrétien', *Annales ESC* XXIV (1969), pp. 1370–90. And see the same author's 'Mariage tardif et vie sexuelle', *Annales ESC* XXVII (1972), pp. 1351–76.

212 M. Riquet, 'Christianisme et population', *Population* IV (1949), pp. 615–30.

213 M. Goodich, 'Sodomy in medieval secular law'.

214 This paragraph is based to a great extent on J. T. Noonan, *Contraception, A History of its Treatment by the Catholic Theologians and Canonists* (Cambridge, Mass. 1965), ch. 5 and pp. 212–35. The problem of the difference in the number of descendants in poor and rich families will be dealt with in the chapters concerning the women in the different social classes.

215 See, e.g., Burchard of Worms, *Decretorum Libri viginti* PL vol. CXL, cols 971–2.

216 C. H. Talbot, *Medicine in Medieval England* (London 1967), p. 136.

217 A. Vauchez, 'Une campagne de pacification en Lombardie autour 1233', *Mélange d'Archéologie et d'Histoire* LXXVIII (1966), p. 533 and note 5; see also Burchard of Worms, op. cit.

218 This paragraph is based to a large extent on J. T. Noonan, ed., *The Morality of Abortion. Legal and Historical Perspectives* (Cambridge, Mass. 1971), pp. 1-42.

CHAPTER 5

1 Humbert de Romans, op. cit., *Sermo* XCV.

2 See M. Bloch, *La Société féodale* (Paris 1949), vol. II, pp. 58-60; G. Duby, *La Société du XIe et XIIe siècles dans la région mâconnaise* (Paris 1963), p. 635; and 'Structure de parenté et noblesse. France du Nord, IXe-XIIe siècles', in *Miscellanea medievalia in memoriam J. F. Niermeyer* (Groningen 1967), p. 159; P. Contamine, ed., *La Noblesse du Moyen Age* (Paris 1976), introduction. In tenth century Catalonia the mother's side was emphasized: see P. Bonnassie, *La Catalogne du milieu du Xe siècle à la fin du XIe siècle* (Toulouse 1975-6), vol. I, p. 279. For the nobility of Metz, see J. Heers, *Le Clan familial au Moyen Age* (Paris 1974), pp. 22-6. *On the other hand*, according to the laws of Brittany, because of woman's inferiority, it was the nobility of the father alone that counted: 'Car il n'est nye saige qui ayde que femme franchise homme, mais homme franchist bien la femme. Car si un homme de grant lignaige prenoit la fille a ung villain les enfens pourroint estre chevaliers.' *La Très ancienne Coutume de Bretagne*, p. 508; see also *Recueil général des anciennes Lois françaises*, vols I-II, pp. 388-9

3 See P. Contamine, op. cit., pp. 23-31.

4 See, e.g., *Chronique latine de Guillaume de Nangis*, ed. H. Géraud (Paris 1843), p. 329.

5 G. Duby, 'Lignage, noblesse et chevalerie au XIIe siècle dans la région mâconnaise', *Annales ESC* XXVII (1972); about the insistence on difference of rank within the nobility by the Early Middle Ages, see J. Martindale, 'The French aristocracy in the Early Middle Ages: a reappraisal', *Past & Present* LXXV (1977), pp. 5-45.

6 E. Morgan, *The Descent of Woman* (New York 1972), pp. 218-19.

7   R. M. Pidal, *La España del Cid* (Madrid 1929), vol. II, pp. 618–20. For examples of women who took part in battles, see J. Verdon, 'Les sources de l'histoire de la femme en Occident aux Xe-XIIIe siècles', *Cahiers de Civilisation médiévale X-XIIe siècles* XX (1977), p. 229.

8   On the Amazons, see B. Roy, 'Le marge du monde connu: les races de monstres', in G. H. Allard, ed., *Aspects de la marginalité au Moyen-Age* (Montreal 1975), p. 73.

9   *La Très ancienne Coutume de Bretagne*, pp. 222, 225. About the beginning of inheritance of fiefs connected with offices by women in southern France and Catalonia, see A. Lewis, *The Development of Southern French and Catalan society (718 –1050)* (Austin 1965), pp. 123–4.

10 About the inheritance of fiefs by women in the different regions: see M. Bloch, op. cit., vol. I, pp. 293–321; F. Ganshof, *Feudalism* (London 1952), pp. 128–9; and *El Feudalismo* (Barcelona 1963), p. 297; H. Thienne, 'Die Frau im öffentlichen Recht und in der Politik', *Rec. Soc. Jean Bodin* XII, 2 (1962), p. 357; J. Gilissen, 'La femme dans l'ancien droit belge', ibid., pp. 282–3; and J. Yver, *Egalité entre Héritiers et exclusion des Enfants dotés; Essai de Géographie coutumière* (Paris 1966), pp. 36–40.

11 P. de Beaumanoir, op. cit., vol. I, §470.

12 *Recueil général des anciennes Lois françaises*, vol. I-II, p. 378; F. Joün de Longrais, 'Le statut de la femme en Angleterre', *Rec. Soc. Jean Bodin*, vol. XII (1962), p. 153; about *paragium* (*pariage*), see F. Ganshof, *Feudalism*, p. 126; M. Parisse, *La Noblesse lorraine, XIe-XIIIe siècles* (Paris-Lille 1976), vol. I, pp. 331–6.

13 J. Heers, op. cit., pp. 220–1.

14 T. H. Hollingworth, 'A demographic study of the British ducal families', *Population Studies* XI (1957), pp. 4–26.

15 J. T. Rosenthal, 'Medieval longevity and the secular peerage, 1350–1500', *Population Studies* XXVII (1973), pp. 287–93; About the violent death of noblemen in north-western France in the twelfth century, see G. Duby, 'Dans la France du Nord-Ouest au XIIe siècle: les "jeunes" dans la société aristocratique', *Annales ESC* XIX (1964), pp. 839–43.

16 About this phenomenon in England, see K. B. McFarlane, *The Nobility of Later Medieval England* (Oxford 1973).

17 M. Gastoux, *Béatrix de Brabant* (Louvain 1943), p. 120; M. Parisse, op. cit., vol. I, p. 615.

18 *Liber Augustalis*, p. 114.

19 D. Herlihy, 'Land, family and women in continental Europe, 701–1200', *Traditio* XVIII (1962), pp. 89–120.

20 A. Longnon, ed., *Documents relatifs au Comté de Champagne et de Brie, 1172–1361. Les Fiefs* (Paris 1901), *inter alia* pp. 32, 56, 59, 146. The last example: 'Comitissa Grandis Pratri fecit homagium ligium de hereditate sua de Espaux nec aliud debet facere homagium. Preterea fecit homagium ligium de dotalitio suo. Fecit etiam homagium de ballio fratris suis.'

21 *Inquisitions and Assessments Relating to Feudal Aids: 1284– 1431 prepared under the Superintendence of the Deputy Keeper of the Records* (London 1973), vol. I, pp. 319, 323, 324, 327, 31, 32, 85, 221; vol. II, pp. 104, 293.

22 D. Herlihy, op. cit., pp. 89–120. For the project of Pierre Dubois, see Pierre Dubois, *De Recuperatione Terre Sancte*, ed. C. Langlois (Paris 1891), pp. 15–16; see also J. Verdon, 'Note sur la femme en Limousin vers 1300', *Annales du Midi* CXXXVIII (1978), pp. 319–29.

23 P. Bonnassie, op. cit., vol. II, pp. 863–4.

24 For examples from the middle and lesser nobility, see J. T. Rosenthal, op. cit., pp. 135–6; M. Parisse, op. cit., vol. I, pp. 331–6.

25 *Liber Augustalis*, p. 18.

26 W. Stubbs, ed., *Select Charters and other illustrations of English Constitutional History*, p. 118, §3–4. See also the Great Charter of Liberties (Magna Carta), §6, 7, 8, ibid., p. 294; J. T. Rosenthal, op. cit., pp. 171–3, 176–7.

27 K. B. MacFarlane, op. cit., pp. 152–3.

28 *Rotuli de Dominabus et Pueris et Puellis de XII Comitatibus*, 1185, ed. J. H. Round (London 1913). The entries also illustrate the system of dowries, child marriages and the number of women who held fiefs and parts of fiefs.

29 'Adam vendit ei predictam Emmam cum terra sua'. Quoted by F. Joün de Longrais, op. cit., p. 159.

30 J. Richard, *Les Ducs de Bourgogne et la Formation du Duché* (Paris 1954), p. 188. M. de Laurière, ed., *Ordonnances des Roys de France*, vol. I, pp. 155–6.

31 F. Ganshof, *Feudalism*, pp. 128–9.

32 About Countess Matilda, see H. E. J. Cowdrey, *The Cluniacs and the Gregorian Reform* (Oxford 1970), pp. 160–1; D. B. Zema, 'The Houses of Tuscany and of Pierleone in the crisis of Rome in the 11th century', *Traditio* II (1944), pp. 155–75; *Selections from the first Nine Books of the Chronica of*

Giovanni Villani (Westminster 1896), pp. 93−6; *Ottonis et Rahewini Gesta Friderici I Imperatoris*, ed. G. Waitz (Hanover and Leipzig 1912), pp. 14, 34, 276. About Eleanor, see A. Kelly, *Eleanor of Aquitaine and the Four Kings* (New York 1957).

33 *The Paston letters*, ed. J. Warrington (London 1956), vol. II, letters 290, 291, 298.

34 See E. Power, *Medieval Women*, ed. M. M. Postan (Cambridge 1975), p. 39. For Littleton's statement, see F. Joün de Longrais, op. cit., p. 148. On the marriage of minors: J. C. Russell, *British Medieval Population* (Albuquerque 1948), p. 156.

35 Cited by E. McLeod, *The Order of the Rose, The Life and Ideas of Christine de Pisan* (London 1975), p. 30.

36 J. T. Rosenthal, op. cit., pp. 177−8.

37 J. C. Russell, op. cit., pp. 157−8. For a criticism of Russell's conclusions, see J. Krause, 'The medieval household, large or small?', *Economic History Review* IX (1957), pp. 420−32. Krause raises the question whether the age of inheritance is necessarily the age of marriage.

38 G. Duby, 'Dans la France du Nord-Ouest au XIIe siècle: les "jeunes" dans la société aristocratique', *Annales ESC* XIX (1964), p. 840.

39 T. H. Hollingworth, op. cit., pp. 4−26.

40 J. Hajnal, 'European marriage patterns in perspective', in *Population in History*, ed. D. V. Glass and E. C. Eversley (London 1965), pp. 101−43, esp. pp. 113, 116−22.

41 G. Duby, 'Structure de parenté et noblesse. France du Nord, XIe-XIIe siècles', op. cit., p. 159.

42 G. Duby, *La Société du XIe et XIIe siècles dans la région mâconnaise*, pp. 266−70.

43 S. Thrupp, *The Merchant Class of Medieval London* (Michigan 1968), p. 263; J. T. Rosenthal, op. cit., p. 89.

44 P. Guichard, *Structures sociales 'orientales' et 'occidentales' dans l'Espagne musulmane* (Paris 1977), p. 92.

45 T. H. Hollingworth, op. cit.

46 J. T. Rosenthal, op. cit., pp. 173−5, 177−8.

47 See, e.g., Gilbert of Nogent, *Histoire de sa Vie*, pp. 133−5; R. Nelli, *La Vie quotidienne des Cathares en Languedoc au XIIIe siècle* (Paris 1969), pp. 90, 211 and note 7.

48 *Liber Miraculorum S. Fidis*, ed. A. Bauillet (Paris 1897), p. 29.

49 Matthew Paris, *Chronica Majora*, ed. R. Luard (RS, London

1880), vol. 57, 5, p. 323.

50 On the small number of offspring in the poorer families in Pistoia and its rural surroundings, see D. Herlihy, *Medieval and Renaissance Pistoia* (New Haven 1967), pp. 90–7, 118; in Tuscany in general, C. Klapisch, 'Household and family in Tuscany in 1427', *Household and Family in Past Times*, ed. P. Laslett and R. Wall (Cambridge 1974), pp. 267, 281; in the English peasantry, Z. Razi, op. cit., pp. 59–60, 66.

51 M. Parisse, op. cit., vol. I, p. 306.

52 G. Duby, 'Lignage, noblesse et chevalerie au XIIe siècle dans la région maconnaise', *Annales ESC* XXVII (1972), pp. 803–23.

53 M. Parisse, op. cit., vol. I, pp. 309–10; G. Duby, *La Société du XIe et XIIe siècles dans la région mâconnaise*, p. 8; and 'Dans la France du Nord-Ouest au XIIe siècle: les "jeunes" dans la société aristocratique', op. cit.; J. C. Russell, op. cit., p. 158.

54 T. H. Hollingworth, op. cit., pp. 4–26.

55 M. Parisse, op. cit., p. 310.

56 J. T. Rosenthal, op. cit., p. 90.

57 On the age of university students, see J. Verger, 'Noblesse et savoir: étudiants nobles aux universités d'Avignon, Cahors, Montpellier et Toulouse (fin du XIVe siècle)' in P. Contamine, ed., *La Noblesse du Moyen Age* (Paris 1976), p. 306. On girls brought up in monasteries and not destined for the nunnery, see E. Rapp, 'Les abbayes: hospices de la noblesse. L'influence de l'aristocratie sur les couvents bénédictins dans l'Empire à la fin du Moyen Age', ibid., p. 315. On girls sent to be brought up in other noble houses, see *The Paston Letters*, vol. I, letter 50. On Catherine of Vadstena, an example of a girl not destined to become a nun who was educated in a nunnery, see *Acta Sanctorum*, March III, p. 504.

58 G. Duby, 'Dans la France du Nord-Ouest au XIIe siècle: les "jeunes" dans la société aristocratique'.

59 G. Longnon, 'La Champagne', in F. Lot and R. Fawtier, eds, *Histoire des Institutions françaises au Moyen Age*, vol. I, *Institutions seigneuriales* (Paris 1957), p. 128.

60 P. Bonnassie, op. cit., vol. I, p. 277.

61 Gilbert of Nogent, *Histoire de sa Vie*, p. 19.

62 S. Sheridan-Walker, 'Widow and ward: the feudal law of child custody in medieval England', in *Women in Medieval Society*, ed. S. Mosher-Stuard (Pennsylvania 1976), pp. 159–72; evi-

dence to the right of the lord to the marriage of wards, both male and female can be found in: *Rotuli de Dominabus et Pueris et Puellis de XII comitatibus*, 1185, ed J. H. Round (London 1913).

63 Héloïse, *Epistola XXI*, PL vol. CLXXXIX, col. 428; E. McLeod, op. cit., pp. 42, 51−5.

64 J. B. Hauréau, 'Le poème adressé par Abélard à son fils Astrolabe', *Notices et extraits de la Bibliothèque nationale* XXXIV, 2 (1895), pp. 153−87.

65 M. Bogin, *The Women Troubadours*, p. 144.

66 *The Paston Letters*, vol. I, letters 28, 65, 72; vol. II, 285. On the attitude towards the sons, see vol. I, 33; vol. II, 228, 237, 239.

67 R. V. Sampson, *The Psychology of Power* (New York 1966).

68 *Acta Sanctorum*, April III (Paris and Rome 1866), pp. 642, 656, See also M. Goodich, 'Childhood and adolescence among the 13th century saints', *History of Childhood Quarterly* I (1973).

69 'pater meae carnis occubuit: et magnas inde tibi gratias, qui hunc hominem sub Christiano, affectu fecisti decedere, providentiae tuae ...' Gilbert of Nogent, *Histoire de sa Vie*, p. 12. About the relationship between Gilbert and his mother, see J. F. Benton, *Self and Society in Medieval France* (New York 1970), Introduction.

70 Jean-Paul Sartre, 'There is nothing better than to produce children, but what a sin to have some! ... among the Aeneases each carrying his Anchises on his shoulders, I cross from one bank to the other alone, detesting those invisible fathers who ride piggy-back on their sons throughout their lives.' *Words*, trans. I. Clephane (London 1964), p. 15.

71 E. Le Roy Ladurie, *Montaillou: Village occitan* (Paris 1975), p. 307 note 1. On the relationship between the mother and her children in patriarchal society, see F. Fromm-Reichmann, 'Note on the mother role in the family group', in *Psychoanalysis and Psychotherapy* (Chicago 1959), pp. 290−305.

72 On the attitude toward the child, mainly in the nobility, see M. M. McLaughlin, 'Survivors and surrogates: children and parents from the 9th to the 13th centuries', in L. de Mause, ed., *The History of Childhood* (London 1974), pp. 101−81. For reference to Frau Ava's poem: ibid., note 10. For St Anselm, see *The Life of St Anselm Archbishop of Canterbury*,

ed. R. W. Southern (London 1962), pp. 171-2; about the noblewoman from Chateauverdun, see *Registre de l'Inquisition de Jacques Fournier*, vol. I, 38a, p. 221.

73 R. G. Glanville, *De Legibus et Consuetudinibus Regni Angliae*, ch. 4, quoted in D. C. Douglas and G. W. Greenway eds, *English Historical Documents* (London 1961), vol. II, p. 941.

74 ibid., p. 938.

75 ibid., pp. 921-2.

76 F. Ganshof, *El Feudalismo*, p. 297.

77 M. Planiol, op. cit., p. 30; see also E. de la Gorgue de Rosny, *Du Droit des Gens mariés dans la Coutume du Boulonnais* (Paris 1910), p. 181.

78 F. Ganshof, 'La Flandre'.

79 *Inquisitions and Assessments Relating to Feudal Aids, 1284-1413*, vol. I, p. 246, Joün de Longrais, op. cit.

80 Y. Labande-Maillert, 'Pauvreté et paix dans l'iconographie romane, X-XII siècles', in M. Mollat drc. *Etude sur l'Histoire de la Pauvreté: Moyen Age-XVIe siècle* (Paris 1973), vol. I, pp. 337-8, fig. 17 (see also note 32 above).

81 H. Regnault, *La Condition juridique du Bâtard au Moyen Age* (Pont-Audemer 1922), p. 118.

82 *Recueil de Documents relatifs à l'Histoire du Droit municipal en France des Origines à la Révolution. Artois*, ed. G. Espinas (Paris 1938-43), vol. II, pp. 338-540, vol. III, pp. 345-54, 368-9, 738.

83 *Recueil de Documents relatifs à l'Histoire de l'Industrie drapière en Flandre*, ed. G. Espinas and H. Pirenne (Bruxelles 1924), vol. I, p. 64, vol. III, pp. 277-8.

84 G. Heers, *Fêtes, jeux et joutes dans les Sociétés d'Occident à la fin du Moyen Age* (Paris 1971), pp. 19-20; M. Mollat drc., *Etudes sur l'Histoire de la pauvreté. Moyen Age-XVIe siècle*, vol. I, p. 29; J. M. Richard, *Comtesse d'Artois et de Bourgogne* (Paris 1887); A. Kemps-Welch, *Of Six Medieval Women* (London 1915).

85 F. Ganshof, 'La Flandre'.

86 *Recueil de Documents relatifs à l'Histoire de l'Industrie drapière en Flandre*, pp. 648-9.

87 E. W. McDonnell, op. cit., pp. 111-12.

88 Cited in P. Contamine and R. Delort, *L'Europe au Moyen Age*, vol. III (Paris 1971), pp. 283-4.

89 *Recueil de Documents relatifs à l'Histoire de l'Industrie*

drapière en Flandre, vol. III, p. 349.

90 P. Bonnassie, op. cit., vol. I, p. 277.

91 R. B. Pugh, *Imprisonment in Medieval England* (Cambridge 1968), p. 351.

92 F. Pollock and F. Maitland, op. cit., vol. I, p. 483.

93 Other examples of women who held fiefs by right of dower or guardianship are Catherine of Clermont – see G. G. Aclocque, *Les Corporations, l'Industrie et le Commerce à Chartres* (Paris 1907), p. 328; and Alice de Verg – see J. Richard, 'Les institutions ducales dans le duché de Bourgogne', in F. Lot and R. Fawtier, eds, op. cit.

94 Chaucer, *Canterbury Tales*, p. 364.

95 E. Power, op. cit., p. 45.

96 *Oeuvres de Froissart, chroniques*, ed. J. M. Kervyn de Lettenhove (Osnabrück 1976), vol. III, pp. 420–3. About Adela of Blois, see J. Verdon, 'Les sources de l'histoire de la femme en Occident aux Xe-XIIIe siècles', *Cahiers de Civilisation médiévale X-XII siècles* XX (1977), p. 239.

97 About the administrative and economic activities of Margaret Paston: *The Paston Letters*, vol. I, letters 16, 47, 65, 133, 145, 148, 149, 151, 155, 170, 171, 174, 178, 195, 198, 199, 219, 220, 222, 223, 237, 239; vol. II, letters 240, 241, 242, 243, 244, 245, 246, 247, 248, 250, 251, 252, 254, 255, 258, 262, 264, 272. On the countess of Norfolk, ibid., vol. I, letter 135.

98 'The Rules of Saint Robert', in *Walter of Henley's Husbandry together with an Anonymous Husbandry, Senechaucie and Robert Grosseteste's Rules*, ed. E. Lamond (London 1890), pp. 121–50.

99 D. Herlihy, 'Land, family and women in continental Europe, 701–1200', *Traditio* XVIII (1962), pp. 89–120.

100 A. Coville, *Gontier et Pierre Col et l'Humanisme en France au temps de Charles VI* (Paris 1934), p. 63.

101 Cited by E. McLeod, op. cit., p. 135.

102 'Post modum vocatus a castellano vel uxore ejus seu ab ejus dapifero'. *Recueil de Documents relatifs à l'Histoire du Droit municipal en France*, vol. III, p. 300.

103 P. Bonnassie, op. cit., vol. I, p. 276.

104 *The Paston Letters*, vol. I, letter 99.

105 E. Power, op. cit., pp. 40–1.

106 John of Salisbury, *Policraticus*, PL vol. CXCIX, col. 393.

107 L. F. Salzman, *English Industries of the Middle Ages* (Oxford 1923), p. 217.

108   About the occupations of the noblewoman according to didactic literature, see R. Mohl, op. cit., p. 47; A. A. Heutsch, op. cit., pp. 45−7.

109   B. Guenée and F. Leroux, eds, *Les Entrées royales françaises de 1328−1515* (Paris 1968), pp. 55, 57, 58.

110   A. A. Heutsch, op. cit., pp. 72−9; R. Nelli, op. cit., pp. 79−83.

111   E. Le Roy Ladurie, *Montaillou*, pp. 379−80.

112   J. T. Rosenthal, op. cit., p. 187.

113   Humbert de Romans, *Sermones* (Venice 1603), pp. 96−7; B. Jarret, *Social Theories in the Middle Ages 1200−1500* (Boston 1926), p. 88; A. A. Heutsch, op. cit., p. 151.

114   ibid., pp. 53−4, 101.

115   Philippe de Novare, *Les Quatre Ages de l'Homme*, §24−5.

116   E. McLeod, op. cit., p. 128.

117   Pierre Dubois, *De Recuperatione Terre Sancte*, ed. C. V. Langlois (Paris 1891), pp. 50−2 57−71.

118   F. Rapp, op. cit.

119   E. W. McDonnell, op. cit., p. 320.

120   *Registre de l'Inquisition de Jacques Fournier*, vol. I, 45b, p. 252.

121   For Peter the Venerable's praise of Héloïse's learning: see *The Letters of Peter the Venerable*, ed. G. Constable (Cambridge, Mass., 1967), vol. I, letter 15, pp. 303−4.

122   See Marie de France, *Lais*, ed. A. Evert (Oxford 1944), pp. v−vi.

123   J. Richard, *Mahaut Comtesse d'Artois et de Bourgogne* (Paris 1887), ch. 8.

124   Cited in P. Ariès, *Centuries of Childhood*, pp. 23−4, 419, notes 20−1.

125   J. Verger, 'Noblesse et savoir: étudiants nobles aux universités d'Avignon, Cahors, Montpellier et Toulouse', in *La Noblesse au Moyen Age*, pp. 289−313.

126   R. Southern, *Saint Anselm and his Biographer. A Study of Monastic Life and Thought* (Cambridge 1963), p. 37.

127   R. R. Bolgar, *The Classical Heritage and its Beneficiaries* (Cambridge 1954), p. 186.

128   A. A. Heutsch, op. cit., p. 47. For examples of women who were patrons of writers and poets, see R. Lejeune, 'La femme dans les littératures française et occitane du XIe au XIIIe siècle', *Cahiers de Civilisation médiévale, Xe-XIIe siècles* XX (1977).

129 'attractiva ad vanitatem mulierum': quoted in J. Heers, *Fêtes, Jeux et Joutes dans les Sociétés d'Occident à la fin du Moyen Age*, p. 48.

130 Simone de Beauvoir, *Le Deuxième Sexe* (Paris 1949), ch. 8.

131 See G. Koch, *Frauenfrage und Ketzertum im Mittelalter* (Berlin 1962).

132 On courtly love as sensual love, see e.g. *Les Poésies de Cercamon*, ed. A. Jeanroy (Paris 1921), pp. 9–12; *Les Poésies de Bernart Marti*, ed. E. Hoepffner (Paris 1929), pp. 10, 13, 24, 31, 33–5. In didactic courtly literature too, sometimes the instructions are not concerned with platonic love: see A. A. Heutsch, op. cit., pp. 56–7. Cynical sensual poems were written by William IX, duke of Aquitaine (as well as others expressing the ideal courtly love): see *Les Chansons de Guillaume IX Duc d'Aquitaine, 1071–1127*, ed. A. Jeanroy (Paris 1927), pp. 8–13. See also E. Kohler, *L'Aventure chevaleresque. Idéal et Réalité dans le Roman Courtois* (Paris 1974).

133 J. M. Ferrante, *The Conflict of Love and Honour. The Medieval Tristan Legend in France, Germany and Italy* (The Hague–Paris 1973).

134 See J. F. Benton, 'Clio and Venus. An historical view of medieval love', in *The Meaning of Courtly Love*, ed. F. X. Newman (New York 1968), pp. 19–43; M. Bogin, op. cit., Introduction. E. Power has dealt with the limited impact of courtly love on everyday life: E. Power, op. cit., pp. 26–9.

135 On the small percentage of noblemen in medieval population, see P. Contamine, ed., *La Noblesse au Moyen Age. XI–XVe siècles*, pp. 31–2.

136 See P. Guichard, op. cit., pp. 164–73.

137 A. Coville, op. cit., pp. 63–5.

138 M. Bogin, op. cit., p. 110.

139 ibid., p. 56; R. Nelli, *L'Erotique des Troubadours* (Paris 1974), pp. 223–34; Andreas Capellanus, *The Art of Courtly Love*, trans. J. J. Parry (New York 1941), p. 100.

140 Hildegard of Bingen, *Liber Scivias*, PL vol. CXCVII, cols 461, 595.

141 Marie de France, *Lais*, ed. A. Ewert (Oxford 1944), pp. 5–6.

142 M. M. McLaughlin, 'Abélard as an autobiographer. The motives and meaning of his Story of Calamities', *Speculum* XLII (1967).

143 E. McLeod, op. cit., p. 135.

144 ibid., pp. 148, 118.
145 Christine de Pisan, *Le Livre de fais et bonnes meurs du Sage Roy Charles V* (Paris 1836), p. 617.
146 *Oeuvres poétiques de Christine de Pisan*, ed. M. Roy, vol. II (Paris 1891), pp. 21–3.
147 E. McLeod, op. cit., p. 117–18.
148 Bartholomaeus Anglicus, *Liber de Proprietatibus Rerum*, L. VI, C. VI; *Acta Sanctorum*, April II (Paris – Rome 1865), p. 159.
149 E. McLeod, op. cit., pp. 130–1.
150 G. Rossi, op. cit., p. 117; D. M. Stenton, *The English Woman in History* (London 1957), p. 29.
151 J. F. Benton, *Self and Society in Medieval France* (New York 1970), p. 23.
152 See, e.g., J. T. Rosenthal, op. cit., pp. 178–9.
153 *Annales Colmarienses* MGHS vol. XVII (Hanover 1861), p. 231.
154 Quoted by J. A. Thomson, *The Later Lollards 1414–1520* (Oxford 1965), p. 8 and note 1.
155 Peter of Vaux de Cernay, *Historia Albigensium, Recueil des Historiens de Gaule et de la France* (Paris 1880), vol. XIX, p. 98.
156 See J. B. Russell, *Dissent and Reform in the Early Middle Ages* (Los Angeles 1965), p. 255.
157 C. Carozzi, 'Une Béguine joachimite. Douceline soeur d'Hugues de Digne', *Cahiers de Fanjeaux* X (1975), p. 173.

CHAPTER 6

1 See, e.g., *Recueil de Documents relatifs à l'Histoire du Droit municipal en France*, ed. G. Espinas, vol. III, p. 315.
2 ibid., p. 236.
3 About the citizenship of women in towns, see *Calendar of Plea and Memoranda Rolls Preserved among the Archives of the Corporation of the City of London at the Guild hall, 1364–1381*, ed. A. H. Thomas (Cambridge 1929), p. lxi.
4 As in the case of a woman in London who asked for a letter of pardon. The mayor was asked by a writ whether she was a citizen of the town. The answer was in the affirmative and she got the letter of pardon: ibid., p. 152. See also *Le Livre Roisin, Coutumier lillois de la fin du 13e siècle*, ed. R. Monier (Paris-Lille 1932), pp. 2–3, 20–1, 41.

5 E. Bourquelot, 'Un scrutin du XIVe siècle', *Mémoires de la Société nationale des Antiquaires de France* XXI (1852), p. 455. One can suppose that women whose husbands' names were not mentioned and who are not referred to as widows were single.

6 E. Boutaric, *La France sous Philippe le Bel* (Brionne 1861), p. 37 and note 7.

7 On the rights of the son domiciled with his father, see W. Stubbs, ed., op. cit., pp. 133–4.

8 See for example A. Ballard and J. Tait, ed., *British Borough Charters, 1216–1307* (Cambridge 1923), p. 133.

9 *Calendar of Wills. Court of Hustings London, 1258–1688*, ed. R. Sharpe (London 1889), vol. I, pp. 418, 420, 430, 678, 682, 686, vol. II, pp. 9, 15, 17, 204, 207, 213, 468, 537, 596.

10 *Calendar of Plea and Memoranda Rolls preserved among the Archives of the Corporation of the City of London at the Guildhall 1364–1381*, p. 294.

11 *Memorials of London and London Life 1276–1419*, ed. H. T. Riley (London 1868), vol. I, p. 68.

12 J. Gilissen, op. cit.; E. M. Meijers and J. J. Salverda de Grave ed., *Le Livre de Droit de Verdun* (Haarlem 1940), pp. 33–4; H. Dillard, op. cit.

13 G. Rossi, op. cit.; A. Pertile, *Storia del diritto italiano* (Torino 1896–1903), vol. IV, pp. 58–9; J. Heers, *Le Clan familial au Moyen-Age* (Paris 1974), p. 108; M. A. Maulde, ed., *Coutumes et Règlements de la République d'Avignon* (Paris 1879), p. 156.

14 J. Heers, op. cit., p. 63; D. Owen Hughes, 'Family structure in medieval Genoa', *Past and Present* LXVI (1975).

15 S. Thrupp, op. cit., p. 192 and note 2.

16 Philippe de Novare, *Les Quatre Ages de l'Homme*, p. 48.

17 For an example from the archers' guild in York, see: *York Memoranda Book*, part I, 1376–1419, ed. M. Sellers (London 1912), p. 54.

18 J. Nooman, *Contraception*, p. 229.

19 See D. Herlihy, *Medieval and Renaissance Pistoia*, pp. 118–20.

20 S. Thrupp, op. cit., pp. 105–6.

21 G. Brucker, ed., *The Society of Renaissance Florence. A Documentary Study* (New York 1971), pp. 29–31.

22 See for example: *Acta Sanctorum*, May I (Paris-Rome 1866), p. 335. See also S. Chojnacki, 'Dowries and kinsmen in early

Renaissance Venice', *Journal of Interdisciplinary History* V, (1975) pp. 571–600; D. Herlihy, 'The medieval marriage market', *Medieval and Renaissance Series* VI (1976). On the other hand in London there was almost an equal contribution by both parties; see S. Thrupp, op. cit., p. 106.

23 T. Smith, ed., *English Guilds* (EETS, London 1870), pp. 194, 340.

24 *British Borough Charters*, P. 134; *Ordonnances des Roys de France*, vol. V, ed. Secousse (Paris 1736), p. 509.

25 D. Herlihy, 'Vieillir au quattrocento', *Annales ESC* XXIV (1969), pp. 1338–52; D. Herlihy and C. Klapisch, op. cit., pp. 205–7, 394–400; S. Thrupp, op. cit., p. 196.

26 *Calendar of Plea and Memoranda Rolls preserved among the Archives of the Corporation of the City of London at the Guild hall 1364–1381*, p. 107; S. Thrupp, op. cit., p. 172 and note 38.

27 We have dealt with the problem in chapters 4 and 5. See also D. Herlihy and C. Klapisch, op. cit., pp. 420–42.

28 Concerning the larger number of offspring in the villages, see D. Herlihy, *Medieval and Renaissance Pistoia*, pp. 117–18.

29 D. Herlihy, 'The Tuscan town in the quattrocento. A demographic profile', *Medievalia et Humanistica* I (1970). In Tuscany in times of plague, the rate of boys' mortality was lower than that of girls. See D. Herlihy and C. Klapisch, op. cit., p. 462; S. Thrupp, op. cit., pp. 197–200.

30 About the rise and decline of the extended family in Italy, see D. Herlihy, 'Family solidarity in medieval Italian history', in *Economy, Society and Government in Medieval Italy*, ed. D. Herlihy, R. Lopez and V. Slessaha (Kent, Ohio, 1969); C. Klapisch and M. Demonet ' "A Uno pane e uno vino": la famille rurale toscane au début du XVe siècle', *Annales ESC* XXVII (1972), pp. 873–901; C. Klapisch, 'Household and family in Tuscany in 1427', in P. Laslett and R. Wall, ed., *Household and Family in Past Times* (Cambridge 1974), pp. 267–81; J. Heers, op. cit., pp. 21–2, 49–58, 65–7.

31 See J. Gillisen, op. cit.

32 *Die Kölner Schreinsbücher des 13 und 14 Jahrhunderts*, ed. H. Planitz and T. Buyken (Weimar 1937), p. 197.

33 D. Herlihy, *Medieval and Renaissance Pistoia*, p. 61.

34 *Borough Customs*, ed. M. Bateson (London 1966), p. 112.

35 See for example the will of Petronilla Ledeney from Gloucester: *Records of the Corporation of Gloucester*, ed. W. H. Stevenson (Gloucester 1893), p. 358.

36 *British Borough Charters*, pp. 90–1.
37 ibid., p. 134.
38 ibid., p. 100.
39 *Calendar of Wills. Court of Hustings. London, 1258–1688*, ed. R. R. Sharpe (London 1889), vol. I, p. 111, vol. II, p. 66.
40 *Bristol Record Society Publications*, ed. E. W. Veale (Bristol 1931), vol. II, p. 264.
41 *Le Droit coutumier de la Ville de Metz au Moyen-Age*, ed. J. Salverda de Grave, M. Meijers and J. Schneider (Haarlem 1951), pp. 134–5.
42 T. Smith, ed., *English Guilds* (EETS, London 1870), p. cxxxii; *Ordonnances des Roys de France*, vol. IV, p. 491.
43 S. Thrupp, op. cit., p. 263.
44 See chapter 4, and also R. H. Helmholz, op. cit., p. 160.
45 D. Herlihy and C. Klapisch, op. cit., p. 594.
46 S. Mosher Stuard, 'Women in charter and statute law: medieval Ragusa' (Dubrovnik), in *Women in Medieval Society*, ed. S. Mosher-Stuard (University of Pennsylvania 1976), p. 204.
47 Wet-nurses are mentioned, *inter alia*, in the ordinance of King Jean II of France concerning wages: see R. de Lespinasse, ed., *Les Métiers et Corporations de la Ville de Paris* (Paris 1886), p. 31.
48 D. Herlihy and C. Klapisch, op. cit., pp. 552–70. About the children handed over to nurses, see R. C. Trexler, 'Infanticide in Florence: new sources and first results', in *History of Childhood Quarterly* I (1973–4), pp. 98–116.
49 V. S. Pritchett, *Balzac* (London 1973), p. 25.
50 *Acta Sanctonum*, April III (Paris-Rome 1866), p. 873.
51 A. Goldthwaite, 'The Florentine palace as domestic architecture', *American Historical Review* LXXVII (1972), pp. 977–1012.
52 D. Herlihy and C. Klapisch, op. cit., p. 569.
53 Thomas de Celano, *Vita Prima* (Rome 1880), ch. 6, p. 17.
54 D. Herlihy, 'Vieillir au quattrocento'.
55 For apprenticeship agreements, see L. F. Salzman. op. cit., p. 339; *Borough Customs*, vol. I, p. 229; *Calendar of Plea and Memoranda Rolls preserved among the Archives of the Corporation of the City of London at the Guildhall*, pp. 107, 219; D. Herlihy and C. Klapisch, op. cit., pp. 573–4.
56 *Acta Sanctorum*, February III, p. 416.
57 Salimbene de Adam, *Chronica*, ed. G. Scalia (Bari 1966), p. 48.
58 B. A. Hanawalt, 'Childrearing among the lower classes of late

medieval England', *Journal of Interdisciplinary History* VIII (1977), pp. 20–1.

59 V. S. Pritchett, op. cit., pp. 26–30.

60 *Complete Works of Thomas More* (Yale 1965), vol. IV, book II, pp. 130–1.

61 See for example, G. Aclocque, *Les Corporations, L'Industrie et le Commerce à Chartres du XIe siècle à la Révolution* (Paris 1917), pp. 108–9.

62 *Règlements sur les Arts et Métiers de Paris rédigés au XIIIe siècle, et connus sous le nom du Livre des Métiers d'Etienne Boileau*, ed. G. B. Depping (Paris 1837), pp. 80–5.

63 ibid., pp. 99–101; R. de Lespinasse, op. cit., vol. III, p. 9.

64 ibid., vol. II, pp. 13–19, 86–7; 556–9.

65 ibid., vol. III, p. 55

66 K. Michäelsson, ed., *Le Livre de la Taille de Paris de l'an 1296* (Göteborg 1958), p. 266, and *Le Livre de la Taille de Paris de l'an 1313* (Göteborg 1951), p. 214.

67 R. de Lespinasse, op. cit., vol. II, pp. 166–7.

68 ibid., vol. III, pp. 303–7.

69 ibid., p. 403, 482, 484. About women producing cushions and coverlets of feathers and head covers, see vol. II, pp. 693–4, 696–7, vol. III, p. 297. For shoemakers, see K. Michäelsson, *Le Livre de la Taille de Paris de l'an 1313*, pp. 84–5. For ironworkers, ibid., p. 87.

70 *Statuti senesi scritti in volgare nel secolo XIIIe-XIVe*, ed. F. L. Polidori (Bologna 1863–77), vol. I, pp. 274, 279, 306, 329. In Perugia at the beginning of the fifteenth century there were 176 women weavers, and twenty-six men weavers. See M. Weber, *The City* (New York 1958), p. 173.

71 E. Staley, *The Guilds of Florence* (London 1906), pp. 68, 353.

72 J. H. Mundy and P. Riesenberg, *The Medieval Town* (Princeton 1958), pp. 175–6.

73 E. W. McDonnell, op. cit., pp. 85, 273.

74 *Calendar of Plea and Memoranda Rolls preserved among the Archives of the City of London at the Guildhall 1364–1381*, p. 102.

75 Cited by H. Cam, 'The legislators of medieval England', in *Historical Studies of the English Parliament*, ed. E. B. Fryde and E. Miller (Cambridge 1970), vol. I, p. 191.

76 S. Thrupp, op. cit., p. 171.

77 *York Memorandum Book. Part I, 1376–1410*, p. 77.

78 T. Smith, ed., op. cit., pp. 182–3.

79 *Borough Customs*, vol. I, p. 229; *Memoranda Rolls preserved among the Archives of the Corporation of the City of London at the Guildhall 1364–1381*, pp. 107, 219.

80 *York Memorandum Book. Part I, 1376–1419*, p. 82.

81 *The Little Red Book of Bristol*, ed. F. B. Brickley (Bristol 1900), vol. I, p. 43; T. Smith, op. cit., p. 343.

82 *Court Rolls of the Borough of Colchester* (Colchester 1921), vol. I, p. xiii. For more examples of women fined for transgression of the Assize of Ale, see ibid., vol. II, pp. 1, 182–4, vol. III, pp. 1–2, 16, 51.

83 T. Smith ed., op. cit., pp. 155–9, 160–1, 178, 194–6; prohibition to participate in the wake, ibid., p. 194. On women members of the fraternity of Marseilles, see P. A. Amargier, 'Mouvements populaires et confrérie du Saint-Esprit à Marseille au seuil du XIIIe siècle', *Cahiers de Fanjeaux* XI (1976), p. 309.

84 *Le Livre de Métiers*, §LXXIII; *Le Droit coutumier de la Ville de Metz au Moyen-Age*, vol. I, pp. 41, 136, 148, 168, 569.

85 *Leet Jurisdiction in the City of Norwich during the 13th and 14th Centuries*, ed. W. Hudson (Selden Society, London 1892), p. 66.

86 P. Grimal, *Histoire mondiale de la Femme* (Paris 1965), vol. II, p. 171.

87 E. McLeod, op. cit., pp. 129–30 and note 8.

88 R. de Lespinasse, op. cit., vol. III, pp. 580–3.

89 ibid., vol. I, p. 45; *Select Cases concerning the Law Merchants*, ed. C. Gross (Selden Society, London 1908), vol. I, pp. 66, 72–3; *The Little Red Book of Bristol*, vol. I, pp. 5, 8; *York Memorandum Book. Part I, 1376–1419*, pp. 6–7, 10–12.

90 ibid., pp. 198–221; *Beverley Town Documents* (Selden Society, London 1900), p. 9; *Leet Jurisdiction in the City of Norwich*, pp. 48–60; *British Borough Charters*, p. 295.

91 K. Michäelsson, ed., *Livre de la Taille de Paris de l'an 1246*, pp. 21, 202; idem, *Le Livre de la Taille de Paris de l'an 1297*, pp. 81, 82, 318, 329; idem, *Le Livre de la Taille de Paris de l'an 1313*, pp. 214, 258; R. de Lespinasse, op. cit., vol. II, p. 243; *Leet Jurisdiction in the City of Norwich*, p. 60.

92 E. Power, *Medieval Women*, pp. 56–7.

93 See for example S. Thrupp, op. cit., p. 173.

94 ibid., pp. 170–1, 262.

95 *Ordonnances des Roys de France*, vol. IV, p. 491.

96 *The Oak Book of Southampton*, ed. P. Studer (Southampton

1910), p. 30. About the connections between the town authorities and the merchant guild, see ibid., p. 60.

97 C. Gross, ed., *The Guild Merchant* (Oxford 1890), vol. I, pp. 50–1, vol. II, pp. 4–5.

98 R. de Lespinasse, op. cit., vol. II, p. 243.

99 *Ordonnances des Roys de France*, vol. II, p. 354.

100 *Memorials of London and London Life*, p. 26.

101 S. Thrupp, op. cit., p. 173.

102 G. Gillisen, op. cit., p. 272; *Recueil général des anciennes Lois françaises*, vol. I, p. 546; p. de Beaumanoir, op. cit., vol. II, 1336; F. Rörig, *The Medieval Town* (London 1967), p. 115; *Calendar of Plea and Memoranda Rolls preserved among the Archives of the Corporation of the City of London at the Guildhall, 1364–1381*, p. 23.

103 A. A. Heutsch, op. cit., pp. 116–17; D. Herlihy and C. Klapisch, op. cit., pp. 582–3.

104 L. F. Salzman, op. cit., p. 329.

105 *Documents relatifs à l'Histoire de l'Industrie et du Commerce en France*, ed. G. Fagniez (Paris 1974), vol. I, pp. 263, 310.

106 L. F. Salzman, op. cit., p. 217.

107 *Recueil de Documents relatifs à l'Histoire de l'Industrie drapière*, vol. I, p. 677.

108 *Documents relatifs à l'Histoire de l'Industrie et du Commerce en France*, vol. I, p. 245.

109 ibid., vol. II, pp. 172–3.

110 *Livre des Métiers*, pp. 69–73.

111 T. Smith, ed., op. cit., pp. 179–80.

112 L. F. Salzman, op. cit., pp. 222, 339–40.

113 G. d'Avenal, op. cit., vol. II, p. 36, vol. III, pp. 608, 611.

114 S. Thrupp, 'Medieval industry', in *The Fontana Economic History of Europe. The Middle Ages*, ed. C. M. Cipolla (Glasgow 1975), p. 266.

115 *York Memorandum Book. Part I, 1376–1419*, p. 54.

116 An example of the sexual morality argument is in *Documents relatifs à l'Histoire de l'Industrie et du Commerce en France*, vol. I, p. 245.

117 Cited in C. H. Talbot, *Medicine in Medieval England* (London 1967), p. 155.

118 R. de Lespinasse, op. cit., vol. I, p. 2.

119 See B. H. Putnam, *The Enforcement of the Statute of Labourers, 1349–1359* (New York 1908), Appendix p. 9, 249–50.

120 *The Peasants' Revolt of 1381*, ed. R. B. Dobson (New York

1970), p. 70; B. H. Putnam, op. cit., pp. 146–9.

121 Cited in S. Thrupp. op. cit., p. 173.

122 In Florence for example the barbers, surgeons and midwives were under the control of the guild of doctors and pharmacists: see E. Staley, *The Guilds of Florence* (London 1906), pp. 238, 241. On accusations of witchcraft, see R. Kieckhefer, *European Witch Trials* (California 1976), p. 56.

123 According to the regulations of the town of York, both men and women had to get a licence to practise from the barbers' guild: see *York Memorandum Book. Part I, 1376–1419*, p. 109. See also V. L. Bullough, *The Development of Medicine as a Profession* (New York 1966), pp. 88–90.

124 C. H. Talbot, op. cit., ch. 7.

125 *Ordonnances des Roys de France*, vol. I, pp. 491–2, vol. IV, pp. 496–7, 499–501. On women surgeons in Paris, see *Livre des Métiers*, pp. 419–20.

126 *Collectio Salermitana*, ed. S. de Renzi (Napoli 1854), vol. III, p. 338.

127 C. H. Talbot, op. cit., p. 96.

128 On the institutionalization of medicine, see V. L. Bullough, op. cit.

129 On the problem of those who practised medicine without a licence, see ibid., pp. 68–72; C. H. Talbot, op. cit., pp. 118, 196, 202. For an example of legislation, see *Recueil général des anciennes Lois françaises*, vol. IV, p. 676.

130 *Cartularium Universitatis Parisiensis*, ed. H. Denifle (Paris 1891), pp. 257–67.

131 ibid., pp. 151–3.

132 ibid., p. 267.

133 ibid.

134 ibid., p. 266.

135 *Acta Sanctorum*, April III, pp. 502–32.

136 A. Memmi, *L'Homme Dominé* (Paris 1968).

137 J. Heers, *Le Clan familial au Moyen-Age*, pp. 49–58, 80.

138 K. Bücher, *Die Frauenfrage im Mittelalter* (Tübingen 1910), p. 6; D. Herlihy, *Medieval and Renaissance Pistoia*, pp. 83–4.

139 *Registre criminel du Châtelet de Paris*, p. 315.

140 R. de Lespinasse, op. cit., vol. I, p. 31.

141 *Ordonnances des Roys de France*, vol. II, p. 370.

142 Women workers in the vineyards, for example, were paid from eight to twelve deniers (pence) a day (without food), but this was, of course, seasonal work: ibid., p. 368.

143 *Select cases concerning the Law Merchant*, vol. I, *Fair Court of St Ives*, ed. C. Gross (Selden Society, London 1908), p. 99.

144 G. d'Avenal, op. cit., vol. III, p. 562.

145 Humbert de Romans, *Sermones* (Venice 1603), *Sermo* LXXVI, p. 75; A. A. Heutsch, op. cit., pp. 107−15.

146 *Le Ménagier de Paris*, vol. II, pp. 53−72.

147 *Calendar of Wills. Court of Hustings London*, vol. I, pp. 669, 677, 679.

148 See A. Memmi, *L'Homme Dominé* (Paris 1968), pp. 173−91, 192−3.

149 St Augustine, *De Ordine*, PL vol. XXXII, col. 1000.

150 Humbert de Romans, *De Eruditione Praedicatorum* C. C., Ad mulieres malas corpore sive meretrices.

151 *Liber Augustalis*, p. 146.

152 J. Bloch, *Die Prostitution* (Berlin 1912), pp. 705−17.

153 The fairs that took place at Scania in the south of Sweden in the thirteenth and fourteenth centuries (called *Mundinae Schaniense*) were famous not only because of the merchants and fishermen who gathered there, but because of the great number of prostitutes too. See J. A. Gade, *The Hanseatic Control of Norwegian Commerce during the Later Middle Ages* (Leyden 1951), p. 16. For examples of prostitutes at fairs, see *Select Cases concerning the Law Merchant, Fair Court of St Ives* (Selden Society, London 1908), ed. C. Gross, vol. I, pp. 14−16. On farmers visiting them, see E. Le Roy Ladurie, *Montaillou*, pp. 30, 217−18.

154 *Le Livre du Chevalier de La Tour Landry*, ed. M. A. Montaiglon (Paris 1854), §127.

155 B. Geremek, *Les Marginaux parisiens aux XIVe et XVe siècles* (Paris 1976), pp. 248−53.

156 J. Bloch, op. cit., pp. 718−20. On the beginning of prostitution in various towns from the twelfth to the fourteenth century, and the different words used for prostitute, see ibid., p. 732−9, 740−7.

157 *Liber Augustalis*, p. 24.

158 J. Bloch, op. cit., p. 760.

159 See B. Geremek, op. cit., pp. 260−1.

160 Examples of the ban on leaving the fixed quarters are in *Recueil des anciennes Lois françaises*, vol. V, p. 320; *Memorials of London and London Life*, p. 535. See also B. Geremek, op. cit., ch. 7 and note 11; D. Herlihy and C. Klapisch, op. cit., pp. 581−2.

161 Thomas de Chobham *Summa Confessorum*, ed. F. Broomfield (Louvain–Paris 1968), Q. Va, De meretricibus, p. 296.

162 Prostitution and public baths: J. Bloch, op. cit., pp. 182–8. Bans on turning the public baths into brothels: *Livre des Métiers*, p. 189; *Ordonnances des Roys de France*, vol. I, p. 441.

163 *Memorials of London and London Life*, p. 484.

164 For examples of royal and town legislation on the subject, see ibid., p. 458; *Recueil général des anciennes Lois françaises*, vol. VI, p. 685.

165 See B. Geremek, op. cit., p. 246.

166 *Coutumes et Règlements de la République d'Avignon* (Paris 1879), ed. M. A. Maulde, p. 200.

167 *Leet Jurisdiction in the City of Norwich during the 13th and 14th Centuries*, p. 59.

168 A. Vauchez, 'Une campagne de pacification en Lombardie autour 1233', *Mélange d'Archéologie et d'Histoire* LXXVIII (1966), pp. 533–5; *Ordonnances des Roys de France*, vol. I, p. 105; *Recueil général des anciennes Lois françaises*, vol. VI, p. 559.

169 *Memorials of London and London Life*, p. 319; *Select Pleas of the Crown*, p. 27.

170 *Livre des Métiers*, p. 378.

171 *Memorials of London and London Life*, p. 347; *Fair Court of St Ives*, p. 83; *Court Rolls of the Borough of Colchester*, vol. I, p. 2.

172 ibid., p. 3; *Calendar of Plea and Memoranda Rolls preserved among the Archives of the Corporation of the City of London at the Guildhall, 1323–1364*, pp. 232–3.

173 ibid., p. 107.

174 On the right to correct an apprentice, see T. Smith, ed., op. cit., p. 390.

175 S. Thrupp, op. cit., p. 164 and note 21.

176 *Fair Court of St Ives*, p. 50.

177 *Borough Customs*, vol. I, p. 80; *Court Rolls of the Borough of Colchester*, vol. II, p. 186, vol. III, p. 4; *Recueil de Documents relatifs à l'Histoire du droit municipal en France*, vol. III, *Saint Omer*, p. 313; *Leet Jurisdiction of Norwich*, pp. 60, 67, 69; *Fair Court of St Ives*, p. 13.

178 J. Heers, *Le Clan Familial*, pp. 114–15, 150–1.

179 *Registre criminel de la justice de St Martin des Champs à Paris*, p. 4; B. A. Hanawalt, 'Childrearing among the lower classes of

late medieval England', *Journal of Interdisciplinary History* VIII (1977), p. 18.

180 J. B. Given, *Society and Homicide in 13th Century England* (Stanford 1977), pp. 48, 116–17, 134–49, 179–83; *Le Droit coutumier de la Ville de Metz au Moyen-Age*, vol. I, p. 268; *Court Rolls of the Borough of Colchester*, vol. I, pp. 10, 18, vol. II, pp. 185, 224, 235, vol. III, pp. 3, 9, 16, 33, 37, 44.

181 *Registre criminel du Châtelet de Paris*, vol. I, pp. 55–61.

182 R. de Lespinasse, *Les Métiers et Corporations de la Ville de Paris* (Paris 1886), vol. I, p. 45.

183 *Registre criminel de Saint-Martin des Champs*, p. 43.

184 *Registre criminel du Châtelet de Paris*, vol. I, pp. 315, 327, 363, 480, vol. II, pp. 60, 64, 337, 393.

185 On women tried for murder, see J. B. Given, op. cit., pp. 179, 182; G. Brucker, ed., *The Society of Renaissance Florence. A Documentary Study* (New York 1971), pp. 140–2; *South Lancashire in the Reign of Edward III as illustrated by the Pleas of Wigan Recorded in Coram Rege Rolls n° 54*, ed. G. M. Tumpling (Manchester 1949), p. 18; *Registre criminel du Châtelet de Paris*, vol. I, p. 268, vol. II, p. 61.

186 *Le Livre Roisin, Coutumier lillois de la fin du 13ème siècle*, p. 138.

187 See J. Huizinga, op. cit., p. 14.

188 M. A. Vauchez, op. cit., p. 509 and note 3.

189 B. Guenée and F. Leroux, *Les Entrées royales françaises* (Paris 1968), pp. 64–5, 87, 143–4, 162; J. Huizinga, op. cit., p. 23.

190 J. Heers, *Le Clan Familial*, pp. 241–3.

191 J. Heers, *Fêtes, jeux et joutes dans les Sociétés de l'Occident à la fin du Moyen-Age* (Paris 1971), pp. 112–13.

192 On the Hokkedays game, see *Memorials of London and London Life*, p. 571.

193 'mulier ebriosa ira magna': Alvarus Pelagius, *De Planctu Ecclesiae* (Venice 1560), f. 85a, col. 1.

194 *The Goliard Poets*, ed. G. F. Whicher (New York 1949), pp. 228–30.

195 J. Heers, *Fêtes, jeux et joutes dans les Societés de l'Occident à la fin du Moyen-Age*, p. 88. For an example of women participating in a drinking party, see T. Smith, ed., op. cit., pp. 182–3.

196 Burchard of Worms, *Decretorum Libri Viginti* PL vol. CXL, L. 19, col. 1010.

197 G. Chaucer, *Canterbury Tales*, p. 305.

198   G. R. Owst, *Literature and Pulpit in Medieval England*, pp. 395–6. For an example, see E. Staley, *The Guilds of Florence*, pp. 90–1.

199   L. F. Salzman, op. cit., p. 339.

200   See M. Jourdain, *L'Education des Femmes au Moyen-Age* (Paris 1871).

201   *Les Chroniques de Jean Froissart*, ed. J. A. C. Buchon (Paris 1835), vol. III, pp. 479, 482.

202   *Chronica di Giovanni Villani* (Florence 1823), pp. 184–5.

203   H. Rashdall, op. cit., vol. II, p. 47 and note 1.

204   Cited in S. Thrupp, op. cit., p. 171.

205   E. Power, *Medieval Women*, p. 86, and ch. 4.

206   E. M. McDonnell, op. cit., pp. 272, 383, 386.

207   ibid., p. 386.

208   M. Jourdain, op. cit., p. 10.

209   *Chronica di Giovanni Villani*, p. 185.

210   J. Verger, op. cit., pp. 289–313.

211   Cited in D. Herlihy and C. Klapisch, op. cit., pp. 566, 597.

212   For an example of guardianship, see *Calendar of wills. Court of Husting, London*, vol. I, p. 671.

213   K. Bücher, op. cit., p. 6; R. Kieckhefer, op. cit., p. 57; J. C. Russell, 'Recent advances in medieval demography', *Speculum* XL (1965); D. Herlihy, *Medieval and Renaissance Pistoia*, pp. 83–4.

214   For some examples of capital-owning women, see S. Thrupp, op. cit., Appendix B.

215   See J. Huizinga, op. cit., p. 11, and Jean Chartier, 'Chronique de Charles VII', cited in L. Tanon, *Histoire de Justice des anciennes Eglises et Communautés monastiques de Paris* (Paris 1883), p. 33.

CHAPTER 7

1   Offices such as that of *forestarius* (forester), *praepositus minor* (manorial agent), or *baillivus* (baillif).

2   Cited in A. Pertile, *Storia del diritto italiano* (Torino 1894), p. 43.

3   See R. Hilton, *The English peasantry in the Later Middle Ages* (Oxford 1975), pp. 105–6.

4   G. Duby, *La Societé aux XIe et XIIe siècles dans la région mâconnaise* (Paris 1953), pp. 369–70.

5   J. Yver, *Egalité entre Héritiers et Exclusion des Enfants dotés; Essai de Géographie coutumière* (Paris 1966); E. Le Roy Ladurie, 'Structures familiales et coutumes d'héritage en France au 16e siècle', *Annales ESC XXVII* 1972), pp. 825–46.

6   E. Le Roy Ladurie, *Montaillou, Village occitan de 1294–1324* (Paris 1975), pp. 66–7, 73–9, 80–1.

7   C. Klapisch and M. Demonet, '"A uno pane e uno vino": la Famille toscane au début du XIVe siècle', *Annales ESC* XXVII (1972), pp. 873–901.

8   R. Hilton, op. cit., p. 98.

9   R. Aubenas, 'Reflex sur les "fraternités artificielles" au Moyen-Age', in *Etude d'Histoire à la mémoire de Noël Didier* (Paris 1960), pp. 8–9; *Court Rolls of the Manor of Hales 1270–1307*, ed. J. Hamphlett and S. g. Hamilton (Oxford 1912), vol. II, pp. 287, 299, 334; F. Maitland, ed., *Select Pleas in Manorial and other Seignorial Courts*, vol. I (Selden Society, London 1889), p. 123; E. Le Roy Ladurie, *Montaillou*, p. 64.

10   J. Gilissen, op. cit., J. Yver, op. cit., p. 37.

11   F. Pollock and F. Maitland, op. cit., vol. II, p. 261.

12   For examples of merchet payments see Z. Razi, op. cit., pp. 45–7, 131–4, 152–3; P. Döllinger, *L'Evolution des Classes rurales en Bavière* (Paris 1949), pp. 254–5. On merchet as control of land tenure inheritance tax rather than over marriage, see E. Searle, 'Seigneurial control of women's marriage: the antecedents and function of merchet in England', *Past and Present* LXXXII (1979), pp. 3–43. On merchet paid by the woman or her husband, H. E. Hallam, *Rural England* (Glasgow 1981), pp. 261–2.

13   *Les Olim ou Registres des Arrêts*, vol. I. pp. 164–5; G. Duby, op. cit., p. 125; Ildefons V. Arx, *Geschichten des Kantons St Gallen* (St Gallen 1810–13) p. 66; P. Hyams, *Kings, Lords and Peasants in Medieval England: The Common Law of Villeinage in the 12th and 13th Centuries* (Oxford 1980), pp. 15–16.

14   E. Le Roy Ladurie, *Montaillou*, pp. 260–6.

15   P. Malansséna, *La Vie en Provence au XIVe et XVe siècle, un exemple, Grasse à travers les actes notariés* (Paris 1969).

16   F. Maitland, ed., *Select Pleas in Manorial and other Seignorial Courts*, vol. I, p. 46.

17   G. C. Hommans, *English Villagers of the 13th Century* (Cambridge, Mass., 1941), p. 175.

18   P. Döllinger, op. cit., p. 208.

19 E. Le Roy Ladurie, *Montaillou*, pp. 221, 270, 272, 273, 403.

20 F. Maitland and P. Baildon, eds, *The Court Baron together with Sellect Pleas from the Bishops of Ely's Court of Littleport* (Selden Society, London 1891), pp. 137–8.

21 See for example *Die exempla des Jacob von Vitry*, ed. G. Frenken, *Quellen und Untersuchungen zur lateinischen Philologie des Mittelalters* V (1914), pp. 128–31.

22 B. Given, op. cit., p. 195; E. Le Roy Ladurie, *Montaillou*, pp. 83, 135, 279, 280, 378.

23 F. Maitland and P. Baildon, eds, op. cit., pp. 54–5.

24 E. Le Roy Ladurie, *Montaillou*, p. 260.

25 ibid., pp. 286, 290, 322, 378; D. Herlihy and C. Klapisch, *Les Toscans et leurs Familles* (Paris 1978), p. 566.

26 F. Maitland, ed., *Select Pleas in Manorial and other Seignorial Courts*, vol. I, p. 32.

27 M. M. Postan and J. Z. Titow, 'Heriots and prices on Winchester manors' in M. M. Postan, ed., *Essays on Medieval Agriculture and General Problems of the Medieval Economy* (Cambridge, 1973), pp. 159–60, 180–3; Z. Razi, op. cit., pp. 43–4. On girls and their dowries, see ibid., pp. 43, 74.

28 J. Hajnal, op. cit., p. 124.

29 Z. Razi, op. cit., pp. 57, 60.

30 E. Le Roy Ladurie, *Montaillou*, pp. 276–7, 532.

31 C. Klapisch and M. Demonet, '"A uno pane e uno vino": la famille toscane au début du XVe siècle', *Annales ESC* XXVII (1972), pp. 873–901.

32 Z. Razi, op. cit., p. 83–5. On the manors of Redgrave and Rickinghall, see ibid., p. 86, and note 178 to p. 164.

33 ibid., pp. 144–9.

34 G. Duby, *La Société au XIe et XIIe siècles dans la région mâconnaise*, pp. 369–70.

35 E. Le roy Ladurie, *Montaillou*, pp. 25, 118, 301; G. Duby, *L'Economie rurale et la Vie des campagnes dans l'Occident médiéval* (Paris 1962), vol. II, p. 569.

36 D. Herlihy, *Medieval and Renaissance Pistoia* (New Haven 1967), p. 97.

37 Alvarus Pelagius, *De Planctu Ecclesiae* (Venice 1560), L. II, f. 84, col. 2.

38 'The Statute of Cambridge', in *A Documentary History of England*, ed. J. J. Bagley and P. B. Rowley, vol. I (London 1966), p. 218; *Acta Sanctorum*, April II, p. 256, March III, p. 520, May III, p. 181, August II, p. 120; *The Miracles of*

Simon de Montfort, ed. J. O. Halliwell (London 1840), p. 87; *The Vita Wulfstani of William of Malmesbury*, ed. R. R. Darlington (London 1928), p. 131.

39   A. Hanawalt, 'Childrearing among the lower classes of late medieval England', *Journal of Interdisciplinary History* III (1977).

40   See for example *Acta Sanctorum*, January I, pp. 896, 345, March II, p. 86, April I, p. 710, April III, pp. 248, 928, 957, May V, p. 103, June IV, p. 782; St Bonaventura, *Legenda Sancti Francisci* in *Opera Omnia* (Quarachi 1898), p. 568; *Analecta Bollandiana* IX (1890), pp. 327-8, 351; *Le Livre de Saint Gilbert*, ed. R. Foreville (Paris 1943), p. 70; *The Vita Wulfstani of William of Malmesbury*, ed. R. R. Darlington (London 1928), p. 121.

41   William Langland, *Piers the Plowman and Richard the Redeless*, ed. W. W. Skeat (Oxford 1901), C. Passus X, 72-9, p. 234.

42   *Der Arme Heinrich* in *Peasant Life in Old German Epics* trans. C. H. Bell (New York 1968), pp. 110-11.

43   *Meir Helmbrecht*, ibid., p. 86.

44   *Le Registre de l'Inquisition de Jacques Fournier (1318-1325)*, vol. I, 77a, p. 382.

45   ibid., 74b, p. 370.

46   ibid., 61ab, p. 320. About another mother who mourned her infant found dead in her bed in the morning, see ibid. 33cd, p. 202.

47   ibid., vol. II, 203cd, pp. 414-15.

48   ibid., vol. I, 105ab, p. 499.

49   ibid., vol. III, 263ab, pp. 188-9.

50   ibid., vol. I, 61bc, p. 321.

51   R. Le Roy Ladurie, *Montaillou*, p. 28.

52   *Registre de l'Inquisition de Jacques Fournier*, vol. III, 295ab, p. 364.

53   ibid., vol. I, 88a, p. 429.

54   E. Le Roy Ladurie, *Montaillou*, p. 52.

55   ibid., p. 86.

56   Z. Razi, op. cit., p. 68-9; F. Maitland, ed., *Select Pleas in Manorial and other Seignorial Courts*, vol. I, p. 173.

57   Robert Gloucester, *Metrical Chronicle*, cited in G. C. Homans, op. cit. pp. 156-7; Robert Mannyng of Brunne, *Handlyng Synne*, cited, ibid., p. 155. On the admonitions, see John Myrc, *Instructions for Parish Priests* (EETS London

1868), p. 54: 'R. Owst, *Literature and Pulpit in Medieval England* (Oxford 1961), pp. 428–9, 460; M. M. McLaughlin, 'Survivors and surrogates: children and parents from the ninth to the thirteenth centuries', in L. de Manse, ed., *The History of Childhood* (London 1976), pp. 120–1.

58 B. A. Hanawalt, 'The female felon in 14th century England', in *Women in Medieval Society*, ed. S. Mosher-Stuard (Pennsylvania 1976), pp. 130–1.

59 See F. Fromm-Reichmann, 'Note on the mother role in the family group', in *Psychoanalysis and Psychotherapy* (Chicago 1959), pp. 290–305.

60 D. Herlihy, op. cit., pp. 83–4; R. Hilton, op. cit., p. 99.

61 J. Z. Titow, *English Rural Society, 1200–1300* (London 1972), p. 87.

62 On the right of dower, see R. Hilton, op. cit., pp. 98–100; R. J. Faith, 'Peasant families and inheritance customs in medieval England', *Agricultural Historical Review* XIV (1966), pp. 77–95. On the customs of Liguria, see J. Heers, *Le Clan familial au Moyen-Age* (Paris 1974), p. 225. For examples of the widower's rights of inheritance, see F. Maitland, ed., *Select Pleas in Manorial and other Seignorial Courts*, vol. I, pp. 37, 29, 121.

63 ibid., pp. 107, 109–10.

64 ibid., pp. 62, 88, 89, 96; F. Maitland, ed., *Select Pleas in Manorial and other Seignorial Courts*, vol. I, pp. 6, 28; G. C. Homans, op. cit., p. 440, note 4.

65 Cited ibid., p. 436.

66 J. Z. Titow, 'Some differences between manors and their effects on the condition of the peasant in the 13th century', *Agricultural Historical Review* X (1962), pp. 1–13; Z. Razi, op. cit., pp. 235, 138–9.

67 G. C. Homans, op. cit., p. 88.

68 ibid., p. 188.

69 E. Le Roy Ladurie, *Montaillou*, p. 186.

70 When Meir Helmbrecht tries to persuade his sister not to marry one of the peasants he mentions all the different kinds of work she would have to do as a peasant's wife. See *Meir Helmbrecht*, pp. 73–4.

71 See for example G. Duby, *L'Economie rurale et la Vie des campagnes dans l'Occident médiéval* (Paris 1962), vol. II, p. 694.

72 R. Hilton, op. cit., p. 101.

73   J. Quicherat, *Procès de Condamnation et de Réhabilitation de Jeanne d'Arc* (Paris 1841), vol. I, p. 51, vol. II, p. 429.

74   On women's work see J. E. T. Rogers, *Six Centuries of Work and Wages* (London 1971), p. 235; R. Hilton, op. cit., p. 101; R. Hilton, *The Economic Development of some Leicester Estates in the 14th and 15th centuries* (Oxford 1947), pp. 145-6; E. Le Roy Ladurie, *Montaillou*, pp. 27-30, 381.

75   J. A. Raftis, *Tenure and Mobility; Studies in the Social History of the Medieval English Village* (Toronto 1964), pp. 67, 90.

76   E. Le Roy Ladurie, *Montaillou*, pp. 139-40.

77   Cited in G. C. Homans, op. cit., p. 436.

78   See for example *The Court Baron together with Select Pleas from the Bishops of Ely's Court of Littleport*, p. 136; E. Le Roy Ladurie, *Montaillou*, pp. 29-30, 381.

79   *Walter of Henley's Husbandry together with an Anonymous Husbandry, Senechaucie and Robert Grosseteste's Rules*, ed. E. Lamond (London 1890), pp. 76, 32, 57, 117, 119, 135.

80   ibid., pp. 64-8.

81   L. F. Salzman, *English Industries of the Middle Ages* (Oxford 1923), p. 55.

82   R. Hilton, *The English Peasantry in the Later Middle Ages*, p. 102.

83   *Ordonnances des Roys de France*, vol. II, p. 368.

84   J. J. Bagley and P. B. Rowley, op. cit., vol. I, p. 217.

85   R. Hilton, op. cit., pp. 101-3.

86   E. Perroy, 'Wage labour in France in the Late Middle Ages', *Economic History Review* VIII (1955), pp. 232-9.

87   G. d'Avenal, *Histoire économique de la Propriété, des Salaires, des Denrées et de tous les Prix en général depuis l'an 1200 jusqu'à l'an 1800* (Paris 1898), vol. II, p. 36, vol. III, pp. 491-4, 518-19, 525-7, 538-9, 550-1.

88   R. Hilton, *The English Peasantry in the Later Middle Ages*, pp. 101-3.

89   According to the research of J. E. T. Rogers men's salaries rose by 50 per cent and women's doubled, generally from 1 to 2 pence a day. See J. E. T. Rogers, op. cit., pp. 233-4, 237.

90   R. Hilton, *The Economic Development of some Leicestershire Estates in the 14th and 15th Centuries*, pp. 145-6.

91   E. Le Roy Ladurie, *Montaillou*, p. 78. One woman servant's poverty can be deduced from what she left after her death: see G. Duby, *L'Economie rurale et la Vie des campagnes dans l'Occident médiéval*, vol. I, p. 755.

92 E. Le Roy Ladurie, *Montaillou*, p. 29.
93 R. Hilton, *The English Peasantry in the Later Middle Ages*, p. 103.
94 E. Le Roy Ladurie, *Montaillou*, p. 332.
95 See for example J. Raftis, op. cit., p. 104.
96 *Court Rolls of the Manor of Hales 1270–1307*, ed. J. Hamphlett and S. G. Hamilton (Oxford 1912), vol. II, pp. 247, 390, 393, 394; F. Maitland, ed., *Select Pleas in Manorial and other Seignorial Courts*, vol. I, pp. 8, 27, 32, 33.
97 ibid., pp. 20, 165, 178; J. Hamphlett, op. cit., p. 246.
98 F. Maitland, ed., *Select Pleas in Manorial and other Seignorial Courts*, vol. I, pp. 12, 14, 15, 36.
99 *The Court Baron together with Select Pleas from the Bishop of Ely's Court of Littleport*, p. 73.
100 See, e.g., F. Maitland, ed., *Select Pleas in Manorial and other Seignorial Courts*, vol. I, p. 143.
101 J. B. Given, op. cit., pp. 167, 169; B. A. Hanawalt, op. cit., pp. 125–40.
102 Photocopy from the proceedings of the royal court in Shropshire, Birmingham Reference Lib. 383853. This reference was given to me by Dr Z. Razi.
103 E. Le Roy Ladurie, *Montaillou*, p. 39.
104 Humbert de Romans, *De Eruditione Praedicatorum*, p. 280.
105 *Walter of Henley's Husbandry*, pp. 101, 114.
106 Cited in C. H. Talbot, *Medicine in Medieval England* (London 1967), p. 150.
107 *Walter of Henley's Husbandry*, p. 8.
108 M. Sahlin, *Etude sur la Carole médiévale* (Uppsala 1940); G. C. Homans, op. cit., ch. 23.
109 Alvarus Pelagius, *De Planctu Ecclesiae* (Venice 1560), L. II, fol. 147b; Humbert de Romans, *Sermones*, Sermo XCIX, p. 98.
110 *Acta Sanctorum*, February III, pp. 298–357. Two more examples of peasant women who were canonized are Margaret the Barefoot, *Acta Sanctorum*, August II, p. 121 f., and Gemma of Solomona, *Acta Sanctorum*, May III, p. 181 f.
111 E. Le Roy Ladurie, *Montaillou*, p. 334.
112 See J. Verger, 'Noblesse et savoir. Etudiants nobles aux universités d'Avignon, Cahors, Montpellier et Toulouse (fin du XIVe siècle)', in P. Contamine, ed., *La Noblesse au Moyen Age* (Paris 1976), pp. 289–315.

CHAPTER 8

1 *Radulphus Glaber, Les Cinq Livres de ses Histoires*, ed. M. Prou (Paris 1886), pp. 74–81; Landulf Senior, *Historia Mediolanensis* II, MGHS, vol. VIII, pp. 65–6; R. I. Moore, 'Family, Community and Cult on the eve of the Gregorian Reform', *TRHS* XXX (1980), pp. 49–69.

2 From *Actus pontificum Cenomannis in urbe degentium*, in *Heresies of the High Middle Ages*, ed. and trans. W. L. Wakefield and A. P. Evans (Columbia 1969), p. 108.

3 *Monumenta Bambergensis*, ed. P. Jaffé (Berlin 1869), pp. 296–300; John of Salisbury, *Historia Pontificalis*, ed. M. Chibnall (London 1956), pp. 62, 64.

4 Gilbert of Nogent, op. cit., L. III, ch. 17; Heribert the monk, *Epistola*, PL vol. CLXXXI, cols 1721–2; Ralph of Coggeshall, *Chronicon anglicanum*, ed. J. Stevenson (Roll Series LXVI, London 1875), pp. 121–5.

5 *Cartularium universitatis parisiensis*, ed. H. Denifle (Paris 1889), vol. I, pp. 71–2.

6 M. D. Lambert, *Medieval Heresy. Popular Movements from Bogomil to Hus* (London 1977), p. 193; S. E. Wessley, 'The 13th century Guglielmites: salvation through women', in D. Baker, ed., *Medieval Women* (Oxford 1978), pp. 289–303.

7 See R. E. Lerner, *The Brothers of the Free Spirit* (California 1972): for the women: see pp. 229–30. About the pseudo-apostles, see Bernard Gui, *Manuel de l'Inquisiteur*, ed. G. Mollat (Paris 1964), pp. 84–104.

8 B. Geremek, *Les Marginaux parisiens au XIVe siècle* (Paris 1976), p. 345 and note 21.

9 See J. A. F. Thomson, *The Later Lollards, 1414–1520* (Oxford 1965): this is a study of the rolls of courts in which men and women suspected of Lollard customs and beliefs were tried. See also C. Gross, 'Great Reasoner in Scripture: the activities of women Lollards 1380–1530', in D. Baker, ed., *Medieval Women* (Oxford 1978), pp. 359–80.

10 G. Leff, *Heresy in the Later Middle Ages* (Manchester 1967), p. 470.

11 Told by Laurentius of Brêjové, in K. Höfler, *Geschichtsschreiben der Hussitischen Bewegung in Bohemen* (Vienna 1856–66), p. 438, §29–33.

12 Alain of Lille, *De Fide Catholica contra Haereticos sui temporis*, PL vol. CCX, col. 379; J. Leclercq, 'Le témoignage de Geoffroy d'Auxerre sur la vie cistercienne', *Studia Anselmiana*

XXXI; *Analecta monastica* II (1953), p. 195; Bernard Gui, op. cit., p. 34; Jacques Fournier, op. cit., vol. I, pp. 1, 2, 7, 33, 34.

13 Burchard of Ursberg, *Chronicon*, ed. O. Holder-Egger and B. von Simson (Scriptores rerum germanicarum in usum scholarum, Hanover and Leipzig 1916), p. 107.

14 *Litterae Episcopi Placentini de pauperibus de Lugduno*, ed. A. Dondaine, in *Archivum fratrum praedicatorum* XXIX (1959), p. 271–4; *Beiträge zur Sektengeschichte des Mittelalters*, ed. J. I. von Döllinger (Munich 1890), vol. II, pp. 6–7; M. Koch, *Frauenfrage und Ketzertum im Mittelalter* (Berlin 1962), ch. 10 and p. 185.

15 Stephen of Bourbon, *Tractatus de diversis materiis praedicabilibus*, ed. A. Lecoy de la Marche (Paris 1887), p. 292; *Registre de l'Inquisition de Jacques Fournier*, vol. I, 7c, p. 74; 3d, p. 56. The witness said that women were not allowed to preach or serve as priests.

16 ibid., 10c. The problem had been discussed by Augustine, whose answer was that each would be resurrected in the body of his/her own sex, because Nature had been good before the Fall, and would be so again at the End of Days. Saint Augustine, *De Civitate Dei*, PL vol. XLI, L. XXII, C. 17.

17 'Deus verus ex patre esset et homo verus ex matre, veram carnem habens ex viceribus matris et animam humanam racionabilem; natus ex Virgine Maria, vera nativitate carnis.' The text is quoted in C. Thouzellier, op. cit., pp. 28–9. About the text, see W. L. Wakefield, op. cit., pp. 204–6.

18 *Registre de l'Inquisition de Jacques Fournier*, vol. I, 9ab, p. 82; *Beiträge zur Sektengeschichte*, vol. II, pp. 9, 99, 307, 339, 620.

19 *Bernardi abbatis Fontis Calidi ordinis Praemonstratensis, Adversus Waldensium sectam liber*, PL vol. CCIV, cols 805–12, 825–6. And see also C. Thouzellier, op. cit., pp. 50–7. Another example of a debate with the Waldenses is Alain of Lille, *De Fide Catholica contra Haereticos sui temporis*, PL, vol. CCX, cols 306–9, 316, 377–80.

20 L. Baudry, *Guillaume d'Occam* (Paris 1950), pp. 171, 176,; G. Lechler, *Johann von Wicliff und die Vorgeschichte der Reformation* (Leipzig 1873), vol. I, p. 127.

21 K. Thomas, 'Women in the Civil War sects', *Past and Present* XIII (1958), pp. 42–62.

22 J. Guiraud, *Histoire de l'Inquisition au Moyen-Age* (Paris 1933), vol. I, p. 291; *Registre de l'Inquisition de Jacques Fournier*, vol. II. 126c, p. 50.

23   About Cathar women, see E. Griffe 'Le Catharisme dans le diocèse de Carcassonne et le Lauragais au XIIe siècle', *Cahiers de Fanjeaux* III (1968), pp. 216, 224, 231; M. Becamel, 'Le Catharisme dans le diocèse d'Albi', ibid., pp. 248–50; Y. Dossat, 'Les Cathares d'après les documents de l'Inquisition', ibid., p. 73, note 8, p. 103, note 9, p. 86, note 82, p. 96, note 138, pp. 98–9, notes 148, 149, 150, 151; H. Blanquière and Y. Dossat, 'Les Cathares au jour le jour, confessions inédites de Cathares quercynois', ibid., pp. 262, 266, 268, 269, 271, 272; Y. Dossat, 'Confession de G. Donadieu', ibid., p. 290–7; R. Nelli, op. cit., ch. 4; J. Guiraud, op. cit., vol. I, pp. 147–8; A. Borst, *Die Katharer* (Stuttgart 1953), p. 207; A. Borst, 'Transmission de l'hérésie au Moyen-Age', in *Hérésies et Société dans l'Europe préindustrielle, XIe–XVIIIe siècles*, ed. J. Le Goff (Paris 1968), p. 276 and notes 13–14; G. Koch, op. cit., ch. 3 and p. 184; about the giving of the *consolamentum* by women, see *Registre de l'Inquisition de Jacques Fournier*, vol. II, 126c, p. 50.

24   R. Nelli, *Dictionnaire des Héresies méridionales* (Toulouse 1968), pp. 206–7.

25   *Cena Secreta ou Interrogatio Iohannis*, ed., J. Ivanof, in *Légendes et écrits bogomiles* (Sofia 1925), p. 82. About 'The Vision of Isaiah', see R. Nelli, *Le Phénomène cathare* (Paris 1925), p. 107 and note 14.

26   *Registre de l'Inquisition de Jacques* Fournier, vol. I, 94b, c, p. 457; vol. II, 202c, d, p. 409.

27   *La Somme des Authorités à l'usage des Prédicateurs méridionaux au XIIIe siècle*, ed. C. Douais (Paris 1896), pp. 125, 119; *Monetae Cremonensis adversus catharos et valdenses libri quinque*, ed. T. A. Ricchini (Rome 1743), p. 5; *Beiträge zur Sektengeschichte*, vol. II, pp. 58, 161, 277.

28   *Cena Secreta*, pp. 78–9.

29   ibid., p. 79.

30   *Registre de l'Inquisition de Jacques Fournier*, vol. II, 218b, c, p. 488; 202b, c, p. 407, vol. III, 268c, d, p. 219.

31   ibid., 209c, pp. 441–2.

32   ibid., 126a, p. 47; *Beiträge zur Sektengeschichte*, vol. II, pp. 149–51.

33   *Registre de l'Inquisition de Jacques Fournier*, vol. III, 251b, p. 130.

34   *Beiträge zur Sektengeschichte*, vol. II, pp. 33, 35, 320; A. Borst, *Die Katharer*, p. 181.

35 *Cena Secreta*, p. 78.

36 *Registre de l'Inquisition de Jacques Fournier*, vol. III, 265c, p. 201, 269b, c, p. 223. About this idea in the early dualistic sects and in John Scotus Erigena, see M. T. d'Alverny, 'Comment les théologiens et les philosophes voient la femme', *Cahiers de Civilisation médiévale Xe–XIIe siècles* (1977), p. 106.

37 *Le Liber de Duobus Principiis. Un traité néo manichéen du XIIIe siècle*, ed. A. Dondaine (Rome 1939), p. 137; Raynier Sacconi, *De Catharis et Pauperibus de Lugduno*, ibid., p. 71; *Registre de l'Inquisition de Jacques Fournier*, vol. III, 268d, p. 220.

38 Y. Dossat, 'Les Cathares d'après les documents de l'Inquisition', *Cahiers de Fanjeaux* III (1968), p. 79, notes 47–50, p. 103.

39 *Un traité cathare inédit du début du 13e siècle d'après le Liber Contra Manicheos de Durand Huesca*, ed. C. Thouzellier (Louvain 1961), p. 90.

40 *Le Nouveau Testament traduit au XIIIe siècle en langue provençale suivi d'un Rituel cathare*, ed. L. Clédat (Paris 1887), p. x.

41 *Fragmentum ritualis*, ed. A. Dondaine, in *Liber de Duobus Principiis*, p. 162.

42 *Registre de l'Inquisition de Jacques Fournier*, vol. III, 272b, pp. 239–40.

43 See for example L. Lowenthal and N. Guterman, *Prophets of Deceit: A Study of the techniques of the American Agitator* (New York 1949).

44 G. Koch, op. cit., ch. 1.

45 For the high percentage of Cathari women who were convicted by a court of the Inquisition, see Y. Dossat, *Les Crises de l'Inquisition toulousaine au XIIIe siècle (1233–1274)* (Bordeaux 1959), pp. 251–7.

46 The *Malleus Maleficarum* was not the first work of its kind. It had been preceded by 'Little hammers', as H. Trevor-Roper called them. A considerable number of these texts were published in *Quellen und Untersuchungen des Hexenwahns und der Hexenverfolgung im Mittelalter*, ed. J. Hansen (Bonn 1901), pp. 38–239. Works that refer to the pact with the Devil: ibid., pp. 423–44.

47 Gregory of Tours, *Historia Francorum*, ed. R. Poupardin (Paris 1913), p. 237.

48 See J. Caro Baroja, *The World of Witches* (London 1964), ch. 3; G. L. Kittredge, *Witchcraft in Old and New England* (Cambridge, Mass. 1929), p. 152; N. Cohn, *Europe's Inner Demons* (London 1975), pp. 149–52.

49 'Quis vero tam stultus et hebes sit, qui haec omnia quae in solo spiritu fiunt, etiam in corpore accidere arbitretur?' Burchard of Worms, *Decretum*, PL vol. CXL, L. 1, C. 1, col. 831; Ivo of Chartres, *Decretum*, PL vol. CLXI, pars. II, C. 2, cols. 746–7; *Corpus Iuris Canonici*, ed. A. Friedberg (Leipzig 1879), vol. I, *Decreti secunda pars*, Causa XXVI, quest. V, col. 1027.

50 R. Kieckhefer, *European Witch trials* (California 1976), pp. 38–9.

51 Gilbert of Nogent, op. cit., L. I, c. 12.

52 N. Cohn, op. cit., pp. 154–5.

53 Some examples of cases of witchcraft accusations made before secular courts in thirteenth- and fourteenth-century England (there are no charges of complicity with the Devil, and the persons who were found guilty had to undergo trial by hot iron, or be pilloried) are in *Pleas before the King or his justices* ed. D. M. Stenton (Selden Society, London 1953), vol. I, p. 45; J. B. Given, op. cit., p. 139; *Memorials of London and London Life*, ed. T. Riley (London 1868), pp. 462, 475. A case when German clergymen intervened to save a woman accused of being a witch from the fury of the mob is recorded in *Annales Colmariensis Maiores*, MGHS, vol. XVII, p. 206. The woman was a nun, and the crowd would have burned her alive. She was saved by the Dominicans.

54 Thomas Aquinas, *Quaestiones Disputatae* (Turin–Rome 1949), vol. II, q. 6, art. X, pp. 185–7.

55 Examples are in Heribert the Monk, *Epistola*, PL vol. CLXXXI, cols 1721–2; Ralph of Coggeshall, op. cit., pp. 121–5; Gilbert of Nogent, op. cit., L. III, c. 17. See also W. L. Wakefield, op. cit., pp. 249–51; J. Caro Baroja, op. cit., pp. 74–8; R. Kieckhefer, op. cit., pp. 40–3.

56 E. E. Evans-Pritchard, *Witchcraft, Oracles and Magic among the Azande* (Oxford 1973), p. 21.

57 About these folk beliefs, see, among others, N. Cohn, op. cit., pp. 209–10, 215.

58 K. Thomas, *Religion and the Decline of Magic* (London 1971), pp. 25–50.

59 See for example P. Brown, 'Sorcery, demons and the rise of Christianity from late antiquity, into the Middle Ages', in

Witchcraft, Confessions and Accusations, ed. M. Douglas (New York 1970); K. Thomas, 'The relevance of social anthropology to the historical study of English witchcraft', ibid., and *Religion and the Decline of Magic*, p. 435f.; J. Bednarski, 'The Salem witch scare viewed sociologically', in *Witchcraft and Sorcery*, ed. M. Marwick (London 1970).

60 R. Kieckhefer, op. cit., p. 96. The study is based in part on records of witchcraft trials during the years 1240–1540, published by J. Hansen, op. cit., pp. 495–613.

61 N. Cohn, op. cit., pp. 198–204; J. Caro Baroja, op. cit., p. 83; R. Lerner, *The Heresy of the Free Spirit in the Later Middle Ages*, p. 70; R. Kieckhefer, op. cit., p. 14.

62 Abel Rigault, *Le Procès de Guichard, Evêque de Troyes (1308–1313)* (Paris 1896), p. 11 and note 6.

63 M. Macfarlane, 'Witchcraft in Tudor and Stuart England', in *Witchcraft Confessions and Accusations*. Out of 270 accused, only twenty-three were men. See also M. Jarrin, 'La sorcellerie en Bresse et en Bugey', *Annales de la Société d'Emulation de l'Ain* X (1877), pp. 193–231, especially pp. 226–7; E. W. Monter, 'The pedestal and the stake: courtly love and witchcraft', in *Becoming Visible. Women in European History*, ed. R. Bridenthal and C. Koonz (Boston 1977), p. 132.

64 P. Mayer, 'Witches', in *Witchcraft and Sorcery*, pp. 47, 62. This is an attempt to explain the charges against women principally as a function of the family and social structures in patrilineal societies. See also C. J. Baroja, op. cit., chs 3–4.

65 E. Goody, 'Legitimate and illegitimate aggression in a West African state', in *Witchcraft Confessions and Accusations*.

66 E. Le Roy Ladurie, op. cit., p. 62; Burchard of Worms, *Decretum*, col. 972.

67 B. Geremek, op. cit., pp. 257–8; *Registre criminel du Châtelet de Paris*, vol. I, p. 327, vol. II, pp. 303–43.

68 R. Kieckhefer, op. cit., pp. 97–100.

69 E. Goody, 'Legitimate and illegitimate aggression in a West African state', p. 240.

70 About witches as a female sect that existed as a protest against masculine domination, see P. Hughes, *Witchcraft* (London 1965), pp. 85–6. The author reached his conclusions principally on the basis of M. Murray, *The Witchcult in Western Europe* (Oxford 1921). According to J. B. Russell, *Witchcraft in the Middle Ages* (Cornell 1972), there was a society of witches which formed an extreme protest movement against the domi-

nant religion, and the role and protest of women was especially strong in it. C. J. Baroja, op. cit., p. 256, did not exclude the possibility that a society of witches did exist, at least in the classical world.

71 B. Malinowski, 'The art of magic and the power of faith', in *Magic, Science and Religion and other Essays* (New York 1955), pp. 79–84.

72 K. Thomas, *Religion and the Decline of Magic*, p. 520.

73 B. Geremek, op. cit., pp. 345–6.

74 ibid., p. 340.

75 K. Thomas and A. Macfarlane explain the witchcraft charges in England in the sixteenth and seventeenth centuries as a result of the disintegration of the traditional mutual aid system. The most vulnerable were the poorest widows. They resorted to begging, and people who turned them away often accused them of being witches. The pathological sexual imaginings and the antifeminine trend did not characterize these charges in England.

76 See K. Horney, 'Distrust Between sexes', in *Feminine Psychology*, ed. H. Kelman (New York 1967), pp. 107–18.

77 M. Goodich, 'Sodomy in ecclesiastical law and theory', *Journal of Homosexuality* I (1976), p. 429.

78 See C. Frugoni, 'L'inconographie de la femme au cours des Xe–XIIIe siècles', *Cahiers de Civilisation médiévale, Xe–XIIe siècles* XX (1977), mainly pp. 180–2, 184.

79 Burchard of Worms, *Decretum*, cols 963, 973.

80 'mulieres solent esse multum pronae ad sortilegia.' Humbert de Romans, *De Eruditione Praedicatorum*, p. 279.

81 Alvarus pelagius, *De Planctu Ecclesiae* (Venice 1560) L. II, C. 44: Ad conditionibus et vitiis mulierum, f. 85 b. col. 2, J. Myrc addresses the question: 'Hast thou had dealings with evil spirits conjuring or witchcraft, or sorcery?' to both men and women. J. Myrc, *Instructions for Parish Priests* (EETS, London 1868), p. 30.

82 *Malleus Maleficarum* (Frankfurt 1582), Pars I, q. 6, pp. 90–105. About the text, its different editions and its authors, see J. Hansen, op. cit., pp. 360–407; *Le Marteau des Sorcières*, trans. A. Donet (Paris 1973), Introduction; *Malleus Maleficarum* trans. M. Summers (London 1928), pp. xvii–xviii.

83 'Sexus fragilitas; propter sexus imbecilitatem; ... cum primis autem effoetas, stupidas, mentemque titubantes, vetulas inducit subdolus ille veterator.' *Iohannis Wieri de Praestigiis Daemo-*

num et incantationibus ac veneficiis Libri Sex (Basle 1568), L. III, C. VI, p. 224–7.

84 See H. Kraus, *The Living Theatre of Medieval Art* (Bloomington, Ind., 1967), p. 57 and note 34.

Index